Concepts and Method in Social Science

Careful work with concepts is a cornerstone of good social science methodology. *Concepts and Method in Social Science* demonstrates the crucial role of concepts, providing a timely contribution that draws both on the classic contributions of Giovanni Sartori and the writing of a younger generation of scholars.

In this volume, major writings of Sartori are juxtaposed with other work that exemplifies important approaches to concept analysis. The book is organized in three sections:

- **Part I: Sartori on concepts and method** – including an examination of the necessary logical steps in moving from conceptualization to measurement, and the relationships among meanings, terms, and observations.
- **Part II: Extending the Sartori tradition** – prominent scholars analyze five key ideas in concept analysis: revolution, culture, democracy, peasants, and institutionalization.
- **Part III: In the academy and beyond** – an engaging autobiographical essay written by Giovanni Sartori and reflections from former students provide a unique context in which to situate this varied and rigorous discussion of concept analysis and qualitative methods.

Concepts and Method in Social Science is an accessible text that is well suited to advanced undergraduates and postgraduates, providing a distinct and coherent introduction to comparative political analysis.

David Collier is Robson Professor of Political Science, University of California, Berkeley.

John Gerring is Professor of Political Science, Boston University.

Contributors: Paul Barresi; David Collier; John Gerring; Edward L. Gibson; Gary Goertz; Christoph Kotowski; Marcus Kurtz; Steven Levitsky; Oreste Massari; Giovanni Sartori; Hector Schamis; Cindy Skach; and Edward Walker.

"Combining the best of a Continental European historical perspective and an Anglo-American analytical focus, this is the most challenging inquiry into the rigorous understanding of concepts to be published in recent years."

Mauro Calise, University of Naples and Theodore J. Lowi, Cornell University, authors of *Hyperpolitics: An Interactive Dictionary of Political Science*

"While much social scientific ink has been spilled over questions of causal inference, such analysis is irrelevant if we do not know what it is we are studying or measuring. Sartori's scholarship is centrally concerned with these challenges, and they are squarely addressed in this book. The volume must be seen in the context of the phenomenally successful resurgence of training in qualitative and multi-method research – and it will be critical for graduate students and scholars not simply in qualitative methods, but also in research design and comparative analysis more generally."

Evan Lieberman, Princeton University

"This is an all-star cast, and the scholarship is outstanding. Sartori is a pioneer in methodology; Collier and Gerring are central figures in the recent renaissance of qualitative methods and have wide experience in presenting technical material to students; and the authors of other chapters are well known for their high-quality scholarship. The book can profitably be read and digested by advanced undergraduates, graduate students, and established scholars."

David Waldner, University of Virginia

"Giovanni Sartori calls for researchers to be 'conscious thinkers' who engage deeply with issues of method, yet are not paralyzed by preoccupation with particular techniques. This volume exemplifies Sartori's approach by bringing together his major essays on concepts and method, along with chapters that show how his framework informs some of the best contemporary social science, and correspondingly yields valuable insights into a series of important substantive topics. Scholars at any stage of their careers should take seriously the insights of this volume."

Melani Cammett, Brown University

"Collier and Gerring have done a great service to the profession by republishing some of Sartori's seminal contributions on concept analysis (and beyond), together with essays of younger scholars who brilliantly continue his tradition in comparative politics. A timely and important contribution to the debate to social science methodology, this book will be compulsory reading – or re-reading – for comparativists."

Giovanni Capoccia, Oxford University

Concepts and Method in Social Science

The tradition of Giovanni Sartori

Edited by
David Collier and John Gerring

Routledge
Taylor & Francis Group

NEW YORK AND LONDON

First published 2009 by Routledge
2 Park Square, Milton Park, Abingdon, Oxon OX14 4RN

Simultaneously published in the USA and Canada
by Routledge
711 Third Avenue, New York, NY 10017

Routledge is an imprint of the Taylor & Francis Group, an informa business

Typeset by Swales & Willis Ltd, Exeter, Devon

British Library Cataloguing in Publication Data
A catalogue record for this book is available from the British Library

Library of Congress Cataloging in Publication Data
Concepts and method in social science: the tradition of Giovanni Sartori /
ed. David Collier and John Gerring.
p. cm.
Includes bibliographical references.
1. Social sciences–Methodology. 2. Social sciences—Philosophy.
3. Social sciences—Comparative method. 4. Sartori, Giovanni, 1924–
I. Collier, David, 1942– II. Gerring, John, 1962–
H61.C528 2008
300.1—dc22
2008028832

ISBN 10: 0–415–77577–9 (hbk)
ISBN 10: 0–415–77578–7 (pbk)

ISBN 13: 978–0–415–77577–9 (hbk)
ISBN 13: 978–0–415–77578–6 (pbk)

Contents

List of illustrations

List of tables

List of contributors

Paul A. Barresi is Associate Professor of Political Science, Southern New Hampshire University

David Collier is Robson Professor of Political Science, University of California, Berkeley

John Gerring is Professor of Political Science, Boston University

Edward L. Gibson is Associate Professor of Political Science, Northwestern University

Gary Goertz is Professor of Political Science, University of Arizona

Christoph Kotowski New York

Marcus J. Kurtz is Associate Professor of Political Science, Ohio State University

Steven Levitsky is Professor of Government, Harvard University

Oreste Massari is Lecturer of Political Science, University of Roma

Giovanni Sartori is Albert Schweitzer Professor of the Humanities, Emeritus, Columbia University

Hector E. Schamis is Associate Professor, School of International Service, American University

Cindy Skach is Professor of Comparative Government and Law, University of Oxford, Official Fellow of Brasenose College

Edward Walker is Executive Director of ISEEES, University of California, Berkeley

Introduction[1]

David Collier and John Gerring

Giovanni Sartori has long been an eminent scholar in the study of democracy and political parties, as well as in research on methodology. He is a leading voice in the study of social science concepts, and his influence is seen in a continuing stream of methodological publications that reflect his contributions.[2] Sartori's work has wide resonance in Europe, the United States, Latin America, and beyond. Although his substantive studies of democracy and parties continue to be available in English,[3] no publication brings together his writings on concepts and methods for an English-speaking audience. Such a publication is now all the more overdue, given the centrality of Sartori's work to the field of qualitative methods – which has recently gained new vitality in political science.

The present volume brings together Sartori's major writings on concepts, method, and comparison, along with examples of scholarship by analysts whose work exemplifies the analytic gains achieved by close attention to concepts. Though in part a tribute to Sartori, this book is not a *Festschrift*.[4] Rather, it republishes a set of writings in this methodological tradition – some substantially revised and adapted for publication here.

Sartori's career

Giovanni Sartori's education and earliest scholarship fall under the rubric of political philosophy. Yet over time, he became better known as an empirical political scientist, and his research on political parties, constitutions, and democracy has left a strong imprint in mainstream journals of political science. He is one of the founders of the contemporary subfield of comparative politics, yet his empirical forays have never lost their theoretical edge or historical underpinnings.

Sartori was born in Florence in 1924. Very inconveniently, he reached his majority – and draft age – just as the crumbling Italian fascist regime was in its final struggle and eagerly sought new military recruits. Motivated by an understandable aversion to joining this struggle on behalf of the government, Sartori went into hiding in a secret room of his family's home, at the risk of being shot on the spot if discovered. Thus sequestered until this regime fell, he passed his time reading Hegel, Croce, and other classics, thereby taking his first major step into political theory. This tale is told, with evident humor, by Sartori himself (Chapter 13, this volume).

After the war, Sartori pursued graduate work at the University of Florence, receiving his degree in social and political science (1946). Shortly thereafter, he became an assistant professor of the history of modern philosophy at Florence, from 1950 to 1956. At that time, the university had a faculty of political sciences; in point of fact, this faculty encompassed teaching in law, history, economics, statistics, geography, and philosophy – but not what would be called political science today. In 1956, Sartori succeeded in having political science added to the purview of this faculty, and managed to have his own appointment moved to this newly created field. In doing so, he established the discipline in Italy and launched his trajectory as the leading Italian political scientist. This trajectory was also evident in his later role as the founding and managing editor of the *Rivista Italiana di Scienza Politica* (1971–2003), which is the main disciplinary journal in Italy, thus continuing his role as architect of Italian political science.

Sartori's close involvement in the US scholarly community began in the second half of the 1960s, when he held visiting professorships at Harvard and Yale. His continuing engagement in the US academy is reflected in his appointment as a Fellow of the Center for Advanced Study in the Behavioral Sciences in 1971–72, and his election as a Foreign Honorary Member of the American Academy of Arts and Sciences in 1975. In 1976, he was appointed as a professor of political science at Stanford, a position he held until 1979. In that year he became the Albert Schweitzer Professor in the Humanities at Columbia University, where he taught from 1979 to 1994. He is now Albert Schweitzer Professor Emeritus.

In the 1960s and 1970s, Sartori was active in the intellectual movement that reshaped the field of comparative politics, collaborating with a large group of scholars including Gabriel Almond, David Apter, Samuel Beer, Robert Dahl, Harry Eckstein, Samuel Huntington, Joseph LaPalombara, Roy Macridis, Fred Riggs, and Henry Teune. Among these colleagues, Sartori was a distinctively European voice, and he played a defining role in setting a basic agenda for the methodology of comparative analysis. He was also active in international scholarly collaboration. For example, from its founding in 1970, Sartori was an important member of the Committee on Political Sociology of the International Political Science Association, which opened new avenues of research in comparative and international studies. This group included Hans Daalder, Mattei Dogan, S. N. Eisenstadt, Juan Linz, Seymour Martin Lipset, and Stein Rokkan. The years at Columbia saw a central continuing engagement in research on parties, democracy, constitutions, and methods, as well as a critical contribution to graduate teaching (Chapter 14). In retirement, Sartori remains actively engaged in the social sciences both in Europe and the US, as well as being a leading commentator on Italian politics.

Methodological contributions: the basic challenge

The biblical story about the Tower of Babel, which offers an explanation for the fragmentation of human language, is an apt metaphor for the confusion of language in the social sciences. It is fitting, therefore, that Sartori adopted it for the title of a major essay (Chapter 3). We have also incorporated this image on the cover of this volume.

Sartori stands at the forefront among scholars who have tackled problems of conceptual confusion. His work poses many questions: What is the basic structure of the concepts in comparative social science? What analytic and practical tools are most useful for working with these concepts? Can uniform standards for concept usage be formulated? How does one persuade scholars to follow these standards?

Sartori's interest in these questions is strikingly reflected in the first book in which he moves beyond the initial concern with political theory. Its arresting title, *Democrazia e definizioni* (*Democracy and Definitions*) (1957), signals his recurring juxtaposition of basic methodological concerns and his substantive focus on democracy and political parties. In numerous subsequent publications, Sartori has continued to address these central questions. He has sought to provide a rigorous approach to methodology – a rigor grounded in the careful use of language, rather than in mathematics. He viewed qualitative work with concepts as essential to achieving such rigor in both qualitative and quantitative research.

We find it helpful to divide into five components Sartori's efforts to pursue this methodological agenda: (1) the foundational statement contained in his *APSR* article on "Concept Misformation and Comparative Politics"; (2) the historical depth of Sartori's thinking about methods; (3) the formulation of rules and procedures for structuring the interplay among concepts, terms, and empirical observations; (4) arguments concerning the logic of inquiry; and (5) his long-term concern with the relation between concept formation and quantitative methods.

Point of departure: concept misformation

Sartori's article "Concept misformation in comparative politics" (Chapter 1) is widely recognized as a foundational statement within comparative politics and political science. In the 1960s and early 1970s, when basic concepts were being extended to political systems across the globe, Sartori provided criteria for thinking about this process of "conceptual traveling," and for avoiding the potential problem of "conceptual stretching." He accomplished this through his now famous discussion of the interplay between the "intension" of a concept, i.e., the meaning it calls forth, and its "extension," i.e., the range of cases to which it can appropriately be applied. Here, Sartori distinguished among low-level concepts, which may be well matched to the contextual specificity of particular countries; medium-level concepts, which may be suited to comparisons within world regions; and high-level concepts, which are useful for broader comparisons. The latter are rightly valued for their role in formulating general theories. Yet Sartori warned that if our concepts become too general, they may be subject to "theoretical vaporization." They may suffer from "defective denotation," in that they cease to offer productive empirical differentiation.

Another important priority in the "Concept Misformation" essay is that careful work with concepts should precede efforts at measurement. Indeed, it is all too easy to construct indicators without careful consideration of what they are measuring.

This problem is addressed through reasoning about a dichotomous form of the concept being measured. Sartori advises scholars to address the question "What is?" before asking "How much?" Thus, meaning before measurement; quality before quantity. This reasoning builds a strong foundation for a graded understanding of the concept being operationalized.

Finally, in formulating his agenda in the "Concept Misformation" essay, Sartori urges scholars to strike an appropriate balance: avoiding the trap of being either an *overconscious* thinker paralyzed by concern with methods, or an *unconscious* thinker oblivious to issues of method. A more appropriate position is that of the *conscious* thinker, who grasps the methodological issues, thereby improving research – without being trapped by excessive preoccupation with methods.

Historical depth

Sartori's methodological contributions are firmly anchored in his knowledge of Western political thought. This facet of his work is reflected in his essay "What Is Politics?" (Chapter 2), which addresses this question by drawing extensively on classical political thought, as well as on the etymology of concepts derived from Latin and Greek. Given his early training and initial faculty positions in philosophy, this focus is hardly surprising.

In addressing the meaning of social science concepts, Sartori returned time and again to their classical origins. He expresses dismay over the loss of etymological anchorage in the methodological work of scholars who lack classical training – an unhappy state that describes most of us today. This dismay is forcefully articulated in "The Tower of Babel" (Chapter 3). In this respect, Sartori plays a bridging role among empirical analysis, the field of comparative politics, and political theory in the classical mode.

Rules and procedures

Establishing explicit rules and procedures for coordinating *concepts*, *terms*, and *observations* is another central point of concern (Chapters 3 and 4). Sartori's rules and procedures build on careful differentiation among alternative forms of definition; the distinction between synonymy and antonymy; and his many warnings about problems in concept usage, including ambiguity (versus univocality), boundlessness, undenotativeness, and vagueness. He is convinced that key terms and concepts, once defined, are too often used inconsistently – a concern reiterated in the work of other authors in this volume, e.g., Collier and Levitsky (Chapter 10).[5] Sartori advocates reconstructing the concepts used in a given study by collecting representative definitions, extracting their component attributes, and forming matrices that present – for example – the contrasts in concept usage employed by different authors in a given literature. Good examples of this reconstruction are found both in Kotowski and in Kurtz (Chapters 8 and 11).

Sartori's concern with rules and procedures leads him to explore the wider semantic field – i.e., the broader set of terms and concepts – within which a given concept is situated. He argues that innovations in terms and meanings should not unsettle this semantic field by creating confusion, overlap, or ambiguity among the constellation of related terms. Since concepts are inevitably nested within this larger field, it must be considered whenever a term is being defined. Concepts are inseparable from the loom of language.

The discussion of rules also extends to Sartori's influential arguments about the ladder of abstraction.[6] Building on Frege and other logicians, Sartori views social science concepts through a classificatory lens. Concepts ought to be ordered through their definitions by *genus et differentia*,[7] with subordinate concepts having smaller extensions (fields of referents) and larger intensions (number of defining traits). This sets up an inverse relationship between the intension and extension of a concept.[8] Vertical movement up and down the "ladder of abstraction" becomes a key tool for building careful comparisons across diverse contexts. Concept definitions should only be as specific as is appropriate to their desired extension.

Finally, Sartori advocates minimal definitions – i.e., those that capture what are understood as core (necessary and sufficient) attributes of a phenomenon. Minimal definitions are thus intended to exclude accompanying or varying properties, whose relation to the core concept seems more productively treated as the focus of empirical investigation rather than as a matter of definition. This approach is explored by Gerring and Barresi (Chapter 9), and the role of minimal definitions in the literature on the third wave of democracy is made clear by Collier and Levitsky (Chapter 10).

Sartori's discussion of rules and procedures springs from a rigorous optimism that scholars can order concepts, terms, definitions, and observations in an analytically productive way. This optimism is central to the contemporary field of comparative politics, and is all the more compelling because it carefully takes into account the heterogeneity of the political world we study. Sartori's rules and procedures seek to address that heterogeneity, rather than sweeping it under the carpet.

And yet we may wonder: can the methodology of concept analysis and concept usage be governed by strict procedures? In quantitative methods and statistics, one finds many rules. Are they equally plausible in qualitative work? We suggest two responses. First, rule-making in *quantitative* methods may be less productive – setting less of a gold standard – than is often presumed (Brady and Collier 2004). One must beware of overdrawing the contrast between quantitative and qualitative methods in this respect. Second, it is worthwhile for scholars to seek standards in working with concepts, even if those standards cannot always be met. The statements by Sartori's former students (Chapter 14) show that the quest for standards can be substantially advanced, for example, by careful teaching.

Broader questions of method and logic of inquiry

Sartori's concerns extend, of course, beyond the specificities of concept analysis to wider issues of methods and logic of inquiry. Several of these concerns are reflected in his pungent article "Comparing and Miscomparing" (Chapter 5). Here, he considers the role of comparison in causal inference, underscoring the centrality of this objective to the entire field. He draws together earlier lines of argument in exploring the question of what is comparable. Relatedly, he discusses how, due to parochialism, scholars may draw from another context of analysis a concept that is inappropriate for their own domain of research. In this new setting, the concept may not refer to anything at all. He considers case studies, underscoring their contribution to generating hypotheses.

Sartori likewise addresses the troubling issue of incommensurability, which in the present context involves the challenge of finding conceptualizations appropriate for diverse cases – i.e., that successfully establishes analytic equivalence. The concern with incommensurability thus frames, in the broadest terms, the issue of conceptual stretching. He observes that this concern potentially challenges the very enterprise of comparative politics. Sartori makes it clear that we have no comprehensive solution to incommensurability, yet a practical solution is possible. Country specialists should avoid dwelling excessively on the uniqueness of "their cases." In doing so, they fail to place them in a wider comparative perspective – and, indeed, they would thereby make a grave mistake, notwithstanding the inevitable challenge of establishing equivalence. In parallel, broad comparativists should take into account detailed knowledge of specific cases. In addressing this detailed knowledge, they may discover that they should refine their own more general concepts. Overall, the solution is not to arrive at a definitive conclusion, but to applaud practical efforts to address incommensurability by juxtaposing the general and the specific.

Concept formation and quantification

Sartori argues forcefully that careful work with a dichotomous form of concepts should be a foundation for quantification. Otherwise, quantitative analysis lacks sound conceptual foundations. To reiterate the framing stated above, the questions "What is?" and "How much?" should be addressed in that order. A pointed expression of Sartori's concern is found in his statement that "statistical technology cannot surrogate what an atrophied formation of concepts does not provide." Sartori's position here might be seen as hostile toward much quantitative research in comparative politics, and in political science more broadly.

We do not agree. First of all, Sartori's insistence on providing strong conceptual foundations for quantitative analysis – based on a categorical understanding of the relevant concepts – is entirely congruent with standard concerns of measurement theory. Take, for example, the form of measurement validation considered necessary with a technique such as factor analysis. It is standard to presume that the quantitative measures produced by this statistical method should be subject to "content validation." Thus, the indicators that go into the quantitative measure should plausibly be elements of the concept being measured, i.e., they should correspond to the "content" of that concept. Factor analysis thus depends on an initial differentiation between what is part of the concept and what is not – i.e., on initially reasoning in dichotomous terms concerning what the concept is "about."

Approaching these issues from another perspective, Collier et al. (2008) have shown that the careful construction of "higher" levels of measurement – i.e., interval, ratio, and absolute scales – is dependent on an initial, dichotomous categorization of the phenomenon under analysis. Relatedly, Collier and Levitsky (Chapter 10) argue that if we are to make sense of the more-or-less gradations they associate with "part–whole" hierarchies, we must have some initial, categorical understanding that addresses the question "Part of what?"

Sartori's position on concept formation as an underpinning for measurement thus coincides with important ideas about validity, levels of measurement, and measurement theory. Further, it should be underscored that Sartori is open to the option of a mathematization of political science, *if* it is constructed on a conceptually rigorous foundation. Of course, a great many formal modelers would likewise insist on a foundation of careful conceptual work. They would certainly agree with the stipulation of "if" in Sartori's formulation.

Organization of this volume

The chapters below present major examples of Sartori's work on concepts and methods, as well as essays by other authors who extend his ideas. In this introduction, we have already discussed key arguments in his essays on "Concept Misformation," "What Is Politics?," "The Tower of Babel," "Guidelines for Concept Analysis," and "Comparing and Miscomparing." The reader is invited to delve further into these essays in Part I of the volume (Chapters 1 to 5). Chapter 6, "Further Observations on Concept Formation, Definitions, and Models," presents excerpts from four essays that further develop important themes in Sartori's work. In "Democracy: 'What Is' vs. 'How Much'" and in "From Classification to Measurement," Sartori concisely articulates his basic arguments about building measurement – i.e., the concern with more and less – on careful concept formation. "Politics as Collectivized Decisions" is an exercise in concept clarification in which Sartori explores different types of decision making and argues that politics distinctively entails collectivized, and not collective, decisions. Likewise, "What Is a Model?" is in part an exercise in concept clarification – exploring the relationship among models, frameworks, and mental constructs – while it also considers the ways in which they should be understood as explanatory. At the same time, Sartori warns against a model mania that fails to distinguish between what he views as real models – for example, the idea of equilibrium or the Downsian model of party competition – as opposed to the evocation of "model" simply as a form of verbal boasting.

Part II presents studies that extend and refine different strands within the Sartori tradition. Gary Goertz (Chapter 7) examines a fundamental point of departure in Sartori's work on concepts: the idea of intension and extension and its application to the challenges of comparative research. Among the questions Goertz considers is the place of ideal types within the intension–extension framework. His chapter also examines specific parts of the analysis offered by Kotowski, Collier and Levitsky, and Kurtz (Chapters 8, 10, and 11), thereby introducing arguments that are developed later in the volume.

The rest of Part II focuses on important social science concepts – revolution, culture, democracy, peasant, and institutionalization – while also exemplifying important ideas of concept analysis. Christoph Kotowski (Chapter 8) engages the concept of revolution, employing a variety of analytic tools, including the matrix of meanings and authors advocated by Sartori, to untangle this concept.

The next two chapters address minimal definitions and conceptual hierarchies. Focusing on the concept of culture, John Gerring and Paul A. Barresi (Chapter 9) juxtapose ideas about ideal types and minimal definitions, thereby exploring the form of definition preferred by Sartori, as well as extending Goertz's discussion of ideal types. David Collier and Steven Levitsky (Chapter 10) push further the idea of conceptual hierarchies. They suggest that Sartori's ladder of abstraction (also called the ladder of generality) can be seen as a "kind hierarchy," which they contrast with a "part–whole hierarchy." This contrast usefully links the discussion with wider arguments about conceptual structure and conceptual change. They illustrate this distinction through an examination of the concept of democracy, as employed in studies of the third wave of democratization in the final decades of the twentieth century. This chapter underscores the value of constructing the analysis of gradations on an initial dichotomous framing of concepts.

The final chapters in Part II demonstrate how careful work with concepts – and especially disaggregation – can clarify and improve causal inference. To use Sartori's terms, through unpacking the intension of their concepts, these authors arrive at a modified extension that groups cases differently, yielding improved leverage in evaluating causal claims. Marcus J. Kurtz (Chapter 11) disaggregates the concept of peasant, thus providing new insight into three major lines of analysis focused on the role of peasants in producing revolutions: the moral economy, political economy, and Marxist perspectives. He unpacks the intension and provides new differentiation of the extension, thereby distinguishing alternative kinds of peasants. Kurtz shows that important parts of the apparent divergence among these explanatory approaches did not involve theoretical differences, but rather a focus on different cases, which came into sharper focus with his disaggregated approach. Writing on institutionalization, Levitsky (Chapter 12) likewise unpacks the concept. In examining explanations for the transformation of political parties, he shows that what appeared to be conflicting accounts in fact derived from different meanings of this concept.

Part III begins with an engaging and informative autobiographical essay, in which Sartori recounts different phases in his career and in the evolution of his thought (Chapter 13). A full biography and bibliography is also provided in the concluding portion of the volume (Chapter 15).

To offer a picture of Sartori the teacher, Part III also includes reflections by scholars who studied methods with him at Columbia University, an experience which they attest had a lasting impact on their analytic skills, their insight into working with concepts, and their careers (Chapter 14). Apparently, for more than a few students who took Sartori's course on "social science concepts," it sounded in principle like an easy class. Yet they were in for a surprise. They describe Sartori as austere and stern in his teaching style, often demanding, and always exacting. Students' ideas were routinely dissected in class meetings, and occasionally Sartori expressed his dismay over their ignorance of Latin and Greek, which limited their capacity to grasp the historical and etymological roots of concepts under discussion.

Yet Sartori was courteous and charming in his teaching. While rigorous and sometimes intimidating, his style is described as gracious and his mentorship unfailing. He would enter the classroom gallantly, wearing tailored Italian suits and clutching his worn briefcase under his arm. With old-world charm and a dry sense of humor, he presided over the class with an elegance of bearing and of mind that fascinated the students. He proved to be a remarkable mentor, with a deep and generous commitment to those with whom he worked closely. Sartori was, and continues to be, a formidable presence, and at the same time a supportive and encouraging teacher and colleague.

Notes

1 For their skilled contributions to the task of transcribing, assembling, coordinating, and checking the chapters in this volume, we are sincerely grateful to Nora Archambeau, Rebecca Baran-Rees, Mauricio Benítez, Erica Hill, Jennifer Jennings, Josephine Marks, Reilly O'Neal, Piero Tortola, and Miranda Yaver. Valuable comments on this introduction were provided by Robert Adcock and Taylor Boas. This volume has been prepared in collaboration with the Consortium for Qualitative Research Methods, as well as the Institute for Qualitative and Multi-Method Research of the Moynihan Institute of Global Affairs, Maxwell School, Syracuse University.
2 See Chapters 7 to 12 in the present volume. A small sampling of related work includes Adcock (2005), Adcock and Collier (2001), Capoccia (2002), Collier and Adcock (1999), Collier and Mahon (1993), Gerring (2001), Goertz (2006), and Schedler (1998, 1999).
3 Sartori (1987, 2005).
4 A *Festschrift* has been published in Italian (Pasquino 2005).
5 Pamela Paxton's (2000) study of inconsistencies in definitions of democracy – a study that fits nicely in the tradition of concept analysis discussed here – offers an outstanding illustration of this problem. She discusses prominent authors who formulated a definition of democracy that included universal suffrage. Yet when these authors analyzed particular countries, at key points their focus extended beyond cases of universal suffrage to encompass countries that had only male suffrage. This failure to hold to initial definitions strongly influenced their conclusions about the emergence and consequences of democracy.
6 This has also been called a ladder of generality (Collier and Mahon 1993; Goertz, Chapter 7). Collier and Levitsky (Chapter 10) frame this in terms of a kind hierarchy. As Collier and Levitsky argue, these alternative labels simply provide alternative perspectives on exactly the same vertical structure of concepts.
7 That is to say, in a conceptual structure in which more generic, superordinate levels stand in a hierarchical relation with more specific, subordinate levels.
8 Sartori strongly emphasizes the idea of inverse variation, while also noting that this pattern does not always pertain and "should not be understood strictly" (Chapter 4, n. 40).

References

Adcock, R. (2005) "What is a Concept?," Paper No. 1, Working Paper Series on Political Concepts of the Committee on Concepts and Methods, International Political Science Association, Mexico City: Centro de Investigación y Docencia Económicas (CIDE).

Adcock, R. and Collier, D. (2001) "Measurement Validity: A Shared Standard for Qualitative and Quantitative Research," *American Political Science Review* 95 (3): 529–46.

Brady, H. and Collier, D. (eds.) (2004) *Rethinking Social Inquiry: Diverse Tools, Shared Standards*, Lanham, MD: Rowman and Littlefield.

Capoccia, G. (2002) "Anti-system Parties: A Conceptual Reassessment," *Journal of Theoretical Politics* 14 (1): 9–35.

Collier, D. and Adcock, R. (1999) "Democracy and Dichotomies: A Pragmatic Approach to Choices about Concepts," *Annual Review of Political Science* 2: 537–65.

Collier, D. and Mahon, J.E. (1993) "Conceptual 'Stretching' Revisited: Conceptual Innovation in Comparative Research," *American Political Science Review* 87 (4): 845–55.

Collier, D., LaPorte, J. and Seawright, J. (2008) "Putting Typologies to Work: Forming Concepts and Creating Categorical Measures," Department of Political Science, University of California, Berkeley.

Gerring, J. (2001) *Social Science Methodology: A Criterial Framework*, Cambridge: Cambridge University Press.

Goertz, G. (2006) *Social Science Concepts: A User's Guide*, Princeton: Princeton University Press.

Pasquino, G. (ed.) (2005) *La scienza politica di Giovanni Sartori*, Bologna: Il Mulino.

Paxton, P. (2000) "Women's Suffrage in the Measurement of Democracy: Problems of Operationalization," *Studies in Comparative International Development* 35 (3): 92–111.

Sartori, G. (1957) *Democrazia e definizioni*, Bologna: Il Mulino.

Sartori, G. (1987) *The Theory of Democracy Revisited*, Chatham, NJ: Chatham House.

Sartori, G. (2005) *Parties and Party Systems: A Framework for Analysis*, Essex: University of Essex, ECPR Classics, European Consortium for Political Research.

Schedler, A. (1998) "What Is Democratic Consolidation?," *Journal of Democracy* 9 (2): 91–107.

Schedler, A. (1999) "Conceptualizing Accountability," in A. Schedler, L. Diamond and M.F. Plattner (eds.), *The Self-Restraining State: Power and Accountability in New Democracies*, Boulder: Lynne Riener Publishers.

Part I
Sartori on concepts and method

1 Concept misformation in comparative politics

Giovanni Sartori

"To have mastered 'theory' and 'method' is to have become a *conscious* thinker, a man at work and aware of the assumptions and implications of whatever he is about. To be mastered by 'method' or 'theory' is simply to be kept from working" (Mills 1959: 27; my emphasis). The sentence applies nicely to the present plight of political science. The profession as a whole oscillates between two unsound extremes. At the one end a large majority of political scientists qualify as pure and simple unconscious thinkers. At the other end a sophisticated minority qualify as over-conscious thinkers, in the sense that their standards of method and theory are drawn from the physical, "paradigmatic" sciences.

The wide gap between the unconscious and the over-conscious thinker is concealed by the growing sophistication of statistical and research techniques. Most of the literature introduced by the title "Methods" (in the social, behavioral or political sciences) actually deals with survey techniques and social statistics, and has little if anything to share with the crucial concern of "methodology," which is a concern with the logical structure and procedure of scientific enquiry. In a very crucial sense there is no methodology without *logos*, without thinking about thinking. And if a firm distinction is drawn – as it should be – between methodology and technique, the latter is no substitute for the former. One may be a wonderful researcher and manipulator of data, and yet remain an unconscious thinker. The view presented in this article is, then, that the profession as a whole is grievously impaired by methodological unawareness. The more we advance technically, the more we leave a vast, uncharted territory behind our backs. And my underlying complaint is that political scientists eminently lack (with exceptions) a training in logic – indeed in elementary logic.

I stress "elementary" because I do not wish to encourage in the least the over-conscious thinker, the man who refuses to discuss heat unless he is given a thermometer. My sympathy goes, instead, to the conscious thinker, the man who realizes the limitations of not having a thermometer and still manages to say a great deal simply by saying hot and cold, warmer and cooler. Indeed I call upon the conscious thinker to steer a middle course between crude logical mishandling on the one hand, and logical perfectionism (and paralysis) on the other hand. Whether we realize it or not, we are still swimming in a "sea of naïveté." And the study of comparative politics is particularly vulnerable to, and illustrative of, this infelicitous state of affairs.

The traveling problem

Traditional, or the more traditional type of, political science inherited a vast array of concepts which had been previously defined and refined – for better and for worse – by generations of philosophers and political theorists. To some extent, therefore, the traditional political scientist could afford to be an unconscious thinker – the thinking had already been done for him. This is even more the case with the country-by-country legalistic institutional approach, which does not particularly require hard thinking.[1] However, the new political science engages in reconceptualization. And this is even more the case, necessarily, with the new comparative expansion of the discipline.[2] There are many reasons for this *renovatio ab imis*.

One is the very "expansion on politics." To some extent politics results are *objectively* bigger on account of the fact that the world is becoming more and more politicized (more participation, more mobilization, and in any case more state intervention in formerly non-governmental spheres). In no small measure, however, politics is *subjectively* bigger in that we have shifted the focus of attention both toward the periphery of politics (vis-à-vis the governmental process), and toward its input side. By now – as Macridis puts it – we study everything that is "potentially political" (Macridis 1968: 81). While this latter aspect of the expansion of politics is disturbing – it ultimately leads to the disappearance of politics – it is not a peculiar concern for comparative politics, in the sense that other segments of political science are equally and even more deeply affected.[3]

Aside from the expansion of politics, a more specific source of conceptual and methodological challenge for comparative politics is what Braibanti calls the "lengthening spectrum of political systems" (1968: 36–7). We are now engaged in worldwide, cross-area comparisons. And while there is an end to geographical size, there is apparently no end to the proliferation of political units. There were about 80 states in 1916; it is no wild guess that we may shortly arrive at 150. Still more important, the lengthening spectrum of political systems includes a variety of primitive, diffuse polities at very different stages of differentiation and consolidation.

Now, the wider the world under investigation, the more we need conceptual tools that are able to travel. It is equally clear that the pre-1950 vocabulary of politics was not devised for worldwide, cross-area traveling. On the other hand, and in spite of bold attempts at drastic terminological innovation,[4] it is hard to see how Western scholars could radically depart from the political experience of the West, i.e., from the vocabulary of politics which has been developed over millennia on the basis of such experience. Therefore, the first question is: how far, and how, can we travel with the help of the available vocabulary of politics?

By and large, so far we have followed (more or less unwittingly) the line of least resistance: broaden the meaning – and thereby the range of application – of the conceptualizations at hand. That is to say, the larger the world, the more we have resorted to *conceptual stretching*, or conceptual straining, i.e., to vague, amorphous conceptualizations. To be sure, there is more to it. One may add, for instance, that conceptual stretching also represents a deliberate attempt to make our conceptualizations value free. Another concurrent explication is that conceptual stretching is largely a "boomerang effect" of the developing areas, i.e., a feedback on the Western categories of the diffuse polities of the Third World.[5] These considerations notwithstanding, conceptual stretching does represent, in comparative politics, the line of least resistance. And the net result of conceptual straining is that our gains in extensional coverage tend to be matched by losses in connotative precision. It appears that we can cover more – in traveling terms – only by saying less, and by saying less in a far less precise manner.

A major drawback of the comparative expansion of the discipline is, then, that it has been conducive to indefiniteness, to undelimited and largely undefined conceptualizations. We do need, ultimately, "universal" categories – concepts which are applicable to any time and place. But nothing is gained if our universals turn out to be "no difference" categories leading to pseudo-equivalences. And even though we need universals, they must be *empirical* universals, that is, categories which somehow are amenable, in spite of their all-embracing, very abstract nature, to empirical testing. Instead we seem to verge on the edge of *philosophical* universals, understood – as Croce defines them – as concepts which are by definition supra-empirical.[6]

That the comparative expansion of the discipline would encounter the aforementioned stumbling block was only to be expected. It was easy to infer, that is, that conceptual stretching would produce indefiniteness and elusiveness, and that the more we climb toward high-flown universals, the more tenuous the link with the empirical evidence. It is pertinent to wonder, therefore, why the problem has seldom been squarely confronted.

Taking a step back, let us begin by asking whether it is really necessary to embark on hazardous worldwide comparisons. This question hinges, in turn, on the prior question, Why compare? The unconscious thinker does not ask himself why he is comparing; and this neglect goes to explain why so much comparative work provides extensions of knowledge, but hardly a strategy for acquiring and validating new knowledge. It is not intuitively evident that to compare is to control, and that the novelty, distinctiveness, and importance of comparative politics consists of a systematic testing, against as many cases as possible, of sets of hypotheses, generalizations, and laws of the "if . . . then" type.[7] But if comparative politics is conceived as a method of control, then its generalizations have to be checked against "all cases," and therefore the enterprise must be – in principle – a global enterprise. So the reason for worldwide comparisons is not simply that we live in a wider world; it is also a methodological reason.

If two or more items are identical, we do not have a problem of comparability. On the other hand, if two or more items have nothing, or not enough in common, we rightly say that stones and rabbits cannot be compared. By and large, then, we obtain comparability when two or more items appear "similar enough," that is, neither identical nor utterly different. But this assessment offers little positive guidance. The problem is often outflanked by saying that we make things comparable. In this perspective to compare is "to assimilate," i.e., to discover deeper or fundamental similarities below the surface of secondary diversities. But this argument equally affords little mileage and conveys, moreover, the misleading suggestion that the trick resides in making the unlike look alike. Surely, then, we have here a major problem which cannot be disposed of with the argument that political theorists have performed decently with comparing since the time of Aristotle, and therefore that we should not get bogged down by the question "What is comparable?" any more than our predecessors. This argument will not do on account of three differences.

In the first place, if our predecessors were culture-bound this implied that they traveled only as far as their personal knowledge allowed them to travel. In the second place, our predecessors hardly disposed of quantitative data and were not quantitatively oriented. Under both of these limitations they enjoyed the distinct advantage of having a substantive understanding of the things they were comparing. This is hardly possible on a worldwide scale, and surely becomes impossible with the computer revolution. A few years ago Karl Deutsch predicted that by 1975 the informational requirements of political science would be satisfied by some "fifty million card-equivalents [of IBM standard cards] . . . and a total annual growth rate of perhaps as much as five million" (1966: 156). I find the estimate frightening, for computer technology and facilities are bound to flood us with masses of data for which no human mind can have any substantive grasp. But even if one shares the enthusiasm of Deutsch, it cannot be denied that we have here a gigantic, unprecedented problem.

In the third place, our predecessors were far from being as unguided as we are. They did not leave the decision about what was homogenous – i.e., comparable – and what was heterogeneous – i.e., non-comparable – to each man's genial insights. As indicated by the terminology, their comparisons applied to things belonging to "the same genus." That is to say, the background of comparability was established by the *per genus et differentiam* mode of analysis, i.e., by a taxonomical treatment. In this contest, comparable means something which belongs to the same genus, species or sub-species – in short to the same class. Hence the class provides the "similarity element" of comparability, while the "differences" enter as the species of a genus, or the sub-species of a species – and so forth, depending on how fine the analysis needs to be. However, and here is the rub, the taxonomical requisites of comparability are currently neglected if not disowned.

We are now better equipped for a discussion of our initial query, namely, why the traveling problem of comparative politics has been met with the poor remedy of "conceptual stretching" instead of being squarely confronted. While there are many reasons for our neglect to attack the problem frontally, a major reason is that we have been swayed by the suggestion that our difficulties can be overcome by switching from "what is" questions to "how much" questions. The argument runs, roughly, as follows: As long as concepts point to differences of *kind*, i.e., as long as we pursue the either-or mode of analysis, we are in trouble; but if concepts are understood as a matter of more-or-less, i.e., as pointing to differences in *degree*, then our difficulties can be solved by measurement, and the real problem is precisely how to measure. Meanwhile – waiting for the measures – class concepts and taxonomies should be looked upon with suspicion (if not rejected), since they represent "an old fashioned logic of properties and attributes not well adapted to study quantities and relations."[8]

According to my previous analysis, a taxonomic unfolding represents a requisite condition for comparability, and indeed a background which becomes all the more important the less we can rely on a substantive familiarity with what is being compared. According to the alternative argument, quantification has no ills of its own; rather, it provides a remedy for the ills and inadequacies of the *per genus et differentiam* mode of analysis. My own view is that when we dismiss the so-called "old fashioned logic" we are plain wrong, and indeed the victims of poor logic – a view that I must now attempt to warrant.

Quantification and classification

What is very confusing in this matter is the abuse of a quantitative idiom which is nothing but an idiom. All too often, that is, we speak of degrees and of measurement "not only without any actual measurements having been performed, but without any being projected, and even without any apparent awareness of what must be done before such measurements can be carried out" (Kaplan 1964: 213). For instance, in most standard textbooks one finds that nominal scales are spoken of as "scales of measurement" (e.g., Festinger and Katz 1953; Selltiz et al. 1959). But a nominal scale is nothing else than a qualitative classification, and I fail to understand what it is that a nominal scale does, or can, measure. To be sure classes can be given numbers; but this is simply a coding device for identifying items and has nothing to do with quantification. Likewise the incessant use of "it is a matter of degree" phraseology and of the "continuum" image leave us with qualitative-impressionistic statements which do not advance us by a hair's breadth toward quantification. In a similar vein we speak more and more of "variables" which are not variables in any proper sense, for they are not attributes permitting gradations and implying measurability. No harm necessarily follows if it pleases us to use the word variable as a synonym for the word concept; but we are only deluding ourselves if we really believe that by *saying* variable we *have* a variable.

All in all, coquetting (if not cheating) with a quantitative idiom grossly exaggerates the extent to which political science is currently amenable to quantification, and, still worse, obfuscates the very notion of quantification. The dividing line between the jargon and the substance of quantification can be drawn very simply: quantification begins with numbers, and when numbers are used in relation to their arithmetical properties. To understand, however, the multifaceted complexities of the notion beyond this dividing line is a far less simple matter. Nevertheless one may usefully distinguish – in spite of the close interconnections – among three broad areas of meaning and application, that is, between quantification as (1) measurement, (2) statistical manipulation, and (3) formal mathematical treatment.

In political science we generally refer to the first meaning. That is to say, far more often than not the quantification of political science consists of (a) attaching numerical values to items (pure and simple measurement), (b) using numbers to indicate the rank order of items (ordinal scales), and (c) measuring differences or distances among items (interval scales).[9]

Beyond the stage of measurement we also have powerful statistical techniques not only for protecting ourselves against sampling and measurement errors, but also for establishing significant relationships among variables. However, statistical processing enters the scene only when sufficient numbers have been pinned on sufficient items, and becomes central to the discipline only when we dispose of variables which measure things that are worth measuring. Both conditions – and especially the latter – are hard to meet.[10] Indeed, a cross-examination of our statistical findings in terms of their theoretical significance – and/or of a "more relevant" political science – shows an impressive disproportion between bravura and relevance. Unfortunately, what makes a statistical treatment theoretically significant has nothing to do with statistics.

As for the ultimate stage of quantification – formal mathematical treatment – it is a fact that, so far, political science and mathematics have engaged only "in a sporadic conversation" (Benson 1967: 132).[11] It is equally a fact that we seldom, if ever, obtain isomorphic correspondence between empirical relations among things and formal relations among numbers.[12] We may well disagree about future prospects,[13] or as to whether it makes sense to construct formalized systems of quantitatively well-defined relationships (mathematical models) so long as we wander in a mist of qualitatively ill-defined concepts. If we are to learn, however, from the mathematical development of economics, the evidence is that it "always lagged behind its qualitative and conceptual improvement" (Spengler 1961: 176).[14] And my point is, precisely, that this is not a casual sequence. It is for a very good reason that the progress of quantification should lag – in whatever discipline – behind its qualitative and conceptual progress.

In this messy controversy about quantification and its bearing on standard logical rules we simply tend to forget that *concept formation stands prior to quantification*. The process of thinking inevitably begins with a qualitative (natural) language, no matter at which shore we shall subsequently land. Correlatively, there is no ultimate way of bypassing the fact that human understanding – the way in which our minds work – requires cut-off points which basically correspond (in spite of all subsequent refinements) to the slices into which a natural or qualitative language happens to be divided.

There is a fantastic lack of perspective in the argument that these cut-off points can be obtained via statistical processing, i.e., by letting the data themselves tell us where to draw them. For this argument applies only *within* the frame of conceptual mappings which have to tell us first of what reality is composed. Let it be stressed, therefore, that long before having data which can speak for themselves, the fundamental articulation of language and of thinking is obtained logically – by cumulative conceptual refinement and chains of coordinated definitions – not by measurement. Measurement of what? We cannot measure unless we know first what it is that we are measuring. Nor can the degrees of something tell us what a thing is. As Lazarsfeld and Barton neatly phrase it, "Before we can investigate the presence or absence of some attribute ... or before we can rank objects or measure them in terms of some variable, *we must form the concept of that variable*" (1951: 155).

The major premise is, then, that quantification enters the scene after, and only after, having formed the concept. The minor premise is that the "stuff" of quantification – the things underpinned by the numbers – cannot be provided by quantification itself. Hence the rules of concept formation are independent of, and cannot be derived from, the rules which govern the treatment of quantities and quantitative relations. Let us elaborate on this conclusion.

In the first place, if we never really have "how much" findings – in the sense that the prior question always is how much *in what*, in what conceptual container – it follows that "how much" quantitative findings are an internal element of "what is" qualitative questions: the claim that the latter should give way to the former cannot be sustained. It equally follows, in the second place, that "categoric concepts" of the either-or type cannot give way to "gradation concepts" of the more-than–less-than type.

What is usually lost sight of is that the either-or type of logic is the very logic of classification building. Classes are required to be mutually exclusive, i.e., class concepts represent characteristics, which the object under consideration must either have or lack. Two items being compared must belong first to the same class, and either have or not have an attribute; and only if they have it can the two items be matched in terms of which has it *more* or *less*. Hence the logic of gradation belongs to the logic of classification. More precisely put, the switch from classification to gradation basically consists of replacing the signs "same–different" with the signs "same–greater–lesser," i.e., consists of introducing a quantitative differentiation within a qualitative sameness (of attributes). Clearly, then, the sign "same–different" established by the logic of classification is the requisite condition of introducing the signs "plus–minus."

The retort tends to be that this is true only as long as we persist in thinking in terms of attributes and dichotomies. But this rejoinder misses the point that – aside from classifying – we dispose of no other unfolding technique. Indeed, the taxonomical exercise "unpacks" concepts, and plays a non-replaceable role in the process of thinking in that it decomposes mental compounds into orderly and manageable sets of component units. Let it be added that at no stage of the methodological argument does the taxonomical unpacking lose weight and importance. As a matter of fact, the more we enter the stage of quantification, the more we need unidimensional scales and continua; and dichotomous categorizations serve precisely the purpose of establishing the ends, and thereby the unidimensionality, of each continuum.

Having disposed of the fuzziness brought about by the abuse of a quantitative idiom, attention should immediately be called to the fact-finding side of the coin. For my emphasis on concept formation should not be misunderstood to imply that my concern is more theoretical than empirical. This is not so, because the concepts of any social science are not only the elements of a theoretical system; they are equally, and just as much, data containers. Indeed data is information which is distributed in, and processed by, "conceptual containers." And since the non-experimental sciences basically depend on fact-finding, i.e., on reports about external (not laboratory) observables, the empirical question becomes what turns a concept into a valuable, indeed a valid, fact-finding container.

The reply need not be far-fetched: the lower the discriminating power of a conceptual container, the more the facts are misgathered, i.e., the greater the misinformation. Conversely, the higher the discriminating power of a category, the better the information. Admittedly, in and by itself this reply is not very illuminating, for it only conveys the suggestion that for fact-finding purposes it is more profitable to exaggerate in over-differentiation than in over-assimilation. The point is, however, that what establishes, or helps establish, the discriminating power of a category is the taxonomical infolding. Since the logical requirement of a classification is that its classes should be mutually exclusive and jointly exhaustive, it follows from this that the taxonomical exercise supplies an orderly series of well-sharpened categories, and thereby the basis for collecting adequately precise information. And this is indeed how we know whether, and to what extent, a concept has a fact-gathering validity.

Once again, then, it appears that we have started to run before having learned how to walk. Numbers must be attached – for our purposes – to "things," to facts. How are these things, or facts, identified and collected? Our ultimate ambition may well be to pass from a science "of species" to a science of "functional correlations" (Lasswell and Kaplan 1950: xvi–xvii). The question is whether we are not repudiating a science of species in exchange for nothing. And it seems to me that premature haste combined with the abuse of a quantitative idiom is largely responsible not only for the fact that much of our theorizing is muddled, but also for the fact that much of our research is trivial and wasteful.

Graduate students are being sent all over the world – as LaPalombara vividly puts it – on "indiscriminate fishing expeditions for data" (1968: 66). These fishing expeditions are "indiscriminate" in that they lack taxonomical backing; which is the same as saying that they are fishing expeditions without adequate nets. The researcher sets out with a "checklist" which is, at best, an imperfect net of his own. This may be an expedient way of handling his private research problems, but remains a very inconvenient strategy from the angle of the additivity and the comparability of his findings. As a result, the joint enterprise of comparative politics is menaced by a growing potpourri of disparate, non-cumulative and – in the aggregate – misleading morass of information.

All in all, and regardless of whether we rely on quantitative data or on more qualitative information, the problem is the same, namely, to construct fact-finding categories that own sufficient discriminating power.[15] If our data containers are blurred, we never know to what extent and on what grounds the "unlike" is made "alike." If so, quantitative analysis may well provide more misinformation than qualitative analysis, especially on account of the aggravating circumstance that quantitative misinformation can be used without any substantive knowledge of the phenomena under consideration.

To recapitulate and conclude, I have argued that the logic of either-or cannot be replaced by the logic of more-and-less. Actually the two logics are complementary, and each has a legitimate field of application. Correlatively, polar oppositions and dichotomous confrontations cannot be dismissed: they are a necessary step in the process of concept formation. Equally, impatience with classification is totally unjustified. Rather, we often confuse a mere enumeration (or checklist) with a classification, and many so-called classifications fail to meet the minimal requirements for what they claim to be.

The over-conscious thinker takes the view that if the study of politics has to be a "science," then it has to be Newtonian (or from Newton all the way up to Hempel). But the experimental method is hardly within the reach of political science (beyond the format of small group experimentation) and the very extent to which we are systematically turning to the comparative method of verification points to the extent to which no stronger method – including the statistical method – is available. If so, our distinctive and major problems begin where the lesson of the more exact sciences leaves off. This is tantamount to saying that a wholesale acceptance of the logic and methodology of physics may well be self-defeating, and is surely of little use for our distinctive needs. In particular, and whatever their limits, classifications remain the requisite, if preliminary, condition for any scientific discourse. As Hempel himself concedes, classificatory concepts do lend themselves to the description of observational findings and to the formulation of initial, if crude, empirical generalization (1952: 54). Moreover, a classificatory activity remains the basic instrument for introducing analytical clarity in whatever we are discussing, and leads us to discuss one thing at a time and different things at different times. Finally, and especially, we need taxonomical networks for solving our fact-finding and fact-storing problems. No comparative science of politics is plausible – on a global scale – unless we can draw on extensive *information* which is sufficiently *precise* to be meaningfully compared. The requisite condition for this is an adequate, relatively stable and, thereby, *additive filing system*. Such a filing system no longer is a wild dream, thanks to computer technology and facilities – except for the paradoxical fact that the more we enter the computer age, the less our fact-finding and fact-storing methods abide by any logically standardized criterion. Therefore, my concern with taxonomies is also a concern with (1) the data side of the question and (2) our failure to provide a filing system for computer exploitation. We *have* entered the computer age – but with feet of clay.

The ladder of abstraction

If quantification cannot solve our problems, in that we cannot measure before conceptualizing, and if, on the other hand, "conceptual stretching" is dangerously conducive to the Hegelian night in which all the cows look black (and eventually the milkman is taken for a cow), then the issue must be joined from its very beginning, that is, on the grounds of concept formation.

A few preliminary cautions should be entered. Things conceived or meaningfully perceived, i.e., concepts, are the central elements of propositions, and – depending on how they are named – provide in and by themselves guidelines of interpretation and observation. It should be understood, therefore, that I shall implicitly refer to the conceptual element problems which in a more extended treatment actually and properly belong to the rubric "propositions." By saying "concept formation" I implicitly point to a proposition-forming and problem-solving activity. It should also be understood, in the second place, that my focus will be on those concepts which are crucial to the discipline, that is, the concepts which Bendix describes as "generalizations in disguise" (1963: 533). In the third place, I propose to concentrate on the vertical members of a conceptual structure, that is, on (1) *observational terms*, and (2) the vertical disposition of such terms along a *ladder of abstraction*.

While the notion of abstraction ladder is related to the problem of the levels of analysis, the two things do not coincide. A highly abstract level of analysis may not result from "ladder climbing." Indeed a number of universal conceptualizations are not abstracted from observables: they are "theoretical terms" defined by their systemic meaning.[16] For instance, the meaning of isomorphism, homeostasis, feedback, entropy, etc., is basically defined by the part that each concept plays in the whole theory. In other instances, however, we deal with "observational terms," that is, we arrive at highly abstract levels of conceptualization via ladder climbing, via abstractive inferences from observables. For instance, terms such as group, communication, conflict, and decision can be used either in a very abstract or in a very concrete meaning, either in some very distant relation to observables or with reference to direct observations. In this case we have, then, "empirical concepts" which can be located at, and moved along, very different points of a ladder of abstraction. If so, we have the problem of assessing the level of abstraction at which observational or (in this sense) empirical concepts are located, and the rules of transformation thus resulting. And this seems to be the pertinent focus for the issue under consideration, for our fundamental problem is how to make extensional gains (by climbing the abstraction ladder) without having to suffer unnecessary losses in precision and empirical testability.

The problem can be neatly underpinned with reference to the distinction, and relation, between the *extension* (denotation) and *intension* (connotation) of a term. A standard definition is as follows: "The extension of a word is the class of *things* to which the word applies; the intension of a word is the collection of *properties* which determine the things to which the word applies" (Salmon 1963: 90–91).[17] Likewise, the denotation of a word is the totality of objects indicated by that word; and the connotation is the totality of characteristics anything must possess to be in the denotation of that word.[18]

Now, there are apparently two ways of climbing a ladder of abstraction. One is to broaden the extension of a concept by diminishing its attributes or properties, i.e., by reducing its connotation. In this case a more "general," or more inclusive, concept can be obtained without any loss of precision. The larger the class, the lesser its differentiae; but those differentiae that remain are precise. Moreover, following this procedure we obtain conceptualizations which, no matter how all-embracing, still bear a traceable relation to a collection of specifics, and – out of being amenable to identifiable sets of specifics – lend themselves to empirical testing.

On the other hand, this is hardly the procedure implied by "conceptual stretching," which adds up to being an attempt to augment the extension without diminishing the intension: *the denotation is extended by obfuscating the connotation.* As a result we do not obtain a more general concept, but its counterfeit, a mere generality (where the pejorative "mere" is meant to restore the distinction between correct and incorrect ways of subsuming a term under a broader genus). While a general concept can be said to represent a collection of specifics, a mere generality cannot be underpinned, out of its indefiniteness, by specifics. And while a general concept is conducive to scientific "generalizations," mere generalities are conducive only to vagueness and conceptual obscurity.

The rules for climbing and descending along a ladder of abstraction are thus very simple rules – in principle. We make a concept more abstract and more general by lessening its properties or attributes. Conversely, a concept is specified by the addition (or unfolding) of qualifications, i.e., by augmenting its attributes or properties. If so, let us pass on to consider a ladder of abstraction as such. It is self-evident that along the abstraction ladder one obtains very different degrees of inclusiveness and, conversely, specificity. These differences can be usefully underpinned – for the purposes of comparative politics – by distinguishing three levels of abstraction, labeled, in shorthand, HL (high level), ML (medium level), and LL (low level).

High-level categorizations obtain universal conceptualizations, regardless of what connotation is sacrificed to the requirement of global denotation – either in space, time, or even both.[19] HL concepts can also be visualized as the ultimate genus which cancels all its species. Descending a step, medium-level categorizations fall short of universality and thus can be said to obtain general classes: at this level not all differentiae are sacrificed to extensional requirements. Nonetheless, ML concepts are intended to stress similarities at the expense of uniqueness, for at this level of abstraction we are typically dealing with generalizations. Finally, low-level categories obtain specific, indeed configurative conceptualizations: here denotation is sacrificed to accuracy of connotation. One may equally say that with LL categories the differentiae of individual settings are stressed above their similarities, so much so that at this level definitions are often contextual.

A couple of examples may be usefully entered. In a perceptive essay which runs parallel to my line of thinking, Smelser makes the point that, for purposes of comparability, "staff is more satisfactory than administration . . ., and administration is more satisfactory than civil service" (1968: 64). This is so, according to Smelser, because the concept of civil service "is literally useless in connection with societies without a formal state or governmental apparatus." In this respect, "the concept of administration is somewhat superior . . . but even this term is quite culture-bound." Hence the more helpful term is "Weber's concept of staff . . . since it can encompass without embarrassment various political arrangements" (1968: 64). In my own terms the argument would be rephrased as follows. In the field of so-called comparative public administration, "staff" is the high level universal category. "Administration" is still a good traveling category, but falls short of universal applicability in that it retains some of the attributes associated with the more specific notion of "bureaucracy." Descending the ladder of abstraction further we then find "civil service," which is qualified by its associations with the modern State. Finally, and to pursue the argument all the way down to the low level of abstraction, a comparative study of, say, French and English state employees will discover their unique and distinguishing traits and would thus provide contextual definitions.

The example suggested by Smelser is fortunate in that we are offered a choice of terms, so that (whatever the choice) a different level of abstraction can be identified by a different denomination. The next example is illustrative, instead, of the far less fortunate situation in which we may have to perform across the whole ladder of abstraction with one and the same term. In illustrating his caution that many concepts are "generalizations in disguise," Bendix comes across such a simple concept as "village." Yet he notes that the term village may be misleading when applied to Indian society, where "the minimum degree of cohesion commonly associated with this term is absent" (1963: 536). Even in such a simple case, then, a scholar is required to place the various associations of "village" along an abstraction ladder in accord with the traveling extension afforded by each connotation.

Clearly, there is no hard and fast dividing line between levels of abstraction. Borders can only be drawn very loosely; and the number of slices into which the ladder is divided largely depends on how fine one's analysis needs to be. Three slices are sufficient, however, for the purposes of logical analysis. And my major concern is, in this connection, with what goes on at the upper end of the ladder, at the crucial juncture at which we cross the border between medium level general concepts and high level universals. The issue may be formulated as follows: how far up can an observational term be pushed without self-denying results?

In principle the extension of a concept should not be broadened beyond the point at which at least one relatively precise connotation (property or attribute) is retained. In practice, however, the requirement of positive identification may be too exacting. But even if no minimal positive identification can be afforded, I do not see how we can renounce the requirement of negative identification. The crucial distinction would thus be between (1) concepts defined by negation or *ex adverso*, i.e., by saying what they are not, and (2) concepts without negation, i.e., no-opposite concepts without specified boundaries. The logical principle involved in this distinction is *omnis determinatio est negatio*, that is, any determination involves a negation. According to this principle, the former concepts are, no matter how broad, *determinate*; whereas the latter are indeterminate, literally *without termination*.

If this principle is applied to the climbing process along a ladder of abstraction, and precisely to the point at which ML categories are turned into HL universals, in the first instance we obtain *empirical universals*, whereas in the second instance we obtain universals which lack empirical value – *pseudo-universals* for an empirical science. The reason for this is that a concept qualified by a negation may or may not be found to apply to the real world; whereas a non-bounded concept always applies by definition: having no specified termination, there is no way of ascertaining whether it applies to the real world or not. An empirical universal is such because it still points to *something*; whereas a non-empirical universal indiscriminately points to *everything* (as any researcher on the field soon discovers).

The group concept serves nicely as an illustration of the foregoing (other examples will be discussed in greater detail later), and is very much to the point in that it represents the first large-scale attempt to meet the traveling problem of comparative politics. In the group theory of politics (Bentley, Truman, and Lathan being the obvious references) it is clear enough that "group" becomes an all-embracing category: not only an analytical construct (as the queer and unclear terminology of the discipline would have it), but definitely a universal construct. However, we are never really told what group is *not*. Not only does "group" apply *everywhere*, as any universal should; it equally applies to *everything*, that is, never and nowhere shall we encounter non-groups.[20] If so, how is it that the group theory of politics since the 1950s has generated a great deal of empirical research? The reply is that the research was not guided by the universal construct but rather by intuitive concrete conceptualizations. Hence the "indefinite group" of the theory and the "concrete groups" of the research are poorly connected. The unfortunate consequences are not only that the research lacks theoretical backing (for want of medium-level categories and especially of a taxonomic framework), but that the vagueness of the theory has no fit for the specificity of the findings. We are thus left with a body of literature that gives the frustrating feeling of dismantling theoretically whatever it discovers empirically.

There is, then, a break-off point in the search for universal inclusiveness beyond which we have, theoretically, a "nullification of the problem" and, empirically, what may be called an "empirical vaporization." This is the point at which a concept is not even determined *ex adverso*. By saying that no-opposite universals are of no empirical use I do not imply that they are utterly useless. But I do wish to say that whenever notions such as groups or – as in my subsequent examples – pluralism, integration, participation, or mobilization, obtain no termination, i.e., remain indeterminate, they provide only tags or chapter headings, i.e., the main entries of a filing system. From an empirical point of view pseudo-universals are only funnels of approach and can only perform, so to speak, an allusive function.

Turning to the middle slice – the fat slice of the medium-level categories – it will suffice to note that at this level we are required to perform the whole set of operations that some authors call "definition by analysis," that is, the process of defining a term by finding the genus to which the object designated by the word belongs, and then specifying the attributes which distinguish such an object from all the other species of the same genus. When Apter complains that our "analytical categories are too general when they are theoretical, and too descriptive where they are not," (1970: 15–16), I understand this complaint to apply to our disorderly leaps from observational findings all the way up to universal categories – and vice versa – by-passing as it were the stage of definition by analysis. Apter is quite right in pleading for "better intermediate analytical categories." But these intermediate categories cannot be constructed, I fear, as long as our contempt for the taxonomical exercise leaves us with an atrophied medium level of abstraction.

The low level of abstraction may appear uninteresting to the comparative scholar. He would be wrong, however, on two counts. First, when the comparative scholar is engaged in fieldwork, the more his fact-finding categories are brought down to this level, the better his research. Second, it is the evidence obtained nation-by-nation, or region-by-region (or whatever the unit of analysis may be) that helps us decide which classification works or which way criterion of classification should be developed.

While classifying must abide by logical rules, logic has nothing to do with the usefulness of a classificatory system. Botanists, mineralogists, and zoologists have not created their taxonomical trees as a matter of mere logical unfolding; that is, they have not imposed their "classes" upon their animals, any more than their animals (flowers or minerals) have imposed themselves upon their classifiers. Let it be added that the information requirements of such an unsettled science as a science of politics can hardly be satisfied by single-purpose classifications (not to mention single-purpose checklists). As I have stressed, we desperately need standard fact-finding and fact-storing containers (concepts). But this standardization is only possible and fruitful on the basis of "multi-purpose" and, at the limit, all-purpose classifications. Now, whether a classification may serve multiple purposes, and which classification fits this requirement best, is something we discover inductively, that is, starting from the bottom of the ladder of abstraction.

The overall discussion is recapitulated in Table 1.1 with respect to its bearing on the problems of comparative politics. A few additional comments are in order. In the first place, reference to three levels of abstraction brings out the inadequacy of merely distinguishing between "broad" and "narrow" meanings of a term.[21] For this does not clarify, whenever this is necessary, whether we distinguish (1) between HL universal and ML general conceptualizations, or (2) between ML genuses and LL species, or (3) between ML and LL categories, or even (4) between HL universal and LL configurative conceptualizations.

In the second place, and more importantly, reference to the ladder of abstraction forcibly highlights the drastic loss of logical articulation, indeed the gigantic leap, implied by the argument that *all* differences are "a matter of degree." This cannot be conceded, to begin with, at the level of universal categories. But all differences cannot be considered a matter of more-or-less at the medium level either. At the top we inevitably begin with opposite pairs, with polar opposites, and this is tantamount to saying that the top ML categories definitely and only establish differences in *kind*. From here downwards, definitions are obtained via the logic of classification, and this implies that a logic of gradation cannot be applied as long as we establish differences between species. Differences in degree obtain only after having

Table 1.1 Ladder of abstraction

Levels of abstraction	Major comparative scope and purpose	Logical and empirical properties of concepts
HL: *High-level categories* Universal conceptualizations	Cross-area comparisons among heterogeneous contexts (global theory)	Maximal extension Minimal intension Definition by negation
ML: *Medium-level categories* General conceptualizations and taxonomies	Intra-area comparisons among relatively homogeneous contexts (middle range theory)	Balance of denotation with connotation Definition by analysis, i.e., per genus et differentiation
LL: *Low-level categories* Configurative conceptualizations	Country by country analysis (narrow-gauge theory)	Maximal intension Minimal extension Contextual definition

established that two or more objects have the same attributes or properties, i.e., belong to the same species. Indeed, it is only *within* the same class that we are entitled – and indeed required – to ask which object has more or less of an attribute or property.

In principle, then, it is a fallacy to apply the logic of gradation whenever ladder climbing (or descending) is involved. If we are reminded that along the ladder we augment the extension by diminishing the denotation (and vice versa), what is at stake here is the presence or absence of a given property; and this is not a matter of degree, but a matter of establishing the level of abstraction. Hence it is only after having settled at a given level of abstraction that considerations of more-and-less correctly apply. And the rule of thumb seems to be that the higher the level of abstraction, the less a degree language applies (as anything but a metaphor); whereas the lower level of abstraction, the more a degree optics correctly and necessarily applies, and the more we profit from gradation concepts.

In the third place, and equally important, reference to the ladder of abstraction casts many doubts on the optimistic view – largely shared by the methodological literature – that "the more universal a proposition, i.e., the greater the number of events a proposition accounts for, the more potential falsifiers can be found, and the more informative is the proposition."[22] The sentence suggests a simultaneous and somewhat natural progression of universality, falsifiers, and informative concepts. It seems to me, instead, that reference to the correct technique of ladder climbing (and descending) confronts us at all points with choosing between a range of explanation (thereby including the explanation of the relationships among the items under investigation), and accuracy of description (or informative accuracy). By saying that the "informative content" of a proposition grows by climbing the abstraction ladder, we should not be misled into understanding that we are supplying more descriptive information. Hence it is dubious whether we are really supplying more potential falsifiers (let alone the danger of "overly universal" propositions of no informative value for which falsifiers cannot be found).

Before concluding it should not pass unnoticed that in this section I have never used the word "variable," nor mentioned operational definitions, nor invoked indicators. Equally, my reference to gradation concepts and to considerations of more-or-less has been, so far, entirely pre-quantitative. What is noteworthy, then, is the length that has been traveled before entering the problems which seem to monopolize our methodological awareness. There is nothing wrong, to be sure, in taking up an argument at whichever point we feel that we have something to say – except that the tail of the methodological argument should not be mistaken for its beginning. Since I have taken up the issue at an early stage, I cannot possibly carry it through to its end. It behooves me, nonetheless, to indicate how I would plug what I have said into what shall have to remain unsaid.[23]

For one thing, it should be understood that by considering concepts – the genus – I have not excluded the consideration of variables, which are a species. That is, a variable is still a concept; but a concept is not necessarily a variable. If all concepts could be turned into variables, the difference could be considered provisional. Unfortunately, as a scholar well versed in quantitative analysis puts it, "All the most interesting variables are nominal" (Rose n.d.: 8). Which is the same as saying that all the most interesting concepts are not variables in the proper, strict sense of implying "the possibility of measurement in the most exact sense of the word" (Lazarsfeld and Barton 1951: 170).[24]

A closely linked and similar argument applies to the operationist requirement. Just as concepts are not necessarily variables, definitions are not necessarily operational. The definitional requirement for a concept is that its *meaning* is declared, while operational definitions are required to state the conditions, indeed the operations, by means of which a concept can be *verified* and, ultimately, measured. Accordingly we may usefully distinguish between definition of meaning and operational definition. And while it is obvious that an operational definition still is a declaration of meaning, the reverse is not true.

The contention is often that definition of meaning represents a pre-scientific age of definition, which should be superseded in scientific discourse by operational definitions. However, this contention can hardly meet the problems of concept formation, and indeed appears to ignore them. As the ladder of abstraction scheme helps to underline, among the many possible ways and procedures of defining the *ex adverso* definitions and taxonomic unfoldings (or definition by analysis) some correspond to different levels of analysis and play, at each level, a non-replaceable role. Moreover, operational definitions generally entail a drastic curtailment of meaning for they can only maintain those meanings that comply with the operationist requirement. Now, we are surely required to reduce ambiguity by cutting down the range of meanings of concepts. But the operational criterion of reducing ambiguity entails drastic losses in conceptual richness and in explanatory power. Take, for instance, the suggestion that "social class" should be dismissed and replaced by a set of operational statements relating to income, occupation, educational level, etc. If the suggestion were adopted wholesale, the loss of conceptual substance would be not only considerable, but unjustified. The same applies, to cite another instance, to "power." To be concerned with the measurement of power does not imply that the meaning of the concept should be reduced to what can be measured about power – the latter view would make human behavior in whatever collective sphere almost inexplicable.

It should be understood, therefore, that operational definitions implement, but do not replace, definitions of meaning. Indeed there must be a conceptualization before we engage in operationalization. As Hempel recommends, operational definitions should not be "emphasized to the neglect of the requirement of systematic import" (1952: 60).[25] This is also to say that definitions of meaning of theoretical import, hardly operational definitions, account for the dynamics of intellectual discovery and stimulation. Finally, it should be understood that empirical testing occurs before and also without, operational definitions. Testing is any method of checking correspondence with reality by the use of pertinent observations; hence the decisive difference brought about by operationalization is verification, or falsification, by measurement.[26]

Speaking of testing, indicators are indeed precious "testing helpers." As a matter of fact it is difficult to see how theoretical terms could be empiricized and tested otherwise, that is, without having recourse to indicators. Indicators are also expedient shortcuts for the empirical checking of observational terms. Yet the question remains: Indicators of what? If we have fuzzy concepts, the fuzziness will remain as it is. That is to say that indicators cannot, in and by themselves, sharpen our concepts and relieve us from composing and decomposing them along a ladder of abstraction.

Comparative fallacies: an illustration

We may now confront in more detail how the ladder of abstraction scheme brings out the snares and the faults of our current way of handling the traveling problem of comparative politics. For we may now settle at a less-rarified level of discussion and proceed on the basis of examples. It is pretty obvious that my line of analysis largely cuts across the various theories and schools that propose themselves for adoption in comparative politics, for my basic preoccupation is with the ongoing work of the "normal science," i.e., with the common conceptual problems of the discipline. Nonetheless it will be useful to enter here a somewhat self-contained illustration which bears not only on discrete concepts, but equally on a theoretical framework. I have thus selected for my first detailed discussion the categories of "structure" and "function," and this precisely on account of their crucial role in establishing the structural-functional approach in the political science setting.[27]

In introducing his pioneering comparative volume, Almond boldly asserts, "What we have done is to separate political function from political structure" (Almond and Coleman 1960: 59). This separation is indeed crucial. But ten years have gone by and the assignment remains largely unfulfilled. Indeed the structural-functional school of thought is still grappling – with clear symptoms of frustration – with the preliminary difficulty of defining "function" – both taken by itself and in its relation to structure.[28] Whether function can be conceived simply as an "activity" performed by structures; or whether it is more proper to construe function as an "effect";[29] or whether function should be conceived only as a "relation" among structures"[30] – this controversy turns out to be largely immaterial in the light of our substantive performance. That is to say, if our attention turns to the functional vocabulary in actual use, a perusal of the literature quickly reveals two things: first, a tantalizing anarchy (more on this later), and second, that the functional terminology employed most of the time by most practitioners definitely carries a purposive or teleological connotation. Skillful verbal camouflage may well push the teleological implication in the background. Yet it is hard to find a functional argumentation which really escapes, in the final analysis, *Zweckrationalität*, what Max Weber called rationality of ends.[31] We may well quarrel about the definition,[32] yet the substance of the matter remains that the definitional controversy has little bearing on our subsequent proceedings. If so, it suits my purposes to settle for the way in which most people use "function" in practice (regardless of how they theorize about it), and thereby to settle for the common sense, unsophisticated meaning.

When we say, somewhat naïvely, that structures "have functions," we are interested in the reason for being of structures: we are implying, that is, that structures exist for some end, purpose, destination, or assignment.[33] This is tantamount to saying that "function" points to a means–end relationship (which becomes, from a systemic viewpoint, also a part–whole relationship), i.e., that function is the activity performed by a structure – the means – vis-à-vis its ascribed or actually served purpose.[34] Conversely, dysfunction, non-functionality, and the like, indicate – from a different angle – that the assigned purpose is not served by a given structure. And this current usage of function goes a long way to explain, in turn, our difficulties with structure.

The major problem with "structure" is, in fact, that political bodies and institutions largely bear, if not a functional denomination, a functional definition. Either under the sheer force of names – which is in itself a tremendous force – or for the sake of brevity, political structures are seldom adequately defined on their own terms – *qua structures*. That is to say, on the one hand, that we dispose of a functional (purposive) vocabulary, whereas we badly lack a structural (descriptive) vocabulary; and that on the other hand, even when we deliberately ask "what is," we are invariably prompted to reply in terms of "what for." What is an election? A means (a structure) for electing office holders. What is a legislature? An arrangement for producing legislation. What is a government? A setup for governing. The structure is almost invariably perceived and qualified by its salient function.[35] This makes a great deal of sense in practical politics, but represents a serious handicap for the understanding of politics.

The plain fact is, then, that the structural-functional analyst is a lame scholar. He claims to walk on two feet, but actually stands on one foot – and a bad foot at that. He cannot really visualize the interplay between "structure" and "function" because the two terms are seldom, if ever, neatly disjoined: the structure remains throughout a twin brother of its imputed functional purposes. And here we enter a somewhat vicious whirl which leads the approach to conclusions which, if true, would be self-denying.

Whatever else the structural-functional scholar may have failed to discover, he feels pretty sure about three points: first, no structure is unifunctional, i.e., performs only one function; second, the same structure can be multifunctional, i.e., can perform across different countries' widely different functions; third, and therefore, the same function has structural alternatives, i.e., can be performed by very different structures. Now, to some extent these points are undeniable – but only to the extent sensed at any time by any perceptive comparative scholar. My quarrel is with the emphasis, which is unwarranted and positively misleading.

Is it really the same structure that functions differently? Or is the functional performance different because the structure is not the same? The thesis generally lacks adequate evidence on the structural side. For instance, "elections" are multifunctional (they may well serve the purpose of legitimizing a despot), but "free elections" are not.[36] That is to say, as soon as the electoral process obtains a structural underpinning – the minute and multiple structural conditions that make for free voting – electoral multifunctionality rapidly comes to an end. If the voter is offered alternatives, if the candidates are free to compete, if fraudulent counting is impossible, then free elections do serve – everywhere – the purpose of allowing an electorate to select and dismiss office holders. In view of this primary, fundamental purpose the same electoral structure (same in providing all the necessary safeties) either approaches unifunctionality, or leaves us with non-functionality, e. g., with the finding that illiterate voters are unable to use electoral mechanisms which presuppose literacy.

While the most serious problem and default is that the structures are inadequately pinpointed and described, let me hasten to add that we are not performing much better from the functional end of the argument. For our functional categories also generally lack adequate underpinning. Surprisingly enough – if one considers the far greater ease with which the functional side of the problem can be attacked – our functions tend to be as unhelpful as our structures.

For instance, if one asks, "Why a party system?" the least challengeable and most inclusive reply might be that parties perform a communication function. And if the problem is left at that, it easily follows that the authorities and the citizens "communicate," in some sense, in any polity, i.e., even when no party system exists. Hence party systems have structural alternatives – *quod erat demonstrandum*. But the problem cannot be left at that, i.e., with an unbounded, no-difference notion of communication which nullifies the problem. And the underpinning of communication brings out, first, that there is an essential difference between upgoing and descending communication, and second, that it is equally important to distinguish between "communication-information" and "communication-pressure." If so, to define a party system as an instrument for "communicating" demands and conveying "information" to the authorities, is to miss the point. A party system is, in reality, a mechanism for sustaining demands – and pressing demands – all the way through to policy implementation. What is at stake, then, is the passage from a two-way (reversible) communication-information to a prevalence of up-going communication-pressure. And for this latter purpose we have not devised, so far, any structural alternative. A party system turns out to be, therefore, a non-replaceable, unique structure as soon as we spell out its distinctive, crucial reason for being.

A more careful scrutiny goes to show, then, that the multifunctional, multistructural argument has been pushed far too far, indeed to the point of becoming erroneous. Aside from the error, the irony of the situation is that, as it stands, the thesis appears self-defeating. If the same structure performs utterly different functions in different countries, and if we can always find structural alternatives for whatever function, what is the use of structural-functional analysis?

Pulling the threads together, I need not spend much time in arguing that the stalemate and the mishandlings of the structural-functional approach have a lot to do with the ladder of abstraction.

On the functional side of the coin we are encumbered by a wealth of haphazard functional categories which are merely enumerated (hardly classified according to some criterion, and even less according to the logical requirements of a taxonomical tree-type unfolding), and definitely provide no clues as to the level and type of analysis (e.g., total versus partial systems analysis) to which they apply.[37] As a result, the global functional argument developed by a number of structural-functionalists remains suspended in mid-air – for lack of a coordinated medium-level taxonomic support – and is left to play with overstretched, if not contentless, functional universals. On the structural side of the coin we are confronted, instead, with little more than nothing. Structures qualified on their own right hardly exist – at least in the Almond line of thinking.[38] This is all the more regrettable in view of the fact that while functions are meant to be (at least in global comparative politics) broad explanatory categories which do not require a low-level specification, structures bear, instead, a closer relation to observables, and definitely need underpinning all the way down the ladder. With structures understood as organizational structures we are required, in fact, to descend the ladder all the way down to low-level configurative-descriptive accounts.

Starting from the top, one can identify – with the help of minor terminological devices – at least four different levels of analysis: (1) structural principles (e.g., pluralism), (2) structural conditions (e.g., the class or the economic structure), (3) organizational patterns (with relation to membership systems), and (4) specific organizational structures (e.g. constitutions). By saying "structural principles," I mean that as an HL category the notion of structure can only point to the principles according to which the component part of polities, or of societies, are related to each other. With reference, instead, to the low level of abstraction it should be clear that constitutions and statutes are not the real structure. Nonetheless, behavior under written rules is easier to pin down than behavior under diffuse rules, and excessive anti-formalism leads us to neglect organizational theory and the extent to which legally enforced regulations do mold behavior.

In summing up, not only has the structural-functional scholar ignored the ladder of abstraction, but he has inadvertently destroyed, during his reckless climbing, his own ladder.[39] So much so that the approach encounters exactly the same perplexity as, say, general systems theory, namely, "Why has no scholar succeeded in presenting a structural-functional formulation which meets the requirements of empirical analysis?" (Flanigan and Fogelman 1967: 82–83). Now, it is hardly surprising that the general systems theorist should encounter great difficulties in deriving testable propositions about politics since he is required to proceed deductively on the basis of theoretical primitives.[40] But this is not the case with the structural-functional approach, which is not necessarily committed to whole systems analysis and enjoys the distinctive empirical advantage of leaning extensively – especially with segmented systems analysis – on observational terms.[41] So, why should the structural-functional scholar remain tied to "a level of analysis which [does] not permit empirical testing?" (Flanigan and Fogelman 1967: 82–83). According to my diagnosis there is no intrinsic reason for this. Quite to the contrary, we may expect very rewarding returns, and the empirical promise (and distinctiveness) of the approach may well near fulfillment, if we only learn how to maneuver along a ladder of abstraction.

Let us now pass on to a further discussion – the second part of this illustration – for which I have selected a somewhat different family of categories: pluralism, integration, participation, and mobilization.[42] While one may think of many other examples that would suit my purposes just as well, the four categories in question are representative in that they are used for significant theoretical developments not only under a variety of different frameworks, but also by the non-affiliated scholar, thereby including – in the case of participation and mobilization – the scholar who happens to be interested only in statistical manipulations.

Given the fact that pluralism, integration, participation, and mobilization are culture-bound concepts which may reflect – as far as we know at the outset – a distinctive Western experience, the methodological caveat here is that the reference area should make for the starting point of the investigation. So to speak, we are required to elaborate our culture-bound concepts in a "we–they" clockwise direction. It is proper, therefore, to start with the question: How do we understand pluralism, integration, participation, and mobilization in their domestic, original context?

At home, "pluralism" does not apply to societal and/or political structure, nor to interplay between a plurality of actors. Pluralism came to be used, in the Western literature, to convey the idea that a pluralistic society is a society whose structural configuration is shaped by pluralistic beliefs, namely, that all kinds of autonomous sub-units should develop at all levels, that interests are recognized in their legitimate diversity, and that dissent, not unanimity, represents the basis of civility. Pluralism is indeed – as already noted – a highly abstract structural principle. Yet the term points to a particular societal structure – not merely to a developed stage of differentiation and specialization – and does retain a wealth of characterizing connotations whenever we discuss, in the Western democracies, our internal policies and problems.

"Integration" can be conceived as an end-state, as a process, or as a function performed by integrating agencies (parties, interest groups, etc.). In any case, in the Western polities integration is not applied to whatever kind of "putting together," to whatever state of amalgamation. For instance, when American scholars discuss their own domestic problems, they have definite ideas of what is, and what is not, integration. They would deny that integration has anything to do with "enforcing uniformity." They are likely to assume, instead, that integration both presupposes and generates a pluralistic society (as qualified above). And, surely, an integrative agency is required to obtain a maximum of coalescence and solidarity with a minimum of coercion.[43]

Similar points can be made with regard to participation and mobilization. Regardless of whether "participation" is used normatively (as pointing to a basic tenet of the democratic ideal) or descriptively (as reflecting a democratic experience), in either case in our domestic discussions participation is not any kind of "taking part." Thus the advocates of a participatory democracy are hardly satisfied by any kind of involvement in politics. To them participation means self-motion; it does not mean being manipulated or coerced into motion. And surely the original definite meaning of the term conveys the idea of a free citizen who acts and intervenes – if he so wishes – according to his best judgment. So conceived, participation is the very opposite, or the very reverse, of mobilization. Mobilization does not convey the idea of individual self-motion, but the idea of a malleable, passive collectivity which is being put into motion at the whim of persuasive – and more than persuasive – authorities. We say that individuals "participate," but we cannot say about the same individuals that they "mobilize" – they *are mobilized*.

It is quite clear, then, that pluralism, integration, participation, and mobilization all have specific connotations which can be pinned down, and are in fact retained – no matter how implicitly – in our Western enquiries and controversies. However, in the context of global comparative politics the specificity of these notions gets lost: there is no end to pluralism; integration is applied indifferently to pluralistic and non-pluralistic settings; and participation and mobilization are turned into largely overlapping notions. There is no end to pluralism, for we are never told what is non-pluralism. Since pluralism exists somewhere, the assumption appears to be that "to a different degree" pluralism will be found to exist everywhere. However, a different degree of *what*? This is indeed the irony of using a degree language – intended when used appropriately to convey precision – for conveying elusiveness. Likewise the meaning of integration changes, and eventually evaporates, en route. Finally, and similarly, the distinction between participation and mobilization only holds at home. With most comparative-oriented scholars, mobilization comes to mean whatever process of social activation and participation is currently applied by the discipline at large, both to democratic and mobilizational techniques of political activation.

At this stage of the argument I need not labor at explaining why and how we obtain these drastic losses of specificity. They result, as we know, from conceptual stretching, which results, in turn, from incorrect ladder climbing: the clumsy attempt to arrive at "traveling universals" at the expense of precision, instead of at the expense of connotation (i.e., by reducing the number of qualifying attributes). What remains to be highlighted are the consequences of this state of affairs.

Take, for instance, the formidable errors in interpretation and prediction which are suggested by the universal, unspecified application of "pluralism" and "integration." If we say that African societies are not pluralistic but "tribalistic," the argument is likely to be that a situation of tribalistic fragmentation hardly provides the structural basis not only for integrative processes to occur, but also for bringing integrative agencies to the fore. Indeed my argument would be that the functional needs, or feedbacks, of a fragmented society are at odds with the functional feedbacks, or needs, of a pluralistic society. In Europe, for instance, medieval fragmentation generated monarchical absolutism. However, if pluralism is vaporized into an empty generality, then we are authorized to call African societies pluralistic, and the unfortunate implication may well be that we expect Africans to solve their problems as if they had to deal with Western-type societies.[44]

"Mobilization" is also a worthwhile example in that it confronts us with a problem that has only been mentioned, so far, in passing. While pluralism, integration, and participation are derived from our experience with democracy – i.e., from the context of the democratic polities – we also dispose of a limited set of terms which originate from a totalitarian context. This is the case of the term mobilization, which derives from military terminology – especially the German total mobilization of World War I – and enters the vocabulary of politics via the militia type of party (as Duverger calls it), and specifically via the experience of fascism and of nazism.[45] Nonetheless the term is currently applied also to the democratic polities – and this means that we have drawn a "reversed extrapolation" (i.e., a counter-clockwise extrapolation). And since we often complain that our terminology is democracy-centered, my first complaint is that we fail to take advantage of the fact that we do have terms which escape the democratic bias. However, the inconvenience resulting from reversed extrapolations is seen best on a broader scale, and with particular reference to what I call the "boomerang effect" of the developing areas.[46]

Western scholars traveling across Africa or Southeast Asia discover that our categories hardly apply, which is hardly surprising. From this they conclude – and this is the boomerang effect – that the Western categories also should not be applied to the West. But this is a strange inference. Granted that global comparative politics requires minimal common denominators, it does not follow that we should escape Western parochialism by masquerading in non-Western clothes. For one thing, it may well be that a number of ancient civilizations appear diffuse and amorphous to the Western observer precisely because he lacks the categories for coping with devious, overly sedimented, "non-rational" structural patterns. On the other hand, and assuming that underdeveloped political societies may be far less structured than others, this is no reason for feeding back shapelessness where structural differentiation does exist. Hence, reversed extrapolations are a fallacy, and the problem of establishing a minimal common denominator does not authorize us to feed primitivism and formlessness into non-primitive settings.

If I may generalize from the foregoing, it appears that much of the ongoing work of the discipline is plagued by "meaningless togetherness," and thereby by dangerous equivocations and distortions. In particular, and especially important, under these conditions we are dangerously exposed to "begging the question," i.e., to assuming what we should be proving: the *petitio principii* fallacy. For instance, if "mobilization" is applied to a democratic polity the suggestion is that democracies mobilize more or less as totalitarian regimes do. Conversely, if "participation" is applied to a totalitarian system the suggestion is that democratic participation also occurs, to some extent at least, in nondemocratic settings. Now this may well be the case. But the case cannot be proven by *transferring the same denomination* from one context to another. For this amounts to pure and simple terminological camouflage: things are declared alike by making them *verbally* identical.

All in all, then, it can hardly be held that our "losses of specificity" are compensated by gains in inclusiveness. I would rather say that our gains in traveling capacity, or in universal inclusiveness, are verbal (and deceptive) while our "gains in obfuscation" are very substantial.

I cannot discuss this further. As LaPalombara vividly puts it, "So many of our generalizations about the political process move with apparent randomness from the micro to the macroanalytic levels" – the result being "messiness caused by confusion as to the level of analysis" (1968: 72). Following this line of complaint I have argued that confusion as to the level of analysis brings about these unfortunate results: (1) at the higher levels, macroscopic errors of interpretation, explanation, and prediction; (2) at the lower levels, a great deal of wasteful data misgathering; and (3) at all levels, confusion of meaning and destruction of the sharpness of our concepts. We do lack words. But conceptual stretching and poor logic have largely impoverished the analytical articulation and the discriminating power of the words that we do have. And my feeling is that only too often major differences are being cancelled on the thin basis of secondary, trivial similarities. It would hardly make sense to say that men and fishes are alike in that both classes share a "swimming capability." Yet much of what we are saying in global comparative politics may not make much more sense.

Let me stress, to conclude, that according to my scheme of analysis all of this is unnecessary. Awareness of the ladder of abstraction shows that the need for highly abstract, all-embracing categories does not require us to inflate, indeed to evaporate, the observational, empirically linkable categories that we do have. Moreover, if we know how to climb and descend along a ladder of abstraction – and thereby know where we stand in relation to the "property space" of the analysis that we are pursuing – not only conceptual stretching is ruled out, but also faulty analogies and the begging-the-question fallacy can be disposed of.

Summary

Especially during the last decade, comparative politics as a substantive field has been rapidly expanding. The scale, if not the scope, of this expansion raises thorny and unprecedented problems of method. But we seem to embark more and more in comparative endeavors without *comparative method*, i.e., with inadequate methodological awareness and less-than-adequate logical skills. That is to say, we seem to be particularly naïve vis-à-vis the logical requirements of a worldwide comparative treatment of political science issues.

My focus is conceptual – about concepts – under the assumption that concepts are not only elements of a theoretical system, but equally tools for fact-gathering, serving as data containers. The empirical problem is that we badly need information which is sufficiently precise to be meaningfully comparable. Hence we need a filing system provided by discriminating, i.e., taxonomic, conceptual containers. If these are not provided, data misgathering is inevitable; and statistical, computerized sophistication is no remedy for misinformation. The theoretical problem can be stated, in turn, as follows: we grievously lack a disciplined use of terms and procedures of comparison. This discipline can be provided, I suggest, by awareness of the ladder of abstraction, of the logical properties that are implied, and of the rules of composition and decomposition thus resulting. If no such discipline is obtained, conceptual mishandling and, ultimately, conceptual misformation is inevitable (and joins forces with data misgathering).

Thus far the discipline has largely followed the line of least resistance, namely, "conceptual stretching." In order to obtain a worldwide applicability the extension of our concepts has been broadened by obfuscating their connotation. As a result, the very purpose of comparing – control – is defeated, and we are left to swim in a sea of empirical and theoretical messiness. Intolerably blunted conceptual tools are conducive, on the one hand, to wasteful if not misleading research, and, on the other hand, to a meaningless togetherness based on pseudo-equivalences.

The remedy resides – I submit – in our combined ability (1) to develop the discipline along a medium level of abstraction with better intermediate categories, and (2) to maneuver, both upwards and downwards, along a ladder of abstraction in such a way as to bring together assimilation and differentiation, a relatively high explanatory power and a relatively precise descriptive content, macro-theory, and empirical testing. To be sure, no level of analysis can be exactly translated and converted into the next level. In this sense, something is always lost (and gained) along the ladder. But a disciplined use of terms and procedures of comparison generates, at each level, sets of propositions which either reinforce or contradict the propositions of the neighboring levels.

The suggestion has recently been put forward that "political scientists turn to mathematics for [the] rules of logic" required "to introduce the necessary deductive power into a paradigm" (Holt and Richardson 1970: 7). I have taken the more sober and indeed counter-perfectionistic view that we should not encourage the over-conscious thinker paralyzed by overly ambitious standards. But surely we cannot expect an unconscious thinker lacking elementary logical training and discipline to meet the intricate new problems arising from global comparisons.

Acknowledgments

I am particularly indebted to David Apter, Harry Eckstein, Carl J. Friedrich, Joseph LaPalombara, Felix Oppenheim, and Fred W. Riggs for their critical comments. I am also very much obliged to the Concilium on International and Area Studies at Yale University, of which I was a fellow in 1966–67. This article is part of the work done under the auspices of the Concilium.

Notes

* Originally published as Giovanni Sartori (1970) "Concept Misformation in Comparative Politics," *American Political Science Review* 64 (4): 1033–53.

1 This is by no means a criticism of a comparative item-by-item analysis, and even less of the "institutional-functional" approach. On the latter, see the judicious remarks of Ralph Braibanti (1968).
2 For the various phases of the comparative approach, see Eckstein's (1963) perceptive "Introduction" in the volume edited by Eckstein and Apter.
3 On the "fallacy of inputism," see Macridis (1968). In his words, "The state of the discipline can be summed up in one phrase: the gradual disappearance of the political" (86). A cogent statement of the issue is Paige (1966: 49 ff). My essay "From the Sociology of Politics to Political Sociology" (1969) is also largely concerned with the fallacy of inputism viewed as a sociological reduction of politics.
4 The works of Fred W. Riggs are perhaps the best instance of such bold attempts (1969, 1970a, 1970b). For a recent presentation, see his "The Comparison of Whole Political Systems" (1970a). While Riggs's innovative strategy has undeniable practical drawbacks, the criticism of Martin Landau (1969) appears somewhat unfair.
5 On the boomerang effect of the developing areas, more in the final section.

6   More precisely in Croce (1942: 13–17), universals are defined *ultrarappresentativi*, as being above and beyond any conceivable empirical representability.

7   For the comparative method as a "method of control," see especially Lijphart (1969). According to Lijphart, the comparative method is a "method of discovering empirical relationships among variables" (2); and I fully concur, except that this definition can be entered only at a later stage of the argument.

8   Carl F. Hempel, quoted in Martindale (1959: 87). Martindale aptly comments that "Hempel's judgments are made from the standpoint of the natural sciences." But the vein is not dissimilar when the statistically trained scholar argues that "whereas it is admittedly technically possible to think always in terms of attributes and dichotomies, one wonders how practical that is" (Blalock 1964: 32).

9   There is some question as to whether it can really be held that ordinal scales are scales of measurement: most of our rank ordering occurs without having recourse to numerical values, and whenever we do assign numbers to our ordered categories, these numbers are arbitrary. However, there are good reasons for drawing the threshold of quantification between nominal and ordinal scales rather than between ordinal and interval scales. (See Tufte 1969, esp. 645.) On the other hand, even if the gap between ordinal scales and interval measurement is not as wide in practice as it is in theory, nonetheless from a mathematical point of view the interesting scales are the interval and, even more, the cardinal scales.

10 Otherwise the comparative method would largely consist of the statistical method, for the latter surely is a stronger technique of control than the former. The difference and the connections are cogently discussed by Lijphart (1969).

11 The chapter usefully reviews the literature. For an introductory treatment, see Alker, Jr. (1965). An illuminating discussion on how quantification enters the various social sciences is in Lerner (1961).

12 A classic example is the (partial) mathematical translation of the theoretical system of *The Human Group* of George C. Homans by Simon (1957: Chapter 7). No similar achievement exists in the political science field. To cite three significant instances, political science issues are eminently lacking in Arrow (1951: Chapter 8); in the contributions collected in Lazarsfeld (1954); and in Kemeny and Snell (1962).

13 Perhaps the mathematical leap of the discipline is just around the corner waiting for non-quantitative developments. If one is to judge, however, from the "mathematics of man" issue of the *International Social Science Bulletin* introduced by Claude Levi-Strauss (1954), this literature is very deceiving. More interesting is Kemeny (1961) and the modal logic developed by the Bourbaki group (1951–). For a general treatment, see Kemeny et al. (1957).

14 Spengler equally points out that, "the introduction of quantitative methods in economics did not result in striking discoveries" (1961: 176). While formal economic theory is by now highly isomorphic with algebra, mathematical economics has added little to the predictive power of the discipline and one often has the impression that we are employing guns to kill mosquitoes.

15 It hardly needs to be emphasized that census data – and for that matter most of the data provided by external agencies – are gathered by conceptual containers which hopelessly lack discrimination. The question with our standard variables on literacy, urbanization, occupation, industrialization, and the like, is whether they really measure common underlying phenomena. It is pretty obvious that, across the world, they do not; and this quite aside from the reliability of the data-gathering agencies.

16 See Kaplan (1964: 56–57, 63–65). According to Hempel, theoretical terms "usually purport to not directly observable entities and their characteristics. . . . They function . . . in scientific theories intended to explain generalizations" (1958: 42). While it is admittedly difficult to draw a neat division between theoretical and observational terms, it is widely recognized that the former cannot be reduced to, nor derived from, the latter. For a recent assessment of the controversy, see Meotti (1969: 119–34).

17 The distinction is more or less the same in any textbook of logic.

18 "Connotation" is also applied, more broadly, to the associations, or associated conceptions brought to mind by the use of a word. As indicated by the text, I intend here the narrower meaning.

19 The space and time dimensions of concepts are often associated with the geography versus history debate. I would rather see it as the "when goes with when?" question, that is, as a calendar time versus historical time dilemma. But this line of development cannot be pursued here.

20 This criticism is perhaps unfair to Truman (1951). However, in spite of its penetrating anatomy the pace of the enquiry is set by the sentence that "an excessive preoccupation with definition will only prove a handicap" (23). For a development of this line of criticism, see Sartori (1959: 742).

21 The same caution applies to the distinctions between micro and macro, or between molecular and molar. These distinctions are insufficient for the purpose of underpinning the level of analysis.

22 I quote Allardt (1968: 165), but the quotation is illustrative of a current mood.

23 In this latter connection an excellent reader still is Lazarsfeld and Rosenberg (1955). See also its largely revised and updated revision (Boudon and Lazarsfeld 1965–66).

24 This notably excludes, for the authors, the application of "variable" to items that can be ranked but not measured.

25 Hempel also writes: "It is precisely the discovery of concepts with theoretical import which advances scientific understanding; and such discovery requires scientific inventiveness and cannot be replaced by the – certainly indispensable, but also definitely insufficient – operationist or empiricist requirement of empirical import alone" (1952: 47).

26 This is not to say that operationalization allows *eo ipso* for quantitative measurements, but to suggest that either operational definitions are ultimately conducive to measurement, or may not be worthwhile.

27 I specify political science setting to avoid the unnecessary regression to Malinowski and Radcliff Brown. This is also to explain why I set aside the contributions of Talcott Parsons and of Marion J. Levy. Flanigan and Fogelman distinguish between three major streams, labeled (1) eclectic functionalism, (2) empirical functionalism (Merton), and (3) structural-functional analysis (1967: 72–79). My discussion exclusively applies to part of the latter.

28 It should be understood that by now the structural-functional label applies to a widely scattered group operating on premises which are largely at variance.

29 This focus was suggested by Merton, whose concern was to separate function – defined as an "observable objective consequence" – from "subjective disposition," i.e., aims, motives, and purposes (1957: 24, and, *passim*, 19–84). In attempting to meet the difficulties raised by the Mertonian focus, Holt construes functions as "sub-types" of effects, and precisely as the "system-relevant effects of structures"; understanding system-relevance as the "system-requiredness" which is determined, in turn, by the "functional requisites" of a given system (1967: 88–90). My own position is that Merton overstated his case thereby creating for his followers unnecessary and unsettled complications.

30 This is the mathematical meaning of function; for example, according to Riggs, in systems theory function refers to "a relation between structures" (1970b). There are problems, however, also with this definition. In particular, while the mathematical meaning of function is suited for whole systems analysis, it hardly suits the needs of segmented systems analysis.

31 Rationality of ends should not be confused with *Wertrationalität*, value rationality, among other reasons because in the former perspective all conceivable ends can be hypothesized as being equally valid. Hence in the *Zweckrationalität* perspective there is little point in unmasking functions as "eu-functions" or, conversely, as "caco-functions." Whether the good goals of one man are the bad goals of the next man becomes relevant only if we enter a normative, *Wertrationalität* discussion.

32 For the many additional intricacies of the subject that I must neglect, a recent, interesting reader largely focused on the "debate over functionalism" is Demerath and Peterson (1967). For a critical statement of the inherent limitations of functionalism, see Runciman (1963: 109–23). Hempel (1959) equally takes a critical view of "the logic of functional analysis," but his standpoint is often far removed from our problems.

33 This is not to fall prey to the subjectivistic fallacy on which Merton (1957) builds his case. Purpose may be a "motivation" of the actor, but may equally be – as it is in teleological analysis – an "imputation" of the observer.

34 "Unintended functions" – the fact that structures may serve ends and obtain results which were neither foreseen nor desired by the structure builders – can be entered, for the economy of my argument, into the list of the purposes actually served. Likewise "latent functions" are immaterial to my point.

35 Riggs makes the same point, namely, that "current terminology quite confusingly links structural and functional meanings" from the opposite angle that expressions such as "legislature and public administrator . . . are normally defined structurally, the first as an elected assembly, the second as a bureaucratic office," but then goes on to say that "the words . . . also imply functions" (Riggs 1970b). It should be understood, therefore, that my "structural definition" calls for a thorough structural description. If the argument were left at defining a legislature as an elected assembly, then it can be made either way, as Riggs does.

36 I cite the title of MacKenzie's book *Free Elections* (1958) to imply that a real structural underpinning may well presuppose a hundred-page description.

37 A sheer list of the functional denominations, roles, or attributions scattered throughout the literature on political parties suffices to illustrate the point, and would be as follows: participation, electioneering, mobilization, extraction, regulation, control, integration, cohesive function, moderating function, consensus maintenance, simplification of alternatives, reconciliation, adaptation, aggregation, mediation, conflict resolution, brokerage, recruitment, policy making, expression, communication, linkage, channelment, conversion, legitimizing function, democratization, labeling function.

38 I make specific reference to Almond because I believe that his very conception of structure is largely responsible for this outcome. For instance, "By structure we mean the observable activities which make up the political system. To refer to these activities as having a structure simply implies that there is a certain regularity to them" (Almond and Powell 1966: 21). In the subsequent paragraph one reads: "We refer to particular sets of roles which are related to one another as structures." Under such porous and excessively sociological criteria, "structure" becomes evanescent.

39 This complaint is ad hoc, but could be expanded at length. On the general lack of logical and methodological status of the approach, two strong critical statements are Dowse (1966: 607–22) and Kalleberg (1966: 69–82). While the two authors are over-conscious thinkers, I would certainly agree with Dowse's concluding sentence, namely, that "to ignore trivial logical points is to risk being not even trivially true" (622).

40 On general systems theory, one may usefully consult Young (1968: Chapter 2). See also Urbani (1968).

41 While there is some controversy on the respective merits and shortcomings of the two strategies, the structural-functional approach is not inherently tied to either one. For the partial versus whole systems controversy, the two stances are well represented by LaPalombara (1970), who favors the segmented approach, and, for the contrary view, Riggs (1970b).

42 The relevant "family difference" is that structure and function are not culture-bound concepts, while the four other categories are. This is also to note that the traveling problem of comparative politics cannot be reduced to the construction of "non-culture bound" conceptualizations. How to use those conceptualizations which cannot help being culture bound is equally a problem.

43 Since we are discussing here macro-problems and macro-theory I need not follow the concepts under investigation all the way down the ladder of abstraction. I should not let pass unnoticed, however, that "integration" also belongs to the vocabulary of sociology and psychology, thereby lending itself to very fine lower-level distinctions. See, e.g., Landecker (1955: 19–27).

44 The point could be extended at great length; e.g., I would assume that only in a truly pluralistic society (i.e., qualified by the characteristics conveyed by the Western use of the term) may differentiation result in, and join forces with, integration. But much of the literature on political development seems to miss this essential condition.

45 Shils and Deutsch relate the notion also to Mannheim's "fundamental democratization" (see especially Deutsch 1961: 494). But while Mannheim may well have provided the bridge across which "mobilization" entered the vocabulary of democracy, the fact remains that in Italy and in Germany in the early 1930s, the term was commonly used to suggest a distinctly totalitarian experience.

46 The boomerang effect is also responsible, in part, for the disappearance of politics (*supra*, note 3).

References

Alker, H.R., Jr. (1965) *Mathematics and Politics*, New York: Macmillan.

Allardt, E. (1968) "The Merger of American and European Traditions of Sociological Research: Contextual Analysis," *Social Science Information* 7 (1): 151–68.

Almond, G.A. and Coleman, J.S. (1960) *The Politics of the Developing Areas*, Princeton: Princeton University Press.

Almond, G.A. and Powell, G.B., Jr. (1966) *Comparative Politics: A Developmental Approach*, Boston: Little, Brown.

Apter, D.E. (1970) "Political Studies and the Search for a Framework," in C. Allen and R.W. Johnson (eds.), *African Perspectives: Papers in the History, Politics and Economics of Africa Presented to Thomas Hodgkin*, Cambridge: Cambridge University Press.

Arrow, K.J. (1951) "Mathematical Models in the Social Sciences," in D. Lerner and H.D. Lasswell (eds.), *The Policy Sciences*, Stanford, CA: Stanford University Press.

Bendix, R. (1963) "Concepts and Generalizations in Comparative Sociological Studies," *American Sociological Review* 28 (4): 532–39.

Benson, O. (1967) "The Mathematical Approach to Political Science," in J. C. Charlesworth (ed.), *Contemporary Political Analysis*, New York: Free Press.

Blalock, H.M., Jr. (1964) *Causal Inferences in Nonexperimental Research*, Chapel Hill: University of North Carolina Press.

Boudon, R. and Lazarsfeld, P.F. (1965–66) *Méthodes de la Sociologie*, 2 vols., Paris and La Haye: Mouton.

Bourbaki, N. (pseud.) (1951–) *Eléments de mathématique*, Paris: Hermann.

Braibanti, R. (1968) "Comparative Political Analytics Reconsidered," *Journal of Politics* 30: 44–49.

Croce, B. (1942) *Logica come Scienza del Concetto Puro*, Bari: Laterza.

Demerath, N.J. and Peterson, R.A. (eds.) (1967) *System, Change and Conflict*, New York: Free Press.

Deutsch, K.W. (1961) "Social Mobilization and Political Development," *American Political Science Review* 55 (3): 493–514.

Deutsch, K.W. (1966) "Recent Trends in Research Methods," in J. C. Charlesworth (ed.), *A Design for Political Science: Scope, Objectives and Methods*, Philadelphia: American Academy of Political and Social Science.

Dowse, R.E. (1966) "A Functionalist's Logic," *World Politics* 18 (4): 607–22.

Eckstein, H. (1963) "Introduction," in H. Eckstein and D.E. Apter (eds.), *Comparative Politics*, Glencoe: Free Press.

Festinger, L. and Katz, D. (eds.) (1953) *Research Methods in the Behavioral Sciences*, New York: Dryden Press.

Flanigan, W.H. and Fogelman, E. (1967) "Functional Analysis," in J. C. Charlesworth (ed.), *Contemporary Political Analysis*, New York: Free Press.

Hempel, C.G. (1952) *Fundamentals of Concept Formation in Empirical Science*, Chicago: University of Chicago Press.

Hempel, C.G. (1958) "The Theoretician's Dilemma: A Study in the Logic of Theory Construction," in H. Feigl, M. Scriven, and G. Maxwell (eds.), *Concepts, Theories, and the Mind–Body Problem*, Minnesota Studies in the Philosophy of Science, vol. 2, Minneapolis: University of Minnesota Press.

Hempel, C.G. (1959) "The Logic of Functional Analysis," in L. Gross (ed.), *Symposium on Sociological Theory*, New York: Harper and Row.

Holt, R.T. (1967) "A Proposed Structural-Functional Framework," in J.C. Charlesworth (ed.), *Contemporary Political Analysis*, New York: Free Press.

Holt, R.T. and Richardson, J.M. (1970) "Competing Paradigms in Comparative Politics," in R.T. Holt and J.E. Turner (eds.), *The Methodology of Comparative Research*, New York: Free Press.

Kalleberg, A.L. (1966) "The Logic of Comparison," *World Politics* 19 (1): 69–82.

Kaplan, A. (1964) *The Conduct of Inquiry*, San Francisco: Chandler.

Kemeny, J.G. (1961) "Mathematics without Numbers," in D. Lerner (ed.), *Quantity and Quality*, Glencoe: Free Press.

Kemeny, J.G. and Snell, J.L. (1962) *Mathematical Models in the Social Sciences*, Boston: Ginn.

Kemeny, J.G., Snell, J.L., and Thompson, G.L. (1957) *Introduction to Finite Mathematics*, Englewood Cliffs, NJ: Prentice Hall.

Landau, M. (1969) "A General Commentary," in R. Braibanti (ed.), *Political and Administrative Development*, Durham, NC: Duke University Press.

Landecker, W.S. (1955) "Types of Integration and their Measurements," in *The Language of Social Research*, Glencoe: Free Press.

LaPalombara, J. (1968) "Macrotheories and Microapplications in Comparative Politics," *Comparative Politics* 1 (1): 52–78.

LaPalombara, J. (1970) "Parsimony and Empiricism in Comparative Politics: An Anti-Scholastic View," in R.T. Holt and J.E. Turner (eds.), *The Methodology of Comparative Research*, New York: Free Press.

Lasswell, H.D. and Kaplan, A. (1950) *Power and Society*, New Haven, CT: Yale University Press.

Lazarsfeld, P.F. (ed.) (1954) *Mathematical Thinking in the Social Sciences*, Glencoe: Free Press.

Lazarsfeld, P.F. and Barton, A.H. (1951) "Qualitative Measurement in the Social Sciences: Classifications, Typologies and Indices," in D. Lerner and H.D. Lasswell (eds.), *The Policy Sciences*, Stanford, CA: Stanford University Press.

Lazarsfeld, P.F. and Rosenberg, M. (eds.) (1955) *The Language of Social Research*, Glencoe: Free Press.

Lerner, D. (ed.) (1961) *Quantity and Quality*, Glencoe: Free Press.

Lévi-Strauss, C. (1954) "The Mathematics of Man," *International Social Science Bulletin* 6 (4): 581–90.

Lijphart, A. (1969) "Comparative Politics and the Comparative Method," paper presented at the Torino IPSA Round Table, September.

MacKenzie, W.J.M. (1958) *Free Elections*, London: Allen & Unwin.

Macridis, R.C. (1968) "Comparative Politics and the Study of Government: The Search for Focus," *Comparative Politics* 1 (1): 79–90.

Martindale, D. (1959) "Sociological Theory and the Ideal Type," in L. Gross (ed.), *Symposium on Sociological Theory*, New York: Harper and Row.

Meotti, A. (1969) "L'Eliminazione dei Termini Teorici," *Rivista di Filosofia* 2: 119–34.

Merton, R.K. (1957) *Social Theory and Social Structure*, rev. edn., Glencoe: Free Press.

Mills, C.W. (1959) "On Intellectual Craftsmanship," in L. Gross (ed.), *Symposium on Sociological Theory*, New York: Harper & Row.

Paige, G.D. (1966) "The Rediscovery of Politics," in J.D. Montgomery and W.I. Siffin (eds.), *Approaches to Development*, New York: McGraw-Hill.

Riggs, F.W. (1969) "A General Commentary," in R. Braibanti (ed.), *Political and Administrative Development*, Durham, NC: Duke University Press.

Riggs, F.W. (1970a) "The Comparison of Whole Political Systems," in R.T. Holt and J.E. Turner (eds.), *The Methodology of Comparative Research*, New York: Free Press.

Riggs, F.W. (1970b) "Systems Theory: Structural Analysis," in M. Haas and H.S. Kariel (eds.), *Approaches to the Study of Political Science*, Scranton, PA: Chandler Publishing Co.

Rose, R. (n.d.) "Social Measure and Public Policy in Britain: The Empiricizing Process," mimeograph.

Runciman, W.C. (1963) *Social and Political Theory*, Cambridge: Cambridge University Press.

Salmon, W.C. (1963) *Logic*, Englewood Cliffs, NJ: Prentice Hall.

Sartori, G. (1959) "Gruppi di Pressione o Gruppi di Interesse?," *Il Mulino* 1: 7–24.

Sartori, G. (1969) "From the Sociology of Politics to Political Sociology," in S.M. Lipset (ed.), *Politics and the Social Sciences*, New York: Oxford University Press.

Selltiz, C. et al. (1959) *Research Methods in Social Relations*, rev. edn., New York: Holt, Rinehart & Winston.

Simon, H.A. (1957) *Models of Man: Social and Rational; Mathematical Essays on Rational Human Behavior in a Social Setting*, New York: Wiley.

Smelser, N.J. (1968) "Notes on the Methodology of Comparative Analysis of Economic Activity," in N.J. Smelser (ed.), *Essays in Sociological Explanation*, Englewood Cliffs, NJ: Prentice Hall.

Spengler, J.J. (1961) "Quantification in Economics: Its History," in D. Lerner (ed.), *Quantity and Quality*, Glencoe: Free Press.

Truman, D. (1951) *The Governmental Process*, New York: Knopf.

Tufte, E.R. (1969) "Improving Data Analysis in Political Science," *World Politics* 21: 641–54.

Urbani, G. (1968) "General Systems Theory: Un Nuovo Strumento per l'Analisi dei Sistemi Politici?," *Il Politico* 4: 795–819.

Young, O.R. (1968) *Systems of Political Science*, Englewood Cliffs, NJ: Prentice Hall.

2 What is politics?

Giovanni Sartori

The concept of "political science" derives its meaning from the interplay of two variables: (1) the state of the organization of knowledge, and (2) the degree of structural differentiation within the framework of human collectivities.

With respect to the first variable, the notion of science makes little sense – or at least no precise sense – unless there exists division and specialization in the cognitive endeavor. Thus, it does not make much sense to speak of political science as long as "science" is indistinguishable from philosophy – i.e., as long as any and all *scire* defines itself as love of wisdom. The notion of science, therefore, achieves precision when scientific knowledge has been weaned from its alma mater, from philosophical knowledge. Of course, science is also different from what is commonly called opinion, theory, doctrine, and ideology. But the first and most fundamental distinction is that between science and philosophy.

With respect to the second variable, the notion of politics applies to everything, and therefore to nothing in particular, as long as the realms of ethics, economics, politics, and society remain united and are not embodied in structural differentiations – that is, in structures and institutions which can be qualified as political in that they are different from those which are declared economic, religious, or social. The most difficult knot to unravel is that between the sphere of politics and the sphere of society. But the knots are many, beginning with the overlapping between the nomenclature that has its roots in Greek – the words derived from polis – and the nomenclature that stems from Latin.

Let us say, then, that the notion of political science varies according to what is meant by science and what is meant by politics. Thus, it is quite futile to speak about a "perennial" political science which is born with Aristotle, reborn with Machiavelli, and which matured into an autonomous discipline in the nineteenth century. Before risking a history of political science *as such*, there must be a science which is "science," and there must be a significant encounter between the idea of science and the idea of politics. Until that moment, a history of political science resolves itself, or divides itself, into a bicephalous history of the concept of science on the one hand, and of the concept of politics on the other.

This separation is necessary not only because science and politics are both variables of great variance, but also because their variations have occurred at different times and at a different speed. We are confronted, therefore, by varying combinations of different notions of science and politics. The stages or periods of political science will be all the more numerous as one pushes back the date of birth of this discipline. But even a short history, confined, for example, to one century, would have to be periodicized. The age of Mosca, Pareto, and Michels is for us already a far-off era. Similarly, the political science of the 1940s appears outdated when compared with that of the 1960s.

I shall *not* attempt to date the birth of the "first" political science. Rather, I will try to single out the elements of the manifold, plausible, "significant encounters" that have taken place between those methods of observing politics which can be qualified as scientific on the one hand, and, on the other, a series of characterizations of the idea of politics.[1] This part of the article deals with the latter.

The name and the idea

It is customary today to make a distinction between the political and the social or between state and society. These are, however, distinctions and contrasts which take shape in their present-day sense only in the nineteenth century. We often hear that, while in Greek thought the political encompasses the social, modern man is inclined to invert this relationship and to have the social subsume the political. But this statement contains at least three errors. First: there was no separation of the sort in Greek thought. Second: things social and "the society" are not equivalent. Third: our noun politics does not have the meaning of the Greek *politiké*, just as our political man is miles apart from Aristotle's "political animal."

If for Aristotle man was a *zoon politikón*, the subtlety that often escapes us is that this was a definition of man, not of politics. It is only because man lives in the polis and, conversely, because the polis lives in him, that he is able to realize his full human potential. Thus Aristotle's political animal expressed the Greek conception of life,[2] a conception that saw the polis as the constitutive unit and the supreme achievement of existence. Therefore, political life and the things political were not perceived by the Greeks as a part or a single aspect of life; they were its essence and totality. Conversely, the nonpolitical man was a deficient, defective being, an *idion* (the original meaning of our word idiot). And this inadequacy stemmed precisely from his having lost – or from his never having acquired – a full symbiosis with his polis. In short, a nonpolitical man was less-than-a-man, an inferior being.

Without delving into the various implications of the Greek conception of man, what needs underscoring is that the political animal, the *polites*, was indistinguishable from the social animal, from that being whom we call societal or sociable. Political life – living *in* and *for* the polis – was at one and the same time collective life or, more intensely, life in *koinonía*, in communion and "community." Hence, it is inaccurate to say that Aristotle thought of the social as being included within the political. The two terms were for him one and the same: neither was contained within the other, because political meant both. In fact, the word social is not Greek, but Latin, and was interpolated into Aristotle by his medieval translators and commentators.

It was Thomas Aquinas (1225–74) who authoritatively translated *zoon politikón* as "political and social animal," observing that "it is the very nature of man to live in a society of many" (*De Regimine Principum*, I, I). But the matter is not as simple as that. Thus Egidius Romano (circa 1285) translated Aristotle as saying that man is a *politicum animal et civile* (*De Regimine Principum*, III, I, 2). At first sight, it might appear as if Thomas were clarifying Aristotle's notion, while Egidius was simply being redundant – after all, *politicum* is a Greek calque for *civile*. However, the appearance of the two terms social and civil merits further commentary, and it would show that both Thomas and Egidius were adding to Aristotle.

It is clear that when the Greeks said *polítes*, the Romans said *civis*. It is just as clear that polis is translated into Latin as *civitas*. But the Romans were absorbing Greek culture at a time when their city had long since surpassed the dimensions that permitted a "political" life as understood by the Greeks. Consequently the Roman civitas is related to the Greek polis as a diluted body politic – and this in two respects. First, the civitas is visualized as a *civilis societas*, thereby taking on a more elastic meaning which broadens its boundaries; and, second, the civitas acquires a juridical organization. The civilis societas thus becomes, in turn, equivalent to a *juris societas*, which permits the Romans to substitute the "juridical" for the "political." Cicero (106–43 B.C.) already maintained that the civitas was not just a random association of men, but that association which was founded upon a consensus concerning the law (*De Re Publica*, I, 25). Already in Cicero's time we are near, therefore, to a civitas in which there is almost nothing of "political" in the Greek sense of the word. The juris societas is to the polis as a condition of depolitization would be to a condition of politization. The cycle is completed with Seneca. For Seneca (4 B.C.–65 A.D.), and for the Stoic conception of the world in general, man is no longer a political animal but, on the contrary, a *sociale animale* (*De Clementia*, I, 3). Here we reach the antithesis of the Aristotelian conception, because the social animal of Seneca and of the Stoics is a man who has lost the polis, who withdraws from it, and who adapts himself for living – negatively more than positively – in a cosmopolis.

The ancient world concludes its cycle bequeathing to posterity not only the image of a political animal, but also the image of a social animal. Yet these two representations in no way foreshadow the disjunction between the political and the social spheres which characterize our time. The first difference is that the social animal does not coexist alongside the politicum animal. The two terms do not point to two facets of the same man, but to two anthropological views which are mutually exclusive and replace one another. The second difference – and the element that needs particular emphasis – is that in the discourse developed thus far politics and politization have never been perceived vertically – i.e., in an altimetric projection which associates the idea of politics with the idea of power, of command and, in the final analysis, with a state superimposed upon society.

The point is that the vertical or hierarchic problem is largely extraneous to the discussion based on Greek nomenclature – polis, polítes, politikós, politiké, and politéia – to its Latin translation and to its medieval development. The Greek title of what we know as *The Republic* of Plato was *Politéia* – an exact translation for the world which thought in Latin, since *res publica* (republic) meant that which is public – i.e., "a common thing" and affair of the community. Res publica, Cicero noted, was *res populi* (*De Re Publica*, VI, 13) – i.e., a thing of the people. Likewise, Aristotle's argument on the good city (often referred to, erroneously, as the optimal "constitution") was calculatedly rendered by its first medieval translators as *de politia optima*, and successively as *de optima republica*, all terms which are connected to a horizontal discourse. This horizontal idea goes into the English common weal and commonwealth, and is rendered today by the notion of common good, public good, and general interest. For this very reason, however, we misunderstand Plato's title, just as we misunderstand the use of res publica in the entire literature from the Romans to Bodin (whose *Six Livres de la République* appeared in 1576). Having become for us a form of state (a form opposed to monarchy), our republic is placed in that vertical dimension which was absent in the ideas of politéia, res publica, and common weal.

This does not mean that we must wait until Machiavelli or Bodin to discover what I have called the vertical dimension, that is, the hierarchical structuring – a sub- and superordering – of associative life. It is quite clear that Plato did imply a verticality. But his ideal was sophocracy: the power of wisdom, not the power of power. And this was not the element received and transmitted by the Aristotelian tradition.[3] On the other hand, if Machiavelli is the first to use the word "state" in its modern sense,[4] it is clear that the perception of verticality – today transfused into the notion of politics – goes all the way back, to say the least, to the Romanistic tradition. But this idea was not expressed by Greek nomenclature, by the word politics and its derivatives. Until the seventeenth century, it was generally and variously expressed by such terms as *principatus, regnum, dominium*, and *gubernaculum*[5] (more so than by such terms as *potestas* and *imperium*, which referred to legitimate power and were used within a juridical frame of reference).

For the medieval and renaissance writers, whether they wrote in Latin, Italian, French, or English, the *dominium politicum* was not "political" in our sense but in the sense of Aristotle: it was the "ideal city" of the polítes, a res publica which served the good of the community and a *res populi* equally removed from the degenerations of democracy and of tyranny. In fact, medieval writers used dominium politicum as the opposite of *dominium regale*, and even more as the opposite of *dominium despoticum*. This is equivalent to saying that the adjective politicum referred to the horizontal vision, while such terms as royalty, despotism, and principality expressed the vertical dimension. Thus, the best way to translate the idea of dominium politicum into modern terminology would be to say "the good society" – except that we are much more naïve or optimistic in this respect than the medieval authors. We could also say that dominium politicum refers to a "stateless society." But the caution would be, here, that the society in question is both a civilis societas and a juris societas, and not just the unqualified and unfettered society spoken of in contemporary sociology.

On the other hand, the term that symbolized more than any other the vertical focus – what we would consider the characteristically political discourse – that term is "Prince." It was no accident that *Il Principe* (1513) was the title chosen by

Machiavelli. *De Regimine Principum* (circa 1260–69) had already been the title of Thomas (as well as of Egidius of Romano), while Marsilius da Padua (circa 1280–1343) had used *principatus* or *pars principans* to indicate the functions which we today call governmental, and might have labeled the kind of government described by Machiavelli as a *principatus despoticus* (*Defensor Pacis*, Chapter XII of *Dictio Prima*).

The conclusion emerging from our sweeping survey is that the complex, tortuous history of the *idea* of politics transcends at every point and in a thousand ways the *word* itself.[6] The politics of Aristotle was, at one and the same time, an anthropology, a conception of man indissolubly linked to the "space" of the polis. With the collapse of the polis, the meaning of the political is variously diluted or turned into something different. In one respect, politics became juridicized and evolved in the direction indicated by Roman thought. In another respect – on which I cannot dwell – the things political became theologized, first conforming to the Christian view of the world, then adapting to the struggle between the Papacy and the Empire, and finally reflecting the schism between Catholicism and Protestantism. In any case, the discourse of, and about, politics develops – beginning with Plato and Aristotle – as a discourse which is jointly and indissolubly ethico-political. The ethics in question could be naturalistic, theological, or juridical – that is, an ethics that debates the problem of the "good" in terms of what is "just," appealing to justice and just laws. The doctrine of natural law, in its successive phases and versions, summarizes quite well this amalgam of juridical and moral norms (see Passerin d'Entrèves 1951). For these and still other reasons, there can be little doubt that it is not until Machiavelli that politics attains a distinctive identity and "autonomy."

The autonomy of politics

When we speak of the autonomy of politics, the concept of autonomy should not be understood in an absolute but rather in a relative sense. Moreover, four theses can be posited with respect to this notion: (1) that politics is different; (2) that it is independent – i.e., that it adheres to its own laws; (3) that it is self-sufficient – i.e., autarchic in the sense that it is sufficient for explaining itself; (4) that it is a first cause, generating not only itself, but, given its causal supremacy, everything else. Strictly speaking, the last thesis is an inference that exceeds the limits of the concept of autonomy. It should also be noted that the second and third propositions often go together even if, rigorously speaking, the idea of autonomy must be distinguished from the idea of autarchy. At any rate, the preliminary thesis is the first.

To say that politics is "different" amounts to stating a necessary, but not a sufficient, condition of its autonomy. Yet the rest of the argument is conditioned by this point of departure. Different from what? In what way? And to what degree?

With Machiavelli (1469–1527), politics established itself as being different from morality and religion. Here is a first, hard and fast separation. Morality and religion are indeed essential ingredients of politics, but as means to an end: they are instrumental to politics. "If a Prince wants to maintain the state, he is often forced to do evil," to act "against faith, against charity, against humanity, and against religion"

(*The Prince*, Chapters 18 and 19). Politics is politics. But Machiavelli does not arrive at his *verità effettuale*, at the actual truth of things, because he is value-free or because he takes a non-normative stand. Let alone the fact that Machiavelli is animated by moral passion, he prescribes to the "new" prince the proper conduct necessary for the preservation or establishment of a state. Machiavelli's greatest originality lies in asserting – with unparalleled theoretical vigor – the existence of an imperative peculiar to politics. Machiavelli not only declares the difference of politics from ethics, but also arrives at a clear-cut affirmation of its autonomy: politics has its laws, laws that the statesman *must* apply.

In the above sense, therefore, it is correct to say that Machiavelli, not Aristotle, "discovered politics." Why Machiavelli? And for what reasons? His discovery can hardly be attributed to a "scientific" spirit (on this point, see Abbagnano 1969; Olschki 1969; Matteucci 1970; generally, see Sasso 1958, 1967). On the other hand, Machavelli was not a philosopher – and this is a major reason why he achieved the directness of vision possessed only by those who begin, or who start again, *ex novo*. Machiavelli "uncovered" what had been covered by the philosophical tradition. Therefore to say that he was neither a philosopher nor a scientist does not detract in the least from his stature, while it goes a long way toward explaining why he succeeds in discovering politics. The point can be highlighted by comparing Machiavelli and Hobbes.

Hobbes (1588–1679) nears "pure" politics even more than Machiavelli. His prince, the *Leviathan* (1651), is the closest and direct precursor of the Big Brother of Orwell: he creates a political order by his own fiat and by his power to create words, to define them, and to impose them upon his subjects. "The first truths," writes Hobbes (1829–45: I, 36), "were arbitrarily made by those that first of all imposed names upon things." From this, Hobbes concludes that political truths are like the arbitrary and conventional truths of geometry. If the prince of Machiavelli governs according to the rules of politics, the leviathan of Hobbes governs by creating these rules and by establishing what politics is. The world of man is infinitely manipulable, and the leviathan – the Grand Definer – is its absolute, ultimate manipulator. Actually, no one had ever propounded a politicization as extreme as that of Hobbes. He not only asserts the absolute independence and self-sufficiency of politics, but affirms a "panpoliticism" in which everything is reabsorbed in, and generated by, politics. If Machiavelli invokes "virtù," Hobbes invokes nothing. If in the pages of Machiavelli one detects a moral passion, Hobbes writes as a detached reasoner coldly intent on constructing a perfect mechanical universe of bodies in motion. If Machiavelli looks upon religion as a buttress for politics, Hobbes gives his monarch – as Comte would later – control over religion.[7]

Not only does Hobbes go beyond Machiavelli in affirming a "pure" politics that is all-pervasive and all-causing; he is also far more science conscious. In the century or more that separates them, there had appeared Bacon (1561–1626) and Galileo (1564–1642). Moreover, Hobbes had been exposed to the method of Descartes (1596–1650), his younger but more precocious contemporary. In its own way, then, Hobbes's thought is pervaded by scientific spirit. His philosophical system is inspired by the mechanistic conception of the universe, and his method – inspired by the model of geometry – flows from the logic of mathematics. At first sight, therefore, we may be tempted to conclude that in Hobbes there exist all the necessary elements for the existence of a "science of politics." According to the canons of Cartesian philosophy, Hobbes uses a scientific method. At the same time, he theorizes the most extreme form of autonomy of politics. If it pleases us, we could also add that Hobbes is value-free. Yet one speaks of Hobbes as being, unquestionably, a philosopher of politics, while Machiavelli is often recognized as the founding father of political science. Why is that?

The answer need not be far-fetched. The element which separates science from philosophy is not afforded by the models of geometry and mathematics. Descartes was a great mathematician, and Leibniz was even a greater one. Mathematics is a rigorous, deductive logic; whereas the sciences are not born of logical deduction but of induction, observation, and experiment.[8] Hobbes was not an observer or, better said, he was not satisfied by observation; he deduced *more geometrico*, as would, a little later, the purest example of a philosopher, Spinoza (1632–77). Hobbes's method, then, was rigorously deductive (see Cassirer 1911: Vol. 2, Chapter 3; Gargani 1971). With this, everything is said. He did not describe and explain the real world. No one can dispute the philosophic greatness of Hobbes. But his "science" is not science. It follows that the autonomy of politics which interests us is not that formulated by Hobbes. And the fact that Hobbes is more value-free than Machiavelli is irrelevant to the matter. In conclusion, if there is as yet no science to be found in Machiavelli, the scientific spirit of Hobbes does not constitute a significant encounter between science and politics. On the other hand, and in particular, the discovery of the autonomy of politics cannot be attributed to a scientific method.

The discovery of society

Up to this point, I have highlighted only a first difference: that between politics and ethics, between Caesar and God. This is a decisive step, but, in retrospect, the simplest and the most obvious. The most difficult – so difficult that it still encumbers us – is to underpin the difference between state and society. Thus far, we have not encountered the separation between the sphere of politics and the sphere of society.[9] When did the idea of society free itself from its multiple associations, thereby positing social reality as an independent and self-sufficient reality?

"Society" is neither *demos* nor *populus*. As a concrete, operating actor, the demos died with its "democracy" – that is, with the demise of the polis. And since the Roman republic never was a democracy, the populus of the Romans never was the demos of the Greeks (Wirszubski 1950). After the fall of the Republic, populus became a juridical fiction and substantially remained a *fictio iuris* throughout the literature of the Middle Ages. On the other hand, Roman and medieval thought in no way expressed an autonomous idea of society. Society was qualified – let it be remembered – as a civilis societas and a iuris societas. To these amalgams, medieval thought added its own strong "organicist" characterization, in such a way as to reorganize society into an articulate multiplicity of "bodies": fiefs, estates, and corporations – a tightly interwoven world regulated by the principle that each man should live according to his status.

The breakdown of this organic, corporate network took place very slowly. It is very telling, for example, that the idea of society had no place in the sixteenth-century literature which upheld the right of resistance and rebellion against the tyrant. For the Monarchomachs, as well as for Calvin and Althusius, it was neither the people nor the society who counterposed and opposed the power of the tyrant, but individuals or specific institutions, such as a church, local assemblies, or particular magistrates. Similarly, the English Revolution was not a revolution in the name and for the sake of the rights of society. Rather, the Great Rebellion, brought back to life – that is, to concreteness – the *fictio iuris* of the people.

It was not by chance, in fact, that the first writer to theorize about the rights of the majority and about majority rule – a rule which gives the notion of the people operational meaning and capacity – was Locke, who wrote at the end of the seventeenth century (see Kendall 1941). Locke is also credited, to be sure, with the first formulation of the idea of society. But this idea is more appropriately attributed, I believe, to the *contractualist* doctrine as a whole, and especially to the distinction that it posits between *pactum subiectionis* and *pactum societatis*, between the (vertical) agreement to obey and the (horizontal) agreement to coexist. In truth, the idea of society is not an idea that is born and strengthened during revolutionary times. Rather, it is a "peaceful" idea that arises along the contractualist development of the school of natural law. It is not the revolt against the sovereign, but the "contract" with the sovereign, which is stipulated in the name of a contractor called society. Nonetheless this "allbody," this society which asserts the "social contract," still is a juridical fiction.

The truth of the matter is that the autonomy of society with respect to the state can hardly be conceived unless another, prior separation takes place – that of the economic sphere. The separation of the social sphere from the body politic occurs through the outgrowth of economics from politics. This is the main stream. Today sociologists in search of an ancestor quote Montesquieu (1689–1755).[10] But it is more appropriate to cite Adam Smith (1723–90), and perhaps to ascend through Smith to Hume (see Bryson 1945; Cropsey 1957: esp. Chapter 1). It was the economists – Smith, Ricardo, and the laissez faire theorists in general – who demonstrated that social life prospers and develops when the state does not intervene, who demonstrated how social life finds its own principle of organization in the division of labor, thereby indicating that social life is largely extraneous to the state and neither regulated by its rules nor by the law. Economic laws are not juridical laws – they are the laws of the market. And the market is a spontaneous automatism, a mechanism which functions on its own. The economists of the eighteenth and nineteenth centuries furnished, then, the tangible image of a social reality capable of self-regulation, of a society which lives and develops according to its own nature. And this is the route through which society becomes self-conscious, or, putting it less philosophically, comes to perceive its own identity.

All this is not meant to deny that Montesquieu too is a precursor of the discovery of society. But he was preceded by the inklings of Locke; and the list of the anticipators is a lengthy one, for it should include liberal constitutionalism in general. All these precursors are such, however, in an indirect and inconclusive fashion. Clearly, the more one reduces the discretion and the space of the absolute state, and the more one obtains the "limited state," the greater the space and legitimacy left for extrastate life. But political liberalism (i.e., constitutionalism) could not and did not have the shattering force of what I have called economic "liberalism" (on this distinction, see Sartori 1965: 361–62). This is so because political liberalism wants the society to be regulated and protected by law. Just as liberalism – classic liberalism, to be sure – concerns itself with neutralizing pure politics, in an analogous way it sees a "pure" society as an exposed, unprotected, and defenseless society. The society of Montesquieu was always, in its own way, *a iuris societas*. The laissez faire economists did not have this problem. They had the opposite problem of breaking the bonds and fetters of medieval corporatism.

It is only in the approach of the economists, therefore, that society is all the more authentic the more it is spontaneous – that is, the freer of political interference and of legal restraints. True enough, the "spontaneous society" of the economists was only the economic society – a part, not the whole. Yet the example and the model of the economic society was easily extendable to the society in general. The premises for the discovery of society as an autonomous reality did not exist, then, in Machiavelli, in Montesquieu, or in the Encyclopedists; they were laid down in full only at the start of the nineteenth century.[11] With the *Industrial System* of Saint Simon (1770–1825), which appears in three volumes in 1821–22, we have the first, prophetic forecast of the industrial society of the second half of the twentieth century. By that time, society becomes an object of an independent science, which is no longer economics, and which Comte (1798–1857) christens "sociology." And Comte does not restrict himself to the baptism of the new science of society: he also proclaims sociology the queen of all sciences. Society is perceived not only as a "social system" which is distinct, independent, and self-sufficient with respect to the political system. In the vision of Comte, it is the social system that gives birth to the political system (on the relation between society and state in general, see Barker 1951; but especially Bendix 1962). We thus come full circle: the pan-politicism of Hobbes is turned upside down and reversed into the pan-sociologism, or the "sociocracy," of Comte. The moment has come for drawing our nets.

The identity of politics

Politics, as we have seen, is not simply different from ethics. It is also different from economics. Nor does politics any longer encompass the social system. In the end, the bonds between politics and law are also severed, in the sense that the political system and the juridical system fall apart. Thus denuded, politics appears different from everything else. But what is it when taken in and of itself?

Let us begin with noting a paradox. For almost two thousand years, the *word* politics – that is to say, the Greek diction – largely falls into disuse; and when we meet it again, as in the expression dominium politicum, it denotes only a small niche, a marginal, if happy, slice of the real world. We must get to Althusius – to the year

1603 – to find an author of note who brings the word politics into his title: *Politica Metodice Digesta*. He is followed by Spinoza; but his *Tractatus Politicus* is only published posthumously in 1677 and hardly leaves a trace. Finally, Bossuet writes the *Politique Tirée de l'Ecriture Sainte* in 1670; but the book is published only in 1709. And the term is not met with, astoundingly enough, in any important titles of the eighteenth century.[12] Nevertheless, during two millennia, there was constant *thought* about politics, for the paramount worldly preoccupation of most thinkers surely was to temper and regulate the domination of man over man. Rousseau went to the heart of the matter when he wrote that man is born free and is everywhere in chains. Thus Rousseau was concerned with the essence of politics, even if the word does not appear in the title of any of his works. Today, instead, the *word* is incessantly on our lips; yet we no longer know how to conceive the thing. In the contemporary world, the word is abused, while the concept suffers from an "identity crisis."[13]

One way to confront the problem is to pose the question that Aristotle did not ask: What makes a political animal different from a religious, ethical, economic, or social animal? Of course, these are ideal types. The question can be, nevertheless, very concrete – namely, whether politics, ethics, and economics can be pinned down behaviorally and in terms of tangible, observable deeds. In what way is economic behavior different from moral behavior? And what distinguishes both from political behavior? To a certain extent, the first question can be answered, but the second one leaves us at a loss.

The criterion of economic behavior is benefit or utility – that is, economic action in such in that it maximizes assets, profit, material, and personal interests. At the other extreme, the criterion of ethical behavior is the good – i.e., moral action is a dutiful, disinterested, altruistic action pursuing ideal ends, not material advantages. But what is the category or the criterion of political behavior? All we can say in this respect is that it coincides with neither the moral nor the economic criteria. We do find – historically – a slackening of the call of "duty" and a growth of the temptation of "profit." Whoever studies voting behavior can well assimilate it, in the aggregate, to economic behavior. Nonetheless how can we deny the enduring presence and recurrent force, in politics, of ideals? When we examine the facts more closely, what strikes us most is the great variety of motives that steer political behavior. And this leads me to suggest that "political behavior" should not be understood literally. The expression does not point to any particular type of behavior; rather, it denotes a locus, a *site* of behavior. Expressions are sometimes very revealing. With respect to moral behavior, it makes little sense to say that it exists and manifests itself in a moral site. Of course, morality has a site: the internal forum of our conscience. But this is hardly a discriminating element, since all behavior must be activated *in interiore hominis*. Hence, there is no behavior "in ethics" in the sense in which we speak of behavior "in politics."

As stated at the outset, in order to find our way in the differentiations among politics, ethics, law, economics, and so forth, it is necessary to refer to the structural differentiation of human aggregations. Perhaps because of a lack of categories, perhaps for other reasons, the fact is that only the field of ethics, which is the most ancient and the most developed, escapes reference to a structural underpinning. Ethics alone escapes because, on closer view, also the discourse on economics is situated structurally. If we draw the distinction between the philosophy of economy on the one hand, and the science of economics on the other, it can be easily seen that philosophers have identified the categories of economy – the useful, the desirable, the pleasurable – by reversing the connotations of ethics, and specifically of the Kantian conception of morality. In other terms, the philosophy of economy is nothing but a branch or an offshoot of moral philosophy. The economic man is inferred *a contrario* from the moral man. If the latter lacks identity, the former cannot be identified. So far, so good. But the science of economics cannot make much headway along these premises. The utility of the economist is not the utility of the philosopher. Likewise, the interest of the economist is a far cry from the interest spoken of in moral philosophy. In particular, and above all, the "value" of the economist is a market value established by market mechanisms – i.e., a value formed by and located within that structure which we call the marketplace. Upon closer inspection, then, the behavior observed by the economist belongs to the site "economic system," which is a constellation of structures, roles, and institutions. In the final analysis, therefore, the economist escapes a crisis of identity only by making reference to those sites summed up by the phrase "in economics."

The same applies to the sociologist. What is the criterion, or category, of social or societal behavior? There is none. Or better, the sociologist answers – as do the economist and the political scientist – it is behavior "in society," or "in the social system," meaning by this that social behavior is what he observes in the institutions, structures, and roles which compose that system. Thus, the political scientist is neither better nor worse off, in identifying political behavior, than any of the other students of man. So-called political behavior is behavior that can be characterized like any other non-moral behavior – that is, in its relation to the sites attributed to the "political system."

It appears, therefore, that the most fruitful way to confront the identity crisis of politics is *not* to ask how the behavior of political man differs from that of social or economic man. Rather, it is to ask what changes take place, structurally, in the organization and differentiation of human aggregations. If this is so, the query becomes what the denotation of "in politics" and of "the political system" are, with respect to the social system or the economic system.

Society, said Bentham in the wake of its discovery by the free-trade exponents, is the sphere of *sponte acta*, of spontaneous actions. But society is a spontaneous reality only with respect to other constraints, only in the sense that it is not regulated by the state, and therefore only in the sense that it denotes a plane where political and other controls give way to social control. This by itself goes to show that the notions of "power" and "coercion" are not sufficient, by themselves, to characterize and circumscribe the sphere of politics. The objection that politics is not only power and coercion notwithstanding, the fact is that, beyond political power, we must also make room for economic, military, religious, and various other powers. The same holds true for the notion of coercion. To political coercion we must add social, juridical, economic, and other kinds of coercion. All these powers and coercions are different, true enough. Yet their diversity cannot be detected without reference to the sites in which the various "coercive powers" become manifest. When one argues, with Max Weber, that political power is the coercive power which monopolizes the legal use of force, this definition presupposes a state apparatus equipped with sites and structures to that end. It may seem that by this route we return to the bygone identification between the political sphere and that of the state. But that is not so.

The farther we depart from the format of the polis and from the small city-state, the more human aggregations acquire, among other things, a vertical structuring. This verticality was – as we know – so foreign to the Greek idea of politics that for centuries it was expressed by Latin notations only, by such words as *principatus, regnum, dominium, gubernaculum, imperium, potestas,* and the like. The fact that, in the nineteenth century, all these terms came together under the word "politics" represents, therefore, a spectacular change, and indeed inversion of perspective. Today we attach the vertical dimension to a word which signifies – in the tradition – the horizontal one. Following this rearrangement, the political sphere is raised and restricted, in the sense of being referred to the activity of government or to the sphere of the state. However, this arrangement, which reflects fairly well the realities of the nineteenth century, collapses under the impact of the realities of the twentieth century. We must face a new fact: the democratization, or at least the "massification," of politics. The masses – hitherto estranged, excluded, or only present intermittently – enter politics, and they enter to remain.

The democratization or massification of politics entails not only its diffusion or, if you wish, its dilution, but above all, the ubiquity of politics. At this point, the horizontal dimension re-enters, superadded to or subtracted from, as it were, the vertical one. After two thousand years of relative stability, we have in little more than a century a succession of earthquakes. It is no wonder, therefore, that the word politics currently evokes a mess. Though the state expands, political processes can no longer be contained within, or brought under, its institutions. Consequently, the concept of the state gives way to the broader and more flexible idea of the political system. To be sure, we may be as unhappy with the notion of political system as we are with the notion of state. At one end, the allegation is that the political system still fails to encompass the ubiquity and diffusion of politics. At the other end, the charge is that the notion of political system is far too broad in that it remains unbounded. Now, a system without boundaries is not, in any proper sense, a "system" (for the technical meaning, see especially Easton 1965a, 1965b; Urbani 1971). Moreover, this leads to a dilution of the concept of politics which comes very close to vaporizing it out of existence. There is more than a grain of truth in these opposite complaints. Yet the two objections, in that they are contrary, neutralize one another and help restore the proportions of the issue. Take the electoral process, which exemplifies well the nexus between the democratization of politics, on the one hand, and the restitution to politics of the horizontal dimension, on the other hand. Clearly, voting belongs to the horizontal plane. Nonetheless, "voting for electing" equally enters the vertical plane, for elections are a means of recruiting the personnel which goes to fill political seats in political sites.

In general, the caution is that we must avoid confusing the *resources of* power, or the *influences on* power, with *having power* (see Dahl 1963: Chapter 5); just as we must distinguish between where and how political power is *generated*, and how and where it is *exercised* (for a general overview, see Passigli 1971). Once these distinctions are made, the difficulties of establishing the boundaries of the political system are no longer insoluble difficulties.

The diffusion of politics does not occur, however, solely at the base of the pyramid, at the level of the demos. We find it also at the apex, at the elite level. Western democracies are increasingly structured as competitive "polyarchies," reflecting a broad pluralistic dissemination (see Dahl 1956). So far there is no problem, in that the notion of political system (with the complement of its subsystems) has the necessary elasticity to embrace a vast and varied dissemination of power. The problem is that, amid these summits, there emerge vertical structures which are not political. This is especially the case of the "giant corporation" – a formidable economic power without property. But we must again remember that to condition or to influence political power is not the same as to wield it. However influential the giant corporations, or their trade union counterparts, it does not follow that their power is "sovereign" and that it outweighs political power. As long as a political system holds together, the binding commands *erga omnes*, directed to all, emanate only from political sites. Only political decisions – whether under the form of laws or not – can be coercively imposed upon the general citizenry. And if by collective decisions we mean the decisions which are not entrusted to single individuals, then political decisions can be defined as the "sovereign" collective decisions from which the individual is less likely to escape, because of both their spatial extension and their coercive intensity.

All in all, my feeling is that the identity crisis of politics is, first and foremost, a "crisis of placement." If we agree on a structural criterion of sorting out politics, and if we do not lose our way in overly peripheral errands – that is, in the diffuseness of politics – the term is definable and identifiable. Political decisions do deal with the most diverse matters: political economy, social policy, the politics of law, of religion, of education, and so forth. If all these decisions are essentially political, it is because they are made by personnel located in *political* sites. This is their political "nature."

Conclusion

There remains one fundamental objection, which concerns less the identity than the very autonomy of politics. The new science of society – sociology – tends to absorb political science, and thereby politics itself, into its own ambit. Sociological reductionism, or the sociologization of politics, is indubitably linked to the democratization of politics and finds in this link its strength as well as its limit. Its strength, because democracy is characterized by ascending vertical processes, results in a "responsive" system typically receptive to demands that come from below. Its limit, however, exists because the sociological explanation breaks down in the case of dictatorial systems, which are "extractive" precisely in that they are characterized by descending processes, by the prevalence of orders coming from above. In substance, sociological reductionism *flattens politics*. In the perspective of the sociologist, the vertical dimension becomes a dependent variable – dependent from, and explained by, the social system and the socioeconomic structure (for a criticism, see Sartori 1969). This leveling out of politics is plausible, as I said, in the case of responsive systems which reflect the power of the people; but it is highly implausible with respect to the political systems characterized by strong verticality. In particular, the sociologization of politics falls short of explaining the dictatorial process – that is, the political systems in which the authoritative allocation of values – as Easton puts it – can in no way be traced to ascending demands, if for no other reason than because these systems impede the autonomous formation and the free expression of the social demand.

The ultimate criticism of the autonomy of politics, however, is not the sociological one; rather, it stems from Marxian philosophy. Marx posits – *qua* philosopher – not only the heteronomy of politics but, more drastically, the "negation of politics." In the economico-materialistic conception of history, politics is a superstructure not only in the sense that it reflects the forces and the forms of production, but also in the sense that it is an epiphenomenon destined to extinction. As the communist society is achieved, the state withers away, and with it the domination of man over man. It is unnecessary to dwell on this wholesale negation of politics. If a philosophy of history is to be measured by the events it generates, then it suffices to note that the "primacy of politics" finds its major confirmation – across the world – in the states founded on the ideology of Marx and his successors. Whoever lives in the communist world has no doubt whatsoever about the identity of politics, nor does he doubt the autonomy or self-sufficiency of politics. In all these countries, it is not the social system that explains the state but, conversely, the state that explains the social system.

As can be seen, the debate about the identity and the autonomy of politics is wide open. One fact is certain: the ubiquity, the growing diffusion, of politics in the contemporary world. This development lends itself, however, to diverse interpretations. It can strengthen the thesis of the heteronomy or, in its extreme form, of the very negation of politics. Or it can strengthen – on the basis of the argument that man has never been politicized as today – the opposite view: a thesis which does not necessarily affirm the supremacy or primacy of politics, but which certainly asserts its autonomy. Between these two opposed interpretations, one can place our uncertain identification of politics, the difficulty of "locating" politics. This uncertainty generates, in turn, the thesis that the diffusion of politics is equivalent to a dilution, and hence leads to the eclipse of the political.

In summary, the current predicament of politics is reflected in at least three discordant views: (1) heteronomy, or outright extinction; (2) autonomy, primacy, or outright triumph; (3) dilution, emasculation, and eclipse. These three views are related in various ways to the ubiquity of politics, reflect different placements of the things political, and, correlatively, different ways of perceiving, identifying, and defining politics. If this is so, it goes to show that, before rushing headlong into the scientific treatment of politics, it is wise to pause and to ask what is being treated. It seems to me, in effect, that the difficulties encountered by the present-day science of politics are derived in no small part from the variable "politics" – i.e., from the object. This article has sought to address that confusion.

Notes

* Originally published as Giovanni Sartori (1973) "What is Politics?" *Political Theory* 1 (1): 5–26.

1   There is no history of political science approached as a set of encounters between science and politics. The relevant material can be found, on the one hand, in works of philosophy, epistemology, and methodology of science, and, on the other hand, in the history of political thought. For the latter, see note 6 below.
2   For the Greek conception of life, Jaeger (1945) remains outstanding. Despite their age and some errors, amended by subsequent historiography, see also Fustel de Coulanges (1885) and Burckhardt (1908).
3   One must bear in mind that the small dimensions of the polis resulted in a network of face-to-face relationships. Magistrates and "superiors" certainly existed, but when the base of the pyramid is narrow, the apex cannot go very high. The horizontal perception of politics should be understood in this perspective and in a relative sense.
4   *The Prince*, Chapters 1 and 3. Machiavelli also used the word "state" in its medieval sense, meaning *status*, rank, or social standing (see Chiappelli 1952: 59–74). The modern use consolidates itself with Hobbes, who uses commonwealth and state as equivalents, and even more so with the translation of Pufendorf into French, in which Barbeyrac renders civitas as *état*.
5   Gubernaculum is characteristic of Bracton, an author of the thirteenth century particularly valued by McIlwain (see note 6) for his distinction between *gurbernaculum* and *iurisdictio*. I have found no traces of the word in the Italian annotators of the time.
6   There is no study that undertakes the complicated, but nevertheless rewarding, task of tracing the terminological evolution of the concept of politics. Among the few encyclopedias that have "politics" as an entry, see the *Grande Dizionario Enciclopedico*, U.T.E.T. (the entry is now in Albertini 1963). Aside from an author-by-author search, the most helpful histories of political thought are: Carlyle and Carlyle (1903–36), McIlwain (1937), Sabine (1961), Wolin (1960), and Ullmann (1961). I am especially indebted to Wolin. Gierke (1900) merits consultation. Also very relevant is McIlwain (1958, 1939).
7   Compare the humanistic interpretation of Polin (1953), which follows Strauss (1952). I follow Wolin (1960: Chapter 8).
8   If we refer to physics, its first development is in terms of *pondere et mensura*; the axiomatic and mathematical phase follows much later.
9   In passing from the autonomy of politics in the Machiavellian sense to that autonomy which separates the political from the social, another dimension is involved. In the first case, we ask what is the specificity of political behavior; in the second, we take stock of a structural differentiation which calls for the delimitation of the respective boundaries. Though logically distinct, the two problems are related.
10   On the issue, see Cotta (1953) and Gentile (1967). Montesquieu was considered the precursor of sociology by Comte; a thesis subsequently developed especially by Durkheim (1953) and recently by Aron (1962: Chapter 3).
11   The history of the discovery of the concept of society remains to be written. For a different interpretation centered on Rousseau, see Dahrendorf (1971). More correctly, the somewhat dated essay of Werner Sombart (1923) places the English (especially Mandeville, A. Ferguson, Adam Smith, and J. Millar) before the French.

12 "Politics" appears, in effect, in the titles of D. Hume, *Essays Moral and Political* (3 vols., 1741–48), and *Political Discourses* (1748–52); but these are minor works. One can also recall Holbach, *La politique naturelle* (1773). The marginality and evanescence of the word politics until the eighteenth century is confirmed by its derivatives: the French word *police* (our "police" comes from polítes) and the expression *parti des politiques*, which was applied, after the night of St. Bartholomew, to those Catholics who deplored the massacre of the Huguenots. Still more telling is the entry "politique" in the *Encyclopédie*, which neglects all the above-mentioned authors and moves – after Machiavelli and Bodin – to Graziano and Boccalini. See in general Hubert (1923: especially Chapters 4–5). See also Derathé (1950).

13 So much so that the entry "politics," while listed in the first *Encyclopedia of the Social Sciences* of 1930–35, disappears in the *International Encyclopedia of the Social Sciences* (1968). Likewise, the entry is no longer listed in the *Encyclopaedia Britannica*. Several attempts at individualization (e.g., Crick 1962; de Jouvenel 1963) are reviewed by Stoppino (1964), who rightly finds them unsatisfactory.

References

Abbagnano, N. (1969) "Machiavelli politico," *Rivista di Filosofia* 60: 5–23.

Albertini, M. (1963) *Politica e altri saggi*, Milan: Giuffré.

Aron, R. (1962) *Dix-huit leçons sur la société industrielle*, Paris: Gallimard.

Barker, E. (1951) *Principles of Social and Political Theory*, New York: Oxford University Press.

Bendix, R. (1962) "Social Stratification and Political Community," in P. Laslett and W.G. Runciman (eds.), *Philosophy, Politics and Society*, Oxford: Blackwell.

Bryson, G. (1945) *Man and Society: the Scottish Enquiry of the Eighteenth Century*, Clifton, NJ: Kelley.

Burckhardt, J. (1908) *Griechische Kulturgeschichte*, Berlin and Stuttgart: W. Spemann.

Carlyle, A.J. and Carlyle, R.W. (1903–36) *A History of Medieval Political Theory in the West*, New York: Barnes and Noble.

Cassirer, E. (1911) *Das Erkentnissproblem in der Philosophie und Wissenschaft der neueren Zeit*, Berlin: B. Cassirer.

Chiappelli, F. (1952) *Studi sul linguaggio de Machiavelli*, Florence: Le Monnier.

Cotta, S. (1953) *Montesquieu e la scienza della societá*, Turin: Ramella.

Crick, B. (1962) *In Defense of Politics*, Chicago: University of Chicago Press.

Cropsey, J. (1957) *Polity and Economy: An Interpretation of the Principles of Adam Smith*, The Hague: Nijhoff.

Dahl, R.A. (1956) *A Preface to Democratic Theory*, Chicago: University of Chicago Press.

Dahl, R.A. (1963) *Modern Political Analysis*, Englewood Cliffs, NJ: Prentice Hall.

Dahrendorf, R. (1971) "Sociologia e societá industriale," in *Uscire dall'utopia*, Bologna: Il Mulino.

Derathé, R. (1950) *Jean Jacques Rousseau et la science politique de son temps*, Paris: Presses Universitaires de France.

Durkheim, E. (1953) *Montesquieu et Rousseau précurseurs de la sociologie*, Paris: Presses Universitaires de France.

Easton, D. (1965a) *A Framework for Political Analysis*, Englewood Cliffs, NJ: Prentice Hall.

Easton, D. (1965b) *A Systems Analysis of Political Life*, New York: Wiley.

Fustel de Coulanges, N.D. (1885) *La cité antique*, Paris: Hachette.

Gargani, A. (1971) *Hobbes e la scienza*, Turin: Einaudi.

Gentile, F. (1967) *L'Esprit classique nel pensiero di Montesquieu*, Padua: Cedam.

Gierke, O. (1900) "Das Deutsche Genossenschaftsrecht," abridged in F.W. Maitland (ed.), *Political Theories in the Middle Ages*, Cambridge: Cambridge University Press.

Hobbes, T. (1829–45) *The English Works of Thomas Hobbes*, London: Molesworth.

Hubert, R. (1923) *Les sciences sociales dans l'encyclopédie*, Paris: Travaux et memoires de l'université de Lille.

Jaeger, W. (1945) *Paideia*, New York: Oxford University Press.

de Jouvenel, B. (1963) *The Pure Theory of Politics*, Cambridge: Cambridge University Press.

Kendall, W. (1941) *John Locke and the Doctrine of Majority Rule*, Urbana: University of Illinois Press.

Matteucci, N. (1970) "Niccolò Machiavelli politologo," *Rassegna Italiana di Sociologia*: 169–206.

McIlwain, H. (1937) *The Growth of Political Thought in the West*, New York: Cooper Square.

McIlwain, H. (1939) *Constitutionalism and the Changing World*, Cambridge: Cambridge University Press.

McIlwain, H. (1958) *Constitutionalism: Ancient and Modern*, Ithaca, NY: Cornell University Press.

Olschki, L. (1969) "Machiavelli scienziato," *Il Pensiero Politico* 2: 509–35.

Passerin d'Entreves, A. (1951) *Natural Law*, London: Hutchinson.

Passigli, S. (ed.) (1971) *Potere e élites politiche*, Bologna: Il Mulino.

Polin, R. (1953) *Politique et philosophie chez Thomas Hobbes*, Paris: Presses Universitaires de France.

Sabine, G.H. (1961) *A History of Political Theory*, New York: Holt, Rinehart & Winston.

Sartori, G. (1965) *Democratic Theory*, 2nd edn., New York: Frederick A. Praeger.

Sartori, G. (1969) "From the Sociology of Politics to Political Sociology," in S.M. Lipset (ed.), *Politics and the Social Sciences*, New York: Oxford University Press.

Sasso, G. (1958) *Niccolò Machiavelli*, Naples: Istituto Italiano per gli studi storici.

Sasso, G. (1967) *Studi su Machiavelli*, Naples: Morano.

Sombart, W. (1923) "Die Anfänge der Soziologie," *Soziologie*, Berlin: Heise.

Stoppino, M. (1964) "Osservazioni su alcune recenti analisi della politica," *Il Politico* 29: 88–905.

Strauss, L. (1952) *The Political Philosophy of Hobbes*, Chicago: University of Chicago Press.

Ullmann, W. (1961) *Principles of Government and Politics in the Middle Ages*, London: Methuen.

Urbani, G. (1971) *L'analisi del sistema politico*, Bologna: Il Mulino.

Wirszubski, C. (1950) *Libertas*, Cambridge: Cambridge University Press.

Wolin, S.S. (1960) *Politics and Vision: Continuity and Innovation in Western Political Thought*, Boston: Little, Brown.

3   The Tower of Babel

Giovanni Sartori

Introduction

Over the years our mutual understanding and lines of communication have not improved, but mightily deteriorated. We often fail to perceive the deterioration because we live with it; we become accustomed to what we are, and we inevitably lack perspective about ourselves. Bluntly put, I sense – and fear – a Tower of Babel trend. The suspicion can be warranted by the four reasons that follow.

The loss of etymological anchorage

Many Western social scientists, especially Americans, no longer know Latin and Greek. This is unprecedented since for some 25 centuries Western authors, even when they began writing in their respective national languages, did know Latin and Greek, and thereby anchored – knowingly or not – their concepts to their Latin and/or Greek roots. The stabilizing and constraining force of this anchorage, of this *semantic viscosity*, can hardly be overstated. If one wonders what provided, for 25 centuries, a "natural," common basis for the Western type of thinking, the single major explanation probably lies in this etymological constraint.

To cite one example out of hundreds, let us take Horowitz's treatment of consensus and cooperation. His definitions are that "cooperation concerns toleration of differences, while consensus demands abolition of these same differences . . . consensus programs the termination of the game by insisting on the principle of unity, whereas cooperation is pluralistic because it programs the continuation of the game" (Horowitz 1962: 177–78). To anyone thinking in Latin, this rearrangement appears inconceivable. Since consensus means, etymologically, "feeling together," whereas cooperation means "working together," it is immediately apparent that the two concepts belong to different dimensions, that the latter concept may (but need not) presuppose the former one, and that it is wholly gratuitous to assert that consensus – i.e., an *idem sentire* – demands the abolition of differences, unity, and the termination of the game. Actually, all of this is lexicographically false.

The loss of historical anchorage

The behavioral revolution, with its ahistorical training and emphasis, has severed another kind of anchorage – our understanding that meanings are not arbitrary stipulations but *reminders of historical experience and experimentation*. Most of our political concepts were shaped and acquired their meaning out of a survival of the fittest process. Terms such as power, authority, violence, coercion, law, constitution, liberty, etc. (thereby including consensus) reflect experiences, behavioral patterns, and perceptions resulting from historical learning; they are, so to speak, *existential reminders*. For instance, when we assert "this is not coercion" (something less than or different from coercion) the *bien fonde* of the argument is that historical experience has assigned the word coercion to things (properties or characteristics) of much greater consequence than those that are declared coercive today.

Thus, political scientists and sociologists – let alone the layman – ignoring the authors of the past have freed themselves not only from the constraints of etymology, but equally from *the learning process of history*. Admittedly, the traditional vocabulary of politics does not always supply a word for what we mean today. But even when the words are supplied, they are often misused, i.e., their historical substance and message are ignored.

The loss of the mainstream of discourse

In addition to the foregoing, the world of words has become a *multipurpose* instrument to a wholly unprecedented extent. We are straining and stretching our instrument – language – in manifold directions, and for purposes which are even at odds.

Until about a century ago, there was a shared mainstream of discourse. The language of poetry permitted "poetic license"; but it was not until the exhaustion of the classic and subsequently of the neoclassic tradition that the language of poetry became a cryptic, *sui generis* language. Similarly, and at the other extreme, the language of philosophy had its own "license," and metaphysical philosophy provided tough reading (Leibnitz's *Monadology* is a good example); yet it was not until the romantic revolution and the philosophy of German idealism (Fichte, Schelling, and Hegel) that the language of philosophy went loose, if not wild. Since then, the diaspora of language has steadily increased, and by now the scattering of what was formerly a common mainstream of discourse is quite fantastic. In principle, the "specialization" of language not only is inevitable – for it follows the equally inevitable process of intellectual division of labor – but should be appraised favorably. I am concerned that this process of specialization has run out of hand, and that its requirements and consequences escape adequate awareness and methodological control. Today the same words extend, without clear underpinning or differentiation, all the way from highly speculative (supra-empirical or metaphysical) to operational meanings – a near astronomic distance. Words such as "structure" and "culture" are used in philosophy, ethnology, anthropology, psychology, sociology, and political science in a way which is chaotic, wasteful, and frequently conducive to cross-disciplinary bastards.

Let me make clear that I am not indulging in a lost paradise mood. I favor the division of labor strategy, and I am skeptical about the "unity of science" program. My point is that, having lost a shared mainstream of discourse, we cannot continue to act as if we still have one. For even our last anchorage – *common* reinforcement – is rapidly losing its hold. On this, as well as on the former scores, we must act – and begin by awakening – or we shall end as did the builders of the Babel Tower.

Novitism

Although my emphasis is on the loss of anchorages (semantic, historical, and common reinforcement), it is obvious that other factors reinforce our diaspora. Not only are we confronted with problems of scale – the growing massiveness of the scholarly profession – but the acceleration of history mightily increases what I call the *frenzy of novitism*: the hypertrophy of innovation.

Until quite recently, scholars usually did not perceive themselves as having to be "new" and original at whatever cost: they understood their main task to consist of transmitting knowledge. Clearly, this is less and less the case. However, it is not easy to be "original," and perhaps the easiest way of appearing to innovate is to play musical chairs with words. One can indeed appear both powerfully destructive of others and mightily innovative, simply by rearranging a string of words with the help of a handful of stipulative definitions. One can easily demonstrate, for example, that not Western societies, but only African societies, are truly "pluralistic," simply by stipulating ad hoc meanings for "consensus" on the one hand, and "conflict" on the other.[1] And one can, by the same token, as easily write a fat book to demonstrate the contrary – and then the contrary of the contrary. At the end of this series, all the contestants will probably be credited with innovative and provocative publications; and another series can be started – but not to the benefit of understanding.

The freezing of language

Assuming that the soft social sciences are sliding – if unawares – toward a vicious circle of incommunicability and frivolous verbalism, it behooves us to give high priority to the search for remedies. This search, however, is immediately confronted with the objections that language is a living reality, and specifically that a science in the making cannot and should not be prematurely frozen with respect to its terminology. Even assuming that this objection carries some weight, it has a weird, untimely flavor. How can we worry about the premature *freezing* of language, when the burning problem is to *contain the proliferation of chaos?*

At any rate, I take the foregoing objection to be wholly misconstrued. First of all, nobody demands a "freezing" (the wrong word!). What is needed is an orderly procedure for the enrichment and refinement of our vocabulary upon stabilized foundations. The pertinent analogy is with all the classificatory sciences, such as mineralogy, botany, zoology, and (in part) medicine, whose vocabularies are almost entirely constructed upon Greek and Latin roots. These roots, and their innumerable combinations, have long furnished an endless source for the invention and addition of new "object terms." Indeed, it is the stability of the primary linguistic units which has permitted the continuous creation of compounded units and the mobility of the overall composition.

Consider, by contrast, the philosophic tradition. Whatever its other differences from the scientific enterprise, one major difference is indisputable: *philosophy is noncumulative*, at least in the sense that science is.[2] The reason is that it suits the purpose of philosophical speculation to have a free hand with language. Fundamentally, each philosopher starts anew. To be sure, he knows what other philosophers have said, and accounts for it; yet he does not begin where his predecessors left off. He rebegins. So do we, in political science. But this does not make us philosophers. It shows, rather, that we are poor scientists, as yet incapable of capitalizing on each other's work.

The cards and the game

In the second place, we should not confuse the dynamics of *language* with the dynamics of *science*. Let us assume that a science has developed its vocabulary to a point at which its stabilization – not its eternal immobility – is taken for granted. (Economics may be a case in point.) In such cases we see that the stabilization of the basic vocabulary has not obstructed, but indeed has favored, scientific growth.

The relation of the linguistic instrument to scientific knowledge resembles – with admitted differences – the relation of cards to a card game. The game (with its near infinite possibilities) can be played only because the cards and the rules of their combination are given – indeed, static. Not too dissimilarly, only a disciplined use of terms and of procedures of composition (and decomposition) permits the scientist to play his game. By contrast, we social scientists invest more and more of our energies simply in *altering the cards*. If so, we are furthering not science, but sheer confusion. We are dismantling, rather than rebuilding, whatever cumulative or additive knowledge we have attained.

Many of us find an alibi in Kuhn: we are undergoing a scientific revolution. But Kuhn (see note 2) has been misread – and has in part changed his own mind. Scientific revolutions are not necessarily "language revolutions" (only the passage from alchemy to chemistry really fits this image), but "paradigm revolutions." Moreover, scientific revolutions occur when "normal science" has exhausted its lines of enquiry and faces insoluble puzzles. Thus, my appraisal of the state of the art is that we are undergoing not a *scientific* but a *verbal* revolution; that, as a consequence, we have yet to enter the stage of a "normal science" type of incremental progress; and that if Kuhn is our alibi, our truer emblem might be Penelope's skein. At this point we no longer know what game we are playing, for every morning we are given a new set of different cards.

The methodologist is generally viewed with impatience as the scholar who is endlessly entangled in preliminaries and never gets to work. But perhaps the time has come to reverse this appraisal: for it is the methodologist who is now entitled to grow impatient at the sterility of the work of the practitioner.

Counteracting chaos

If language is no longer stabilized by semantic viscosity ("The loss of etymological anchorage"), by historical testing ("The loss of historical anchorage"), or by the reinforcement of unquestioned consensus ("The loss of the mainstream of discourse" and "Novitism"), then our problem is not to shy away from the "ideal" of a stabilized basic vocabulary – under various pretexts ("The freezing of language" and "The cards and the game") – but to give serious thought to how this ideal can be pursued. Obviously it cannot be approached by fiat. We have an unprecedented problem, so new and so huge that we are just beginning to grasp it. I have no miraculous solution to offer, aside from suggesting that "novitism" can be curbed, and card reshuffling counteracted, by becoming serious about *standards*: whether an author submits himself to, and passes the test of, a given set of standards.

One such standard is obvious: *new stipulations* must be not only declared but *justified*, and this implies that the stipulator must show that his proposal is prompted not by his ignorance (a very frequent case) but by his knowledge (see "Arbitrariness in defining").

Another crucial standard relates to the *semantic field* (see especially Ullmann 1962: Chapter 9). If we alter the meaning of a key term, then *a whole constellation of neighboring terms needs reallocation and redefinition*, for terms come in "strings." If this were a required test, my guess is that "novitism" would largely founder on this reef. Only Lasswell and Kaplan (1952) have deliberately launched themselves in such an enterprise – and even they have not fared too well.

A third set of standards will be expounded at length (see "Conceptual analysis"): the standards provided by *logical rules*. When we assert, e.g., "let us classify," the standard is that a classification should be a classification, whereas most so-called classifications do not live up to their claim. Note, incidentally, that classifications do not violate our intellectual freedom or our desire for novelty. Since each classification is only the ordering based on its own criterion, there is in principle no end to the possibilities of reclassification, i.e., of establishing other classes with other criteria. Yet, each conceivable classification must meet at least two standards: its classes must be mutually exclusive and empirically useful. Meeting only these two requirements is far more easily said than done, and it actually imposes all the discipline we need.

In general, we might call the standard of logical analysis – as illustrated by the case of classifications – the *do what you claim to be doing* test: a test, or a burden, from which we have relieved ourselves far too easily.

The model–paradigm juncture

Thus far discipline has been my main recommendation. The questions now are: at what point is freedom of creativity to be recommended, and when indeed does it become necessary? While I do not praise the freedom of unsettling the vocabulary, nor the freedom of disregarding logical rules, I believe the acid test of real creativity comes at the *modeling stage*, as construed by Anthony Judge (1972: especially 14, 16–20).[3] Other authors refer to much the same thing by speaking of paradigm and "paradigmatic level" (see, e.g., Holt and Turner 1970: Chapter 2). Provided that our political or social-science paradigms are brought down to proportion (with respect to Kuhn's meaning) and thereby understood as "quasiparadigms" or "microparadigms," I have no quarrel with this label either. Let me thus say that the juncture at which we fruitfully diverge is the *model-paradigm level.*[4]

A good illustration of how fundamental disagreements can be imputed to, and derived from, alternative "model-paradigms" is provided by the notion of "interest." This notion is conceived and developed, in the contemporary literature, either within the frame of a "conflict model" (paradigm), or within the frame of a "consensus model" (paradigm). Once these different paradigmatic premises are spelled out, it becomes clear why and how two entirely different lines of argumentation coherently follow (Connolly 1973).

Appreciation of inventiveness and creativity at the model-paradigm level is not the same as encouraging every man to go loose. Quite to the contrary, by asking a novitist, "Please outline your paradigm," we are making things very difficult for him. After all, there are not that many models or paradigms around. The model-paradigm standard, or clause, thus seemingly suggests an optimal balance between "normal science," which grows cumulatively upon a stabilized vocabulary, and "innovation in science." In short: if the test of originality is "another model," this is a more than sufficient standard and anchorage – and indeed the *discrimen* between real creativity and prestidigitation (if not cheating).

Concepts, words, phenomena

Which is the start?

In any process of understanding, at least three elements are involved: (i) *concepts*, (ii) *words*, (iii) *phenomena*. We may wish to make the assertion somewhat more precise. If so, we may distinguish between (i) concepts, conceptions, and meanings, (ii) words and terms, (iii) phenomena and data. These distinctions are based on the following stipulations:

1   *Idea* is a mental image, a meaning.
2   *Conception* is a set of ideas associated with, or elicited by, a given word.
3   *Concept* is a conception treated according to logical rules. In an example given by Riggs, the *conception* of a bird embraces all the multifarious ideas signified by the word "bird," while one *concept* called "Aves" is "feathered vertebrates."
4   *Terms* are words which unambiguously refer to concepts. Example: if "bird" (or Aves) is defined as "feathered vertebrate," it becomes a term. If "bird" refers to a dozen possible meanings, then it is a word which elicits a manifold conception.

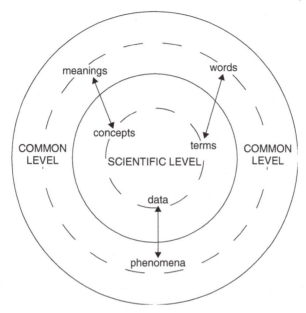

Figure 3.1 Two levels: common versus scientific discourse.

The above stipulations sort out two levels of discourse – common (ordinary) and scientific. In *common discourse* the three elements are: (a) meanings, (b) words, (c) phenomena-or-facts. In *scientific discourse* the three elements become: (a) concepts, (b) terms, (c) data. The interrelations among the two sets (levels of discourse) are depicted in Figure 3.1.

For some purposes, it is important to distinguish the two levels and the corresponding stipulations are very useful. For a preliminary argument, however, the wording of my initial assertion is clear enough and suffices to make my point – that concept-words-phenomena are linked *in that order*. The reasons why these elements are best construed as a unidirectional sequence in which the concept takes precedence, or the lead, are stated by Riggs (1975). They need not be repeated here. To be sure, the sequence is actually a circular one, for phenomena or data do feed back into concepts. However, the return from the phenomena to the concepts occurs via hazardous and somewhat mysterious inductive processes – a feedback loop more than a simple feedback.

Language and thinking

In the above framework, *words* are symbols to be allocated in the most economical and unequivocal fashion to carry ideas, i.e., to "serve" the *unit of thinking*, which is the concept. Yet we must ask how words and thinking – more inclusively, language and understanding – relate to each other.

There are four possibilities: (a) no intrinsic relation; (b) the relation is so intrinsic that the two elements are indistinguishable; (c) words are only tools, i.e., neutral instruments, for communicating thoughts; (d) words are tools of thinking (not merely of communicating), and are by no means neutral, for they powerfully orient, in and by themselves, our perceptions and interpretations.

These four possibilities, with additional shades, are examined in semantics, and need no further discussion here. It should be pointed out, however, that the COCTA[5] strategy is easier to accept under the third (c) than the fourth solution (d). Since I happen to subscribe to the latter, it behooves me first to emphasize the importance of "naming" (the choice of the word) and, second, to explain why I nonetheless adhere to the precedence of the concept.

The impact of words

As the old maxim goes, *nomina si nescis, peril et cognito rerum*: if one does not have or know the names, there is no knowledge of things. We are thus being reminded that if a language does not provide a name for an object, the object passes unnoticed. But there is much more to it. Words are not simply means for identifying objects. Words intervene in our *perception* of objects, and indeed convey *interpretations* and attach *significance* to their referents. A classic example is provided by the various words for moon. In archaic Greek, moon was *men* (from the verb *menai*, to count), and the implication was that the moon was perceived as an instrument for counting time. The Romans, who already had a calendar, called the moon *luna* (from *lucere*, to provide light), and thus the moon was perceived as a means of illumination.[6]

It should now be clear why I insist that we perform mentally across three phases, one of these being the word phase in its irreducible distinctiveness. However, the importance of *name choosing* (or of assigning terms) does not imply that words come first. Since we are required to pick up the "right word,"[7] the beginning is in the choosing, and the choosing is part and parcel of the concept.

From these semantic considerations comes my distress with what I have called playing "musical chairs" with words, or careless card reshuffling. By rebaptizing an object (moon, in the example) we give it a new interpretation, and this is or may be of great consequence. Thus too much rebaptizing, if at whim, results not only in fuzzy identifications but also in a disarrangement of the whole field to which the object (or the object-term) belongs. If "mammal" is defined as "having sizeable breasts," or if we replace the term mammal with the word "breastal," then whales might be considered fishes and zoology would have to be reorganized.

The neo-Baconian start

Reverting to the sequence, concepts-words-phenomena, what if the order is reversed? This is in effect what Holt and Richardson describe as "twentieth century Baconianism," i.e., as "atheoretic approaches to theory development" (Holt and

Turner 1970: 58–69). Since I agree with their exposition and criticism, only a few additional comments are in order.

Putting it simplistically, but perhaps not unfairly, the neo-Baconian formula is: *from the data back to science*. It will be noted that this is not only a reversed but a shorter sequence: where words stand, and how they relate to concepts, all of this passes under a huge whitewash of silence. It would seem therefore that "data" are something leaping into our sense from a real world *an sich* and *fur sich*. Epistemologically speaking, this is monumentally naïve, as I shall attempt to show by arguing that data are nothing but information and observations collected within and processed by ad hoc "conceptual containers" (see "An illustration").

The neo-Baconian counter-argument is likely to be that I neglect the novelty, the fact that we now own powerful statistical techniques which can, from the data end, do what formerly had to be done at the conceptual end, i.e., detect errors and shape, or reshape, the resulting theory. Thus, the implicit contention is that statistical analysis surrogates, for the better, logical analysis. But statistical controls control only the variable in *use*. They do not control the variables that are kept constant, and even less variables that have yet to be conceived. In particular, multiple-regression analysis detects spurious correlations only for those variables actually controlled. Hence, it does not discover other variables which, once discovered, might account for the observed correlation.

In sum, statistical techniques and computer programs cannot supply what concept formation does not provide. And, if the foregoing is correct, then our precise measures are a *precision masking imprecision*, i.e., the vagueness of the terms used both for collecting the data and for specifying what is being measured. Furthermore, "our problems derive from the need to make inferences from quantitative observations when we have only very limited ability to specify the processes which generated them. The likely results are faulty inferences" (Cnudde 1972: 131). Unless we are alert, we may well be entering a gigantic enterprise of self-delusion.

Conceptual analysis

Terms as concepts and terms in sentences

Many authors do not use "term" for the word allocated to a concept, but as the most inclusive word for speaking about words. Under this broad usage, "term" can be understood either as a synonym for *word*, or as a synonym for *concept*. If so, we have a fundamental bifurcation. If a term is a *word* (not a concept), then the meaning of a term can only be given in context and specified by the sentence (statement, proposition) in which the word is employed. Hence, terms refer us to *sentences*. Dictionary makers and linguists first collect sentences in which a given word is used. All such statements are then sorted out so as to cluster together those in which the word seems to have the same or a similar meaning. Subsequently, definitions – appropriately called "lexicographic" – are prepared to describe each of these meanings.

Nobody questions this approach. It is not only very useful, but the appropriate one for ascertaining what people may mean by the words they use. Its limits are the limits of grammars and inherent in mere *reconstructions*. For this is by no means the way in which knowledge is *actually constructed*. In particular, this procedure dramatizes the overlapping and unnecessarily erratic multiplicity of meanings attributed to most words. Furthermore, this approach freezes out of consideration those concepts for which we currently lack words. Simply put, dictionaries themselves enhance the enormous looseness and ambiguity of language.

If, on the other hand, a term is a *concept* (stands for a concept), then meanings can be attached to the *terms as such* and the lexicographic procedure is reversed and/or severely curtailed. It is reversed in that the concept shapes the sentence (not the sentence the concept); and it is curtailed in that a large number of lexicographic meanings are dropped. In short, in this procedure the concept is the guideline. This entails that meanings are "structured" by logical rules and "systematic" coordination. This is equally to say that *concepts* (terms as concepts) can be treated out of context, or at least *above context*: for the concept is the rider, and the sentence which declares its meaning is the horse.

Logical systematizing

That the concept should be the guideline is more easily said than done. How can it be said *and* done? Only the *force of logic* overrules the force of words. That is to say that concepts are the guidelines if, and only if, we are guided by *logical rules*. By saying logical rules, I do not intend, however, that we should become involved in the minutiae which delight professional logicians. My concern is with a necessary and sufficient *minimal logic* (subsequently called "applied logic") for the layman. Social scientists are not logicians, just as they are not mathematicians. But they should neither be totally ignorant of mathematics (as we now concede), nor of elementary logic (as we still fail to realize).

For the moment, however, I shall merely speak of *conceptual* analysis – with the understanding that "analysis" should be taken seriously, that is, as *logical analysis*. So conceived, conceptual analysis points to two major areas of concern, or application: (a) the logical systematizing of ensembles, and (b) the logical treatment of single concepts, or of discrete conceptual clusters.

Logical systematizing can be dealt with quickly. Aside from and long before "systems theory," any science is required to be "systematic." We endlessly ask: what do we *call* this, and *why*? The answer lies in *systematic considerations* which in turn relate to a given *semantic field*. Since words come in strings, any allocation or reallocation of meanings entails a systematic arrangement or rearrangement guided by logical considerations.

Analysis by classification

Passing to the logical treatment of concepts or of conceptual clusters – which I take to be the central part of conceptual analysis – the oldest and simplest technique is analysis by classification.

As is well known, a classificatory treatment requires, and leads to, *mutually exclusive* classes: objects or events *either* fall into one class *or* they fall into another class. The other requirement is that a classification should be *exhaustive*; a requirement easily met by inserting the residual class "other." What is far more important is that a classificatory analysis presupposes at least *one criterion*. A classification is in fact an either-or arrangement *of*, or according to, the chosen criterion. When more than one are combined together, we often speak of taxonomy – thus leaving the word classification for the single-criterion analysis.[8] Classifications and taxonomies should be carefully distinguished from mere enumerations, or *checklists*, of items. Checklists are often handy, but obstruct the cumulation of knowledge.

If we take the view that classificatory analysis is obsolete, then it must be replaced by a different method of analysis. But if the disrepute of classifications leads – as it often does – to pseudo-classifications, then we obtain only the worse of two worlds. Many so-called "nominal scales" are only incomplete or incorrect classifications; we are confronted by a crescendo of mere enumerations which fail to meet the logical standards of classificatory analysis.

Vertical classification

Classifications are not necessarily hierarchical, i.e., classes may simply be arranged horizontally. Vertical classifications – with classes and sub-classes – are more powerful than horizontal ones. Again, vertical classifications do not necessarily lead to a tree-type arrangement. If they do, then the rule of decomposition, or unfolding, of the general class (the genus) is known as the *per genus proximum et differentiam specificam* mode of analysis. At times the tree does not come out well; its base appears to have a narrow, insufficient spread. In the social sciences this is often the case – frequently because the logical decomposition is hampered by a lack of names, by classes for which we do not have a term.

In spite of the prevailing contrary view, I submit that hierarchical classifications, or taxonomies, remain a major, non-replaceable, logical backbone of scientific (empirical) enquiry. The genus and differentia unpacking of concepts not only helps us detect – via the unnamed cases – our cognitive voids; it also appears to be the only systematic technique for arriving at standardized fact-seeking and fact-sorting data containers (see "Concepts as data containers").

Rules of transformation along a ladder of abstraction

Whenever we have a vertical arrangement, the implication is that our concepts belong to different *levels of abstraction*. The most inclusive concept is thus the more abstract one; the least inclusive is the one located at the lowest level of abstraction. This is no great discovery, unless we have a rule of transformation for moving upward (composition) and downward (decomposition) along such a *ladder of abstraction*. The rule of transformation is provided by the inverse relationship between the extension (denotation) and the intension (connotation) of concepts.

The *extension* of a term is the class of *things* to which it applies; the *intension* of a term is the collection of *properties* which determine the things included in the concept (Salmon 1963: 90–91).[9] Our rule of transformation can be specified, therefore, as follows: the extension grows as the intension diminishes – and vice versa. This means that the *more abstract*, or the more general (inclusive) a concept, *the fewer its properties* or attributes. Conversely, the more numerous the attributes or properties of a concept, the lower its level of abstraction and the less its inclusiveness or generality (see "Concept misformation in comparative politics," Chapter 1 of this volume).

Note that whenever we generalize and attempt to theorize on the basis of empirical evidence, the underlying logical operation is, whether we realize it or not, of the "ladder-climbing" type. But unawareness of the rule of transformation leads to what I call *conceptual stretching*, i.e., to augmenting the extension (inclusiveness) of a concept without reducing its properties, and thereby to extending the denotation by obfuscating the connotation. If one follows instead the rule that a concept is made more inclusive by reducing its attributes, then a more "general" concept can be obtained without loss of clarity. The larger the class, the fewer the differentiae; but those differentiae that remain, remain precise. Moreover, following this procedure we obtain conceptualizations which, no matter how all-embracing, still bear a traceable relation to a set of specifics and therefore still lend themselves to empirical testing.

Unless I am mistaken, the foregoing goes a long way to bridging the much-lamented gap between research and theory. We rightly complain that our categories are too general (and much too vague) when they are theoretical, and too minute and descriptive when they are not. This happens because we leap from observational findings all the way to universal categories (and vice versa), bypassing as it were the rules of ladder-climbing (and descending). Indeed, most of the time we do not even identify the level of abstraction with which we are dealing, and the argument develops randomly all the way up to a macro-level, and all the way down to a micro-level.

It should be clear that the inverse relation between extension and intension holds only for a vertical arrangement. If no such arrangement is sought, a single attribute may define a very narrow class, and several attributes a larger class. However, a narrow class defined by a single attribute generally leaves unstated (and to common sense) a host of implied attributes. To illustrate with the classic swan example, one might say that a black swan (indeed a narrow class) is qualified only by the attribute "black." But this is incorrect, for several unstated attributes have to be added to identify the subspecies "swan." With look-and-see terms such as swan and black, it would be pedantic to do this logical exercise in full. But look-and-see terms do not afford much mileage in the social sciences.

An illustration

Let us illustrate by considering, for example, "family." Since the family is a minimal social unit, according to the *per genus et differentiam* mode of analysis we are already at the low end (the subspecies level) of a hierarchical classification whose genus might be "mankind." Our problem is, thus, how to start anew (establish another hierarchy) from this low end.

Let the word "family" represent a concept defined as "a social group characterized by legitimate heterosexual intercourse with a function of rearing children." One might want to make explicit in such a minimal definition that "family" implies cohesiveness and/or enough durability to ensure the survival of its children. Whether in the shorter or longer version, this definition serves its purpose if it includes whatever social unit is conceived, around the world, as being a family, and excludes all social groups that fall under different categories.

The next question is: what do we want to know about families? Families can be monogamous or polygamous, patriarchic or matriarchic; they can be fertile or sterile; they can be "nuclear" or extended to varying degrees and in many ways. Moreover, families vary in intensity and nature of bonds, motivations, duration, role allocation, etc. Now, information about families is all the more detailed (discriminating or disaggregated) the more it conveys each and all of the properties or attributes mentioned above. And the problem is how this slicing can be arranged hierarchically according to orderly criteria and simple rules of decomposition and recomposition. A solution is represented in Table 3.1 (which covers, to be sure, only one hierarchical line, and should be completed on the right side).

The scheme can be read as a typology constructed vertically (taxonomically). But the point is that it is constructed according to the *extension–intension* criterion. Therefore, the interesting question is: why is this a ladder of abstraction? The reply is disarmingly simple: because it is arranged as it is. Nonetheless, the hierarchy does abide by criteria and does follow a rationale. The highest level of abstraction (1) is such because it must be answered dichotomously (Yes–No). Levels 2 and 3

Table 3.1 Ladder of abstraction: an example

Levels	Family	Nature of information
1	Patriarchal/matriarchal	Yes – No
2	Monogamous/polygamous, etc.	Yes – How many
3	Sterile/fertile	Yes – How many
4	Stable-to-unstable	Yes – Duration in time, number of remarriages
5	Nuclear-to-extended	Yes – To whom (e.g., kinship), how much (measure)
6	Patrimonial-to-romantic	Types of motivation
7	Internal role structure	How wife relates to husband and children to parents (e.g., who works for whom)
8	Degree of cohesiveness	Assessed on some scale or continuum
9	Other	Other

are, admittedly, interchangeable; except that fertility (how many families have an x number of children) extends more (with respect to the universe) than the number of wives. Levels 4 and 5 are equally interchangeable – and nobody would quarrel with that – except that the stability of families can be measured (albeit in various ways), whereas the extension of families (from nuclear to broad kinship networks) calls for a typological answer. Thus levels 1 to 4 are more abstract because their classes can be very broad (populated) in that they can all be reaggregated dichotomously (either sterile or fertile, etc.), even though there is a presumption that the disaggregated measures will be more scattered as we descend the ladder.

From level 5 or 6 downwards, we generally find soft data and, moreover, many alternative ways of slicing. Hence, the information may turn out to be quite minute (richness of intension and therefore narrowing of extension). One might wonder why the degree of cohesiveness is placed at the lowest level (8). The reason is that – in spite of the wording – this is not a comparatively reliable measure: it has to be assessed, largely on the basis of single country yardsticks, impressionistically, whereas 6 and 7 can be handled, with more precision, typologically.

To sum up: ladders of abstractions enable us to collect highly disaggregated information which can be endlessly recombined – not only across countries but also over time – in an orderly, simple, and systematic fashion. In the above example, at level 5 just one numerical value would yield how many families are patriarchal, monogamous, fertile, stable, and nuclear – or not. Reading upwards from level 7, one would quickly learn how the families in which, e.g., the children are a source of support, are characterized by, and relate to, patrimonial motivations, stability, size, fertility, monogamy or polygamy, etc.

The example also demonstrates the earlier point (see "Counteracting chaos" above) that logical rules and logical analysis are in themselves a powerful means for counteracting chaos. Going downwards along a ladder of abstraction, the members of the lower classes include all the attributes of the higher classes, plus one. Conversely, i.e., going upward, the members of the higher classes are qualified, at each level, by one attribute less. Therefore, the allocation of words to classes is subject to a *stringent logical testing*: it cannot be done at whim.

Concepts as data containers

Conceptual analysis and emphasis on concept formation do not imply that my concerns are more theoretical than empirical. I would instead argue that it is precisely research and research findings that end up suffering the most from conceptual atrophy. Let me take up the question, therefore, from its data end.

What are data? There is no such thing as crude, uncontaminated, unspoiled facts. "Facts" are, at their crudest, objects or events as perceived and sliced by the *words* of a given semantic field in a given language. But little can be done with such facts. This is why we speak of facts suitable for scientific enquiry as *data*. Thus, data are facts which have been refined. And such refinement follows from having transformed mere words into concepts. More exactly, data are information processed by, and distributed in, *conceptual containers*. This is tantamount to saying that data are observations collected and arranged according to how concepts are defined by the fact-finder, or by the information-seeker. Concepts are not only, then, the units of thinking; they are also, just as much, *data containers*.[10] The relevant question thus becomes: what turns a concept into a valid *fact-finding container*?

There are many possible answers, one being that this is what operational definitions are for. One prior condition, however, is that "data containers" (i.e., concepts) should be (a) *standardized*, and that they should be standardized with (b) *high discriminating power*. If they are not standardized, the information is not cumulative. On the other hand, standardization is self-defeating unless the data containers are discriminating enough to allow for *multi-purpose utilization*, i.e., to serve the varied needs of a variety of consumers.

I insist on the discriminating power, for the poorer the discrimination of fact-seeking containers, the more the facts are misgathered, and therefore the greater the *misinformation*. Conversely, the greater the discriminating power of fact-finding categories, the finer, and thus the more multipurpose, the information. The finer the better, also, because data can always be aggregated, but cannot be disaggregated beyond the discriminating power of the class (container) under which the information was collected.

How can all these requirements be met? They can be met if and only if our concepts are unpacked *per genus et differentiam* (*supra*, "Vertical classification" to "An illustration") into mutually disjoined classes that become, as we descend the ladder of abstraction, always more specific (i.e., qualified by additional properties) and thereby more discriminating.

Somewhere along the line, we also need the help of indicators and operational definitions. However, operational definitions alone are not conducive to standardization – they tend very much to be ad hoc. Moreover, we need a frame of reference for realizing how much conceptual richness operational definitions leave out, or have to neglect. And classificatory unpacking provides, also for this purpose, a systematic frame of reference.

Theory poor and data cheated

My major grievance with the neo-Baconian view (*supra*, "The neo-Baconian start") should now be clear. The underlying assumption of the maxim, "from data back to science," must be that we are theory poor and data rich. But the quality of our data does not sustain this assumption. For one thing, increasing amounts of research and survey data are matched by an increasing lack of comparability and cumulability for they almost invariably result from fishing expeditions guided by non-standardized, single-purpose checklists. On the other hand, most of the cheap and dirty quantitative data provided by institutionalized statistical agencies hopelessly lack discrimination. Moreover, it is clear that our standard variables on literacy, social class, occupation, industrialization, etc., do not really measure, around the world, common underlying phenomena. If this is so, then our major problem is to improve the quality of the data *at its source*. Computer "cleaning" is no remedy for hopelessly vague fact-seeking categories. Yet the neo-Baconian adept is apparently content to remanipulate "masses of data."

Some years ago, Karl Deutsch argued that we were theory rich and data poor. My fear is that, along the neo-Baconian path, we wind up being both theory poor and data cheated.

Measurements and quantification

How does measurement relate to pre- or non-measurement? Once we have dealt with conceptual analysis, this is the crucial issue. It raises two questions. First, where does non-measurement end, i.e., *where does measurement begin*? Second, how do the two things *relate* to each other? Are they complementary, in the sense that the latter adds to, or extends, the former? Are they, instead, mutually exclusive? Or are they, perhaps, related by rules of transformation, so that one can be converted, without loss, into the other?

The broad meaning

A majority of social scientists understands "measurement" very broadly, so as to include: (a) a sheer quantitative idiom, (b) so-called nominal scales, and (c) operational definitions. I object to all three inclusions.

The *quantitative idiom* which is nothing but an idiom, and indeed a verbal abuse, has been disposed of by Kaplan, from whom I borrow the expression (Kaplan 1964: 13). For instance, we can repeat at every line, "this is a matter of degree," without nearing measurement by a hair's breadth. But more on this shortly (see "Objections" and "Pros and cons"). So-called "nominal scales" can be viewed as another example of this abuse, for their distinctive characteristic is to be *nominal*, and hence not to be *scales*. If it pleases us to call them scales (the tyranny of fashion!), the fact remains that they measure nothing.

Turning to *operational definitions*, the tendency is to equate them with "measurement operations" and to argue that a definition is operational if and only if it lends itself to actual measurement. I take the view that this reduction is wrong on at least two counts. By definition, a definition is "operational" when it indicates the "operations" through which a term is applicable to a particular thing or – more broadly – the operations through which empirical statements can be tested (verified or falsified). That a verification (finding out whether something is true or false) should consist only of "measurement operations" is untrue by definition and – let it be added – untrue, i.e., empirically false, to a very large part of our actual operationalizations.

The argument could be rephrased by saying that the more operationalism turns quantitative, the better. But I am not sure. The fundamental objection is that "operationalism" belongs to the *theory-research dimension*, i.e., addresses the long and complex passage from theory to empirical research. Quantifications and measurement do not belong to this dimension. With respect to how theory becomes "empirical," and to how empirical theory extends into and is enriched by research, measurement enters only as a tail-end, as adding "precision."

This is not to downgrade what measurement accomplishes but, quite the contrary, to upgrade its role and importance by placing it in another dimension, namely, *mathematization* (the passage from counting to mathematical transformations).

The narrow meaning

If we exclude verbal camouflages, nominal scales, and operational definitions, we are left with a precise meaning: measurement consists of *using numbers* (i.e., attaching numerical values to items) in terms of their *arithmetical properties*. In practice, this implies that measurement begins at least with ordinal, but especially with interval, scales.

The above definition is only initial and minimal. Among other things, it applies only to *quantitative science* (the science that measures), not to *mathematical science*, which represents a further step, and consists of bringing our numerical values and measures under the concepts and rules of mathematics.

However, here I am only interested in establishing where quantification begins in order to tackle the crucial question: how quantitative science (that measures) relates to qualitative science (that does not). Putting it the other way around, the central issue in this section is how do *what is* questions relate to *how much* questions? This is the same as asking how differences in kind relate to differences in *degree*.

Kinds and degrees

During the last twenty years or so the prevailing mood has been to do away with "an old-fashioned logic of properties and attributes not well adapted to study quantities and relations." This was Hempel's recommendation (as synthesized in Martindale 1959: 87). Its substance is generally expressed by the familiar saying: this is not really a difference in *kind*, but a difference in *degree*, of more or less. More technically put, the recommendation is to replace dichotomous characteristics with "continuous characteristics."

So far, so good. The ultimate question is: do we mean that *all* differences should be transformed into differences in degree, and that *all* characteristics should be construed as continuous? The reply tends to be: yes, as much as possible. What remains obscure, however, is whether the "as much as possible" points to a *pro tempore* limitation in feasibility, or to some intrinsic gnoseological frontier.

Before entering this debate, let us approach the issue by illustration, taking the example of equality. One frequently hears: there is no such thing as absolute equality or inequality – the problem is always more or less equality. Fine, but this is no great discovery unless we proceed further. How? There is no next step unless a conceptual analysis reveals that equality applies to (a) an end state (equal conditions), and to (b) a treatment (rules of allocation), and that when we come to the notion of equal treatment, we are confronted with several different and often conflicting rules of allocation. The example suggests that if conceptual analysis does not provide the breakdowns, the "degree discovery" (if it is a discovery) remains a sheer platitude.

To be sure, equality is a matter of more or less. But more or less with respect to which property (wealth, education, opportunity, intelligence, strength, sex, color, longevity, etc.), and resulting, or not resulting, from which rule of allocation?

Upon further inspection, moreover, the example testifies to another point: that we get to the "degrees" of the matter because *all the contours have been previously drawn dichotomously*. Equal with respect to which property? If all the attributes were in turn transformed into continuous characteristics, we would open up a near *endless regression*. For there is almost no end to the attributes according to which people may be declared unequal.

A retort might be that my example is tailored to my purposes. However, I can think offhand of some thirty concepts, all central to macro-theory, which would have to be tackled exactly like my equality example. A haphazard enumeration brings to mind the following: development, modernization, social class, status, society, culture, ideology, pluralism, integration, power, participation, consensus, conflict, authority, structure, function, system, coercion, repression, violence, collectivism, liberty, democracy. . . .

Consider another example, the simplest one I can think of: centralization and decentralization. Here again, we have "discovered" that centralization and decentralization are a matter of degree, not dichotomous attributes. Fine. But what next? Presumably, we must raise questions of this sort: which power, or other attribute, is placed at the lower levels (decentralization), and which is retained at the higher levels (centralization)? Take trade unions – a largely uncharted topic. The "powers" at stake here are at least the following: who declares a strike, who controls the strike funds, who nominates (or elects) the union officials (at which level)? If such an analysis is carefully worked out, then we obtain a scale of centralization–decentralization. But if each element of the problem had, in turn, to be "graded," then the problem itself would explode in our hands. It is precisely because hosts of questions are previously decided on a binary yes-or-no basis that we can subsequently measure, or at least rank order, centralization and decentralization (see Riggs 1975; "Quantities of what?" and "Truth-operators and quantifiers").

Objections

We are now better able to decide whether *all* differences not only can (feasibility), but should (ultimately) be construed as *degree differences*. Logically and gnoseologically speaking, I would definitely reply no, on both counts.

The logical objections can be formulated as follows. If two (or more) things – as defined by their properties – are no longer declared, in the first instance, *different-or-same*, but are declared *more-or-less different* – then the next man is entitled to declare them *more-or-less same*. (Incidentally, this is the scheme according to which much of our "novitism" has been flourishing.) Are the latter two expressions equivalent? Most authors imply that they are not; and indeed many disputes consist of nothing else than keeping constant the "more-or-less," and substituting "different" for "same" (and vice versa). If this is so, then we are trapped in a vicious circle

– for the only way of establishing that the two expressions are not equivalent, and of deciding which is the appropriate one, is to ask first the question that the "degreeists" (another neologism which is needed) have dismissed: whether things are different-*or*-same.

A second type of objection bears on how far we want the study of politics and of society to be removed from the grasp of those studied. Quite aside from the demand for "relevance" (which implies, *inter alia*, that social and political matters should be made as meaningful as possible to all those concerned), here we are ultimately confronted with the question: what about *natural language*? At some point, quantities and whatever we measure must be reconverted into their meaning for *life experience*. To experience something as "hot" is very different from knowing a number on the temperature scale; and forty-five degrees on the centigrade scale is, for human beings, "death." How do we know it unless we say it? It would seem to follow that our gnoseological needs are not furthered by jettisoning natural language, but by feeding back into the world of words the precision of the world of measures.

Pros and cons

Whatever the merit of the foregoing objections, they do indicate that the problem is far more complex than we generally realize. Awaiting a better logical and gnoseological probing, it should be conceded that we have yet to understand where to draw the line between the proper use and the abuse of "degree language."

There are merits, but there are also drawbacks, in transforming dichotomies into continuous characteristics. The merits are not automatic, and relapse rather than progress ensues unless we keep an eye precisely on the demerits.

To illustrate this, a first example is wealth and poverty. When wealth and poverty are conceived dichotomously, the argument is that there is more-or-less wealth on the one hand, and more-or-less poverty on the other. However, if wealth and poverty are construed as continuous characteristics, then the argument becomes that there is more-or-less "wealth-poverty." This is better for two reasons: first, that wealth and poverty can indeed be quantified and, second, that the poor and the rich themselves perceive their status in monetary and, thus, quantitative terms. (This, incidentally, is the great advantage economists have over the other social scientists: their quantities are not "reconstructions.")

A second example is democracy and dictatorship. When the two things are considered different in kind, the argument is that democracies vary in attributing more-or-less power to the people, while dictatorships vary in the amount of discretionary power exercised by the dictator. If, on the other hand, democracy and dictatorship are construed as continuous characteristics, then the argument revolves about more-or-less "democracy-dictatorship." Here I fail to perceive the gain. Even though some of the properties of democracy and dictatorship can be quantified and measured, this does not warrant inferences from the properties that can be measured to the whole wealth of meanings that qualify "democracy" and "dictatorship." Hence statements over the world that "democracy-dictatorship" is *different*, or the *same*, to *a different degree*, leave us with just *one* more-or-less (which remains largely verbal and impressionistic) to cover a *double distance* in variation (that is, both variations within democracies and variations within dictatorships) – surely a net loss.

Quantities of what?

I began by asking how "what is" questions relate to "how much" questions, and outlined three possible relationships: (a) complementarity and implementation, (b) mutual exclusion, (c) transformation.

Our previous discussion shows that the transformation of dichotomies into continuous characteristics, or variables, has been largely overdone. Some of these transformations are for the better, but some may well be for the worse; and abuses are difficult to contain unless we gain a clearer gnoseological grasp of the whole matter. Perhaps this gnoseological grasp in turn depends on a better understanding of the logical structure of concepts. Meanwhile, I submit that the fundamental relation between concepts and measurement is that the latter *implements* the former. More precisely, concept formation stands prior to quantification and measurement, and the rules of the former are independent of the rules of the latter. Simply put, we cannot measure until we know what we are measuring. In the words of Lazarsfeld and Barton, "Before we can rank objects or measure them in terms of some variables, we must form the concept of that variable" (1955: 155). That is to say, we cannot ascertain whether x has property p to a higher (or lower) degree than y until we establish (according to some rule of concept formation) that x and y share the same property, p.

In conclusion, "how much" questions – no matter whether they lead to non-metric ordering or to ordinal, interval, or even to cardinal scales – can be asked only of things which belong (with respect to a given property) to the same *class*; the implication being that a classificatory treatment is presupposed. (See "Conceptual analysis", *passim*.)

Applied logic

Science and logic

Why should social scientists become concerned with the problems raised in the foregoing sections? In particular, why should social scientists attempt to do (worse) what logicians and methodologists are supposed to do (better)?

The reply to the first question is – in the words of Cohen and Nagel – that "logic is involved in all reasoned knowledge," and that this "enables us to regard all science as *applied logic* [my emphasis], which was expressed by the Greeks in calling the science of any subject, for example, man, or the earth, the logic of it – anthropo*logy* or geo*logy*" (1934: 191). Logic is thus a *necessary* condition – though by no means the sufficient one – of all scientific knowledge. This reminder is all but superfluous. We say socio*logy*: but is there a logical component in our science of things social? Likewise, political science is often called – in German, French, and Italian – "polito*logy*," logic of things political. But can we say that the "politologist" is aware of the *logic* of his science? The answer is, clearly, no: both sociology and "politology" do not live up to the claim of being a *logos* – they remain "dismal sciences," in no small part for that reason.

The foregoing may be granted, and yet the question remains, why should, and how can, social scientists themselves remedy this gap? The specialization of knowledge entails that matters of *logos* belong to the jurisdiction of logic (proper), of philosophy of science (or epistemology), and of methodology. Hence, the remedy lies in introducing these disciplines to social science curricula.

While I do deplore the narrowness and incompleteness of most social science curricula in the above respects, nevertheless I do not believe in such a remedy. To begin with, logic has recently become excessively inbred, and indeed of little practical (or applied) avail for the layman. In turn, philosophy of science actually is, at base, the philosophy of the exact or natural sciences. As for methodology, the label has been unduly appropriated for research and statistical "techniques." There is little "logical method" in most of what is being delivered under that title.

Given this state of the art, no *applied logic* tailored to the needs of the practitioner is likely to develop, unless it is developed by social scientists *themselves* as a theoretical reflection emerging from *within*, from their problems and failures. What I shall now attempt to sketch, then, is the applied logic, or the operational logic, of the sciences of man.

To be sure, an applied logic remains "logic." Among other things, we should not rediscover the umbrella, that is, things which have already been discovered. On the other hand, an applied logic will not only be "minimal" (see "Logical systematizing") and greatly simplified, but also a reconstruction guided by the *practical value* of the elements that are retained. Furthermore, along the way we shall discover that professional logicians and philosophers have neglected or mishandled a number of matters. At the end, therefore, an applied logic will also be a *different* and somewhat new logic.

A strategy of allocation

I have dealt earlier with "conceptual analysis." An applied logic embraces, however, many other matters. But before plunging into additional complexities, it is wise to pause and to decide an overall strategy for allocating our problems. A perusal of the literature shows, in the aggregate, that no such strategy exists. The various problems usually are revealed in the course of *analyzing sentences*. This is nice, but engenders an enormous overlapping (the same problems are taken up over and over again from different angles) and becomes very confusing for lack of adequate coordination. Individual logicians and philosophers may indeed follow a consistent line, but the textbooks are encumbered by a sedimentation of too many layers – old and new – which are simply juxtaposed or superimposed. If so, *cleaning* is badly needed, and the cleaning business in turn requires a strategy for assigning the various problems.

The strategy proposed here is to allocate as many problems as possible either to the domain of (a) *logical treatment* or (b) *definitional treatment*. What I call logical treatment hinges on *logical connectives* and on the *nature of concepts* (metaconcept analysis). A definitional treatment bears instead on the *types* and *methods of definition*.

The implication is that I wish to reduce as much as possible the *space of sentences* qua sentences, that is, in their irreducibility to (a) conceptual analysis, (b) logical connectives, (c) nature of concepts, and (d) defining procedures.

The enormous variety and possibility of variation of sentences is well known to anyone familiar with the work of linguists. When logicians enter, they do away with stylistic and grammatical variations and reduce sentences to "standard forms" which bear exclusively on the *form* (logical structure) of sentences, regardless of content. However, logicians *transform*, but hardly *reduce*, judging by the wealth of "formalized sentences" which make up most of the contents of their books. Hence, the third recommendation of my strategy is to leave sentences (qua sentences) as a *residual element*. Let us see first how many problems can be settled *before* stumbling into the maze of "propositional forms."

Truth-operators and quantifiers

There is no standard meta-language for what I have just called "logical connectives."[11] With respect to sentences (not to argument and inferences, i.e., the process of drawing conclusions from premises), most logical connectives are either *truth-operators* (and, or, if . . . then, not)[12] or *quantifiers* (all, no, some). The basic truth-operators are: (a) *conjunction* ("and," whose sign is a dot, and whose grammatical equivalents are: also, still, besides, but . . .); (b) *disjunction* ("either-or," whose sign is the wedge "V"); (c) *negation* ("it is not the case that," whose sign is the bar '-'); and (d) *implication* ("if . . . then," whose sign is the horseshoe '⊃').

As we know from the previous section, a current major issue in the social sciences involves what I have previously called the "logic of classification," and may now call, more technically, the sentences disjoined by the truth-operator "either-or" – in short, *disjunctions* and *disjuncts*.

While the logical status of any sentence having the form "p V q" is pretty well established, the same cannot be said of the logical status of what I have previously called the logic of graduation, that is, the logical status of the connective "more-less."

If "all," "no," and "some" are *quantifiers*, one might suspect that "more-less" should also be conceived as a quantifier. Strangely enough, however, all the textbooks I have consulted are remarkably thin, if not silent, on the matter. A typical treatment – with reference to "probability" – is as follows:

> Given the concept of probability, if it is . . . characterized by numerical values, we may say we are considering a *quantitative concept* of probability. . . . Alternatively we might investigate a concept of probability which is used merely to classify things into . . . *probable* or *not probable, i.e.,* we might

consider a *qualitative concept* of probability. Examples of other qualitative concepts are hot or cold, large or small, male or female, rich or poor, etc. Finally, we might investigate a concept which is used to compare things with respect to their being *more* or *less probable*, *i.e.*, we might consider a *comparative concept* of probability. Examples of other comparative concepts are warmer, colder, larger, smaller, richer, poorer, etc.[13]

Unless I am badly mistaken, the quotation goes to show that even the logic of logicians can sometimes be very feeble. The counter-argument is as follows: first, the concept is one and the same, and the difference lies in the treatment (quantitative, qualitative, and comparative). Second, only the qualitative treatment is logically grounded (for it rests on sentences having the form "p V q," in which V is the disjunction sign for the truth-operator either-or), whereas the so-called comparative treatment lacks any equivalent foundation (the logical nature of the connective "more-less" is never underpinned). Third, the examples of qualitative concepts are repeated for the comparative concepts, except for "male-female," which is simply dropped. Granted that male-female cannot be treated as hot-cold, the task of the logician is to explain why.

However that may be, it turns out that logical connectives do not suffice to carry the weight of the argument and that what enters – when our truth-operators or quantifiers fail us – is (in the illustration) a tripartition between three kinds of concepts: quantitative, qualitative, and comparative. Let us turn, then, to the "nature" of concepts.

Theoretical terms and observational terms

Our understanding of the nature of concepts hinges on our metaconcepts – the concepts for analyzing concepts. A first, fundamental distinction is the one between (a) *theoretical terms* and (b) *observational terms*. Theoretical terms can be defined only by the part they play in a theoretical argument, or by their systemic meaning (see, e.g., Kaplan 1964: 56–57, 63–65). The only clear, and by now widely recognized, characteristic of theoretical terms is that they cannot be reduced to, nor derived from, observational terms and primitives. Observational terms are, instead, amenable, no matter how indirectly, to observables. Let it be noted that an observational term is not necessarily concrete. For example, group, communication, conflict, decision, can be "concrete" in that they are defined ostensively (Robinson 1965: 117–26; Russell 1948: 63) or in observational, look-see terms; but they can also be used for very abstract meanings, i.e., as "analytic" terms, obtained via reductive inferences from observables. Let it also be noted that when we speak of *empirical concepts* we mean, presumably, that we are dealing with observational terms.

The borderline between theoretical and observational terms is highly controversial and, at least for the time being, very fluid. One may equally say that a number of terms are neither theoretical nor observational, but this is hardly a reason for dismissing the distinction. The fundamental purpose of metaconcepts is to sort out differences in the *nature* of concepts, that is, those differences that indicate *which logical treatment is appropriate*,[14] and, surely, the treatment of theoretical concepts is different from the treatment of observational concepts. For instance, the rules of transformation along a ladder of abstraction (see "Rules of transformation along a ladder of abstraction") apply to observational, not to theoretical, concepts.

Object concepts and property concepts

Teune (1975: Sections 6 and 8) elaborates on another distinction – between (a) *object concepts* and (b) *property concepts* which is not established in the literature and yet provides a helpful compass for the practitioner as he muddles through. As I understand the distinction, in the first instance, object concepts point to or stand for *physical objects* – which indeed constitute a large part of the natural sciences – while property concepts can be used only as *predicates*, for they have no physical referent. To illustrate, beauty, color, age, shape, weight, rate, are (in spite of their noun form) property terms. Empirically speaking, there is no "beautiness," "yellowness," or "rateness" – these are properties or attributes of objects.

One difference brought out by this distinction – and therefore a logical reason which sustains it – is that property concepts lend themselves to the more-or-less treatment, while object concepts peremptorily require the either-or treatment. Something cannot be, except in loose, metaphorical parlance, more-or-less tree, more-or-less tiger, more-or-less train, more-or-less money.

One retort may be that as we pass from the natural to the social sciences, the distinction loses force, for most social science concepts are neither "real" objects nor "pure" properties. However, as already noted with respect to the distinction between theoretical and observational concepts, our metaconcepts cannot pretend to be exhaustive: they are useful to the extent that they alert us to differences in the nature of concepts, which in turn help us to handle the in-between no-man's land.

From this vantage point, so called "collective terms" and the *social objects* spoken of by Teune can well be defended, and it makes a great deal of sense to say, e.g., that *object-properties* are those used to define classes of objects, while *non-object properties* are those whose variance across a set of objects is being examined. Take, e.g., "democracy." Democracy is not, per se, an object concept: it is a "property of properties," i.e., it is construed as such by combining properties. Yet it can either be treated as an "object" (a set of properties which define it as an object), or as a predicate that varies across objects and over time – two treatments which should not be confused.

To pursue the example, if democracy is construed as an object (a social object, to be sure), its object-properties are its *definitional properties* (which are true by definition) while its non-object properties are its *variable properties* (to be assessed empirically and, if possible, measured). The definitional properties serve the purpose of deciding whether the concrete cases are democracies or not (binary, either-or treatment). The variable properties serve, instead, to rank cases as being more-or-less democratic with respect to some or all of the variable properties.

To be sure, if the definitional properties (which define the object) are changed, then the cases classified as "democracies" also change. And one might note that here the assimilation between physical objects and social objects breaks down. However, the greater fixity or stability of physical objects is hardly explained by their physical referents. Physical objects also are perceived and identified by their definitional properties. If social objects have less fixity, this is because the world of man is fluidified and stirred by interests, passions, and values. But physical objects are construed, logically, just like social objects.

Reverting to the "male-female" example (see "Rules of transformation along a ladder of abstraction") – which was left at the unanswered question, why are these qualitative but not comparative concepts? – the reply can be that male and female are construed as object concepts for the purpose of establishing which beings have sex, and what is their sex. Although we could also say more-or-less male, or more-or-less female, we are not interested in this finding. We want clear-cut two-valued answers: who is male or not, who is female or not, who is neither, and who is both (hermaphrodite). And indeed four classes (male, female, neither, both) are more informative than degrees or continuous characteristics.

The next question could be: are male or female physical or social objects? We could reply both – and this because the difference is immaterial. We do not see a "male" unless the state of being male is identified by certain definitional properties or characteristics. The point is that the transition from simple physical objects to complex social objects is continuous.

Entities should not be multiplied

We can go on at length to discover and enumerate different kinds or different "natures" of concepts. Beyond theoretical/observational and object/property concepts, a perusal of the literature yields many more.

For instance, Hempel distinguishes between: (a) relation terms ("x is a husband of y"); (b) property terms ("x is a husband"); (c) observable and observation terms ("hard, liquid, blue"); (d) disposition terms ("magnetic"); (e) classificatory concepts ("hard"); (f) comparative concepts ("harder than"); while (g) "theoretical constructs" are entered as a sideline with reference to "metrical concepts in their theoretical use" (Hempel 1952: 13, 22, 24, 32, 54–56). The argument is developed in a very disorganized fashion, and the examples are – at least to me – confusing. Thus "husband" is (a) relational, and also (b) a property term; "hard-harder" is (c) observable, (e) classificatory, and (f) comparative (but also, undeniably, a property and a relational term); "magnetic" is (d) dispositional (but also, undeniably, a property and an observable term).

Let us remember that our concern here is with the concepts that organize concepts, whereas Hempel seemingly gives us a wholly disorganized and non-organizable enumeration. In such a case, the golden rule has long been Occam's, namely, that "entities should not be multiplied."

Let us take up again the recurrent example of hardness. As we have just seen, for Hempel "hard" is classificatory (or qualitative), while "harder than" is both comparative and relational – thus hard-harder are conceived as different concepts. My explication would be, instead, that the concept is always the same – "hardness" – that "hard" is an observable property concept (not an object concept), and that "harder" remains a property concept. The difference lies only in the logical treatment. The sentence, "x is hard" is established by the *either-or* connective, for it results from the sentence, "x is either hard or non-hard (soft)." This implies, in turn, that we are defining (with respect to its attributes or properties) an object concept. The question here is: which properties enter (qualify) object x? Unless the answer is of the *yes-no* type, the object remains undetermined and inadequately identified.

The sentence "x is harder than" utilizes, instead, the *more-or-less* connective, which in turn presupposes that our problem is to rank-order (and ultimately measure) a property concept. The question now is: how does hardness vary? (Not necessarily between x and y, but also within x itself, i.e., between x_1, x_2, x_3, etc.)

In my explication everything is said, then, without recourse to *comparative concepts* or *relational concepts*. According to Occam's razor, these are unnecessary metaconcepts. We may well want to distinguish between relational/non-relational concepts, or between comparative/non-comparative concepts. But we have already seen that the logical underpinning of so-called comparative concepts is deficient – and the same is even truer for relational concepts. Furthermore, from the vantage point of an applied logic, the question is whether the practitioner needs to be warned on this score, or whether his unawareness is immaterial, since no mishandling is likely to follow. And I submit that I do not feel illuminated by realizing that some concepts are relational and/or comparative, while others are not. As for our last metaconcept – dispositioned concepts – I will argue shortly (see "The allocation of dispositional terms") that it can be reduced to a definitional problem.

So much for some of the metaconcepts which have gained – in my opinion – an undue currency. But new metaconcepts are also being proposed which are not only superfluous but untenable. A pertinent illustration is the distinction drawn by Holt and Turner between (a) *conceptual element*, which is declared neither true nor false, but theoretically useful or not, and (b) *theoretical element*, which is, instead, amenable to empirical verification, and thereby true or false (Holt and Turner 1970: 24).

Why this major reshuffling? Surely Holt and Turner know that in the philosophy of science and for most authors, "theoretical terms" are precisely the concepts which are *not* amenable to empirical verification. Therefore, their stipulation is bound to be misunderstood and to create misunderstandings. Turning to the substance, the second question is: does the distinction hold? Holt and Turner divide "theoretical element" into two sub-elements – axioms and theorems – and the authors acknowledge that the axioms are confirmed (empirically verifiable) only via the theorems. If so, the distinction appears undermined and internally inconsistent. Axioms fall under the definition of the conceptual element (theoretically useful or not). Conversely, the conceptual element can be entered as a component sub-element of the theoretical element.

My headache grows when I find that the conceptual element is made equal to "propositions which are logical and true by definition" (Holt and Turner 1970: 35).

I fail to grasp why "logical propositions" should be conceptual and not theoretical. Why not both, for instance? The point is that all the foregoing complications are wholly unnecessary; Holt and Turner's intent can be made perfectly clear with no meta-language reshuffling (e.g., on the basis of the distinction between theoretical and observational concepts).

As can be seen, if we are not doing well with language, we are not doing better with meta-language. Another Babel Tower within the Tower of Babel? I would say, yes. The disorderly proliferation of metaconcepts requires us to call even more on Occam's razor and to explore how much ground can be covered by a parsimonious and coordinated set of "relevant" constructs. A metaconcept is relevant (this being the first rule of parsimony) only to the extent that it sorts out, in the "nature" of concepts, an element *which entails a sui generis treatment*. And whatever reason one may give for shunning the stabilization of language (see "The freezing of language"), no such reason exists for avoiding the standardization of meta-language.

The allocation of dispositional terms

In this section I am trying to allocate our problems between logical treatment and definitional treatment. (See "A strategy of allocation".) Before passing from the first to the second, the case of *disposition* or *dispositional* concepts can well be discussed in this perspective.

Hempel's example of a disposition term is "magnetic." Arthur Pap dwells on "soluble," and points out that many terms ending in "-uble" and "-able" are dispositional (1962: Chapter 2, Section F and Chapter 15, Section C; see also Bergmann 1957: 59–62; Pap 1958, vol. 2: 196 ff). Teune's examples are: hostile, aggressive, efficacious, intelligent, authoritarian. On the basis of these examples, let me immediately press the issue: should "dispositions" be construed as a particular genus of *concepts*, or are they best allocated and understood as a particular genus of operational *definitions*?

Magnetic, soluble . . . intelligent, authoritarian, are, to begin with, "property concepts" which – like many other property concepts – cannot be directly observed. What makes for the distinctiveness of *dispositional properties* is not that they are different qua properties, but that they lend themselves to a particular kind of testing: they may be defined by an *if-then* type of statement (often called "conditional"). The "if" specifies the test conditions; the "then" specifies what we expect (or predict) to observe when the object having that property is placed under the test conditions. (With reference to "soluble," the statement would be, e.g., "*If* a piece of sugar is placed in a cup of water, *then* it will melt.") But this is nothing else, or nothing more than a satisfactorily codified type of operational definition. The only reason why most property terms cannot even approach this ideal type of operationalization is that the test conditions in question are experimental, or near laboratory, conditions. The point remains, nonetheless, that what is at stake is a *definitional treatment*, not a *conceptual essence*.

Simple definitions

Whenever one asks, "What do you mean?" or asserts, "By this word I mean," *definition* is at stake. Thus, the definition of "definition" is *specification of meaning*. To be sure, this is the simplest definition of "definition." Definitions can become complex and, if so, we discover various kinds of definitions. Teune (1975: Section 5.1) distinguishes between simple and complex definitions. My points can be recast within his distinction – except that they are intended to be more general.

If the requirement of simple definitions is only to declare and specify meanings, we immediately need a definition of "specification," or at least of the extent of specification required – which is the *specification of boundaries*, i.e., delimination, *assigning limits*. Thus, any definition must provide an indication of what it includes and, by implication, what it excludes.

Within the ambit of simple definitions, the current dislike of definition is hard to justify, and indeed ill-founded. When an author avoids defining his key terms, the odds are that his argument will rest on the *word*, not on the *concept*. If this is so, he is unnecessarily exposed, among other things, to the risk of changing his meanings as his argument proceeds. This is no small risk, if we are to judge by the fact that "meaning inconsistency" – the error of using the same word with different meanings (fallacy of equivocation) – is the most classic and most denounced of all the logical fallacies.

No doubt, a good mind is always clear. But we cannot expect normal science to be a science under bad advice. Presumably, when we are advised to leave a concept broadly defined, or to avoid getting bogged down by definitions, what is intended is a warning against *premature closure*, and specifically premature closure caused by "the *reduction* of meaning brought about by strict definition" (Kaplan 1964: 70–73). However, "premature closure" is a liability for science, or a scientific process, *as a whole*. To the single scholar it is bad advice; for individual scholars playing with "indefiniteness" have worsened, not improved, the state of the social sciences.

Definitions which merely declare and specify meanings (i.e., simple definitions) are a *sine qua non* both for enabling a scientific community to *communicate*, and for helping the single scientist to be *consistent*, i.e., keep his meaning constant. Definitions are then a liability only when they lead us to solve empirical problems, or matters of fact, *by definition*. (See "Minimal definitions".) But the error of "solving" empirical problems by definition should not be rectified by the counter-error of shunning definitions.

Varieties of definitions

The literature about definitions usually starts with discussing *nominal* versus *real* definitions, and attributes a major importance to the distinction between *lexical* (lexicographic) and *stipulative* definitions.

The first distinction is medieval and bears on the relationship between "logic" and "ontology." Once this metaphysical (ontological) background subsides, the argument that "real definitions" seek the "essence" of things hits on a straw man, the distinction becomes of secondary importance, and could be easily settled – within the ambit of the philosophy of science – by conceding that all definitions are "nominal" in that they relate to concepts expressed by words,[15] even though some may be called "real" in the sense that they employ observational terms and are conceived as pointers to "objects." My own preference is to leave the argument at that. However, if it is pursued (Riggs 1975: Section 1) then we should not confuse the traditional, Aristotelic meaning of this distinction with its rejuvenation for new intents and in entirely new meanings.

The second distinction – between lexical and stipulative definitions – is, instead, far more recent, and actually presupposes the exhaustion of the ontological debate, i.e., assumes that all definitions are nominal. If so, how can we avoid concluding that all definitions are "arbitrary" conventions? The distinction between lexical and stipulative definitions was invented, then, as a dike against the destructive implications of conventionalism. Granted that all definitions are "conventions," some (the lexical ones) are not "arbitrary"; they are found in, and stabilized by, dictionaries (lexicons). Fine. But how one can really build a dike on this difference endlessly elicits my amazement.[16]

In any event, here my concern is only to explain why I do not dwell on nominal, real, lexical and stipulative definitions, and why I shall confine myself to discussing, (a) *operational definitions*, (b) *minimal definitions*, and, conclusively, the problem of (c) *arbitrariness in definitions*.[17] For these are indeed differences and issues to which the practitioner needs to be alerted.

Operational definitions

A major type of complex definition is one in which the composition (or decomposition) rule is by genus and differentia (see "Analysis by classification"), also called "definition by analysis." One important characteristic of definitions by genus and differentia is that they are dictated by logical rules of sytematic import *regardless of testability*. Operational definitions are guided, instead, by the criterion of testability, regardless of other criteria. They clearly stand out, therefore, as a distinct type of definition.[18]

It goes without saying that operational definitions are crucial to an empirical science. And I have already made the point that the requirement of operational definitions is *testability*, not *measurability* (see "The broad meaning"). Far more often than not, operational definitions take this form: let x be what can be checked via the indicators a, b, c. . . . I abide, thus, by a relatively broad definition of "operational definition" which broadens, in turn, its ambit of application. Even so, at least three cautions are in order.

In the first place, we should be aware of how peripheral operational definitions remain, at least *pro tempore*, with respect to our macrotheory. Felix Oppenheim cites to this effect the claim of Karl Deutsch that each of his concepts "is defined in terms of some operation that can be repeated and tested . . . ," and then makes the following appropriate comment: "One may wonder what 'operations' are referred to by his definitions: *politics*, 'the making of decisions by public means'; *interest*, 'anyone's interest in a situation consists in the rewards which he can extract from it'; *liberty*, the ability to act in accordance with one's own personality, without having to make a great effort at self-denial; *legitimacy*, 'the terms legitimate and just will be used interchangeably'" (Oppenheim 1975: vol. 1, 297; reference is made to Deutsch 1970: ix, 3, 10, 13, 14).

In the second place we should also beware of undue haste, in the sense that operational definitions need the prior guidance of conceptual analysis. For example, party cohesion is often measured by this indicator: the frequency of vote against party leadership. It is easy to realize, however, that this index measures "discipline," and that whether party discipline stems from "cohesion" (rather than from, e.g., sanctions) remains to be demonstrated. A previous conceptual analysis would have easily avoided the equivocation.

My third and major point, however, is that conceptual analysis stands not only prior to operationalization, but also independently. This rejoins Hempel's warning that operational definitions should not be "emphasized to the neglect of the requirement of systematic import," and that the "discovery of concepts of theoretical import . . . cannot be replaced by . . . the operationist or empiricist requirement of empirical import alone" (1952: 47, 60; see also 1965: 123 ff).

Operationalism not only entails a drastic curtailment in the range of properties and attributes of concepts – including their theoretical and explanatory power – but also introduces a distortion (its own distortion) in this process of selection. Operationally, beauty can be defined as whatever wins or passes a beauty contest. Quite aside from the circularity, an operationalization of this sort fantastically impoverishes the concept. Taking Teune's example, "political 'liberalism' can be defined as a preference for political change." Yes; except that liberalism connotes, historically, a wealth of meanings that make "preference for change" appear an ill-focused characterization. In sum, conceptual analysis should not be distorted by the preoccupation with operationalization. Operationalization is not the sole requirement, but one of the many requirements of an empirical science. And it fares better when guided by a prior conceptual unfolding which abides by its own rules.

Minimal definitions

Definitions are not an unmixed blessing in that we are easily misled into solving empirical problems by definitional fiat. We are thus reminded of the distinction between *definitional properties* (which define the object or, more exactly, terms construed as "object terms") and *variable properties*. (See "Object concepts and property concepts".) Definitional properties are *true by definition*, whereas variable properties are best treated as *hypotheses*.

On these premises the question is: what is the optimal strategy for empirical enquiry, and particularly for the appropriate use of definitions? My answer is: *minimal definitions*. The minimal definition strategy consists of reducing to a minimum the defining properties and of handling as many properties as possible by testable propositions. In the light of this strategy, conceptual analysis can no longer be accused of leading to definitional encumbrances and/or rigidity.

The minimal definition recommendation cannot, however, be pushed too far. Definitional properties must not fall below a minimum that suffices to identify the object (in terms of the specification requirement of simple definitions, i.e., "delimitation"). In principle, at the very least one attribute or property must be retained by definition. In practice, this is seldom sufficient: the definitional properties generally are more than one.

To illustrate, take the concept "party." One course is to consider party whatever is called such; but this leaves us to float with the word, with a vague conception. The alternative course is to provide a minimal definition, i.e., the most inclusive definition that still permits separating party from "nonparty" (e.g., from pressure group, trade union, faction, sect, clique, etc.). To this end, Janda defines party as "organizations that pursue a goal of placing their avowed representatives in government positions" (1970: 2). To the same end – providing a minimal definition – but with a different boundary in mind, Fred Riggs has defined party as "any organization which nominates candidates for election to a legislature" (1968: 51).

The foregoing examples suggest, among other things, that minimal definitions are not easy to come by and that they cannot be that "minimal" if all the boundaries of the object under consideration have to be taken into account. For instance, Janda's definition blurs the difference between parties and factions, and eventually between parties and labor unions. Riggs supplies a boundary on this side; but his definition includes parties that are nothing but labels (parties on paper).[19]

Arbitrariness in defining

The distinction between lexical and stipulative definitions is misleading rather than illuminating, for it creates a major problem for which it provides a poor remedy. Since all definitions are (when first proposed) stipulations, and thereby (according to the stipulative theory) arbitrary, the remedy against arbitrariness is found in the possibility of dismissing a new stipulation as *lexically false* – i.e., not found in lexicons. Quite aside from this frivolous notion of truth and falsity, this is a poor remedy since lexicons take stock of numberless meanings in a haphazard fashion. A second, and even feebler, remedy is to point out that while stipulations are neither true nor false, nevertheless they must be *useful* – in some sense of the term. Unfortunately, "useful" is (lexically: for we must be consistent) a highly ambiguous term, and arbitrary stipulations are indeed "useful" for scholars who otherwise would have nothing to say. As noted at the outset, novitism (see "Novitism") finds a powerful incentive in the principle and practice of "stipulating" meanings.

To avoid a cheap originality and a Babel Tower regression, we are left, therefore, to establish more precise conditions and restrictions than "usefulness," under which terminological and definitional innovations are not only permissible, but indeed *necessary*. Some restrictions have already been suggested earlier (see "Counteracting chaos"); but I now propose to formulate them so as to afford practical guidance.

First, there is no point in creating new words, or in stipulating new meaning, for existing words, unless we actually identify new phenomena, or things as yet unnamed. This may be called, in brief, the *naming the unnamed clause*.

Second, awaiting contrary proof, no word should be used as a synonym for any other word. Given our terminological shortage, this practice represents an intolerable waste for the economy of language and impairs the articulation of thought. This may be called the *anti-synonymity clause*.

Third, the contrary proof clause implies that the burden of proof rests on the propounder of what would turn out to be, otherwise, either a "superfluous naming," or a "superfluous coextensiveness." This may be called the *burden of proof clause*: a condition that applies to all assertions whose form either is, "let the word x mean something which it never meant before," or "let the term x be interchangeable with the term y."[20]

Fourth, no new stipulation is acceptable in isolation, that is, without regard to the semantic, systematic, and/or theoretical *field* to which a given term belongs. Terms, I have said, come in strings (see "Counteracting chaos"). We may equally say that each field of inquiry consists, at base, of a set of independent-interdependent terms – not defined by the others, but sustained and implemented by the others – which represent the "conceptual structure," or the "conceptual framework" of a given field. This may be called, then, the *field clause*. For instance, if we stipulate that birds are "flying animals," it follows that bats become birds and that ostriches cannot be classified as birds. Hence, the stipulation cannot be accepted without overhauling the criteria of the whole field.

The difference brought about by the foregoing clauses can be illustrated by taking the example of "ideology" – a word which immediately confronts us with the following string: idea, belief, opinion, creed, myth, utopia, and the like. Now, under the awaiting contrary proof clause we are required to demonstrate the equivalence of, not the difference between, any of the aforementioned terms. This blocks the easy way out, which is to stipulate that "ideology will be used interchangeably with . . . ," and prompts us, instead, to decompose ideology into its various dimensions and properties. What we find is, at least in my experience, that the term is useful, and can be used without ambiguity precisely because, and to the extent that, it is *not* made synonymous with any other contiguous term. At the end of this exercise, it turns out that the entire semantic and theoretical field reverts from shapelessness to shape (this exercise is pursued in Sartori 1969).

Concluding thoughts

Heraclitus versus Descartes

Throughout my *fliegende Blatter*, indeed my floating and inchoate notes, one can easily detect a Cartesian bias. Thus my defense of classifications, of the genus and differentia mode of analysis, and, lastly, of definitions as "specification of boundaries" admittedly reveals a liking for clear and distinct ideas. I must anticipate, therefore, the objection that phenomena are, per se, unbounded, continuous, and in endless flux. This was said first by Heraclitus, and has been repeated innumerable times over the millennia – but with no great consequence for our techniques of enquiry and our methods of understanding.

To be sure, we realize that understanding must not only be "static," but also "dynamic." It is, moreover, undeniable that we are better able today than ever before to cope with a "continuous," as against a "discontinuous," grasp of phenomena. Nonetheless, the premise that "reality" is, as such and in itself, a state of flux cannot warrant the conclusion that our concepts must also be constructed as continua without boundaries. No such conclusion follows, for this much can be summarized with reasonable confidence: there is infinitely more in our head than there is in an eyeball (and, conversely, infinitely more in "reality" than our senses can sense).

Without entering the gnoseological argument, the elemental point to be borne in mind is that the attribute space – i.e., properties, attributes, or characteristics – is of the concept, not of the phenomena. Heraclitus may well be right, and yet we do not acquire a mental control over "reality" by mirroring it (whatever the "it" may be assumed to be). Wherever we have arrived, as mental animals, in controlling the world of nature, we owe it to the Cartesian approach.

The missing bridge

Needless to say, my points apply only to concepts that are central to the subject we are investigating. Since we *are* swimming in a sea of naïvete, in any argument a number of terms are, or must be treated as, "primitives." Let me simply call them *regression stoppers*, and note that we do need them. The best we can do, in this respect, is to make a deliberate rather than an unthinking decision as to which terms are our primitives or can be best used as regression stoppers.

My intent has nothing in common, then, with conceptual pedantry. Rather I have made a first try at sorting out *attention sharpeners* both for reviewing the conceptual and methodological fallacies of others, and for helping us to avoid such fallacies in our own work. My hope is that, in the long run, COCTA will provide – as a joint endeavor – the missing linkage, or the *missing bridge*, between specialists in logic, methodology, and the philosophy of science on the one hand, and social science practitioners on the other. As I have said (see "Science and logic"), I conceive of COCTA as promoting an *applied logic*, or, if you wish, an *applied methodology*. The logical and methodological discussion among specialists is far too esoteric and remote from the actual problems of the practitioner. We should attempt, therefore, to build the bridge from the practitioner's end. In the words of C. Wright Mills, the "over-conscious" scholar never gets any work done; but we do need, at this point, "conscious" scholars who know what they are doing.

Acknowledgments

I wish to acknowledge my very great debt to the meticulous comments and the careful editing of Professor Fred W. Riggs. I have also benefitted from the advice of my colleague Professor Alessandro Bruschi, and from the criticism of Professor Felix Oppenheim.

Notes

* Originally published as Giovanni Sartori (1975) "The Tower of Babel," in G. Sartori, F.W. Riggs, and H. Teune (eds.), *Tower of Babel: On the Definition and Analysis of Concepts in the Social Sciences*, International Studies Association, Occasional Paper No. 6, University of Pittsburgh, Chapter 1.

1 The example is inspired by Kuper and Smith (1969).
2 To be sure, science (normal science) is cumulative until a scientific revolution occurs, in Kuhn's (1962) sense. On this and many other differences between a philosophical and a scientific treatment, I dwell on Sartori (1974).
3 Judge conceives a model as both a preliminary to and a component of "classifications," with an emphasis on "model" conceived as a "structure of relationships," or as a network of relationships.
4 By connecting the two terms, "model" (indeed a hopelessly vague metaconcept) becomes less imprecise, and "paradigm" less ambitious.
5 The present chapter was originally written for a volume sponsored by COCTA, the Committee on Conceptual and Terminological Analysis of the International Political Science Association.
6 The example is from Wilhelm von Humboldt, the originator of a line of linguistics which is eminently represented now by Whorf (1953). Both on Humboldt and in general, see Cassirer (1953: vol. 1, pp. 155 ff., and *passim*), which is an unduly neglected work.
7 The objection of a pedantic stipulativism is, of course, that there are not "right words." Anyone who takes this argument seriously should, if consistent, experiment with "artificial words," i.e., consonant-vowel-consonant forms which are pronounceable but meaningless in the sense that no community-wide rules exist for defining them. A classic example is the form (syllable) *mel* invented by Edward Sapir for his experiments.
8 Strictly speaking, one should distinguish between: (a) classification, (b) taxonomy, and (c) typology. In the light of this tripartition, a taxonomy is an intermediate ordering between the classificatory and matrix type orderings.
9 Very similar definitions can be found in most textbooks. For instance: "The totality of things denoted by a word is called its *denotation* or *extension.* . . . The totality of characteristics anything must possess to be correctly denoted by a word is called the word's *connotation* or *intension*" (Michalos 1969: 388). Cohen and Nagel, in their classic *Introduction to Logic and Scientific Method* (1934), put it thus: "A term may be viewed . . . either as a class of objects . . . or as a set of attributes or characteristics which determine the objects. The first aspect is called the denotation or *extension* of the term, the second is called the *connotation* or *intension*" (31).
10 Oppenheim (1973) argues that "words or concepts cannot be data containers" on the premise that "if what we perceive is shaped by the way we perceive it, including by our concepts and by our language, there can be no solid bridge connecting words with objects, language with 'reality'" (5). While Oppenheim's premise is also my premise, his conclusion (or negation) sorely does not follow. By asserting that concepts are data containers I am not positing a "solid bridge"; quite to the contrary, I am implying that many social scientists have remained at a very naïve epistemology. I fail to understand, therefore, Oppenheim's objection.
11 The expression "logical connectives" is used, however, by Blanche (1957). Another text from which I draw the meta-language employed here is Michalos (1969).
12 Truth "operators" are called such because they permit logical "operations." They are also called "truth functors."

13 Michalos (1969: 184). The author simply repeats here Hempel (1952: 54–58). But see again Hempel 1952: 13, 22, 24, 32, 54–56.
14 Likewise, "the analysis of propositions is undertaken for the purpose of discovering what inferences may be validly drawn from them" (Cohen and Nagel 1934: 34).
15 *Contra*, Hempel (1952: 2), who utterly misrepresents the issue (historically) by asserting that "a nominal definition . . . is a convention which merely introduces an alternative – and usually abbreviatory – notation for a given linguistic expression . . ." and that "it may be characterized as a stipulation to the effect that . . . the *definiendum* is to be synonymous with a certain other expression, the *definiens*, whose meaning is already determined." (See also Chapter 2, note 11.)
16 See Sartori (1962: 207–20), where I spell out my objection in detail. But see also "Arbitrariness in defining," where the argument is pursued.
17 For the complexities that are left out, see, e.g., the analysis of Scriven (1958: 99–195).
18 Operationalism and operational definitions are a standard topic throughout the contemporary literature. An interesting discussion among various authors is in Frank (1957: Chapter 2).
19 For more on the definition of parties, see Riggs (1975: Sections 3.7–3.9). In personal correspondence, Riggs clarifies that he "deliberately" sought a definition which includes them. "I want to include non-functioning parties in my concept so that I can develop a theory to handle the question, 'What determines a party's effectiveness?' If I had no ineffective parties in my concept, and all were effective by definition, then I could not well discover, by comparative analysis, what conditions are related to the mal-performance of paper parties, and which are essential for effective party activity. By contrast, Janda's definition includes entities he does not want in his theory – in fact, he uses my concept in his project." Thus what appears an open boundary represents, instead, an openness suited to, and required by, a research problem.
20 See in a narrower and more technical sense, Hempel: "The introduction of certain kinds of nominal definition into a given theoretical system is permissible only on condition that an appropriate non-definitional sentence, which might be called *its justificatory sentence*, has been previously established" (1952: 18). My "burden of proof clause" is much broader, but incorporates, as a special case, Hempel's "justificatory sentences."

References

Bergmann, G. (1957) *Philosophy of Science*, Madison: University of Wisconsin Press.
Blanche, R. (1957) *Introduction a la logique contemporaine*, Paris: Colin.
Cassirer, E. (1953) *The Philosophy of Symbolic Forms*, New Haven, CT: Yale University Press.
Cnudde, C.F. (1972) "Theories of Political Development and the Assumptions of Statistical Models," *Comparative Political Studies* 5 (2): 131–50.
Cohen, M.R. and Nagel, E. (1934) *Introduction to Logic and Scientific Method*, London: Routledge and Kegan Paul.
Connolly, W.E. (1973) "Theoretical Self-Consciousness," *Polity* 6: 5–35.
Deutsch, K. (1970) *Politics and Government*, Boston: Houghton Mifflin.
Frank, P.G. (ed.) (1957) *The Validation of Scientific Theories*, New York: Collier Books.
Hempel, C. (1952) *Fundamentals of Concept Formation in Empirical Science*, Chicago: University of Chicago Press.
Hempel, C. (1965) *Aspects of Scientific Explanation*, New York: Free Press.
Holt, R.T. and Turner, J.E. (eds.) (1970) *The Methodology of Comparative Research*, New York: Free Press.
Horowitz, I.L. (1962) "Consensus, Conflict and Cooperation: A Sociological Inventory," *Social Forces* (41): 177–78.

Janda, K. (1970) *ICPP Coding Manual,* 2nd edn., Evanston, IL: Northwestern University.

Judge, A. (1972) "Relationships between Elements of Knowledge," COCTA paper no. 3, mimeograph.

Kaplan, A. (1964) *The Conduct of Inquiry*, San Francisco: Chandler.

Kuhn, T.S. (1962) *The Structure of Scientific Revolutions*, Chicago: University of Chicago Press.

Kuper, L. and Smith, M.G. (eds.) (1969) *Pluralism in Africa*, Berkeley: University of California Press.

Lasswell, H.D. and Kaplan, A. (1952) *Power and Society: A Framework for Political Inquiry*, London: Routledge and Kegan Paul.

Lazarsfeld, P.F. and Barton, A.H. (1955) "Qualitative Measurement in the Social Sciences: Classification, Typologies and Indices," in D. Lerner and H.D. Lasswell (eds.), *The Policy Sciences*, Stanford: Stanford University Press.

Martindale, D. (1959) "Sociological Theory and the Ideal Type," in L. Gross (ed.), *Symposium on Sociological Theory*, New York: Harper and Row.

Michalos, A.C. (1969) *Principles of Logic*, Englewood Cliffs, NJ: Prentice Hall.

Oppenheim, F. (1973) *A Meta-Tower of Babel?*, paper presented at the COCTA panel, International Political Science Association World Congress, Montreal,

Oppenheim, F. (1975) "The Language of Political Enquiry: Problems of Clarification," in F.I. Greenstein and N.W. Polsby (eds.), *Handbook of Political Science*, Reading, MA: Addison-Wesley.

Pap, A. (1958) "Disposition Concepts and Extensional Logic," in H. Feigl, M. Scriven, and G. Maxwell (eds.), *Concepts, Theories and the Mind-Body Problem*, Minnesota Studies in the Philosophy of Science, vol. 2, Minneapolis: University of Minnesota Press.

Pap, A. (1962) *An Introduction to the Philosophy of Science*, New York: Free Press.

Riggs, W.F. (1968) "Comparative Politics and the Study of Political Parties," in W. Crotty (ed.), *Approaches to the Study of Party Organization*, Englewood Cliffs, NJ: Allen and Bacon.

Riggs, W.F. (1975) "The Definition of Concepts," in G. Sartori, F.W. Riggs, and H. Teune (eds.), *Tower of Babel: On the Definition and Analysis of Concepts in the Social Sciences*, Pittsburgh: International Studies Association, Occasional Paper 6.

Robinson, R. (1965) *Definition*, Oxford: Clarendon Press.

Russell, B. (1948) *Human Knowledge*, New York: Simon & Schuster.

Salmon, W.C. (1963) *Logic*, Englewood Cliffs, NJ: Prentice Hall.

Sartori, G. (1962) *Democratic Theory*, Detroit: Wayne State University Press.

Sartori, G. (1969) "Politics, Ideology and Belief Systems," *American Political Science Review* 63 (2): 398–411.

Sartori, G. (1974) "Philosophy, Theory and Science of Politics," *Political Theory* 2: 133–61.

Scriven, M. (1958) "Definitions, Explanations and Theories," in H. Feigl, M. Scriven, and G. Maxwell (eds.), *Concepts, Theories and the Mind-Body Problem*, Minnesota Studies in the Philosophy of Science, vol. 2, Minneapolis: University of Minnesota Press.

Teune, H. (1975) "On the Analysis of Concepts," in G. Sartori, F. W. Riggs, and H. Teune (eds.), *Tower of Babel: On the Definition and Analysis of Concepts in the Social Sciences*, Pittsburgh: International Studies Association, Occasional Paper 6.

Ullmann, S. (1962) *Semantics: An Introduction to the Science of Meaning*, Oxford: Blackwell.

Whorf, B.L. (1953) *Language, Thought and Reality*, Cambridge, MA: MIT Press.

4 Guidelines for concept analysis

Giovanni Sartori

> A good part of the work called "theorizing" is taken up with the clarification of concepts – and rightly so. It is in this matter of clearly defined concepts that social science research is not infrequently defective.
>
> (Merton 1958: 114)

The semantic import

Whatever we know is mediated by a language, if not by the language in which we know it. And if language is the *sine qua non* instrument of knowing, the knowledge-seeker had better be in control of the instrument. Bad language generates bad thinking; and bad thinking is bad for whatever the knowledge-seeker does next. Despite the much proclaimed quantitative turn of the social science endeavor, the fact remains that the bulk of our knowledge of ourselves is expressed in a natural language – not in a formal, formalized, or uninterpreted language. Whatever we measure refers to "named" variables; and formalization (i.e., the construction or application of uninterpreted systems of signs) plays a collateral and instrumental role in the social science enterprise. So the basic fact is and remains that we stand on, and walk with, a natural, interpreted language. And the central trait of a natural language consists of its semantic properties. First of all, then, we are peremptorily required to master the *meaning function* of words – that is, semantics.

Semantics is a sort of crossroad discipline and thus has, understandably, many facets. It can refer to the development and change of meaning (historical semantics), to the interlocking of meaning and logic (truth-conditional semantics), to how language relates to "culture" (as in the Sapir–Whorf hypothesis), and so forth. In the systematization proposed by Morris (1946), semiotics (the general theory of signs) is subdivided into (1) syntactics, the relation of signs to signs regardless of their meaning function; (2) pragmatics, the relation of signs to behavior; and (3) semantics. The distinction between semantics and syntactics is the important one. What has followed from this distinction is, in the summation of Hilary Putnam (1975, vol. 2: 139), an "enormous progress . . . in the *syntactic theory* of natural languages," but hardly a "comparable progress . . . in the *semantic theory* of natural languages." There are many reasons for the lag of the latter. One of them has to do with the distinction between semantics and pragmatics. The distinction is, in itself, valuable and acceptable; but it has been drawn in ways that impoverish semantics and overextend pragmatics. On the one hand, logicians tend to attribute to the realm of pragmatics whatever cannot be handled in terms of truth-value, thus restricting the ambit of semantics to true-false "propositions." On the other hand, linguists tend to reduce semantics to what they would do anyhow as linguists. On account of the resulting amputations (which result, in turn, from the way in which disciplinary fiefs happen to be drawn), much of the present-day treatment of semantics misses, I submit, what matters most.

For want of an established label let me propose as the nucleus to which I give prominence the notions of *projective semantics* and, derivatively, of *semantic projection*. Moreover, since the expression "semantic meaning" has been utterly trivialized, I shall say, more pointedly, *semantic import*. In a nutshell, the semantic import of words entails that (1) what is *not named* largely remains *unnoticed* or, in any event, impervious to cognitive development; and that, (2) the *naming choice* (selecting a given word within a given semantic field) involves a far-reaching *interpretive projection*. All told, then, projective semantics brings to the fore both the *constraints* and the *pathways* that any given natural language imposes upon and affords to our perceiving, thinking, and knowing. But let us proceed orderly.

My premise is that in the beginning is the word, that is, *naming*. We express what we mean (what we have in mind) by picking from within the ambit of our natural language the "right words." Conversely, we are unable to express exactly what we mean unless we find words for it. By affirming that in the beginning is the word, I am simply asserting that we cannot form a sentence unless we already know the meanings of the words it contains.[1] It is not that words *acquire* their meaning via the sentences in which they are placed. It is the case, rather, that the meaning of a word is *specified* by the sentence in which it is placed. If "context" is applied to "sentence," then words out of context (as itemized, e.g., in dictionaries) have signification just as much as words in context. The difference is that words out of context are (in a natural language) polysemes, whereas words in context are less multi-meaning for the context (sentence) suggests which meanings are not intended and, conversely, intended.[2]

Even though it goes without saying, it is safe to say it: Not all words have semantic meaning. For one, personal names (of persons and also of places) do not enter the purview of semantics. Also, connectives (conjunctions, sentence-forming operators, etc.) have only a syntactic meaning. So, semantic considerations apply to words that can be used – in sentences – as subjects or predicates (and, derivatively, to the verbal forms which have a corresponding noun form). Furthermore, it should be well understood that in this writing we are not interested in any and all words but specifically in those "important words" that are carriers of concepts, that can be said to constitute, in some meaningful sense, *units of thinking*.[3]

Bearing the foregoing qualifications in mind, I take the central tenet of semantics to be that "language is constitutive of the reality, is essential to its being the kind of reality it is" (Taylor 1971: 24). The author that makes the point as forcefully as it can possibly be made is Whorf, who writes: "We dissect nature along lines laid down by our native languages . . . we cut nature up, organize it into concepts, and ascribe significances as we do, largely because we are parties to . . . our speech community." Thus, "facts are unlike to speakers whose language background provides for unlike formulation of them." Still more comprehensively, thinking "is in a language – in English, in Sanskrit, in Chinese. And every language is a vast pattern-system . . . by which the personality not only communicates, but also analyzes nature, notices or neglects types of relationship and phenomena, channels his reasoning" (1956: 213, 235, 252).

Whorfianism (or the Whorf–Sapir hypothesis) is often criticized quite unfairly.[4] It does upset the view that thinking is the master and language its infinitely versatile slave; it does not uphold, however, a linguistic "determinism." Whorf's linguistic and/or cultural relativism may well be excessive; it does not endorse, however, "untranslatability" in principle (nor can the problem be disposed of by noting that translations and cross-cultural communications do in fact occur). This having been said in fairness to Whorf, my own view (Sartori 1979: 23–28) is that it is our thinking that monitors our language, even though thinking, language, and culture largely interpenetrate each other and evolve in feedback fashion. Be that as it may, ultimately the fact remains that as each individual thinks about something at each point in time, he or she does relate to a particular linguistic system as a "given." Hence, at that moment his natural language is his *thought-molding instrument*. It is thought-molding in the sense that he is thinking via a vocabulary that embodies an overall way of *perceiving* and *conceiving* reality.

In order to establish the point, let me single out two aspects of the semantic import of words (the ones amenable to semantic consideration): (1) a *slicing aspect*, and (2) the *interpretative aspect*. All words provide some kind of cutting up or slicing of the real world. In addition some words (especially the ones amenable to conceptual rank) also shape the perception and/or the interpretation of whatever we take cognizance of. The notion of semantic projection may be said to apply with full force, or more specifically, to the perceptive-interpretative "track" that words (some words) provide. Does the distinction between slicing and interpreting correspond to the one between object-words and concepts? Roughly, yes. However, it is worthy to note that even words of natural objects may have a semantic projection. In the classical example of Wilhelm von Humboldt, the word for moon in primitive ancient Greek was *mene* (from a root that meant "to measure"), whereas in Latin it was *luna* (from *lucere*, "to illuminate"). This entails that the primitive Greeks interpreted the moon as an instrument of measuring time, as a substitute for a calendar, whereas the Romans perceived it as a surrogate of light, as performing an illuminating function (at night). Note that *mene* and *luna* have exactly the same denotation (i.e., point exactly to the same object). They differ, however, in their connotation. The example shows that words "interpret" things precisely because their denotation is filtered by their connotation.

However, most words for natural kinds or physical objects do not embody an interpretative projection; their semantic import generally resides in how broad or how thin their cutting up of phenomena is. The easiest illustration of "slicing difference" is provided by colors. While no language appears to have more than twelve color categories (English has eleven), some languages have only two: "black" and "white." Does this entail – it has been asked – that a two-name vocabulary renders its user color-blind to other colors? Almost certainly not. It does imply, however, that the colors that are named acquire perceptive prominence and, secondly, that the fewer the categories, the greater the range and diffuseness of the colors that are being singled out. Other examples of slicing differences relate to the presence or absence of abstract, general terms. For instance, the Eskimos do not have the general word "snow," but a variety of specific words for specific states of snow. Contrariwise, the Aztecs (who did not have to worry about arctic weather) had just one and the same root word for ice (the noun), cold (rendered by icy, the adjectival form), and snow (rendered as ice mist). Likewise, Bedouins do not have the general term "camel," but a very extensive and minute terminology for specific features and varieties of camels. Finally, and more strikingly, counting systems may not have the numerals "one," "two," "three," and so on. There is a Brazilian language in which the counting field is divided into: none, one or two, three or four, and many. Here – one may suspect – "individualism" (the conception) is not likely to fare well.[5]

It will be noted that none of the foregoing examples – the ones that are generally found in the semantics literature – refer to the important words that acquire conceptual rank. Yet it is at this level that words condition and channel our reasoning and, therefore, that their semantic projection comes to the fore. Since my agenda in this essay is a crowded one, I can afford two examples only – the simplest ones I can find.

Consider the words state and government. For quite a long time English has preferred "government" to "state," and has indeed translated the French *état* and the German *Staat* into "government." Much of the continental European literature has taken the opposite course, thus considering "government" one of the partitions of the state (the general term). As one changes language one obtains, then, the configurations that are contrasted in Figure 4.1.

In the first part of the figure "government" covers the whole (i.e., is the general term); it is also a subclass of itself (when government is restricted to mean "the executive"); and may be (especially in translations) a synonym of "state." On the right the configuration is, instead, a straightforward one: "State" is the general and abstract term, while government is one of its component elements and unequivocally indicates the executive branch (of the state). What are we to make of this contrast?

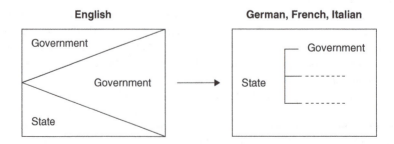

Figure 4.1 Differences in semantic configurations.

Compounding a somewhat subtler argument, that whoever addresses the topic in English is handicapped in two respects: he or she is more exposed to ambiguities and, second, covers less ground in that much of what has been elaborated in the other languages in terms of an abstract, juridical and also philosophical theory of the state will be missed. Conversely, Continental Europeans will miss much of the concreteness (real governments, real people) that characterizes the Anglo-American literature. To be sure, one may always contend that these differences reflect cultural traits. If so, we are simply pushing the argument back to a highly elusive prime mover (the culture), and the additional assumption is entered that it is the culture that generates the language. At the end of this detour the point remains as it is: whatever the ultimate and distant causal factor, the proximate one is that the linguistic eyeglasses of an English author prompt him to approach the topic in a way that radically differs from the track suggested by German, Italian, or French. In short, in English I do not "see" the state; an Italian that only knows Italian does (or so believes).

My second example will be handled even more simply. "People" is in English a plural, whereas *Volk, peuple,* and *popolo* are, grammatically, singular. So what? Well, English authors have difficulty in understanding and seldom accept "people" conceived as an oversoul, or as an organic indivisible entity – a notion that has been largely entertained by the German, French, and Italian speech community. A sheer coincidence? Or is it not the case that when we say "people *are*" we are semantically prompted to perceive and conceive a multiplicity, a sum total of "each body," while those who say "people *is*" are predisposed and encouraged to conceive an "allbody," a whole that subsumes its parts?

Another angle from which to grasp the semantic import of words is, of course, to look into the words that give trouble to the translator. Take the German *Aufhebung*, which is the key term of Hegelian and idealistic dialectics. We have settled for translating it, in English, with "superseding" – hardly a term that conveys the Hegelian concept. Indeed, Hegel translated into English is ludicrous. We have never been able to convey what the Ancient Greeks meant by *polis* and derivatives (another key word). Conversely, ancient Greek has no word for "intelligent" (the closest term would be *sophos*). The English "spirit" (at times weirdly rendered as "ghost") is only an empty calque of the French *esprit* or the Italian *spirito* which are (like the German *Geist*) terms of highly significant conceptual richness.

However, let us not overshoot the mark. That speakers in different languages cannot form (conceive) the same concepts is certainly not true for all concepts, and very much depends on which are the languages in question. English, incidentally, is a good receiver for its vocabulary draws extensively from Saxon, Latin, Greek, and French. A number of European languages have also interpenetrated one another for centuries, if not for millennia. I, for one, do manage to rethink myself across SAE (standard average European). However, when I read how English has to be rendered in Chinese, Japanese, Hopi, Navaho, and other non-SAE languages – and conversely how these languages are rendered in English – I feel pretty sure that I miss a great deal precisely because thinking is language-wrapped.[6]

To sum up, our knowing is, intrinsically and inextricably, *onomatology* – logos about (mediated by) names. This is what my notions of semantic projection and semantic import bring into prominence. In order to make my case as simply as it can possibly be made, my unit of analysis has been the word. But, as will be apparent in the subsequent proceedings, the full case extends to, and actually stems from, a linguistic system in its entirety. Actually, my crucial concept will be the one of *semantic field*, conceived as a manageable breakdown and the most meaningful subunit of a whole linguistic *system*. For the time being let me simply stress that when semantics is taken seriously, then we are fully entitled to assert, "this is the wrong word," for the assertion renders the constraints of language (as a system) with respect to the semantic projection of words.

The basic scheme

Clear thinking requires clear language. In turn, a clear language requires that its terms be explicitly defined. In order to avoid cumbersomeness, and also on grounds of expediency, the terminology (and metaterminology) of our enquiry is brought together and defined in the glossary. It should be well understood, then, that the aforesaid glossary is an integral and indeed constitutive part of this writing: whatever is in need of being defined is defined there.

On this proviso, let us immediately come to the strategy of conceptual analysis that I shall employ. The most useful scheme of "concept unraveling" from which to start is, I submit, the one outlined by Ogden and Richards and known, therefore, as the Ogden and Richards "triangle" (1946: 11). Following their lead (although not their terminology), the frame of the argument is that the knowing and the known can be broken down into three basic component elements: (1) *words*, (2) *meanings*, (3) *referents*. In turn, words, meanings, and referents are best distinguished by addressing the following two fundamental questions:

How do meanings relate to words? How do meanings relate to referents?

With respect to the first question, the relation between meanings and words can either be *equivocal* or univocal, either *ambiguous* or clear. With respect to the second question, the relation between meanings and referents can either be *vague* or not,[7] either *undenotative* or adequate.[8]

Generally, "word" is used interchangeably with *term* (with the implicit understanding that "word" is broader and all-encompassing because also connectives or conjunctions are words); "meaning" is often called *connotation*; and "referent" is frequently rendered as *object*. We also speak of the connotation of a concept as its *intension*. When we say "connotation," its complement is *denotation*; and when we say "intension," the complement is *extension* (in a technical meaning of the term). Our basic metaterminology can now be organized as in Ogden and Richards (except that their triangle is now an angle) and represented as in Figures 4.2–4.5.

Figure 4.2 is my redrawing – with amendments – of the Ogden–Richards triangle. It indicates, in particular, that "term" is preferred to "word" (since we shall

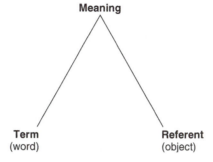

Figure 4.2 The basic scheme.

stipulate that "term" is a word allocated to a concept), and that "referent" is preferred to "object" (let alone "reference"). But what does the word referent mean? I shall define it: whatever is *out there* before or beyond mental and linguistic apprehension. So to speak, referents are the real-world counterparts (if existent) of the world in our head.

Figure 4.3 addresses the important and yet troubling notions of intensionextension and/or connotation-denotation.[9] As the figure indicates, in this analysis intension is (means) the same as connotation, and extension is the same as denotation. There is no problem with defining *intension* or connotation: it consists of the ensemble of characteristics and/or properties associated with, or included in, a given word, term, or concept. Within this generally agreed upon signification let my own definition be the following: the intension (or connotation) of a term consists of all the characteristics or properties of that term, that is, assignable to a term under the constraints of a given linguistic-semantic system.[10]

So far, however, we have not added much to the plainer notion of meaning, for also the "meaning of meaning" could be defined as we have just defined the intension. What is it, then, that we gain by saying intension or connotation? The gain comes from the pairing, that is, from the fact that "intension" goes with "extension" (just as connotation goes with denotation), that these notions are complementary and crucially interrelated. The important question thus becomes: what is the *extension*, or the denotation? A perusal of the literature detects two very different replies. Hospers, for instance, asserts, "The entire denotation of a word is the complete list

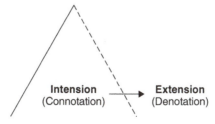

Figure 4.3 Intension and extension.

of all the things to which the word applies," and emphatically denies that words denote classes of things: "The denotation of a word is always an individual thing" (1967: 40, 42). Now, if "denotation" is extralinguistic, Hospers's point is correct.[11] But Salmon (1964: 90) and others define the extension as follows: "The extension of a word consists of the class of all objects to which that word correctly applies."[12] And when "things" is replaced by "class of things," the implication is that the ambit of the extension is just as linguistic (and mental) as the ambit of the intension.

Clearly, the relation between the intension and the extension addresses the gnoseological problem. How do we reach out? How do we pass from what is "in our mind" to what is "out there"? (Or, conversely, how does the outer world enter into our mind?) The solution suggested in Figure 4.3 shuns the epistemological controversy. What the figure conveys is that the complementarity of intension and extension (or of connotation and denotation) purports to cross the border between the mental and the extramental, between what is already apprehended linguistically and what is extralinguistic (a pure and simple "referent"). Hence, the right side of the angle is segmented and allows for a breach. To be sure, if we were to confront the gnoseological issue we would need a second arrow that goes back from the outer world into the mental one. However, it is not for us to decide if and how our knowing "seizes the object" out there. The point that bears on our concerns simply is that "the denotation of a term clearly depends upon its connotation" (Cohen and Nagel 1936: 32). A conclusion that also applies, I submit, to object terms.[13]

Once the relationship between intension and extension has been appraised, the next step is to ask ourselves whether the ensemble of characteristics of a term (i.e., its intension or connotation) is amenable to some kind of organization. In this connection it should be borne in mind that some concepts (or terms) may display a dazzling number of characteristics. How are we then to handle the wealth of connotations that enter, or may enter, the concepts that we are addressing? Figure 4.4 suggests that the overall pool of characteristics, properties, or attributes of a concept may be conveniently disaggregated into two clusters. A first cluster (on the left side) brings together the *non-observable* or *least-observable characteristics*, while the second cluster (on the right side) brings together the properties that

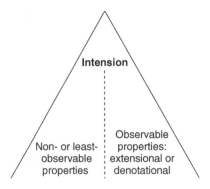

Figure 4.4 Observable versus non-observable properties of intension.

are amenable to observation. In accord with our previous discussion and as a follow-up of Figure 4.3, in Figure 4.4 the latter cluster, or subset, is labeled *extensional* or *denotational properties*. These are the properties that appear to be suited, or relatively more suited, for "seizing the object."

The implication of Figure 4.4 is that whoever addresses empirical and research problems is well advised to extract from the overall heap of the intension the subset of properties that I have called "extensional" and/or "denotative"; whereas the more theoretically oriented scholar will be largely dealing with the subset of characteristics that our representation places in the proximity of "term" rather than in the proximity of "referent."

Let us turn to Figure 4.5, which deals with what goes wrong (the defects) and is largely self-explanatory. The argument visually represented in the figure is, in brief, the following. The meaning-to-word relation is defective when it is ambiguous and/or equivocal. To be sure, in a natural language almost no word is univocal (i.e., endowed with only one meaning): all words are polysemic, or polysemes. Therefore the defect is not in the multiplicity of the meanings of each word per se (out of context) but resides in their entanglement, in the fact that it is unclear (in context) which meaning is intended. In short, the problem is *confusion of meanings*.[14] The activity that we have come to call disambiguation does not purport, then, to attain univocity – a one-to-one correspondence between meaning and word – but clarity (of meaning). Thus, univocal meanings are, eventually, an ideal objective. The concrete problem that we confront is reducing ambiguity and dispelling equivocation.

On the right side of Figure 4.5 the argument is that the meaning-to-referent relation is defective in that it is vague. As I have said, the problem here is to seize the object. Thus a concept that lacks "denotative adequacy" is a concept that obtains unbounded or fuzzy referents. If so, the remedy consists of increasing its denotative and/or discriminating power.

The last suggestion is to superimpose, mentally, Figure 4.4 upon Figure 4.5. Figure 4.4 may now be said to convey that the left side of our angle centrally addresses the *terminological problem* (the problem of "terming the concept"), whereas its right side centrally addresses the *denotational problem*. This entails –

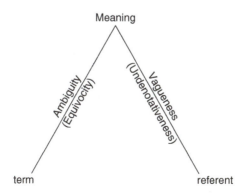

Figure 4.5 Defects: ambiguity and vagueness.

in relation to Figure 4.5 – that we now have a compass for deciding which properties are to be extracted from the overall pool of all the characteristics (that can be predicated of a concept) for which purpose: either the primary intent of disambiguating the concept, or the intent of increasing its denotative power. In short, we now have a compass for making sure that we are not extracting (from the inner area of our angle) the wrong characteristics for the wrong purpose.

It may strike the reader that our figures do not mention "concept." Now, one may certainly say that a concept has meaning, needs a term, and, if empirical, points to referents.[15] The implication is that whatever is predicated of one of the three component elements of the scheme can also be more broadly predicated of "concept." I take it, though, that the crucial point is how "concept" relates to "sentence." In this purview, concept is defined: the basic unit of thinking. This is, admittedly, a loose definition. It does bring out, however, that it is the concept that *circumscribes* whatever we apprehend into meaning-centered units. To be sure, concepts are defined, shaped, and explicated via sentences. Yet, it is the concept that structures the sentences it governs – not the other way around.

Our overall scheme of analysis assumes, then, that the defectiveness of a concept is best seen as, and actually results from, its ambiguity and/or its vagueness. The basic layout of my guidelines can thus be summarized and expressed in a "practice-oriented" rule form, as follows:

Rule 1: Of any empirical concept always, and separately, check (1) whether it is ambiguous, *that is, how the meaning relates to the term; and (2) whether it is* vague, *that is, how the meaning relates to the referent.*

The first part of Rule 1 addresses the question: what is *the meaning* of a concept? This question confronts the problem of confused and many-to-one relations among meanings and words. Its purpose is to achieve *clarity*, to identify ambiguities and correct errors of equivocation. The second part of Rule 1 addresses the question: what is *the referent* of a concept? This question confronts the problem of inadequate linkages among meaning and referent. Its purpose is to achieve *denotational adequacy* or denotativeness. Rule 1 specifies "empirical concept" in order to underline that it does not address concepts that lack extension. A concept is empirical if, and only if, it can be rendered in *testable propositions* that confirm it (in some respect or extent); and a concept cannot be so confirmed or falsified – with respect to the propositions it generates – unless we identify its extension.

In the following sections we shall look in some detail into the following: the causes and remedies of ambiguity ("Defining"); the organization of the intension ("Ambiguity, homonyms, and synonyms"); and the causes and remedies of vagueness ("Organizing the intention"). But before exploring these three problem areas one by one, let us complete our scheme of analysis.

Defining

Having identified two kinds of conceptual faults, the question is how do we cure these defects? The first reply is this: one way of curing concepts lies in *defining*.

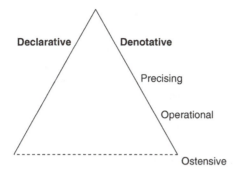

Figure 4.6 Definitions: declarative versus denotative, and types of denotative.

Granted, this reply is not very helpful unless we know (1) how to define, and (2) for what purpose. That is to say that we need not only a typology, but also a map of where various kinds of definitions are located. For this latter purpose our initial scheme of analysis (Figures 4.2–4.4) can be converted into Figure 4.6.

The simplest definition of definition is a declaration of meaning – hence, *declarative definition*.[16] The objection might be that a simple declaration of meaning is less than a definition (in the proper or more technical meaning of the term). However, this objection applies even more to ostensive definitions, that are nonetheless called definitions.[17] Moreover, if we consider that declarative, or declaratory, definitions cover the entire left side of our scheme, it is clear that there are many ways of handling the meaning-to-word relationship, many of which do consist of definitions in a more strict or proper sense.

Let us exemplify with reference to the concept of man. A declaration of meaning might be "by 'man' I intend males but not females." We might say that this is a stipulation, hardly a definition; yet it already serves the purpose of declaring a meaning. In any event, most declarative definitions pick up a lexical definition (that cannot be challenged as not being definitions). Example: by man I intend a rational animal. The common element of all declarative definitions resides in "disambiguation," in the fact that they reduce or eliminate equivocation.

Turning to the meaning-to-referent relationship, along this side Figure 4.6 locates four kinds of definitions: denotative, precising, operational, and ostensive. The general class (the symmetric vis-à-vis of the declarative definition) is here *denotative definition*, which I define as follows: all the definitions intended to seize the object (by increasing the denotativeness).[18] However (as we shall see in detail in "Undenotativeness (vagueness)"), denotative definitions confront different problems – namely (1) establishing the boundaries; (2) sorting out the membership of any given denotatum; and (3) deciding the cut-off point vis-à-vis marginal entities.

Since the requisite of any extensional definition is to include-exclude, it can be assumed that a denotative definition is such (i.e., adequate) when it sets the boundaries. This is the same as saying that a denotative definition serves the general requirement of whatever defining occurs along the meaning-to-referent side of the angle. Yet, boundary setting is not all. In the first place, within our borders we may obtain a fuzzy membership and/or weird bedfellows. For instance, "mammal" has, in zoology, well-demarcated boundaries; but we must be able to discriminate, for most purposes, between whales and human beings. For this specific and quite distinct purpose I propose the label *precising definition*.[19] It may be argued that precising definitions are a trivial subclass of denotative definitions in the sense that the latter are obtained via the same procedure as the former, which is in essence to augment the number of the defining characteristics. Yes and no, however. If "table" is defined as a flat surface sustained by four legs, then six-legged or three-legged or even one-legged tables are not tables. We may wish to solve the problem by defining table as characterized by having between one and eight legs. It seems neater, however, to define table as a surface sustained by legs (denotational definition), and to enter a specification of the number of legs (precising definition) when a problem of fuzzy membership arises.

The insertion along the meaning–referent relation of precising definitions helps, in turn, to give a more accurate destination to *operational definitions*. In the mapping of Figure 4.6, operational definitions are located in the lower right end of the scheme. This does not imply that they are subordinated to precising definitions. What the mapping is meant to convey is that operational definitions are *another* subclass of denotative definitions located at a different point (in greater proximity of the referent) than precising definitions. In any event, and regardless of whether one accepts the proposed insertion of precising definitions, the indication conveyed by the overall mapping is that far too much is omitted when we leap, as it were, from declarative definitions to operational definitions. The operationalization of a concept often entails a drastic and eventually distorting curtailment of its connotation. For instance, "rational man" may be defined operationally as the capability of responding to, and of being scaled by, an IQ test. This is fine, but is also an enormous impoverishment of a wealth of connotations. The point is, then, that the alternative is not either operationalize or perish. We may not be able to operationalize a concept, and yet we can satisfactorily proceed toward seizing the object on the basis of denotative definitions supplemented by precising definitions.[20]

Let us continue with our example. A denotative definition of "man" could be the following: man is a two-legged animal (*animal erectus*), without feathers, that symbolizes (Cassirer's [1944] *animal symbolicum*). This is an adequate denotative definition for it suffices to exclude all the living beings that are not human beings. Had I only said, instead, "man is a two-legged animal without feathers," the object would not have been adequately seized, for this definition would have excluded birds but would still have included apes. The question that might arise in connection with the example at hand is, why is it that "man as a rational animal" is considered a declaratory and not a denotative definition? The answer is that "rationality" loses too much of its connotative richness when reduced to observable characteristics; and that if rationality is defined with a minimum of tightness, then it is very likely that many human beings would not pass the test of such a definition (and would thus have to be excluded from the class "man"). Conversely, two-leggedness and featherlessness are highly visible characteristics; and this entails that the "symbolic test" (our third defining condition) would only be necessary for marginal cases (e.g., in order to exclude apes). Let it also be noted that I have chosen Cassirer's characterization (symbolic animal) instead of *animal loquax* (speaking animal), because the latter property would compel us to exclude one who is incapable of speech.[21]

We may now revert to *operational definitions*. As their placement in Figure 4.6 implies, I suggest that operational definitions should not be intended loosely (this purpose is already served by denotative and precising definitions) but narrowly – that is, as definitions that restrict themselves to possible *measurement operations* and thus to the properties that lend themselves to actual measurements.[22] Note that this narrow acceptation also uncovers the *sui generis* nature of operational definitions, for definitions that involve measurement also involve error and "validity."

As for *ostensive definitions*, Bertrand Russell (1948: Chapter 2) conceived them as extralinguistic modes of communicating, as mere look-and-see shortcuts. For instance, to understand "round," look at a billiard ball. In our example, the ostensive definition of man is, "Look, this is a man." Ostensive definitions are called such because they assume a capacity of abstraction (from seeing a concrete man, one abstracts the concept of man). However, definition by ostension amounts to a "pointing" (from a word to an object) which is, as such, of very thin linguistic substance. This is why in Figure 4.6 we have an incomplete triangle (the base is dotted), and why ostensive definitions are placed below the dotted line. And, once again, the recommendation is to understand ostensive definitions in a narrow rather than in a diluted and overstretched sense. The overstretching becomes unnecessary when, along the meaning–referent relation, we sort out other types of defining.

In Figure 4.6 the central area is left blank. As we know, here we find all the properties or characteristics that are associated with a given concept, that is, its *full* connotation or intension. This overall pool of characteristics may be highly populated. Take, once again, the concept of man. To the observable properties picked out (above) by the denotative definition one may add, for example, characteristics such as these: man is (1) a free agent; and (2) a speaking animal; (3) capable of infinite learning; (4) one that masters nature. Another set of characteristics may focus, instead, on the social, political, and religious nature of man. One will also find in the pool a set of metaphysical characterizations: For example, man is a spiritual animal, endowed with an immortal soul, and so on. Let us say, for the sake of argument, that if a computer were to scan the literature in search of all the characteristics associated with the word man, it would collect hundreds of associated words. An "intelligent animal" (man) may reduce them to, say, 50, and a particularly intelligent man may meaningfully reduce them further by *organizing them in clusters of connotations*.

The question remains whether there are logical differences among the characteristics or properties encompassed by, or associated with, a concept. The reply is yes. The pool contains two kinds of properties – namely (1) *defining properties*, and (2) *accompanying properties* (or contingent, accidental, or variable properties). While this distinction may be difficult to draw in practice, it is an essential one in principle. If too much is declared "true by definition," empirical research is stultified. Conversely, if the necessary properties are not stated, a word simply does not apply

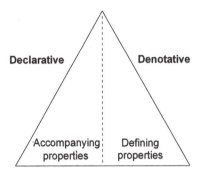

Figure 4.7 Types of definition and defining properties.

– that is, we are unable to decide to what it applies. If "state" is declared not to have necessary or defining properties, we cannot ascertain whether a given entity is or is not a state.

The issue as to which properties are the defining ones will be confronted later (in Reconceptualization"), where I will suggest that within the context of an empirical science, the defining properties are the ones that identify the referent and establish its boundaries. If this suggestion is accepted, then the blank of Figure 4.6 can be filled as in Figure 4.7, which places the defining (necessary) properties on the referential (right) side of our angle. If the suggestion is not accepted or in all the cases in which we are not dealing with an empirical science, the distinction would have to be assessed differently.

It goes without saying that the definitions singled out in this section by no means exhaust the typology of definitions. But our mapping in Figure 4.6 singles out, it seems to me, the ones that are crucial for practitioners and that best alert them to which definitions are appropriate for what purpose. In particular, the social scientist especially needs to realize that he or she is confronted with three distinct definitional problems: first, the *border problem* (to be settled by denotative definitions); second, the *membership problem* (precising definitions); and third, the *measurability problem* (operational definitions which generally hinge in turn on the search for valid indicators).

I was just saying that my typology of definitions is far from being exhaustive.[23] Social scientists are very familiar with, for example, the notions of *lexical* and *stipulative* definitions. While this is a useful distinction, it is being largely overworked and abused. For instance, that lexical definitions are true or false (depending on whether they are actually found in lexicons) whereas stipulative definitions are neither true nor false (since they are mere proposals) is a grand way of stating, at best, a triviality. Lexical definitions are all born, when first proposed, as stipulations; and their general acceptance simply makes them lexical (in no way an addition to whatever true value they might have). We have also come into the habit of saying "I stipulate" simply to say that we select one among the set of definitions carried in lexicons. By saying so, however, we are canceling the distinction that we are employing. Since almost all words are multi-meaning, in order to be lexically grounded should we adopt all such meanings? Clearly, we always do choose among the lexical meanings – and if this is "stipulating," then everything is: every definition is a stipulation. In order, then, to have a distinction that carries a difference, a stipulative definition must be a non-lexical one: The two categories are of analytical avail only if employed as mutually exclusive complements of each other.

In conclusion and also to summarize on the route traveled thus far, a concept can be unsatisfactory – either muddled or inadequate – on three grounds:

1   Defects in the intension (disorganized or trivial characteristics).
2   Defects in the extension (undenotativeness or vagueness).
3   Defects in the term (ambiguity).

If so, a complete conceptual and terminological analysis involves three steps. Their logical order is as follows:

1   Establishing the connotative definition (by characteristics) of the concept.
2   Determining its referents (denotative definition).
3   Making sure that the term for it is understood univocally (declarative definition).

Ambiguity, homonyms, and synonyms

Let us now probe our scheme of analysis, beginning with the left side of Figure 4.4 and precisely with the problem of ambiguity, of confusions(s) of meaning(s). These confusions result from homonymy – from the use of a same word for different meanings. The caveat is, thus, that *homonymies are not homologies*, that a same word does not entail sameness of *logos*.

However, even the simple assertion that ambiguity arises from homonyms must be immediately qualified. In the first place, homonyms hardly create ambiguity when they fall into different disciplinary fields. The fact that *canis* applies to a constellation in astronomy and means "dog" in zoology is hardly a matter of concern. It should be understood, therefore, that our concern generally is with within-field or within-discipline ambiguities.[24] In the second place, it is important to distinguish between individual and collective ambiguity. *Individual ambiguity* is a single author's confusion, his own obscurity and/or inconsistency of meaning. *Collective ambiguity* attests, instead, to an infelicitous state of a discipline as such: it is a situation in which (at the limit) each scholar ascribes his own meanings to his key terms. To be sure, individual equivocation worsens collective ambiguity. Yet collective ambiguity can be rampant – to the point of destroying a discipline as a cumulative fabric of knowledge – even if no individual ambiguity subsists. We are confronted, therefore, with two problems that require separate treatment.

The recipe for combating individual ambiguity is no great discovery. Since we have (in mind) more meanings than available words, homonyms are inevitable; and the ambiguity thus resulting can only be cured by surveillance – and this in two steps. First, we must check if and how the key terms (in the subject under investigation) are defined with respect to the meaning–term relationship – that is, check if and how their meaning is declared; and, second, we must check whether the meaning assigned to a given term is kept constant – whether the same word is actually used, throughout the argument of each author, in the same meaning. In rule form,

Rule 2a: Always check (1) whether the key terms (the designator of the concept and the entailed terms) are defined; (2) whether the meaning declared by their definition is unambiguous; and (3) whether the declared meaning remains, throughout the argument, unchanged (i.e., consistent).

More succinctly (2a and 2b are one and the same rule),

Rule 2b: Always check whether the key terms are used univocally and consistently in the declared meaning.

But what about collective ambiguity? Collective ambiguity does not result only from homonymies; *it may also result from synonymies* (different words with same meaning). However, before looking into how synonymies relate to ambiguity it is appropriate to consider synonymy per se.

Two preliminary provisos are in order. The first one is that my discussion is not a lexical discussion – that is, it does not bear on lexical synonymies. The lexicographer's unit is a "word entry," and it is his or her business to report on *similarity in meaning* (of words). As Quine (1963: 25) puts it, his definitional activity is confined "to the reporting of preexisting synonymies" – to be sure, of preexisting synonymies that have been intersubjectively accepted. To clear my way, I shall say that lexical synonymies are givens, and that I take them, as everybody generally does, for granted.[25] The logical point is that "similarity" in meaning is a far cry from "sameness" in meaning[26] and, moreover, that a synonymy of words has little to do with establishing a *conceptual synonymy*.

Let us now move from the word (as the unit) to the sentence (as the unit). In this case we speak of *synonymity sentences*; and the proviso is, again, that much of this activity is irrelevant to our concern. For instance, sentences that take the form "we shall use the terms A, B, and C indiscriminately or interchangeably" simply attest to how sharp an analysis needs to be and point to what is peripheral to the analysis at hand. Likewise, most sentences that take the form "means the same as,'' or "this is the same as saying," simply pick up lexical synonymies and are, generally, context-embedded: they do not entail in any way, and certainly do not suffice to demonstrate, that two concepts have the same meaning. The question thus becomes, when is it that a synonymity sentence establishes or purports to establish a conceptual synonymy?[27]

When this is the case we say (or intend to say) that the "true meaning," the "correct meaning," or the "proper meaning" of A is x. These expressions, let it be stressed, do not necessarily reflect an ontological or metaphysical conception of language. They may simply and appropriately reflect the fact that a semantic universe is a system structured by rules of meaning which are, for all practical intents and purposes, givens. (To call them "conventions" engenders a naively anthropomorphic and misleading interpretation.) Thus, a correct meaning is a meaning that complies with these rules, while an incorrect (wrong) meaning violates them. And this is what we endlessly discuss under the form of *interpretative sentences*[28] – that is, sentences that address, in the final analysis, the issue as to whether a word is used according to the rules of language or not. So far, so good. That is to say, if two terms are given the same meaning via interpretative sentences, synonymities are, in principle, unimpeachable. But are all synonymities (of terms) so established? The reply is that this has been less and less the case under the aegis of the very convenient dictum that "all meaning is arbitrary" and, if so, that we are free to define as we wish (i.e., to freely stipulate meanings). But a synonymy that is not warranted by interpretative sentences is an *arbitrary synonymy*: a synonymy that is simply declared, without further ado, in the name of freedom of stipulation.[29]

Having brought out the point of controversy, or the sore spot, let us pass on to the overall relationships between homonymy and synonymy.

Homonymy (one word–many meanings) obtains this relation:

Synonymy (many words–one meaning) obtains the reverse relation:

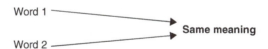

Now, let us assume that a homonymy is confusing, that it produces ambiguity. (Note that I am not assuming that a natural language should resemble, ideally, a predicate calculus. One can fully appreciate the virtues of the polysemantic richness of words and yet combat, at critical junctures, its drawbacks.) In that case, the golden rule is to have one word for each meaning, as follows:

If the same scheme is applied to the case of synonymy, the difference is that the end result is indeterminate, as in the following representation:

To be sure, there are many good answers that one can give to the above "what for?" For instance, that entities should not be multiplied; or that one kind of "explanation" consists precisely in demonstrating that A is nothing other than B (and thus that two terms are synonymous).[30] Moreover, as I have previously pointed out, most synonymies are lexical givens – and that is that. The point remains that synonymies are not simply the reverse of homonymies – they bring up the question, what is their merit? If we break down a homonymy, the worst that can happen is to propose a trivial distinction, a distinction with no difference: the sin, if any, is of little consequence. Contrariwise, if a *conceptual synonymy* is not demonstrated in accord with accepted and controlling procedures (not only interpretative sentences but, as we shall see, the "semantic field rules" formulated in "Selecting the term within a semantic field"), then we are apt to incur a sin of very great consequence: the sheer *unsettling of a semantic field*. Indeed, the best indicator of *stipulative arbitrariness* is that it unsettles, *without resettling*, the semantic field to which the stipulation belongs.

But this argument is premature at this stage. For the time being, the fact that synonymy is a risky affair and that its eventual demerits are of no small consequence warrants two caveats – one very general, and one very specific.

The general caveat about giving the same meaning to different words is that this appears to be, in the aggregate, a *terminological waste*. That is to say, that from the vantage point of what may be called economies of language, synonymies should not be encouraged for they add up, on balance, to providing "fewer words" which are in turn burdened with "more meanings." The specific caveat is that collective ambiguity is generated by and is the inevitable outcome of *stipulating synonymies at whim* – by now a widespread practice in the social sciences. To this effect, at this stage I shall simply note that any synonymy that is stipulated without adequate "interpretative support" (in terms of interpretative sentences) should be refused. At a later stage, however, I shall indicate (under Rules 8 and 9) a crucial test condition, or controlling procedure.

With respect to the first caveat (that is, to the problem of *terminological waste*) the recommendation is to make sure that synonymies do not hamper the articulation of language. This recommendation can be expressed under an "awaiting contrary proof" clause (that implies that a net advantage should be demonstrated), as in the allowing rule form:

Rule 3a: Awaiting contrary proof, no word should be used as a synonym for another word.[31]

Rule 3b: With respect to stipulating synonymies, the burden of proof is reversed: what requires demonstration is that by attributing different meanings to different words we create a distinction of no consequence.

As can easily be seen, the difference between 3a and 3b – the anti-waste rule – is simply that the latter formulation spells out the clause "awaiting contrary proof." Let it also be stressed that Rule 3 should be interpreted with a grain of salt. The crucial reminder is that my concern is about *conceptual synonymy* (not about lexical or sentential synonymies). This means, in practice, that Rule 3 does not apply to that which is peripheral to an investigation: it is intended only for the core of what is being investigated. It is appropriate to conclude on the point with a note of caution. Even when we encounter "accepted synonyms" (givens) their identity-similarity of meaning can be accepted if (and only if) it passes two tests, namely: (1) sameness of the major meaning component of different words, and (2) sameness in the value connotation (whether a word is evaluative or neutral) of different words. For instance, if political class is neutral and if political elite is either appreciative (in past usage) or derogatory (in recent usage), then the two words are not synonymous: their extension can be the same, but their intension is not (evaluatively). Likewise (this was Hobbes's favorite example) "regicide" and "tyrannicide" may both denote the killing of a same person; yet tyrannicide renders lawful and laudable a regicide (i.e., the unlawful act of killing a king). Again, while the denotation of the two terms may be exactly the same, they are not synonyms for their evaluative connotation is different.

I have left out or to the very end the obvious recipe for combating ambiguity in general – namely, *neologisms*. The point here is a very simple one. The remedy of creating new words is excellent in principle, but fails in practice – unless three conditions are respected: parsimony (few inventions), gradualness (few at a time), and, possibly, easy intelligibility. Maybe we should combine – in a strategy of reciprocal correction – neologisms with "neovalents" (a new meaning given to an existing word). A neologism involves a memory cost, but is (in its very reason for being) unequivocal. Conversely, a neovalent adds to the ambiguity of a word but has no memory cost. The recommendation is, thus, to accompany the more equivocal but familiar form (the neovalent) with the more forgettable but unequivocal form.

Organizing the intension

It will be recalled that a concept *is* its intension, for the intension (or connotation) encompasses all its characteristics or properties. From this starting point the query is this: how do we handle a maze of characteristics and, to begin with, how do we know which are these characteristics?

In order to reply a distinction must be drawn between (1) reconstructing a concept, and (2) forming a concept. In reconstruction we are interested in canvassing the history of a concept (if it happens to be an old one) and in assessing its current state in the literature. In the perspective of formation, we formulate instead *our* concept and, it is hoped, an improved concept. Here we shall dwell on the reconstruction under the assumption that it should precede the formation and indeed that a prior reconstruction helps concept formation. So, the first question is, how do we know which are the characteristics, properties, or attributes of any given concept? Scholars find this out by searching in the pertinent literature for the definitions that are given of a concept. On this simple consideration, let me immediately submit the rule that applies to the reconstruction of a concept, as below:

Rule 4: In reconstructing a concept, first collect a representative set of definitions; second, extract their characteristics; and third, construct matrixes that organize such characteristics meaningfully.[32]

Rule 4 is deliberately (and by necessity) loose because it is simply intended to call attention to the fact that the process of reconstructing a concept requires, at a minimum, three steps: first, the canvassing and listing of existing, authoritative definitions; second, the clustering and transformation of these definitions into a set of extracted characteristics; third, a matrix (or matrixes) that organizes on the basis of meaningful criteria the characteristics so extracted. It is probably vain, I believe, to search for standard patterns for our matrixes. Different concepts (or concepts subjected to different treatment – e.g., "property concepts" versus "object concepts") are likely to require different organizing matrixes left to the perceptiveness and ingenuity of the analyst. Maybe we can go beyond mapping devices and eventually land at full-fledged "conceptual trees." The argument is only, then, that a reconstruction is incomplete and loses much of its fruitfulness unless it leads, at a minimum, to an organization of characteristics that somehow compounds the similarities and the differences in how a given concept is conceived.[33]

   A comment is appropriate with respect to the first recommendation of Rule 4: "Collect a representative set of definitions." This formulation applies, as such, to relatively recent concepts (e.g., culture, ideology). With respect to old concepts (such as alienation or power), the set must also be representative historically – that is, historical depth and sequencing appear to be an important thread. This preliminary canvassing involves three aspects: (1) establishing the etymology; (2) following the *Geistesgeschichte* of the word; and (3) a text analysis of key authors or sources. Regardless of how we go about collecting definitions, the essential part of the exercise consists of *extracting the characteristics*. One can find more than 50 definitions of "power." However, all these definitions exhibit, in various combinations and shades, a far smaller number of characteristics. And when we come to the core characteristics, I surmise that very few concepts would display as many as, say, ten.

Undenotativeness (vagueness)

We may now turn to the extension or to the denotation – that is, to how the meaning relates to the referent. Along this side of our scheme of analysis the problem is *denotativeness*, and the defect has thus been labeled *undenotativeness*. With respect to the referent, the basic question is, which objects or entities are included and which are excluded? As we have already seen in our mapping of definitions ("Defining" and Figure 4.6), this question can be underpinned in three different directions, namely:

1 Boundary indefiniteness.
2 Membership indefiniteness.
3 Cut-off indefiniteness.

The boundary problem is, we may say, the "sine qua non" problem. Boundary indefiniteness results from, or can be imputed to, insufficient characteristics in number – other conditions being, of course, equal.[34] That is to say, that a concept is unbounded (no matter how well we perform otherwise) when it is not given a sufficient number of characteristics for identifying its referents with respect to all their boundaries.

However, the boundaries may be drawn and yet we may remain confronted with a "fuzzy set," with membership indefiniteness. When we complain – as we very often do – that a concept does not have a sufficient discriminating power, it seems to me that this complaint is particularly appropriate when it addresses the membership problem. To illustrate with reference to "elite": the concept is defective with respect to its boundaries when it fails to sort out elite as a distinct kind of group; and is defective with respect to its membership when no within-elite "precising" is possible.[35] The latter is the problem – we have suggested in "Defining" – that is specifically addressed by precising definitions. Let us now say that precising definitions are intended to provide or increase a within-concept discriminating capability. The foregoing can be summarized in rule form as follows:

Rule 5: With respect to the extension of a concept, always assess (1) its degree of boundlessness, and (2) its degree of denotative discrimination vis-à-vis its membership.

While there is a difference between boundary vagueness and membership vagueness, both defects are amenable to the same cure, as in Rule 6:

Rule 6: The boundlessness of a concept is remedied by increasing the number of its properties; and its discriminating adequacy is improved as additional properties are entered.

The rationale of Rule 6 will be explained in the next section (and by Rule 7). The objection could be that increasing the number of properties is not enough in the sense that what is also and concurrently involved is the "sharpness" of the characteristics in question. I concur, but I do not know how to handle this problem any better than I have done in "Organizing the intension." Allow me simply to specify, therefore, that my Rule 6 applies under the following *ceteris paribus* clause: provided that the sharpness of our characteristics is equal, then vagueness of boundaries and/or of membership becomes a function of the number of the properties.[36]

We are left with the cut-off indefiniteness. The boundaries may be well drawn conceptually, and yet the researcher on the field may still be in trouble. At this point his trouble will be of a residual kind, to be formulated as follows: despite adequately drawn conceptual frontiers, we must ask which marginal entities or borderline entities are to be included or excluded. Take, again, the elite example. The membership problem may have been resolved according to Rule 6, and yet the researcher may still have to decide how to sort out all the concrete groups that should either be included or excluded. To cite another instance, with "political party" where is the cut-off point? Failure to achieve representation? At 2, 3, or 5 percent of the total vote? A given percentage in seats? And when does a hill end and a mountain begin? At what point is a city a city?

The borderline problem cannot be settled in general. I mention it for two reasons. The first one is that much can be done about "membership indefiniteness" before coming to the cut-off point, and this implies that the two things should not be confused. The second reason is that the inclusion-exclusion of marginal entities is, conceptually, a residual issue. No doubt, it troubles the researcher; but it does not arise until we come to operationalization. That is to say, that it is a problem to be settled by operational definitions. On the other hand, the more theoretically oriented scholar may prefer to speak, in this connection, of the *open texture* of concepts.[37] And the idea that concepts are so characterized does not displease him at all. Quite to the contrary, open texture is often conceived as a conceptual asset.

Ladder of abstraction and universal concepts

Up to this point we have not touched explicitly upon the vertical organization of knowledge. The classic instance of vertical organization is given by hierarchical classifications of the *per genus et differentiam* type: genus, species, subspecies.[38] However, hierarchical classifications are only a special case of a more general structure that is generally identified as a difference in *levels of abstraction*.

We are all aware of the fact that the theorist performs at a higher level of abstraction than the researcher; and we are even more aware of how poorly our theory generally relates to our research (and vice versa). This is so – I submit – because we do not know how to descend or, conversely, how to climb along a *ladder of abstraction*. This is tantamount to saying that from a logical standpoint the problem is to convert a discrete and often messy superimposition of levels of abstraction into a ladder of abstraction – that is, into orderly rules of transformation (composition and decomposition) from one level to another.[39] To this latter effect, the rule of thumb seems to be that we climb a ladder of abstraction by reducing (in number) the characteristics of a concept. Conversely, we descend a ladder of abstraction by augmenting (in number) the characteristics of a concept. In rule form:

Rule 7:   The connotation and the denotation of a concept are inversely related.[40]

As already noted, the inverse relationship between connotation and denotation provides a rationale to our previous Rule 6 – namely, that the undenotativeness of a concept is remedied by increasing the number of its extensional properties. It can now be seen that Rule 6 belongs to the broader context of how theory (i.e., a high level of abstraction) relates to field research (i.e., a low level of abstraction). The denotative and discriminative power of a concept is increased by increasing its properties, because this is how we descend a ladder of abstraction in order to meet research (and verification) needs.

Clearly, a concept can be (and indeed is) treated by different authors at different levels of abstraction. If so, Rule 7 helps us in reconstructing into one concept what may appear as a congeries of concepts. On similar grounds, the notion of levels of abstraction alerts us to a possible way of organizing our matrixes of characteristics ("Organizing the intension").

Rule 7 also enables us to underpin the strength and the weakness of the all-inclusive, highly abstract concepts philosophers call, or have called, *universals*. Any concept can be "universalized" in this sense: whenever it obtains the most inclusive definition it can (semantically) obtain.[41] For instance, the universal definition of republic is any form of state which is not monarchic. While this definition is all-inclusive (no state qualified as republic would be missed), it hardly is very telling, (i.e., non-monarchic is not a very interesting characteristic). Yet, the "entry" into a discourse about republics or the "genus" for classifying republics into species and subspecies is afforded by the universal definition.

While each concept has its own upper limit (some concepts are "more universal" than others), under this proviso it can be generally said that universals are nothing other than what remains of a concept at its highest level of abstraction. According to Rule 7, this means that the ladder of abstraction has been climbed to the point at which a concept is connoted by only one characteristic. This is so because in order to extend the denotation we must reduce the connotative characteristics; and the denotation of a concept reaches the point of all-inclusiveness precisely when all its characteristics but one have been removed. For instance, "group" becomes a universal when defined, "any collection of more than two individuals" (where more-than-two is the only remaining characterization).

Universal concepts (as defined above) are looked upon with suspicion by empirically oriented scholars. However, they too can hardly perform without them. They will argue – with reason – that highly abstract concepts are of no avail on research and testing grounds. Nonetheless, a highly abstract concept may turn out to have a high explanatory or heuristic value; and, in any case, universals do serve mapping and organizational purposes. Universal concepts are often thought of as being hopelessly imprecise. If this means that they are necessarily ambiguous, this charge cannot be sustained. A universal concept need not be ambiguous, for the one characteristic that it retains may be expressed and defined unequivocally. Yet Rule 7 implies that a universal concept must be, in some respect, *defective in denotation*.[42] This necessarily follows from the abstractive (ladder climbing) process: When we are left with one characteristic only and when this characteristic is selected precisely for its all-inclusiveness (or greater inclusiveness), the other side of the coin is that we are left with poor boundaries and/or with poor discriminating power. Conversely, the more we descend the ladder of abstraction by entering additional characteristics, the more a concept obtains boundaries and denotative discrimination (thereby suiting the needs of the researcher).

Of course a universal concept can be, all in one, ambiguous and utterly undenotative. Take again, to illustrate, the concept of group in the "group theory" of politics of David Truman et al. In order to be a universal key, "group" was conceived in the 1950s as any significant interacting unit resulting from the aggregation of two or more (up to billions) individuals. And even this characteristic ("any significant unit") was destroyed by the introduction of so-called latent or potential groups. At this point the universal is indeed universal, but its boundlessness is staggering; and to use "group" to mean any amount of individuals serves no purpose other than the one of unsettling the semantic field to which the term belongs.

The reconstruction of concepts

In "Organizing the intension," I pointed out that our major reason for dwelling on the intension of a concept is that we are interested in reconstructing it. However, the reconstruction of concepts was left (in Rule 4) at the recommendation of constructing matrixes of characteristics. This is indeed the most crucial part of the exercise; but we still have to confront the complexities of a full-fledged reconstruction.[43]

The rebuilding of a concept begins with looking into its literature. Here, the referent is library "references." It is only to be expected, therefore, that the extraction of the characteristics (from our list of definitions) will leave us with a sheer enumeration of characteristics that appears intractable: we simply see no way of bringing this enumeration together into some meaningful kind of organization. In order to grasp the nature of the difficulties that might confront us at this juncture, it is helpful to imagine – as in Figure 4.8 – some typical configurations of characteristics. Note that the figure is merely illustrative. As for its interpretation, a circle indicates a cluster of characteristics that are internally congruent, that hang together; overlapping circles indicate clusters of characteristics that can be derived from one another; and isolated circles point to the most intractable configuration. The circles are included in boxes that represent the pool of all the conceivable connotations of a concept.

The configurations in boxes (a) and (b) are, for our purposes, the more pleasing ones. Under box (a) we have a common core of characteristics (the shaded area), three adjacent areas of overlapping, and a periphery that poses, as it stands, no problems. Under (b) we have, instead, a central common core that originates strings of characteristics that go in very different, mutually independent, and yet connected (string by string) directions.[44] The trouble begins when we obtain a configuration as under (c), for here we do not seem to have a common core, and the interconnections

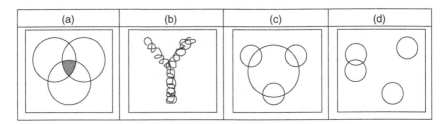

Figure 4.8 Possible configurations of characteristics.

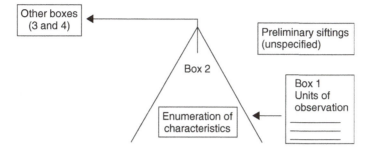

Figure 4.9 Ordering of definitions (input side).

between the four circles (clusters) are difficult to establish. And, of course, the worst possible configuration is the one under (d). So, we may be in trouble. If we are, should we lift our arms in despair and simply conclude that the concept under investigation is a morass, an impossible mess, or a bottomless swamp? Not at all – and surely not yet. Let it be stressed that here we are reconstructing a concept *from its literature*. This suggests that a first sifting must occur before we enter our standard scheme of analysis (as we have left it in the initial figures). Let us thus expand the right side of the scheme, as in Figure 4.9.

What does Figure 4.9 convey? Very simply, that the disorder (intractability) in box 2 – our overall pool of characteristics – might well depend from a disorder in input: that is, from having neglected to order, in a preliminary way, the set of definitions from which we subsequently extract the characteristics. In box 1, the suggestion is specifically pinned down to a criterion – namely, which is the unit observed by each author and thus reflected in his definition? For instance, if the concept of power is focused on the unit "diadic relationships," it will be conceived differently than when the unit is a "one-to-many" relationship. Likewise, the integration of the unit "household" is not the integration of the unit "nation." And so forth. What is recommended as a first step is, then, to ask the following question: power, integration, alienation, consensus, culture, and so on, *with respect to what*? That is, with respect to which unit of observation and/or analysis? And if this question or other siftings of the kind[45] are asked on the entry side of our scheme, it may well be that also the characteristics assembled in box 2 (the domain of the intension) fall into place. But let me continue to play the devil's role. Let us assume that box 1 does not bring any order into box 2. What next? The subsequent steps, that may be called – for the symmetry of the argument – steps in output, are outlined in Figure 4.10 under the general heading of "contexts."

Figure 4.10 suggests that our inability to find any order in box 2 may also depend on the fact that a concept adapts itself to, or is changed by (1) the *disciplines* (political science, sociology, anthropology, economics, psychology, etc.) within which it is developed, and/or (2) the *theoretical contexts*, frameworks, and approaches (e.g., cybernetics, decision making, functionalism, structuralism) that employ it. Figure 4.10 also allows a box for field contexts – that is, for within-discipline slicings (such as comparative versus non-comparative).

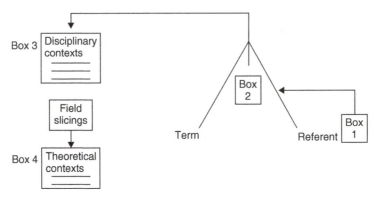

Figure 4.10 Ordering by concepts (output side).

The question, or the objection, might be this: why are disciplinary and theoretical contexts treated in my sequencing as a last resort fitting? I grant that – in principle – all four boxes could be placed on the entry (right) side of the scheme. However, I have reasons for placing them where they are. First, it is impractical and confusing to clog the entry with too many siftings. Second, the "unit of observation" criterion is a neat one, whereas disciplines and theoretical contexts are, as criteria, very untidy ones. Let us, therefore, check first how much mileage is afforded by our best sorting device. Third, and in particular, passing references to "theoretical contexts" appears to be a very convenient alibi for unfinished jobs or (still worse) issue-escapism. In any event, I am interested in finding out to what extent the social science "theoretical contexts" really do affect our conceptualizations.[46] So, let us see first how much of the variance is explained by the previous boxes.

A final reflection is in order. A "real science" does not devote any special attention to concept reconstruction. The need for *reconstruction* results from *destruction*, from the fact that our disciplines have increasingly lost all "discipline."[47] Amidst the resulting state of non-cumulability, collective ambiguity, and increasing incommunicability, it is imperative to restore or attempt to restore the conceptual foundations of the edifice. This is not to say that an exercise in conceptual reconstruction will restore consensus – we are far too disbanded for that. However, if the exercise succeeds, it will restore intelligibility – and, with intelligibility, an awareness of the enormous intellectual waste brought about by our present-day indiscipline (and methodological unawareness). This is why I insist on the reconstruction of concepts. But, of course, this is not an end in itself.

Concept reconstruction is a highly needed therapy for the current state of chaos of most social sciences. Moreover, it helps each individual scholar in deciding what to do on his own. Unless a reconstruction precedes the construction, he is not only liable to waste time and energy in rediscovering the umbrella (I mean something already discovered) but also to add a "meaning 51" to some other 50 preexisting meanings, thus adding, at best, profusion to confusion. Nonetheless, the fact remains that concept reconstruction is a means whose ultimate purpose is to provide a cleaned-up basis for construction – that is, for the *formation* of concepts.

Forming the concept

Since the reconstruction has involved us in a somewhat distracting detour, it is important to recall – with reference to the initial scheme of analysis – that also the formation of the concept hinges on the distinction between the meaning–word problem (ambiguity), and the meaning–referent problem (undenotativeness). The point concerning ambiguity is that "many meanings in one word" are conducive to equivocations. In order to minimize them, the golden rule (incorporated in my anti-waste Rule 3) is that "different things should have different names" – as much as is possible, of course. Hence, stipulating synonymies without proof – that is, in disregard of the "burden of proof" clause – is both a waste of language and a way of aggravating ambiguity. Undenotativeness, instead, cannot be condemned as such. It points, true enough, to some kind of empirical weakness of a concept. But this may simply mean that an author is a theorist, that he is not concerned with the extension, denotation, and, in the final analysis, operationalization of concepts. There is nothing inherently sinful in that.

Even so, how we cure vagueness or undenotativeness (as handled by Rules 5 and 6) remains an important question – also for the theoretically oriented scholar. This is so because nobody ever really addresses a concept by asking, what are *all* its conceivable characteristics or properties? The empirically oriented scholar asks, Which are the apt and sufficient properties for marking the boundaries? His problem, as we have phrased it at the outset, is to seize the object. As for the theoretically oriented scholar, he may well want to do more than seize the object. Yet it will not harm him to do so.

On the basis of the foregoing, which is the next step? We are seemingly close to the point at which we are in a position to decide, on warranted grounds, the designator of the concept – that is, the *allocation of the term*. This is a very crucial step because "terms" are the carriers of the stability of language and of the cumulability of knowledge. Moreover, when we settle for a given term (the term that designates the concept) our selection has a *semantic projection*, and this means – as we have seen at the onset – that our choice entails a way of conceiving and perceiving (things or processes). It is precisely because language is not only a means of expression but also a *molder of thought* that allocating the term to a concept – terming the concept – is a most central decision.

Selecting the term within a semantic field

How do we go about, then, selecting the term that designates the concept? The reply crucially hinges on the fundamental notion of *semantic field*. A natural language in its entirety is – I have said – a semantic *system*. But we cannot involve, when we deal with a single concept, the entire linguistic system. If this were the case, the undertaking would be unmanageable. However, a linguistic system can be conveniently broken down into manageable subunits, into relatively small semantic fields.

A semantic field should not be confused with Wittgenstein's "family resemblances." While it consists of a clustering of terms, it remains a subsystem of the overall linguistic system and, therefore, it remains characterized by *systemic properties*. A semantic field is, then, a clustering of terms such that each of its component elements interacts with all the others, and (as with all systems) is altered by any alteration of the others. In other words, a semantic field consists of a set of associated, neighboring terms that *hang together* under the following test: when one term is redefined, the other terms or some other term also need to be redefined.[48] The notion of semantic field entails, then, that the selection of the term that designates the concept must be submitted to the following rule:

Rule 8: In selecting the term that designates the concept, always relate to and control with the semantic field (to which the term belongs) – that is, the set of associated, neighboring words.

Let the above be called the *semantic field rule*, and let me dwell on it via examples. First example: the term that designates the concept is *elite*, and the set of neighboring words is, at a minimum, aristocracy, oligarchy, ruling class, political class, power class. Now, if elite is not defined as required by the anti-waste rule (Rule 3), then we shall find in all likelihood assimilations such as elite is nothing other than power class (those in power). If so, Rule 8 requires us to readjust the whole semantic field, and particularly to make sure (1) that no meaning is cancelled when the word elite swallows another member of its set, and/or that (2) by declaring a synonymy (e.g., that elite and power class have the same meaning) we do not, in fact, increase the ambiguity of the concept.

Second example: the term allocated to the concept is *power*, and a first set of associated words is influence, authority, coercion, force, sanction, or even persuasion. Now, if Rule 3 is respected, Rule 8 does not apply. But if the anti-waste rule is disregarded, then we shall probably end up with assimilations such as power is influence, and influence is power. If so, Rule 8 requires us to resettle the semantic field in such a way as to show (1) that power is not coercion (since it is influence), (2) what is influence without power (surely a conceivable possibility), and (3) how we relate power-influence to authority, force, and sanction. At the end, we are likely to discover that any assimilation has a "field cost": it obfuscates, in part or totally, the rest of the set.

Third example: the designator of the concept is *ideology*, and here the associations indeed loom large because they touch on idea, doctrine, theory, science, belief, affect, value, creed, myth, utopia, truth and cognition, class interest, and more. In this instance my own experience is that Rule 3 and its "awaiting contrary proof" clause is decisive; it is its incessant violation that has reduced "ideology" to a morass.

The foregoing illustration suffices, I trust, to sustain the following sub-rule of practical implementation:

Rule 9: If the term that designates the concept unsettles the semantic field (to which the term belongs), then justify your selection by showing that (1) no field meaning is lost, and (2) ambiguity is not increased by being transferred into the rest of the field set.

This semantic field rule is by no means intended as a reconceptualization blocker.[49] Quite to the contrary, the ultimate purpose of our guidelines is to sustain concept formation. But a reconceptualization cannot consist of a single-shot stipulation. Not only must we confront the "unsettling costs," but the merit of a reconceptualization consists precisely in demonstrating that the resettling advantages *for the whole field* largely outweigh these costs.

While the crucial considerations for "terming of the concept" are given by the semantic field Rules 8 and 9, a concomitant, expedient way of assessing whether a concept is ill-termed (or could be termed better) is provided by what I shall call the *substitution test*. The substitution test may be formulated as follows: if, in any given defining sentence(s) the word A can be substituted by the word B not only without alteration of the presumably intended meaning but indeed with a gain in clarity and/or precision, then the word A is being misused or inappropriately used. This test is well illustrated by F. W. Riggs in his analysis of the concept of development, and consists (in the semantic field under scrutiny) of taking a series of definitions of "development" and of substituting, in such definitions, the word development with other neighboring words, such as "change," "growth," "expansion," "modernization," "progress," and many more. It turns out that in a number of instances the definitions so tested become clearer (less ambiguous) when "development" is substituted with another word that conveys a more precise meaning of what the author seemingly intends.[50] To say the least, the substitution test shows that fashionable words may only add to obfuscation, or that whatever improvement in conceptual clarity is brought about at the outset is subsequently lost when popularity turns a word into sheer verbiage. Let it be stressed, however, that while the substitution test is a most useful and expedient *test* (i.e., detector of abuse and sloppy usage) it cannot replace – as a guide for concept formation – the semantic field rules.

Reconceptualization

I have insisted on the allocation of the term because it prejudges (semantically) what follows – namely, *reconceptualization*, the definition that formulates and forms the concept, our conclusive step.

Does concept formation, as defined, amount to "legislating" over concepts? This is often said, and often used as a scare word or as an indictment. But legislating is a wrong word. (Remember that semantic systems do entitle us to dispute the correctness of words.) If "legislating" conveys, as it does, that somebody imposes and enforces something upon someone else, then the word misrepresents the process of knowing – as I shall stress in the final section. For the time being, let me simply note that the reconceptualizing that I recommend is different from the one in which everybody is engaged all the time in one respect only – that it is guided (it is hoped for the best) by methodological alertness and procedural rules.

There appear to be two pathways to concept formation that owe their distinctiveness to the fact that each science actually consists of two component parts: the pure science (theoretically oriented), and the applied science (research-and testing-oriented).[51] In the pure science precedence is given to the *theoretical fertility* of a concept, whereas the applied science must give precedence to the *empirical usefulness* of a concept, that is, to its extensional or denotational adequacy. While these two orientations are not mutually exclusive – a scholar can be equally sensitive to both – the bearing of the point is that it is perfectly legitimate to end up either with a definition of theoretical import, or with a definition of empirical utility. And while I have no recipe for theoretical fertility, empirical reconceptualization remains, instead, amenable to rules.

As we already know from "Defining," the crux of defining consists of separating the *defining properties* (or necessary characteristics) from the *accompanying properties* (contingent or accidental characteristics). The defining properties (carried in defining sentences) are *true by definition*; this entails that a concept without defining properties, or necessary characteristics, cannot be applied with any certainty and consistency.[52] The contingent or variable properties are the ones that may, but also may not, accompany the object (entity, process, relation) being defined; and this implies that their presence must be ascertained by investigation – not declared to exist by definition. Our current neglect or even rejection, in the social sciences, of defining is ominous; yet it finds a justification in previous abuses, in the malpractice of outflanking problems by solving them "by definition." But this malpractice attests only to the difficulty of sorting out the necessary from the contingent characteristics.[53] The point remains that what must be settled by definition cannot be settled by investigation; and, conversely, that what can be settled by investigation should not be settled by definition.

The crucial question thus is, How do we decide which characteristics belong to the defining properties? With respect to empirical knowledge (not in other domains and respects) I answer: *defining properties are those that bound the concept extensionally*. To illustrate, if the ability to fly were considered a defining property of birds, then an ostrich could not be classified as a bird. As a consequences, either we unsettle (and resettle differently) the criteria according to which zoologists classify all living beings, or we must make "ability to fly" an accidental, if very frequent, property. Note that a minor borderline problem relating to marginal entities (mainly ostriches and turkeys) wins over the visible property that most people would consider the characteristic of birds. So, the defining properties are the bounding ones – not the most frequent or ostensively obvious ones.

This is, then, the *logic of defining* that social scientists have long forgotten. What has come to replace it is the recommendation of *parsimony in defining*. I do concur with this recommendation. Yet parsimony is no guide – it remains an exhortation without content, unless it is spelled out as follows: confine your defining to the necessary properties. And the same applies to the concurrent recommendation of settling for *minimal definitions*, for definitions that leave the maximum conceivable room to findings. Again, in order to be of guidance "minimal" must be specified as follows: exclude from your defining the accompanying properties. And if this is the case, then the practice-oriented rule derived from the logic of defining can be formulated as below:

Rule 10: Make sure that the definiens of a concept is adequate and parsimonious: adequate in that it contains enough characteristics to identify the referents and their boundaries; parsimonious in that no accompanying property is included among the necessary, defining properties.

Clearly, the rule satisfies the requirement of empirical adequacy, not the requirement of theoretical fertility. With respect to the latter, I must leave the argument by noting that after a conceptual reconstruction we are likely to be far better equipped than otherwise for looking into the characteristics that serve the advance of the "pure science."

At the end of our "guideline journey," it is appropriate to ask: should we say, by way of conclusion, that *a concept has many meanings*, or instead that *each one of these meanings is a concept?* The first way of putting it implies that we are reporting on how a discipline as a whole stands on any given concept. The second way of putting it appears more accurate,[54] but may not help a discipline in trying to restore common conceptual foundations. All things considered, I suggest that both formulations are permissible if understood with a grain of salt. Since my overarching concern is with counteracting chaos, my preference is to say that a concept has many conceptualizations.[55] But this statement is in no way intended to contradict the statement that each conceptualization is a concept.

It is also appropriate to stress, at this point, that guidelines are simply guidelines. The adoption of a *core method of analysis* and of replicable analytic procedures is necessary for a joint, incrementally oriented endeavor. But a modicum of discipline is not inimical to variations and inventiveness. Indeed, variations and inventiveness are an essential part of the exercise. In this connection it is well to note that my guidelines owe little to the philosophy of science literature and to the resulting methodology. The model of the current philosophy of science is (with exceptions, to be sure) physics. Unfortunately, there is very little in such a model that social scientists are able to imitate or even to approximate. As a result social science practitioners are taught what they do not need to know, and are not told what is needed for their own knowing. In order to fill this gap I have in fact worked back from the science (as we are best able to practice it) to the method. That is to say, that my guidelines are largely extracted from the problems that the social scientist actually confronts. This entails, in turn, that the method outlined in this writing is monitored by and fully open to feedback. If, along the course of concrete conceptual analyses, worthy reasons are given for dismissing a particular rule, it will have to be dismissed. If, on the other hand, the concrete analyses come up with better and/or different rules, they shall have to be incorporated. As more and more analyses of concepts are performed, they will not only engender a more sophisticated method but may also suggest alternative methods. As I was saying, variations and inventiveness are no less necessary to our endeavor as a modicum of discipline. But a method we must have.

Fallacies: a coda

It is an easy prophecy that what is being proposed here will be challenged from a variety of quarters. Some of the foreseeable objections have been implicitly accounted for along the way. Even so, it is well to explicitly bring them together. It is also the case that many of the foreseeable objections can be neatly dismissed as fallacies – or so I believe. There is no particular ordering in the fallacies that I am about to expose, except that the simpler ones are introduced first. Let it also be understood that when a fallacy is brought back to the major author under whose authority it is held, my quarrel is not necessarily with the author itself but, more often, with a false witnessing.

The language-in-use fallacy

One of the celebrated dictums of Wittgenstein is that "the meaning of a word is its use in the language" (1953: 43). The dictum is easily extended to concepts. If so, it cannot be left at that. To which "language use" should we bow? To the one of ordinary language? Much of the analytic and linguistic philosophy inspired by Wittgenstein has in fact followed this cue. To the extent that this is so, however, the philosophers in question have segregated themselves from any understanding of how a scientific knowledge is formed and actually develops. Whatever else "science" may be, its necessary, preliminary condition resides in the formulation of a *special and specialized language* (not to be confused with a calculus or a formalized language) whose distinctive characteristics are precisely to correct the defects of ordinary language. The various sciences – both the hard and soft ones – took off by inventing neologisms (their own technical vocabulary), by reducing by definition the ambiguity of their key terms, and by consistently abiding by syntactical rules. What is the relevance, then, of Wittgenstein's stand for the realm of science? The reply either is absolutely none, or must be that his stance is as misleading as can be.[56] This is less readily apparent for mechanics (after Galileo and Newton) and for the physical sciences in general – once they are firmly established and so long as their practitioners perform within the ambit of Kuhn's (1962) "normal science." But a soft social science that bows to Wittgenstein's dictum negates the very possibility of its ever becoming a science. If would-be social scientists, like the Wittgenstinian philosopher, "may in no way interfere with the actual use of language; [they] can . . . only describe it" (1953: 124), then they are only left to get lost in a Tower of Babel which they, if only by omission, are in fact aggrandizing. Let me insist: if there is one thing that new sciences in the making do incessantly, and more than any other, this is tampering with language. Such "interference" can be for the better, when the end in view is one of creating a specialized and more precise language; or will be for the worse, when no such end is acknowledged and pursued.

However that may be, on the point Wittgenstein holds that meaning and context are inextricably interwoven and, therefore, that to define terms apart from context is to misunderstand how language works. The fallacy is, then, that Wittgenstein is indeed interpreted out of context. Wittgenstein addresses the question, "What is meaning?" We can accept his reply to his query, and yet ask a subsequent and different question: how are meanings actually treated in *scientific usage*, that is, within the specialized vocabularies (languages) that each science constructs for itself? If this becomes the question, then to quote Wittgenstein amounts to a false witnessing – extending the authority of an author beyond his realm of competence.

The disambiguation-by-context fallacy

This is a shorthand for the dictum (which can be read as an implication of the Wittgenstein fallacy) that "words are disambiguated by context, and *by context only.*" While it is trivially true that the context (sentence or sequel of sentences) helps to disambiguate (even though at times it does not), the error lies in the *only* and, thereby, in missing the crucial point that the more meanings must be surmised by contextual investigation, the less we are dealing with a scientific kind of knowledge. In any science worthy of the name, it is not the context that disambiguates the word (to be sure, the key words); this tricky encumbrance has been disposed of once and for all.

The imprecision fallacy

Popper's warning is that "precision" may be a "false ideal"; a warning that is being twisted into a praise of imprecise language. The issue addressed by Popper is how non-formalized discourse (natural language) relates to a formalized one. In addressing this issue, Frege (1949) and Russell (among others) took the view that natural language was a hopeless tool which had to be banished and replaced by formal languages. And this is the issue-context within which Popper holds that the precision exemplified by uninterpreted axiomatic systems such as mathematics is a false ideal. This is a view with which I very much concur; but does it have anything to do with recommending *imprecision* for natural languages (i.e., for languages which already are intrinsically imprecise)? Certainly not. Such a recommendation actually amounts to adding imprecision to imprecision; and it is a wholesale distortion to call upon Popper to support a crescendo of terminological and logical sloppiness. The dismal state of natural language imprecision into which the social sciences have allowed themselves to drift surely does not need to be reinforced by an imprecision-pursuing program.

The literary fallacy

In resisting the quest for greater precision or lesser imprecision – this being, let me insist, my sole claim – even social scientists make at times reference to the "poetic" force of poetry and, more generally, of literary language in order to sustain the universal virtues of allusive, evocative, metaphoric, and, all in all, loose language. But why should that be so? As ordinary or maternal language is refined by a spontaneous division of labor strategy into diversified special and specialized languages, it is in fact the case that the literary use (specialization) of language pulls in the direction of an *affect load*, whereas the scientific use (specialization) of language pulls into the opposite direction of *emotive unloading* (Sartori 1979: 12–13). The great poet scores low in the "logic form" of his syntax; the great scientist scores low in "non-logical" syntax. In short, what is good for the former is bad for the latter – and vice versa. That poetry attains "truth" may be true; but in none of the meanings which "truth" obtains in science. Whoever calls upon literary witnessing (for science) fails to understand the process of specialization of language and confuses, therefore, the two most distant cases of "special usages."

The arbitrariness fallacy

This compounds all the fallacies inherent in the stipulative theory of language and is expressed by the dictum that all definitions are arbitrary since word meanings are all arbitrary. If "arbitrary" meant "not necessitated by logic," then the argument would simply be trivial (nobody has ever held, to my knowledge, that there is a logical necessity in calling a cow a "cow") and much fuss would be made about nothing. But the stipulative theory of language abides by a different understanding of "arbitrary," for its message is that we are free to make words mean whatever we wish.

The reduction to absurdity of this stance is that since arbitrariness itself must be defined arbitrarily, this being a logical implication true by definition – then the assertion "all meanings are arbitrary" can never be falsified (shown to be in fact false) because each testing can be offset by another arbitrary (free) definition of arbitrariness, and so on *ad infinitum*. On the other hand, if it is true that words have a semantic import and themselves provide *interpretative eyeglasses* (incidentally, a statement fully open to verification), then it is a warrantable assertion that "arbitrariness," "convention," and "freedom" are *wrong words* – that is, words which mislead our understanding of a linguistic system. Note that even in a genetic type of explanation the leap from "arbitrariness" conceived as historical hazard (and, thus, received by us as a sedimentation solidified by millennia) to "individual arbitrariness" (freedom of stipulation) is not only an acrobatic inference but also an inference faulted by ambiguity, for the first meaning of arbitrariness is utterly different from the second one. Contrary, then, to the tenets of stipulativism, our thinking and knowing crucially hinge on fishing out from the universe of discourse the *right words*. While I would not go as far as Condillac in saying that science is nothing but a well-made language, I would certainly hold that as we are (semantically) prisoners of the words we pick, we had better pick them well. Sentences such as "no matter what word we chose" are intended to make a point of substance and are appropriate shortcuts across trivial verbal bickerings. Yet, at base, it does matter what word we chose: the "terming" of a concept is a decision of central consequence.

The general point is as follows. One can always say of human artifacts that they are just that: things that have been done (*facere*) and susceptible of being undone – nurture and not nature. This premise in no way permits the inference that therefore all of this is arbitrary. In effect, arbitrariness is the "waste aspect" of the process (i.e., the element which gets lost, which is not built-in in whatever is being built). An arbitrary bridge (free from the law of gravity) is a bridge that falls down. An arbitrary ship sinks. And if language really were arbitrary (in the meaning intended by the stipulativists), this would simply mean that we have no language.

The ultimate implication of the arbitrariness fallacy and of what I call *stipulative arbitrariness*, is that on such premises the universe of discourse can no longer be said to contain analytic statements (i.e., statements whose truth follows from the definition of the words which occur in it).[57] This implies, in turn, that deductive inferences have no firm ground on which to stand; and deduction – let it be recalled – is the very core of logic.

The premature closure fallacy

Under this heading I bring together arguments which only express a *pro tempore* strategy: namely, the view that while a stabilized vocabulary is necessary for a grown-up science, it is detrimental to a science at its inception. In this connection we hear talk of the "freezing" of language, and the resulting warning is that such a freezing hampers the "dynamics" not only of the language but also of the science. However, statics and dynamics are totally beside the point. A linguistic system is such an overpowering entity that only a welding of Hobbes's Leviathan with Orwell's Big Brother might entertain the illusion of freezing it, of a static immobilization. So, nobody holds that natural languages should or can be frozen: language is, whether we like it or not, an ever-changing, quasi-living, dynamic entity. The point at issue is an infinitely narrower one – namely, whether a relatively stabilized "special vocabulary" may, at any stage, hamper the science that it is required to serve. And there is overwhelming evidence, in the history of all the sciences, that this is not the case. That a "fixed language" in no way "blocks the science" is monumentally evident in the instances of Euclidean geometry or, more generally, of the development of mathematics. Likewise, music has long frozen in a highly mechanical fashion its written language (a serial order of semitones), and yet musicians freely and inventively compose; and chemistry was born only when another serial order (of electrons) was firmed up once and for all. With reference to natural languages, the analogy that quickly illustrates the point is the game analogy. Card games or chess are based on a very small number of units and on very firm rules of movement: yet these games allow, precisely on account of the invariance of their "conventions," an infinite sequel of combinations. If anything, then, it is the relative invariance of its language base that "dynamizes" the cumulative growth of a science.

The legislative fallacy

This is expressed by the dictum that language cannot be legislated upon and that any attempt at disambiguating and standardizing a scientific language amounts to a normative-legislative abuse. Here the fallacy simply resides in calling legislation something that does not bear any resemblance to law-making and law-enforcing. "Legislation" is, in short, a misnomer. Galileo, Newton, or Lavoisier – to cite only three names – proposed winning concepts and conceptions which in due course received the *consensus scholarum* on their intrinsic merits. No scholar "legislates." Important scholars settle for definitions of theoretical or empirical fertility; and irrelevant scholars hold on to their irrelevance under various pretexts – of which the anti-legislative banner simply represents the version a la mode. To be sure, any ter-minological house-cleaning has normative implications (and hopes) in some per-fectly respectable sense of the term; but to propose rules is not to enforce rules, is not legislation. And if a critic were to retort, "to me normative means legislative," I would in turn feel perfectly comfortable with rejecting his stipulation as semanti-cally arbitrary, unfounded, and confusing.

An enumeration of fallacies displays two limitations: on the one hand, it imputes to each one of them more analytic distinctiveness than they may in fact have; on the other hand, it underrates how they are variously combined in a mutually reinforc-ing vortex of errors. To illustrate the latter point, let me single out a characteristic passage of Feyerabend: "Without a constant misuse of language there cannot be any discovery and any progress" (1970: 25). This is, I submit, a statement that con-joins three fallacies.

In the first place, I would say that "misuse of language" belongs to, and is sustained by, the literary fallacy. From the vantage point of a scientist, it can well be said that the poet "misuses" language. Conversely, the poet is perfectly entitled to retort that science sterilizes and impoverishes language. This having been granted, the fact is that Feyerabend is taking a methodological stand against methodology. On his ground, therefore, he is getting off his own hook with a false witnessing. Turning, in the second place, to the "discovery" element of the statement, Feyerabend equivo-cates here between context of discovery and context of validation.[58] On the assump-tion that there is no "method of discovery" (in some grand sense of the expression), it is easy to state that anything – including misuse – may generate discovery. But this begs the question, which bears – in scientific methodology – on confirmation or val-idation. As for Feyerabend's "progress," the query is, which progress? Ruling out "discovery" – for which there is no rule, not even the one that language is to be mis-used – we are left with the "cumulative progress" of a normal science. Let me stress that this, and little more, is what methodology can best deliver. If so, it is demonstra-bly false that a constant misuse of language contributes to the cumulative progress of science. Quite to the contrary, Feyerabend singles out what makes for the destruction of any sustained, collective, and intersubjective progress of scientific knowledge.

Appendix: Rules

Rule 1: Of any empirical concept always, and separately, check (1) whether it is ambiguous, that is, how the meaning relates to the term; and (2) whether it is vague, that is, how the meaning relates to the referent.

Rule 2a: Always check (1) whether the key terms (the designator of the concept and the entailed terms) are defined; (2) whether the meaning declared by their def-inition is unambiguous; and (3) whether the declared meaning remains, throughout the argument, unchanged (i.e., consistent).

Rule 2b: Always check whether the key terms are used univocally and consistently in the declared meaning.

Rule 3a: Awaiting contrary proof, no word should be used as a synonym for another word.

Rule 3b: With respect to stipulating synonymities, the burden of proof is reversed: what requires demonstration is that by attributing different meanings to different words we create a distinction of no consequence.

Rule 4: In reconstructing a concept, first collect a representative set of definitions; second, extract their characteristics; and third, construct matrixes that organize such characteristics meaningfully.

Rule 5: With respect to the extension of a concept, always assess (1) its degree of boundlessness, and (2) its degree of denotative discrimination vis-à-vis its membership.

Rule 6: The boundlessness of a concept is remedied by increasing the number of its properties; and its discriminating adequacy is improved as additional properties are entered.

Rule 7: The connotation and the denotation of a concept are inversely related.

Rule 8: In selecting the term that designates the concept, always relate to and control with the semantic field to which the term belongs – that is, the set of associated, neighboring words.

Rule 9: If the term that designates the concept unsettles the semantic field (to which the term belongs), then justify your selection by showing that (1) no field meaning is lost, and (2) ambiguity is not increased by being transferred into the rest of the field set.

Rule 10: Make sure that the definiens of a concept is adequate and parsimonious: adequate in that it contains enough characteristics to identify the referents and their boundaries; parsimonious in that no accompanying property is included among the necessary, defining properties.

Glossary

This glossary is cross-disciplinary and settles for a modicum of precision – the more intuitively intelligible formulation is preferred to the more technical one. The following symbols are used:

ST   Synonymous term, surrogate term, or near-synonym
OT   Opposite term (antonym)
TM   Technical meaning
*   Stipulation

Accompanying property   Any property that is not treated as a defining property. ST: contingent property, accidental property, variable property.

Accuracy (of a measure)   A measure that is free of systematic (as opposed to random) error.

Adequacy   Short form for "extensional adequacy." A concept (or its definition) is adequate when it obtains the denotative power that is necessary and sufficient for the enquiry at hand.* OT: undenotativeness.

Aggregate   Any set which is not a system.

Ambiguity   Having several meanings which can be mistaken for each other, thus producing fallacious argumentation. Ambiguity is a defect that pertains to the meaning-to-word linkage and results from *homonyms* and *synonyms*. OT: clarity, univocity. ST: equivocity.

Analytic statement   A statement whose denial involves self-contradiction. More broadly, a statement true by definition. Specifically, analytic statements are true by virtue of their logical form alone, or by virtue of both their logical form and the meaning of their constituent terms (e.g., "all bachelors are unmarried"). OT: synthetic statement.

Antonymy   Oppositeness of meaning. Words that are opposite (opposites) are antonyms. Opposites or antonyms are the basis of definitions *a contrario* in which each term of a pair is reciprocally defined by its contrary or contradictory.

Applied science   The performing part of a scientific knowledge. Derivatively, the applied science also contributes to the testing of the hypotheses of the "pure science." See: Scientific theory.

Approach   A theoretically sustained vantage point for analyzing a subject matter. An approach is more encompassing (but generally less precise) than a conceptual framework: it determines the sets of concepts, questions, and perspectives of an inquiry. An approach may also be seen as a quasi-theory or as a pretheory, a path to theory.

Arbitrariness (in stipulation)   See: Stipulative arbitrariness.

Arbitrary synonymity   A synonymy unsupported by *interpretative sentences*, that is, established by mere stipulative *fiat*.* ST: unfounded synonymy.

Artificial language   TM: any language whose vocabulary and syntax are determinately specified. Often an artificial language is an "uninterpreted" language. See: Formalization, Calculus. In ordinary parlance, Esperanto would be an artificial language. OT: natural language.

Associated terms   Terms that belong to (cluster within) a same *semantic field*. ST: neighboring terms. Not to be confused with entailed terms.

Attribute   Whatever may be predicated of an entity.

Axiom   Statement assumed to be true (asserted without proof) in order to prove other statements (theorems). Vulgarly: unproven assumption.

Boundlessness (of a concept)   Not having boundaries for establishing what is included in or excluded from its extension.

Calculus   An uninterpreted axiomatic system or, more broadly, a constructed logical system. A calculus is expressed in formalized language. See: Formalization.

The major types of logical calculi are (1) propositional, or sentential; and (2) functional, or predicate.

Categorical statement   A simple proposition having a subject, verb, predicate form. ST: subject-predicate statement.

Characteristic   Can be used interchangeably with *property*. TM: characteristics are properties included in the definition of a concept.

Checklist   A mere enumeration of items that abides by no logical criterion.

Classification   An ordering whose objects are assigned to mutually exclusive and jointly exhaustive classes. At each step of a classificatory analysis (division) its objects are treated dichotomously: they *either* fall *or* do not fall into a given class. A classification thus requires a single criterion called *fundamentum divisionis*, the basis of division. When multiple criteria or dimensions are involved, we have a typology and/or a taxonomy. See: Hierarchical classification.

Cognitive meaning   A non-emotive meaning of heuristic value.

Concept   The basic unit of thinking. It can be said that we have a concept of A (or of A-ness) when we are able to distinguish A from whatever is not-A.

Concept construction   The forming, or formulating, of a concept.

Concept reconstruction   The sorting out of the meanings of a concept. More precisely, an explication that consists of extracting (and ordering) the *characteristics* from the definitions of a term.

Conception   A concept, (1) in the early process of being conceived, or (2) all the compatible meanings associated with a word. A conception is thus a loose or unstructured concept.

Conceptual framework   A scheme of defined and differentiated concepts used for (and confined to) the study of a particular subject. See: Approach.

Condition   See: Necessary condition, Sufficient condition. A condition is not a cause, even though "condition analysis" prefaces causal analysis.

Conditional statement   A compound proposition that takes the form, "If A, then B." ST: hypothetical statement.

Connective   Any sentence-forming operator. The most common sentential (or propositional) connectives are negation, conjunction, disjunction, implication (not, and, or, if/then); but also: as, but, because, and the like. Connectives only function syntactically; they do not have extralinguistic referents, but rather intralinguistic uses.

Concreta   Objects susceptible to direct observation. OT: ideata.

Confusion   A defect resulting from ambiguity.

Connotation   See: Intension.

Context   Any setting in which a word is used, to be specified as follows: (1) author's context, (2) disciplinary context, (3) field or subfield context, (4) theoretical context.

Context of discovery   The context that precedes the context of validation and is not subject, therefore, to the strictures of the latter. Popper's "conjectures" largely belong to the context of discovery.

Context of validation   The context within which normal science performs. Logic, methodology, and statistical techniques largely apply to the context of validation or of verification, not to the context of discovery. Popper's "refutations" belong to the context of validation.

Contingent   Logically possible, or what is not logically necessary.

Contradiction   The joint assertion of a proposition and its denial. The *law of noncontradiction* is that nothing can both be P and not-P.

Contradictory   Two terms are contradictory if they are mutually exclusive and exhaustive (e.g., the contradictory of blue is not-blue). When two propositions are contradictory, if one is true the other is false, and if one is false the other is true. The principle of the *excluded middle* (see: Excluded middle) applies to contradictories, not to contraries.

Contrary   Two terms are contrary if they are mutually exclusive but not exhaustively so. With respect to contrary propositions, if one is true the other is false, but if one is false the truth-value of the other is indeterminate. ST: opposite, contrasting term.

Cutting-off indeterminacy   A defect of the extension that leaves undecided the inclusion-exclusion of marginal entities.

Declarative definition   A definition that simply declares the meaning that is intended. ST: declaratory definition.

Definiendum   What is to be defined.

Definiens   Whatever serves to define. TM: expression giving the *characteristics* of a concept that follows the symbol of definitional equality.

Defining characteristic   A characteristic or property in the absence of which a word is not applicable: we are unable to decide to what it applies.

Defining properties   The necessary characteristics of a concept (in its definition).

Definition   In natural language, any conveyance of meaning expressed as an equivalence between a *definiendum* and a *definiens*. Ostensive and operational definitions convey meaning, but are not definitions in the sense defined above. Definitions *a contrario* also require a definition of their own. In a formalized or uninterpreted language, definitions do not convey meaning: they determine the notational system. See also: Declarative definition, Denotative definition, Precising definition, *Per genus et differentiam*.

Definition a contrario   A binary definition expressed in the form; "x is the opposite or the contradictory of y." Definitions by contrary or by contradictory are negative: they assert what something *is not*.

Denotata (of a term)   The objects that can be classed under a term.

Denotation   See: Extension. The denotation of a word is the ensemble of things (objects) to which the word applies.

Denotative discrimination   The extensional property that enables us to sort out the membership of a referent. ST: discriminative adequacy, discriminating power.

Denotative definition   Any extensional definition. Vulgarly: definitions intended to "seize the object."

Dimension TM: A characteristic that takes on more than two values (i.e., treated as a variable). Basically, a dimension is unidimensional when its values range across binary outermost opposites. A multidimensional dimension is ill-suited for measurement.

Discriminative adequacy See: Denotative discrimination.

Disjunctive statement A compound proposition that takes the form, "A or B."

Dispositional definition Extensional definitions in which some test is specified as a means of identifying denotata. They apply to dispositional words – such as irritable, soluble, combustible, elastic, habit – which ascribe a tendency or pre-disposition.

Empirical concept Any concept that is amenable, no matter how indirectly, to observations. Thus empirical concepts involve observational terms and *referents*. Contrasted with theoretical terms, logical concepts (e.g., "analytic") and metaphysical concepts (e.g., "absolute being").

Entailed term A term that belongs to the *defining characteristics* of the concept being defined. Not to be confused with associated term.

Entity General name for whatever is. ST: object. Entities are not "things," for the latter are usually conceived, more restrictively, as material substances.

Entry term A term used as the heading (or lemma) in a concept definition.

Equality A relation between terms or sets which is either of *identity* or, more loosely, of *equivalence*. ST: sameness, similarity.

Equivocation Fallacy resulting from *ambiguity*.

Etymology The investigation of earlier or original meanings of words. The etymology of "etymology" conveys that what is discovered is the true meaning.

Evaluative connotation Class of connotations characterized by positive or negative value-loading. Also called "emotive meaning." OT: cognitive meaning.

Explication Carnap's renaming of logical analysis or rational reconstruction. An explication sentence (or an explicative definition) does not simply exhibit the commonly accepted meaning of an expression (concept) but proposes a new and precise meaning for it. Explication aims at reducing the limitations, ambiguities, and inconsistencies of the ordinary usage of terms by propounding a reinterpretation intended to enhance the clarity and precision of their meanings as well as their ability to function in hypotheses and theories with explanatory and predictive force (Hempel). An explicative sentence can thus be contrasted with an *interpretative sentence*.

Extension The referent or referents to which a term applies. ST: denotation.

Falsifiability Possibility of being disproved. See: Verification.

Falsification While a generalization cannot be finally established by any number of supporting instances, it is falsified by counter-instances (e.g., "All swans are white," is falsified by finding one black swan). See: Verification.

Formalization Making the logical structure of a language explicit by replacing descriptive terms with variables (x, y, z). Formalization also involves formation rules and transformation rules. A formalized language is a language (in a metaphorical sense of the term) whose logical structure is explicitly and completely formulated. See: Calculus.

Fuzziness   A defect resulting from undenotativeness.*

Glossary   A dictionary of the terms used in a specified context. Glossaries apply to a specialized language (see: Specialized language).

Heuristic value   A property that applies to the context of discovery rather than to the context of validation. Thus, a heuristic value is not a truth-value (e.g., Weber's ideal types are said to have heuristic value).

Hierarchical classification   A classification (see) whose classes are either successive divisions of a *summum genus* (the all-inclusive kind) or, conversely, successive aggregations from an *infima species* (the lowest, indivisible class). The in-between classes are called *subalterna genera*. Hierarchical or vertical classifications assume transitivity and employ the mode of analysis (and definition) called *per genus proximum et differentiam specificam*. Vulgarly: an ordering in which a genus (the all-inclusive class) is divided into species and subspecies.

Homonymy   A same word for different meanings. In dictionaries *hymonyms* have separate entries while *polysemes* are treated under a single entry.

Ideal type   Heuristic construct that does not reflect frequency or probability of empirical occurrence. When construed as a polar end of a continuum or of a serial order, it coincides with a *polar concept*. When construed as a parameter or model (archetype) an ideal type is also called "pure type."

Indefiniteness   See: Undenotativeness. Etymologically: diffuseness of boundaries.

Indicator   A variable that stands for another factor in order to facilitate its measurement (TM). Indicators help operationalization.

Intension   The ensemble of characteristics of (included in) a concept. Vulgarly: the associations a word has in the mind of its users. ST: connotation. The intension may be extensionally opaque.

Interpretative sentence   A sentence that relates a *definiendum* to the rules of language, thus establishing a "correct meaning." Not to be confused with explicative sentences (see: Explication).

Interpreted language   The same as "natural language" or, more precisely, any meaning-based language. OT: uninterpreted language.

Key term   The designator of a concept.* But see: Entailed term.

Language   See Interpreted language, Artificial language, Formalization. While formalized languages (i.e., constructed logical systems) are frequently referred to as languages, it is more precise to call them calculi (see: Calculus).

Lexical definition   A definition reported in dictionaries. Thus a lexical definition employs a meaning that a word already has. OT: stipulation, stipulative definition.

Lexical field   A set of words in their ordinary usages as studied by linguists. Not to be confused with *semantic field* as defined here: the emphasis of lexical field analysis is not on the thought-molding weight of words.

Lexical primitive   See: Primitive.

Loaded word   A word with strong evaluative connotation, whether positive or negative. OT: neutral word.

Logic The study of the validity of inferences (see: Validity). Thus logic deals with the relationship between premises and conclusion, not with the truth of the premises. Vulgarly: logic applies to the form, not to the substance of arguments.

Logical words Logical constants, namely, the symbols employed in valid deductive argument. Logical words include connectives, quantifiers, and all the notational forms used for logical operations.

Marginal entity indefiniteness A denotative inadequacy bearing on the cut-off points.*

Meaning What is predicated or conveyed by a word or term. Vulgarly: any mental content.

Measure A unit in terms of which quantitative differences applicable to entities or properties can be compared and assigned numerical values.

Measurement Vulgarly: establishing quantities of something.

Membership The relation between a set and its elements. Do not confuse the relation of set-membership with the relation of set-inclusion.

Membership indefiniteness A defect resulting from insufficient denotative discrimination.*

Metaphor A "transferred" meaning.

Minimal definition A definition that includes the defining properties (or characteristics) and excludes the accompanying properties. See: Parsimony.

Model (1) a drastically simplified representation of the real world endowed with strong explanatory power; or (2) an exemplary, paradigmatic, idealized case. Neither are technical meanings.

Necessary characteristic See: Defining characteristic (ST).

Necessary condition In causal explanation a condition in the absence of which an event (effect) cannot occur. A necessary condition is not sufficient for an event to occur or for a thing to exist (see: Sufficient condition).

Neighboring terms See: Associated terms.

Neologism A new word for a new meaning.* Vulgarly: any new word.

Normative statement Statements that are neither factual nor hypothetical. Normative statements can be (1) instrumental, when they establish means-to-end relationships thus expressing a *Zweckrationalität*; or (2) evaluative (*Wertrationalität*). Therefore "normativism" is not the same as "value normativism" (as expressed by value statements). For the latter, see: Evaluative connotation. Normative statements should not be confused with laws. ST: prescriptive statement.

Object concept A concept treated as an object, that is, employed for identifying a discrete object.* Object concepts belong to the logic of *classification*. Not to be confused with empirical concept. OT: property concept.

Object words That class of words that actually denotes material objects (B. Russell). Object words are learned ostensively (see: Ostensive definition). The class of object words is narrower than the class of observable terms.

Objective validity Intersubjective truth-value resulting from two conditions: (1) verifiability by any researcher (observer); (2) having in fact been confirmed (or not disconfirmed) by other observers. Objective validity does not apply to analytic truths or statements.

Open texture   An extensional indefiniteness. Open texture is looser than cut-off indeterminacy.

Operational definition   An extensional definition hinged on measurable properties and leading to measurement operations. More broadly, a definition that establishes the meaning of the definiendum in terms of observable-measurable indicators. Operational definitions involve validity.

Operator   A symbol with no independent meaning. *Existential quantifiers* (to be read: "there exists") and *universal quantifiers* (to be read: "for all") used in combination with a variable are common examples of operators. See: Quantifiers.

Opposites   Pairs of words with contrary or contrasting meanings. An opposite word is an antonym (see: Antonymy). Some opposites are gradable (e.g., wide–narrow, big–small); other opposites are not, for they are members of two-term sets (e.g., alive–dead, married–single). In the latter case to say, for example, that somebody is not alive, married, and so on, is to say that he or she is dead, single, and so forth. In the former case, to say, for example, that something is not big does not necessarily entail that it is small: it may be neither big nor small.

Ordinary language   The natural language in current use. Lexical considerations generally refer to ordinary language. OT: specialized language. See also: Artificial language.

Ostension   The designation of objects by non-verbal means, such as pointing.

Ostensive definition   A definition based on pointing to existents.

Paradigm   In Kuhn's sense, the scientific community's consensus on what constitutes the scientific procedure, and the basic axioms or findings thus resulting. More loosely, a framework that gives organization and direction to scientific investigation. The Platonic sense, which is entirely different, may be rendered by "prototype."

Paradox   TM: a statement whose truth leads to a contradiction, and the truth of whose denial leads to a contradiction (e.g., the paradox of the liar: "this statement is false").

Parsimony (in defining)   A definition that includes only the necessary properties of a concept. See: Minimal definition.

Per genus et differentiam   Aristotle's standard procedure of definition: giving what is common (the *genus*, the kind) and what makes for the difference (*differentia*). For example, in the statement "man is a rational animal," the genus is "animal" and the difference (the specificity) is "rational." See: Hierarchical classification.

Polar concept   An empirical concept construed as a polar extreme on a continuum. See: Ideal type.

Polyseme   Word with many meanings. Most natural language words are polysemes, or polysemic.

Precising definition   A subclass of denotative definitions that specifically addresses the problem of membership indefiniteness, or of membership fuzziness.*

Predicate Term designating a property. Predication: attribution of a property to something.

Primitive Any undefined term. Reference is generally made to (1) the undefined word that exhausts a line of regression, or (2) a look-and-see word, or (3) a lexical primitive (i.e., one of the standard, established dictionary definitions of a word).

Property See: Characteristic. TM: a property is either (1) an attribute of the referent, or (2) a second-order metaconcept for what can be said about a concept.

Property concept A concept treated as a variable possessing more than two ordered values.* OT: object concept (e.g., democratic is a property concept, while democracy is an object concept). Property concepts belong to the logic of *gradation*.

Proposition What a sentence asserts or states. See: Statement. Truth is a property of propositions, not of sentences. Sentences are only meaningless or meaningful (and need not be assertive, i.e., propositions). Different sentences may assert a same proposition. Propositions can be (1) simple (or atomic), or (2) compound (or molecular) depending on whether they do not or do have other propositions as component parts. Among simple propositions, the more important types are the categorical (see: Categorical statement) and the relational (affirming or denying that a relation holds). Instances of compound propositions are the disjunctive and the conditional propositions (see: Disjunctive, Conditional propositions).

Pure science See: Scientific theory.

Quantifiers In natural language, the forms "all" (every), "many," "some" (few), and "none."

Recognitor A discriminable feature of the object world used as symptomatic of some object or class of objects. See: Operational definition. ST: indicator.

Reductio ad absurdum The reduction to absurdity as a method of indirect proof argues that the denial of A (together with accepted propositions B1, B2 . . .) leads to contradiction. The force of the argument resides in using premises that are far better established than the denial of A. The reduction to absurdity is equally a method of indirect disconfirmation.

Referent The real world counterpart of words (i.e., the objects, entities or processes denoted by words). Short form for "extralinguistic referent." Referents pertain to the extension of a concept.

Reliability The extent to which measurements yield, when repeated, similar or confirming results.

Requisite characteristic See: Defining characteristic. ST: necessary characteristic.

Root word An indivisible form which can be written by itself or in various combinations to create derivatives. Usually the "etymon."

Sameness See: Equality.

Scientific theory A theory is scientific when it provides the following: (1) specified concepts, (2) a set of general assumptions, (3) a connection between its theoretical statement and observable phenomena – that is, "testability in principle" (Hempel) or "falsifiability" (Popper). The scientific theory of a science is often called the "pure science," as contrasted to the applied science.

Semantic field   A covarying ensemble of associated and neighboring terms that constitute a *system of terms*. A linguistic system as a whole best displays the systemic property of covariance at its subsystem level (i.e., when subdivided into semantic field units). A semantic field analysis may coincide in extension, but not in intension, with a lexical field analysis: for it is the former, not the latter, that brings out the semantic import (see below).

Semantic import   The interpretative weight of words. See: Semantic projection.

Semantic projection   That words condition the conceiving and perceiving of things. More technically, the interpretative bearing of the connotation on the denotation.

Semantics   The study of language in its meaning function. In Carnap and Tarski, a logical theory of meaning (TM not followed here). Quine breaks down semantics into a theory of reference (bearing on the denotation) and a theory of meaning (bearing on the connotation). This distinction obfuscates the notion of semantic projection. From the latter vantage point, semantics accounts for the *thought-molding* and *thought-slicing* impact of a given linguistic system.

Set   A cluster of items with shared attributes that does not presuppose ordering or sequencing. A set is "fuzzy" if its membership is not clear. A "nul set" is a set with no members. Not to be confused with "string," nor with "class."

Setting   The context, environment, and/or language within which concepts are created and used. See: Context.

Sign   Anything that suggests the existence of something else. If sign is distinguished from "signal," then it is the same as "symbol."

Specialized language   Any language that refines ordinary use with respect to a specific area of inquiry or interest. A specialized or *special language* is still a natural language, characterized, however, by a technical terminology. Not to be confused with artificial language.

Statement   Either what is asserted by a proposition, or a sentence that expresses a proposition. Statement and proposition are often used interchangeably (see: Proposition).

Stem word   Root word (ST).

Stipulation   A definition not found in dictionaries (i.e., not a reportive or lexical definition) proposed for future observance. OT: lexical definition. If the mere selection of one of the lexical meanings is called a stipulation, then almost every definition is stipulative.

Stipulative arbitrariness   A stipulative definition not sustained by *interpretative sentences* and/or proposed without consideration of the semantic field; that is, a definition that unsettles, without resettling, the semantic field to which a term belongs.*

String   A sequence of items. ST: chain. Not to be confused with set.

Substitution test   Substituting a neighboring word (to the one employed by the author of the sentence under inspection) in order to assess whether the substituted word improves the clarity and sharpens the meaning intended by the author.

Sufficient condition In causal explanation, that condition which suffices to bring a thing into existence or to generate an event (effect). Note that different sufficient conditions can lead to the event (i.e., a given sufficient condition is neither exclusive nor exhaustive) (e.g., lack of oxygen is a sufficient condition of death; but death can occur on account of many other conditions).

Surrogate term A term that can be used interchangeably with another (regardless of whether it is a synonym or a near-synonym) in order to avoid pedantic repetition.*

Symmetry A relation is symmetric when it takes the form "if a = b, then b = a." Conversely, a relation can either be asymmetric (e.g., causality), or non-symmetric.

Synonymy A same meaning of (or stipulated for) different words. Synonymy assumes similarity (not identity) of meaning.

Syntactics Study of linguistic signs in relation to each other, without consideration of their meanings. Formalized languages are syntactic.

System Any bounded set whose elements are interdependent with each other.

Tautology Literally, saying the same thing. A tautology is not a logical fallacy and should not be confused with the fallacy of *petitio principii* or circular reasoning.

Term The form used to signify the concept – that is, a word allocated to a concept.* Etymologically, the terminal element (*terminus*) of analysis.

Terminological analysis TM: explication of the meanings of words leading to the selection of appropriate terms for concepts.*

Theoretical term A term made meaningful by (and giving meaning to) the theory to which it belongs (i.e., characterized by a theoretical function). Theoretical terms are often contrasted with "observables," or observational terms. It can also be said that theoretical terms have an intensional, not an extensional, meaning. Examples: system, structure, function, equilibrium, homeostasis.

Theory A body of systematically related generalizations of explanatory value.

To denote To identify the denotata of a concept.

To term To select the term(s) for a concept.*

Truth A property of single statements or propositions (while validity is a property of inferences and arguments).

Unboundedness Lack or insufficiency of boundaries. ST: boundlessness. See: Undenotativeness.

Undenotativeness Defect that pertains to the meaning-to-referent linkage. Specifically, undenotativeness can be of two sorts: (1) unboundedness, or (2) discriminative inadequacy.*

Uninterpreted language A language in which meanings are unassigned. Formalized languages are uninterpreted. See: Formalization, Calculus.

Univocal Unambiguous. A univocal word is a word with only one meaning.

Vagueness In ordinary parlance, any kind of looseness and indeterminacy. TM:

extensional indefiniteness: a word is vague if there are objects (referents) which are neither includable in, nor excludable from, its extension. ST: undenotativeness.

Validation   The process by which scientific theories become accepted. ST: confirmation.

Validity   In logic an argument is valid when its conclusion correctly follows (inferentially) from its premise. A measurement is valid (empirically) if it measures what it purports to measure.

Value(s)   With reference to a variable (see: Variable), the elements over which it ranges. Not to be confused with value connotations and the ethical meaning of the term.

Variable   TM: anything that may take on more than two values, or successive values. However, "sex" is generally called a variable even though it may take only one of two values.

Verification   Testing the empirical validity of assertions, generalizations, laws, and theories. Since the number of supporting instances is indefinite, a process of verification is never final. In practice, therefore, verification is upheld by non-falsification (Popper). See: Falsification.

Word   Any form used in a natural language to convey meaning.

Notes

* Originally published as Giovanni Sartori (1984) "Guidelines for Concept Analysis," in G. Sartori (ed.), *Social Science Concepts: A Systematic Analysis*, Beverly Hills, CA: Sage, Chapter 1.

1   This remains the point no matter how much we stress that "meaning is generally attached not to words in isolation, but to expressions" (Oppenheim 1981: 4). Even so, an expression is meaningless – it can neither be formulated nor understood – unless we know what its words mean in isolation. That meaning is generally "attached to expressions" cannot be construed as an objection to my argument.

2   Even so the sentence context does not suffice, as such, to establish a precise (unequivocal or unambiguous) meaning. For this we need ad hoc sentences, that is, defining sentences. Thus, sentences in general "specify" meanings in the sense that they narrow the total meaning range; they do not specify in the sense of providing a single, well-defined meaning.

3   To call any word – except proper names and syntactic terms – a concept is simply to say that any word involves some degree of abstraction. Yet is "pear" (admittedly, an abstraction) in any way assimilable, for example, to "consensus"? In order not to drown into a Hegelian night, I say the "idea" of pear and the "concept" of consensus.

4   See, for example, Max Black, "Some Troubles with Whorfianism" (1969: 30–35). Black's attack carries to the extremes and exemplifies the a priori rejection of semantics as a disturbance. For a fair discussion, see, in Harry Hoijer (1954), the chapters of Fearing, Hoijer, and Hockett. In conjunction with Whorf, see also Sapir (1921, 1949).

5   For the color example, see Palmer (1981: 70–75). The example of the Eskimos and Aztecs is drawn from Whorf (1956: 216). For the Brazilian counting system, see again Palmer (1981: 70).

6   That translators somehow manage to translate, if imperfectly and at times awkwardly, has no bearing on the point at issue. The polyglot "rethinks" in each of the languages he masters. The monoglot, however, is truly closed into the semantic properties of his language.

7 In common parlance, vagueness is any unclarity or indeterminacy; and even in its technical meaning it is far from established that "vagueness" applies *only* to the referential problem. Kaplan (1964: 65–68) speaks of "internal vagueness." Similarly, Copi (1972: 110–11) uses "vagueness" ambiguously – namely (1) simply to say "clarification of the meaning of a term," and (2) specifically for "borderline cases." But the prevalent usage, followed here, is to restrict vagueness to "extensional vagueness." (See, e.g., Quine 1960: 125–29).

8 Adequacy is the term used for their triangle by Ogden and Richards (1946). "Undenotative" is my coinage that I propose in order to avoid the ambiguity associated with the ordinary meaning of "vagueness."

9 The distinction between connotation and denotation was introduced by John Stuart Mill; the one between intension and extension derives from Frege (whose distinction applied only to proper names and actually was between *Sinn* and *Bedeutung*, often translated as "sense" and "reference") but was generalized by Carnap (1956). For the complexities that are involved, see Lyons (1977: vol. 1, Chapter 7). The intension–extension mode of analysis is currently attacked by the "new theory of reference." (See Schwartz [1977], which brings together contributions of Putnam, Quine, Saul, Kripke, et al.) This new theory basically deals with proper names and "natural kind" terms (i.e., with classes of terms that are largely irrelevant to the social sciences).

10 It will be noted that I do not define the intension in terms of the extension, as most authors do. For example, "The intension of a word consists of the properties a thing must have in order to be in the *extension* of the word" (Salmon 1964: 91, my emphasis). Similarly, "A word connotes each and every characteristic anything must possess to be correctly *denoted* by that word" (Michalos 1969: 388, my emphasis). The two definitions are standard ones, but I find them excessively circular.

11 To exemplify, in this view the denotation of "cow" consists of the individual animals so designated. It may also be said that the denotation of "rodent" is to look at mice, squirrels, rabbits, beavers, porcupines, and so on. All is well so long as reference is made (as is invariably the case) to "things" – names for material objects, natural kinds, and the like – amenable to sense perception, in short, to things that can be identified ostensively. The problem arises when we pass from object-words to what Bertrand Russell called "dictionary words," that is, to all the rest and the most.

12 This definition remains in the second revised edition of 1973, p. 123.

13 Therefore I do not concede that what can be identified ostensively (see the notion of ostensive definition in this glossary) is entirely extralinguistic. As argued in "The semantic import," even sense experience is largely molded – in terms of slicing, when not of semantic projection – by the linguistic system.

14 When an argument is stated in syllogistic form, the taking of a same word in two different meanings enters the list of fallacies under the name of "paralogism."

15 This formulation assumes (with Hempel 1965: 173 fl) that "theoretical terms" whose meaning is established by their function in a theoretical argument are in no way reducible to observational terms. If one assumes, instead, that all concepts can be turned, at least in principle, into empirical (observational) concepts, then "if empirical" is redundant. On the debate concerning the "theoretical–observational" distinction, see Shapere in Achinstein and Barker (1969: 115–31).

16 See John Stuart Mill: "The simplest and most correct notion of a definition is a proposition declaratory of the meaning of a word: namely, either the meaning which it bears in common acceptation, or that which the speaker or writer . . . intends to annex to it" (1898: Book 1, Chapter 8: 86).

17 Similarly, so-called "nominal scales" are not scales at all. Yet, when the item is "scales" authors always begin with nominal scales.

18 Note that "denotative definition," as defined, does not correspond to what is commonly understood by "definition by denotation." The difference follows from our assessment of how the denotation relates to the connotation.

19 I draw the "precising definition" from Copi (1972: 139–40). However, in Copi, a precising definition is a definition that helps decide borderline cases, and actually corresponds to what I call "denotative definition." Since we lack a label for the specific problem of membership indefiniteness, I narrow Copi's meaning to this more specific purpose.

20 I drop at this point the issues of membership fuzziness and of the cut-off point, for they will be taken up in "Undenotativeness (vagueness)."

21 The objection might still be that a symbolic capability is not an observable characteristic. It can be detected, however, by means of indicators. The example must also be subjected to the caveat that any denotative defining must be prefaced by "initial conditions."

22 This is not as restrictive as to imply (as did P. W. Bridgman's original formulation in *The Logic of Modern Physics*, 1927) that an operational definition must specify a testing "operation" (such as the scratch test for defining "harder than"). On the other hand, "operationalism" certainly calls for something more, and more precise, than sheer observability.

23 Many of my omissions are, however, deliberate. For example, what do we gain, as long as we deal with natural languages, by calling a definition "semantic"? This is, at best, a redundancy that impoverishes, in turn, the meaningfulness of "semantics." Also, and furthermore, what is the point in opposing "real" to "verbal" definitions? Is "definition by context" anything else than recommending to infer from a context a definition that is not explicitly given? The standard treatment of definitions in textbooks appears obsolete and needs rethinking.

24 To be sure, we may also have to account for interdisciplinary ambiguities. For example, concepts that lack disciplinary distinctiveness (e.g., structure, culture, alienation) may well have to be reconstructed across disciplines.

25 Let it be added that languages that draw from many sources do have "true synonyms." English disposes of "kingly" (Anglo-Saxon), "royal" (French), and "regal" (Latin), that do mean the same thing. For the same reason, in English "freedom" and "liberty" are synonyms.

26 This is not to detract from the further point, forcefully made by Goodman in "Seven Strictures on Similarity" (1970), that "similarity" is hard to define with any precision.

27 The "sentence game" often loses sight of this difference, thus ending up with dismembering the concept (and my complaint bears on the "game" excesses of the exercise). One can write a 450-page analysis of synonymy (as Arne Naess) in which the conceptual point never comes up, and is indeed drowned in an ocean of synonymity sentences.

28 See Naess (1953: 9, 41, and *passim*). Interpretative sentences are generally contrasted to "explicative sentences" that improve upon the definiendum by refining or supplementing its meaning.

29 My objections to stipulativism are given at the end, in "The fallacy of arbitrariness." Russell (1921: 190) nicely ridicules the stipulativist-conventionalist explanation of language: "We can hardly suppose a parliament of hitherto speechless elders meeting together and agreeing to call a cow a cow and a wolf a wolf."

30 This is a feeble meaning of "explanation." Most logicians require the *explanans* to be a covering law under which the *explanandum* can be subsumed.

31 I first proposed this rule, with reference to the analysis of the concept of ideology, in Sartori (1969: especially 399).

32 "Representative" is not intended technically. In connection with this rule, the objection could be that previously advanced explicit definitions of a concept might not be the best material for a systematic explication of its meaning(s). This suggests a reformulation of Rule 4 in terms of *usage* (in accord with the tenets of ordinary language philosophers), as follows: "In reconstructing a concept, first collect a sample of *usage*." Quite aside from my qualms about ordinary language, for the time being following two routes would be confusing; but this is not to affirm in principle that ordinary usage should be discounted.

33 A good illustration of what happens when no such organizational design is pursued is

Kluckhohn and Kroeber (1952) which leaves us – with respect to the concept of culture – with a wealth of undigestible material.

34 Among the other conditions that must be equal, the obvious one is that the characteristics in question should not be ambiguous. Adding one ambiguous characteristic to another worsens, if anything, boundary indefiniteness.

35 See Zannoni (1978: 1–30). This article well illustrates the method of analysis proposed by the present "Guidelines."

36 The limit (i.e., too many properties) is that we should not obtain empirically empty sets.

37 For "open texture," see Harrison (1972: 128–52). See also Waisman (1952).

38 The classic illustration of this mode of analysis is provided by the so-called Tree of Porphyry. See, for example, Cohen and Nagel (1936: 236).

39 The suggestion was initially outlined in Sartori (1970). But now see Sartori et al. (1975: 17–19, see Chapter 3 of this volume) where a step-by-step illustration is provided by the concept of family.

40 It should be understood that this is so because we are now considering a vertical ordering. See Cohen and Nagel (1936: 33): "When a series of terms is arranged in order of subordination, the extension and intension vary inversely." I say "inversely related," which is a more flexible formulation because Cohen and Nagel themselves immediately issue the caveat that the "law of inverse variation" must not be understood strictly.

41 It is apparent that I am not interested in the ontological or epistemological status of universals. By "universal" I simply intend the upper limit of an abstractive treatment. For the current relevance of the Medieval dispute, see, for example, Quine (1963: 14 fl). Popper discusses more than most contemporary authors the notion of universal (especially 1959).

42 As Popper puts it (1962: 262), "Every scientific language must make use of *genuine universals*, i.e., of words . . . with an indeterminate extension, though perhaps with a reasonably definite intensional 'meaning.'" In my argument, the extension is maximal but not necessarily indeterminate.

43 "Reconstruction" is intended broadly as the complement of "construction," and therefore not in the specific meaning proposed by Oppenheim (1981: 1), for whom to reconstruct concepts is to "provide them with explicative definitions." I do concur, however, with Oppenheim's emphasis on explication.

44 These are the configurations that Wittgenstein addresses with his image of the artichoke and its leaves. When the leaves are peeled off, there remains a common core.

45 For example, descriptive versus evaluative or normative versus non-normative. It is important to underline, in this connection, that a normative statement need not be an evaluative statement. As Max Weber pointed out, a *Zweckrationalität* (rationality of ends) is very different from a *Wertrationalität* (value-rationality) in that the former addresses means-to-ends relationships that can be expressed in the conditional "if-then" form.

46 Feyerabend (1962, *passim*) contends that the meaning of a term is solely a function of the "theory" containing the term. (See the rebuttal of Putnam [1975: Chapter 6]). My scheme (Figures 4.9 and 4.10) suggests how such a contention might be tested. Of course, much depends on which theory is deemed "theory." Feyerabend's reasoning can well leave us with ideologically untouchable sanctuaries.

47 I have given in *The Tower of Babel* (Chapter 3 of this volume) four reasons for this progressive deterioration: the loss of etymological anchorage, the loss of historical anchorage, the loss of the mainstream of discourse, and the "frenzy of novitism."

48 This is the case in principle. In practice, because our semantic fields are all in disarray, it may well happen that by redefining one term the associated ones regain an ordered placement.

49 It can be read, however, as a rule that blocks "stipulative arbitrariness" and thus as an implementation of Rule 3. In this connection, my semantic field rules are illustrative of what is required from "interpretative sentences."

50 As the text implies, my notion of "substitution test" is drawn from Riggs (1975) and is to be credited to him.
51 The distinction between pure and applied science is a standard one in the natural sciences. More specifically, it can be said that "science" includes a "scientific theory" that consists, according to Hempel, of three elements: (1) specified concepts; (2) a set of general assumptions; and (3) a connection between theoretical statements and empirical phenomena, namely, "testability in principle." See Hempel (1965: 150). The "applied science" is not, then, the sheer activity of practical problem solving.
52 Note, however, that specification of necessary characteristics for a term's applicability does not determine its "full meaning" (its intension). For example, "animal is any warmblooded organism" may be a minimal definition of "animal" (as defined), but certainly does not exhaust the characteristics of the concept nor does it imply that no alternative minimal definition can be offered (e.g., "animal is any organism with a backbone").
53 It will not escape notice that reference is made only to necessary, not to "sufficient" characteristics. The latter requirement would involve us in unnecessary, if not also unmanageable, intricacies.
54 In particular, if "concept" is identified with "meaning," it would be contradictory to hold that a concept – that is, a meaning – can have many meanings.
55 This is certainly the case when a concept can be formulated in altogether different fashions. For example, Euclidean geometry can be axiomatized in a number of equivalent ways; and, similarly, the logic of propositions can be presented in equivalent ways that still represent the same concept.
56 Reference is especially made to the late Wittgenstein of the *Philosophical Investigations*. However, it is very dubious whether even the earlier Wittgenstein of the *Tractatus Logico-Philosophicus* of 1921–22 had any interest in or understanding of what science is about.
57 For example, "nobody has yet killed his own successor" is analytically true (i.e., its truthvalue hinges entirely on the definitions of "successor" and "killing"). A successor, in order to be such, must be alive. Hence, he has not been killed and, indeed, must not (by definition) be dead.
58 The importance of this distinction can hardly be exaggerated. It was Reichenbach (1947) who first distinguished between context of discovery and context of justification. However, most authors currently substitute the latter expression with "context of validation" or confirmation.

References

Achinstein, P. and Barker, S.F. (eds.) (1969) *The Legacy of Logical Positivism*, Baltimore: Johns Hopkins Press.

Black, M. (1969) "Some Troubles with Whorfianism," in S. Hook (ed.), *Language and Philosophy*, New York: New York University Press.

Bridgman, P.W. (1927) *The Logic of Modern Physics*, New York: Macmillan.

Carnap, R. (1956) *Meaning and Necessity*, Chicago: University of Chicago Press.

Cassirer, E. (1944) *Essay on Man*, New Haven, CT: Yale University Press.

Cohen, M.R. and Nagel, E. (1936) *An Introduction to Logic and Scientific Method*, London: Routledge and Kegan Paul.

Copi, I.M. (1972) *Introduction to Logic*, New York: Macmillan.

Feyerabend, P.K. (1970) "Against Method: Outline of an Anarchist Theory of Knowledge," in M. Radnerand and S. Winokur (eds.), *Theories and Methods of Physics and Psychology*, Minnesota Studies in the Philosophy of Science, vol. 4, Minnesota: University of Minnesota Press.

Frege, G. (1949) "On Sense and Nominatum," in H. Feigl and W. Sellars (eds.), *Readings in Philosophical Analysis*, New York: Appleton-Century-Crofts.

Hoijer, H. (ed.) (1954) *Language in Culture: Proceedings of a Conference on the Interrelations of Language to Other Aspects of Culture*, Chicago: University of Chicago Press.

Goodman, N. (1970) "Seven Strictures on Similarity," in L. Foster and J.W. Swanson (eds.), *Experience and Theory*, Amherst: University of Massachusetts Press.

Harrison, B. (1972) *Meaning and Structure*, New York: Harper & Row.

Hempel, C.G. (1965) *Aspects of Scientific Explanation*, New York: Free Press.

Hospers, J. (1967) *An Introduction to Philosophical Analysis*, Englewoods Cliffs, NJ: Prentice Hall.

Kaplan, A. (1964) *The Conduct of Inquiry: Methodology for Behavioral Science*, San Francisco: Chandler Publishing Co.

Kluckhohn, C. and Kroeber, A.L. (1952) *Culture: A Critical Review of Concepts and Definitions*, New York: Vintage Books.

Kuhn, T.S. (1962) *The Structure of Scientific Revolutions*, Chicago: University of Chicago Press.

Lyons, J. (1977) *Semantics*, vol. 1, Cambridge: Cambridge University Press.

Merton, R.K. (1958) *Social Theory and Social Structure*, New York: Free Press.

Michalos, A.C. (1969) *Principles of Logic*, Englewood Cliffs, NJ: Prentice Hall.

Mill, J.S. (1898) *System of Logic*, Book I. London.

Morris, C.W. (1946) *Signs, Language, and Behavior*, New York: Prentice Hall.

Naess, A. (1953) *Interpretation and Preciseness*, Oslo: Jacob Dybwad.

Ogden, C.K. and Richards, I.A. (1946) *The Meaning of Meaning*, New York: Harcourt Brace Jovanovitch.

Oppenheim, F. (1981) *Political Concepts: A Reconstruction*, Chicago: University of Chicago Press.

Palmer, F.R. (1981) *Semantics*, Cambridge: Cambridge University Press.

Popper, K. (1959) *Logic of Scientific Discovery*, London: Hutchinson.

Popper, K. (1962) *Conjectures and Refutations*, New York: Basic Books.

Putnam, H. (1975) *Mind, Language and Reality*, vol. 2, Cambridge: Cambridge University Press.

Quine, W.V. (1960) *Word and Object*, New York: Wiley.

Quine, W.V. (1963) *From a Logical Point of View*, New York: Harper & Row.

Riggs, F. (1975) "The Definition of Concepts," in G. Sartori, F. Riggs and H. Teune (eds.), *The Tower of Babel: On the Definition and Analysis of Concepts in the Social Sciences*, Pittsburgh: International Studies Association, Occasional Paper 6.

Russell, B. (1921) *The Analysis of Mind*, London: Allen and Unwin.

Russell, B. (1948) *Human Knowledge*, New York: Simon and Schuster.

Salmon, W.C. (1964) *Logic*, New York: Prentice Hall.

Sapir, E. (1921) *Language: An Introduction to the Study of Speech*, New York: Harcourt.

Sapir, E. (1949) *Selected Writings in Language, Culture, and Personality*, Berkeley: University of California Press.

Sartori, G. (1969) "Politics, Ideology, and Belief Systems," *American Political Science Review* (June): 398–411.

Sartori, G. (1970) "Concept Misformation in Comparative Politics," *American Political Science Review* 64 (4): 1033–53.

Sartori, G. (1979) *La Politica: Logica e Metodo in Scienze Sociali*, Milano: SugarCo.

Sartori, G., Riggs, F.W. and Teune, H. (eds.), (1975) *Tower of Babel: On the Definition of*

Concepts in the Social Sciences, Pittsburgh: International Studies Association, Occasional Paper 6.

Schwartz, S.P. (ed.) (1977) *Naming, Necessity, and Natural Kinds*, Ithaca, NY: Cornell University Press.

Shapere, D. (1969) "Notes Toward a Post-positivistic Interpretation of Science," in P. Achinstein and S.F. Barker (eds.), *The Legacy of Logical Positivism*, Baltimore, MD: Johns Hopkins University Press.

Taylor, C. (1971) "Interpretation and the Sciences of Man," *Review of Metaphysics* 25: 24.

Waisman, F. (1952) "Verifiability," in A. Flew (ed.), *Logic and Language*, Oxford: Blackwell.

Whorf, B.L. (1956) *Language, Thought, and Reality*, Cambridge, MA: MIT Press.

Wittgenstein, L. (1922) *Tractatus Logico-Philosophicus*, London: Routledge and Kegan Paul.

Wittgenstein, L. (1953) *Philosophical Investigations*, New York: Macmillan.

Zannoni, P. (1978) "The Concept of Elite," *European Journal of Political Research* 6 (March): 1–30.

5   Comparing and miscomparing

Giovanni Sartori

In the early 1950s, when Roy Macridis blasted the traditional comparative politics of the time, his first and major charge was that it was "essentially non-comparative" (1953, 1955). Much, or indeed more of the same, can be said as of 1991, since the field (in the United States) defines itself as studying "other countries," generally just one. Thus, a scholar who studies only American presidents is an Americanist, whereas a scholar who studies only French presidents is a comparativist. Do not ask me how this makes sense – it does not.[1] The fact remains that a field called comparative politics is densely populated by non-comparativists, by scholars who have no interest, no notion, no training in comparing. Thus, the preliminary point must be to establish the distinctiveness of comparative politics as a field characterized by a method.[2]

It is often held that comparisons can be "implicit" and/or that the scientific approach per se is inherently comparative. I grant that a scholar *can be* implicitly comparative without comparing – that is, provided that the one-country or one-unit study *is* embedded in a comparative context. But how often is this really the case?[3] I equally grant that, in some sense, the scientific method itself assumes a comparing; but this is a long shot. The short of the matter is that *if* a scholar is implicitly (though not unwittingly) comparative, this doubtlessly makes him or her a better scholar. But the difference between the implicit and the explicit cannot be slighted to the point of automatically making the "unconscious comparativist" a comparativist. On this criterion, there has never been a behavioral revolution because students of politics have always implicitly observed behavior. There has never been a quantitative revolution because even the simpletons of the past said much, little, greater, lesser, and were thus, implicitly, quantitativists. This absurdity is attested by the blatant fact that under the "inevitably comparative" cover-up, the social sciences are actually inundated with parochial yardsticks and hypotheses that would flounder in a second if ever exposed to comparative checking.

Why compare?

Indeed, comparative *checking*. Have I not already answered my first question, namely, *Why compare?* While I am surely not the first to assert that comparisons *control* – they control (verify or falsify) whether generalizations hold across the cases to which they apply – nonetheless, this is a seemingly forgotten answer. According to Przeworski, a "consensus exists that comparative research consists *not of comparing but of explaining*. The general purpose of cross-national research is to understand . . ." (1987: 35, my emphasis). Przeworski appears to be right about the current consensus. In similar fashion, Ragin (1987: 6) holds that comparative knowledge "provides the key to understanding, explaining and interpreting," and Mayer (1989: 12) "redefines" (in his title) comparative politics as a field whose goal is "the building of empirically falsifiable, explanatory theory." Well, one can hardly disagree with an intent described as understanding and explaining; for all knowledge, none excluded, is aimed at understanding and all knowledge seeks to explain.[4] But then, why compare? What is the specific reason for being of a comparative route to knowledge? What are comparisons *for*? Against the loss of purpose that appears by now to dominate the field, let a purpose be forcefully reinstated, namely, and to repeat, that *comparing is controlling*. To be sure, one may engage in comparative work for any number of reasons, but *the* reason is control.[5]

Take the statement, "Revolutions are caused by relative deprivation"; or the statement, "Presidential systems are conducive to effective government, while parliamentary systems result in feeble government." True or false? How do we know? We know by looking around – that is, by comparative checking. Granted, comparative control is but *one* method of control. It is not even a strong one. Surely experimental controls and, presumably, statistical controls are more powerful "controllers."[6] But the experimental method has limited applicability in the social sciences, and the statistical one requires many cases.[7] We are often faced, instead, with the "many variables, small N" problem, as Lijphart (1971: 686) felicitously encapsulates it; and when this is the case our best option is to have recourse to the comparative method of control.[8] *The* reason for comparing is thus, in its basic simplicity, a compelling one. To this reason one may sensibly add that comparing is "learning" from the experience of others and, conversely, that he who knows only one country knows none. Quite so.

What is comparable?

The second question is, *What is comparable?* We frequently argue that apples and pears are "incomparable"; but the counterargument inevitably is: how do we know unless we compare them? Actually, with pears and apples, the issue is easily solved. But are stones and monkeys comparable? We may still reply that in order to declare them "incomparables" we have, if for only one second, compared them. Nonetheless, if the entities[9] being compared have nothing in common, there is nothing more to be said, and this is what we mean when we declare that stones and monkeys are not comparable: the comparison is of no interest, it ends where it begins. Returning to pears and apples; are they comparable or not? Yes, they are comparable with respect to some of their properties, i.e., the properties they share, and noncomparable with respect to the properties that they do not share. Thus, pears and apples are comparable as fruits, as things that can be eaten, as entities that grow on trees; but incomparable, e.g., in their respective shapes. Making the point in general, the question always is: *comparable with respect to which properties or characteristics*, and incomparable (i.e., too dissimilar) with respect to which other properties or characteristics?

It will be appreciated that the foregoing establishes that to compare is both to assimilate and to differentiate *to a point*. If two entities are similar in everything, in all their characteristics, then they are the same entity, and that is that. If, on the other hand, two entities are different in every respect, then their comparison is nonsensical, and again that is that. The comparisons in which we sensibly and actually engage are thus the ones between entities whose attributes are in part shared (similar) and in part non-shared (and thus, we say, incomparable).

Does the above simply push the problem back to the Osgood question, namely, "When is the same really the same?" and, conversely, "When is different really different?" (1967: 7). Many authors have been struggling without avail with this question, and much research has foundered on these reefs. Yet the question does have a sound answer if we remember that it is answered by classifications and/or by the *per genus et differentiam* mode of analysis. To classify is to order a given universe into classes that are mutually exclusive and jointly exhaustive. Hence, classifications do establish what is same and what is not. "Same" brings together whatever falls into a given class; "different" is what falls under other classes.[10] Let it also be underscored that classes do not impute "real sameness," but *similarity*. The objects that fall into a same class are more similar among themselves – with respect to the criterion of the sorting – than to the objects that fall into other classes. But this leaves us with highly flexible degrees of similarity.

As a rule of thumb, the smaller the number of classes yielded by a classification, the higher its intra-class variation (its classes incorporate, so to speak, very different sames). Conversely, the greater the number of the classes, the lesser the intra-class variance. If we divide the world just into monarchies and republics, we have two classes that are, if anything, impossibly large and excessively varied. Still, the example shows that there is no merit in the objection that to classify is to freeze sameness. Any class, no matter how minute, allows for intra-class variations (at least of degree); and it is up to the classifier to decide how much his classes are to be inclusive (broad) or discriminating (narrow).

The gist is – let it be reiterated – that what is comparable is established by putting the question in its proper form, which is: comparable *in which respect?* Under this formulation, pears and apples are, in a number of respects (properties), comparable. So are, but less so, men and gorillas (they are, e.g., both erect animals with *prensilis* hands); and so are, at the limit, even men and whales (both are mammals, and neither can breathe under water). But, of course, the incomparables grow as we pass from the first to the third example. When and how is it, then, that we go wrong? I do not claim that the only way of playing the comparative game without error is to rely on classificatory orderings. However, the route along which much of the profession has chosen to embark in the last twenty years or so is clearly unsafe and easily conducive to shipwreck. I call it the cat-dog route and make it into a story (I hope an amusing one).

The cat-dog

Mr. Doe is ready for his dissertation, but he must be original and must have, he is insistently told by his advisers, a hypothesis. His subject is the cat-dog (one cannot be original, nowadays, just with cats or just with dogs), and his hypothesis, after much prodding, is that all cat-dogs emit the sound "bow wow." The adviser says, "Interesting," and a foundation gives him $100,000 for worldwide research. Three years later, Mr. Doe shows up in great dismay and admits that many cat-dogs do emit the sound "bow wow," but many do not – the hypothesis is disconfirmed. "However," he says, "I now have another hypothesis: all cat-dogs emit the noise 'meow meow.'" Another three years go by, another $100,000 are dutifully spent in researching. Yet, once again, the hypothesis is not sustained: many cat-dogs do emit the noise "meow meow" but many do not. In deep despair, Mr. Doe visits the oracle of Delphi at dusk. On that day, she had grown tired of making up sibylline responses. "My friend," the oracle says, "to you I shall speak the simple truth, which simply is that the cat-dog *does not exist*." End of story, and back to non-fiction.

How does the cat-dog come about? It is fathered, I submit, by four mutually sustaining sources: (1) parochialism, (2) misclassification, (3) degreeism, and (4) conceptual stretching.

Parochialism refers, here, to single-country studies *in vacuo*, that purely and simply ignore the categories established by general theories and/or by comparative frameworks of analysis, and thereby unceasingly invent, on the spur of the moment, an ad hoc, self-tailored terminology. For example, the wording of the title of a recent article by Sundquist (1988) deals with "coalition government in the United States." Now, throughout the world, "coalition government" stands for parliamentary systems (not American-type presidential systems) in which governments are voted into office and supported by parliaments, and happen not to be single-party governments. Not one of these characteristics obtains in what Sundquist calls coalition government. Thus, a cat-dog (or, worse, a dog-bat) is born; and as soon as the misnomer is entered into our computers, it is bound to mess up whatever is correctly known of coalition governments (proper).

Misclassification and degreeism

In the example above, a cat-dog results from a mislabeling, which results in turn from parochialism. A second source is misclassification – pseudo-classes. Take the one-party category in the literature on political parties, a huge basket that has long included: (1) the so-called one-party states in the United States, Japan, and, off and on, Sweden, Norway, and India; (2) Mexico; and (3) the Soviet Union, China, and Eastern European countries. The above collapses into three utterly different animals and thus is, I submit, a cat-dog-bat.[11] Suppose now that we wish to explain what causes unipartism. Huntington suggests that, "the social origins of one-party systems are to be found . . . in bifurcation." That is to say, "one-party systems . . . tend to be the product of either the cumulation of cleavages . . . or the ascendancy in importance of one line of cleavage over the others" (Huntington and More 1970: 11). Right? Wrong? We shall never find out. Neither his hypothesis nor any other will ever pass the test of the cat-dog-bat, for no generalization can conceivably hold up under the joint assaults of such a three-headed monster. What might apply to cats will apply only in part to dogs, and in almost no respect whatsoever to bats (and vice versa). One may wonder why, here, the culprit is misclassification. Well, because classifications are orderings derived from a single criterion. In the case in point, under a correct classificatory treatment, "one" will include only the polities in which "second" (more than one) parties neither exist nor are permitted to exist. Under a classificatory treatment, therefore, the United States, Japan, India, etc., could not possibly fall into the one-party box. But under a pseudo-class, anything goes.

A third producer of cat-dogs and further – in increasing order of teratological messiness – of dog-bats and even fish-birds is, I have suggested, "degreeism." By this I mean the abuse (uncritical use) of the maxim that differences in kind are best conceived as differences of degree, and that dichotomous treatments are invariably best replaced by continuous ones. To exemplify, under a continuous or continuum-based treatment, democracy cannot be separated from non-democracy. Rather, democracy is a property that to some (different) degree can be predicated of all political systems and, conversely, non-democracy is always more or less present in any polity. We may thus obtain a worldwide continuum ranging, say, from 80 percent democracies, to semi-democracies, to 80 percent non-democracies, whose cut-off points are stipulated arbitrarily and can, therefore, be moved around at whim. This is wonderful, for the exceptions that might cripple a hypothesis generally lie in the vicinity of the cutting points. Thus, in the continuous treatment, the exceptions (disconfirmations) can simply be made to disappear by cutting a continuum at astutely doctored points. Along this route we obtain, then, the Cheshire cat-dog – it appears, grins at us, and vanishes before we catch it.

Concept stretching

Fourthly, comparative futility and fallacies simply and generally result from definitional sloppiness and "conceptual stretching" (Sartori 1970). Take *constitution*. If the term is stretched to mean "any state form," then the generalization "constitutions obstruct tyranny" would be crushingly disconfirmed (while it would be confirmed under a narrower meaning). Take *pluralism*. If all societies are declared, in some sense, pluralistic, then the generalization "pluralism falls and stands with democracy" no longer holds. Another good example is *mobilization*. If the concept is stretched to the point of including both self-motion (participation as a voluntary act) and its obverse – namely, hetero-motion, being coerced into motion (mobilization proper) – then not only do we have a perfect cat-dog, but we may also end up with a cat-dog fight in which the two components eat up each other. *Ideology* would be a further excellent instance of a concept deprived of all heuristic validity, let alone testability, by having been stretched to a point of meaninglessness. As currently used and abused, the word ideology never ceases to apply (it has no opposite), everything is ideology, and thus a worthy tool of analysis is turned – following up on the dog-cat imagery – into zoology in its entirety.

It may look as though I have already moved from the question, *What is comparable?* to the question, *How compare?* Even so, a number of method-specific issues still lie ahead.

Compare how?

There are many possible ways of conceiving the basic, general strategy of scientific inquiry. My favorite is the one outlined by Smelser. The initial picture of any phenomenon that a social scientist attempts to explain, he writes, "is one of a *multiplicity* of conditions, a *compounding* of their influences on what is to be explained (the dependent variable) and an *indeterminacy* regarding the effect of any one condition or several conditions in combination." In order to reduce the number of conditions, isolate them, and specify their role, the investigator is required (1) to organize the conditions into independent, intervening, and dependent variables, and (2) to treat some causal conditions as *parameters*, parametric constants, or givens (as when we invoke the *ceteris paribus* clause) that are assumed not to vary, while treating other conditions as *operative variables* that are instead allowed to vary in order to assess their influence upon the dependent variable(s) (1976: 152–54). To be sure, no variable is inherently independent or dependent, and "what is treated as a parameter in one investigation may become the operative variable in another" (154).[12]

Another general point bears on research designs. By and large, "at times comparativists will emphasize similarities, at times differences. They will tend to look for differences in contexts that are roughly similar, or . . . will try to find analogies in contrasting political systems" (Dogan and Pelassy 1984: 127). But shifts in emphasis can also become distinct research methodologies. Most comparativists adopt a "most similar system" design; but as Przeworski and Teune point out, one can also abide by a "most different system" design (1970: 31ff). In the most similar system strategy, the researcher brings together systems that are as similar as possible in as many features (properties) as possible, thus allowing a large number of variables to be ignored under the assumption that they are equal. Simply put, a most similar strategy (as with area studies, Anglo-American countries, and the like) assumes that the factors that are common to relatively homogeneous countries are irrelevant in explaining their differences. The recommendation thus is: choose entities that are similar, if possible, in all variables, with the exception of the phenomenon to be investigated. Sure. But the reverse way of attacking the problem is to choose the most different systems – that is, systems that differ as much as possible but that do not differ on the phenomenon under investigation. In the example of Przeworski and Teune, if rates of suicide are the same among the Zuni, the Swedes, and the Russians (utterly different systems), then systemic factors are irrelevant for the explanation of suicide can be disregarded (35). Again, fine.[13]

Rules and exceptions

Entering more troubled waters, an issue that recurs without convincing answers is when and to what extent exceptions kill a rule – that is to say, law-like generalizations endowed with explanatory power. Of course, if we assume that a law is "deterministic," just one exception suffices to kill it. But far more often than not, we declare our law-like generalizations "probabilistic," and this appears to let us off the hook. Does it? Note, first, that the argument is not reserved for statistical laws, for which it is impeccable, but extended to any law-like explanation. If so, what does probabilistic mean when no mathematical power is attached to the notion? I believe it can only mean that we are dealing with "tendency laws" with respect to which one or few exceptions do not entail rejection. Even so, exceptions are disconfirming; but it is too easy to leave the point at that.

Assume that our laws are given the *if-then* form, a formulation conducive to condition analysis. Assume further that "if" does not stand for sufficient, but rather for necessary conditions without which a law does not apply. Thus, the spelling out of necessary conditions specifies when a law is, or is not, applicable; and the addition of further necessary conditions restricts the ambit of its applicability. For the issue at hand, this means that exceptions are handled (reduced) by limiting the range of application of a rule on the basis of its necessary conditions. For instance, Galileo's law of falling bodies was bound to be experimentally disconfirmed unless the necessary condition "falling in a vacuum" was entered. There is, however, another way of handling the problem, which is to reformulate a law such that it incorporates its exceptions.[14] And it is only when both strategies have been pursued to their reasonable point of exhaustion that a rule may be retained (if at a low level of confidence) by explaining away its exceptions on ad hoc grounds.[15] But it is impermissible, I submit, to declare a law "deterministic . . . with the exceptions noted" (Riker 1982: 761). This statement, as stated, compounds two logical errors.

The case study

Another unsettled issue bears on how case studies – especially of the "heuristic" and the "crucial" variety[16] – relate to the comparative method. I must insist that as a "one-case" investigation, the case study cannot be subsumed under the comparative *method* (though it may have comparative *merit*). On the other hand, comparison and case study can well be mutually reinforcing and complementary undertakings. My sense is that for the comparativist, case studies are most valuable as hypothesis-generating inquiries. They cannot confirm a generalization (one confirmation adds confidence, but cannot add up to a confirming test), and they can only disconfirm a regularity to a limited degree. But heuristic case studies do provide an ideal – perhaps the best – soil for the conceiving of generalizations. If so, however, case studies are, first and foremost, part and parcel of theory-building (as Eckstein underscores), not of theory-controlling.[17]

Incommensurability

We are ready for the most crucial and, at the same time, most unsettled issue of the lot. Let us go back, in order to confront it squarely, to the knock-down question: is the comparative enterprise at all possible? There have been all along many ways of formulating this fundamental objection. The more recent one rallies the negators under the banner of a so-called "incommensurability of concepts." In my understanding, incommensurable basically conveys that we have no measure, or no common measure, for something. If so, what I have been saying is hardly affected by an incommensurability indictment. However, "incommensurability" is currently brandished in a strong sense that implies that all our concepts are context-embedded to the point of being inescapably idiosyncratic.[18] This is an overkill; if anything, concepts are generalizations in disguise, mental containers that amalgamate an endless flow of discrete perceptions and conceptions.

But to dismiss incommensurability in its extreme claim is not to dismiss the one-century-old distinction, put forward by Rickert and Dilthey, between idiographic and nomothetic sciences. In their understanding (which preceded the *Annales* school), historians addressed the unique, thus coming in on the side of what we call a configurative, context-embedded focus. Conversely, the natural sciences were nomothetic, sought laws, and thus dissolved singularity into generality. Here, then, we do not have inescapable prisons of closed incommensurables, but an alternative that allows for tradeoffs between gains and losses. On balance, case studies sacrifice generality to depth and thickness of understanding, indeed to *Verstehen*: one knows more and better about less (less in extension). Conversely, comparative studies sacrifice understanding-in-context – and of context – to inclusiveness: one knows less about more.

Is there no way of bridging this gap? In theory, that is, methodologically speaking, we do have to choose between alternative strategies of inquiry. In practice – that is, in our actual proceedings – the comparativist is required to draw on the information provided by single-country, configurative studies. Conversely, the single-country specialist who ignores comparative findings harms his own endeavor.

Take, to illustrate, the topic of corruption. To the contextualist, corruption in, say, Egypt is only corruption in Egypt and is not, furthermore, corruption at all, since "paying for a service" is not perceived as Westerners perceive it, i.e., as an illicit and harmful social practice. Right. The finding of the comparativist will be, instead, that corruption is "normal" (and quasi-universal) in the Middle East, Asia, and Africa; "endemic," though deprecated, in Latin America and other parts of the world; and counteracted with some (different) modicum of success in, say, some twenty to thirty Western-type countries. Wrong? No, because his point is to assess the extent to which, across the world, bureaucrats, politicians, and eventually judges provide their services on the basis of payments or gifts. The context-ignorant comparativist is likely to be wrong, however, in the interpretation and, in its wake, in the explanation. What he observes – his common denominator – is *a particular class of exchanges*, not corruption as bribery, not the subclass "illicit exchanges." Should we leave this at saying that the contextualist and the comparativist both discover half-truths? Certainly not. But we now need a theoretical framework that accommodates the two halves. In such a framework, the general category would be exchange, its subsets "economic" versus "extra-economic" exchanges, and the explanation (leading, in its refinements, to a causal argument) might roughly be that extra-economic exchanges become dysfunctional, illicit, and morally wicked when polities reach the stage of structural differentiation that provides – in Max Weber's terminology – for a "rational-legal" bureaucracy. It is only when a civil service is paid for by the state (i.e., by tax revenues), only when judges become civil servants (on a payroll), and when, in turn, politics is no longer conceived as a wealth-making resource, that the citizen comes to expect services in exchange for nothing and that corruption and bribery are perceived as wrongdoings. Note, incidentally, that this framework not only endows the comparativist with the amount of contextual understanding that he needs; it also suggests that the Egypt-only specialist might be wrong in overstressing Egypt's uniqueness.

Individualizing vs. generalizing

The methodological point remains, to be sure, that we *are* confronted with an alternative between individualizing and generalizing. Even so, the alternative is not intractable and bridges do exist that help us to switch from generalization to context, and vice versa. In a much quoted passage, Sidney Verba makes this convergence appear as a self-defeating sort of vortex, as an entanglement that ends in strangulation (of comparative politics):

> To be comparative, we are told, we must look for generalizations or covering laws that apply to all cases of a particular type. . . . But where are the general laws? Generalizations fade when we look at the particular cases. We add intervening variable after intervening variable. Since the cases are few in number, we end with an explanation tailored to each case. The result begins to sound quite idiographic or configurative. . . . As we bring more and more variables back into our analysis in order to arrive at any generalizations that hold up across a series of political systems, we bring back so much that we have a "unique" case in its configurative whole.
>
> (1967: 113)

The foregoing may be a truthful account of how we have been messing things up, but should not be taken as a recipe for making headway. "Where are the general laws?" Well, nowhere – for even if we were capable of formulating them (and we are not: see Sartori 1986) the cat-dog would kill them. "Adding intervening variable after intervening variable" certainly is a wrong way of proceeding. My suggestion has long been (Sartori 1970: 1040–45, 1984: 44–46; Sartori et al. 1975: 16–19) that an orderly way – indeed, method – of relating universals to particulars is to organize our categories along a *ladder of abstraction* whose basic rule of transformation (upward aggregation and, conversely, downward specification) is that the connotation (intension) and denotation (extension) of concepts are inversely related. Thus, in order to make a concept more general, viz. of increasing its traveling capability, we must reduce its characteristics or properties. Conversely, in order to make a concept more specific (contextually adequate), we must increase its properties or characteristics. As I was saying, the problem is not intractable,[19] but some routes are more difficult to travel than others. The one that I propose admittedly requires painstaking thinking, while it is infinitely easier to behead problems by invoking incommensurability or by letting computers do our work while we relax.

Conclusions

Vis-à-vis the high hopes of three decades ago, comparative politics is, to say the least, a disappointment. In the early 1960s, the survey of Somit and Tanenhaus (1964: 55–57) indicated that comparative politics was seen as the field in which "most significant work was being done." But only a few years later, Verba asked himself, "Why has there been so much movement and so little movement forward?" (1967: 113). In part, he replied, "the answer is in the toughness of the problem" (ibid.). Quite. The other part of the answer is, however, that a discipline without logical, methodological, and linguistic *discipline* cannot solve, but only aggravate problems for itself.

In the last forty years or so, we have enjoyed moving from one "revolution" to another: behavioral, paradigmatic, "critical," post-positivist, hermeneutic, and so on. But revolutions (in science) just leave us with a new beginning – they have to be followed up and made to bear fruits. We have, instead, just allowed them to fade away, as ever new beginnings hold ever new promises which remain, in turn, ever unfulfilled. In the process the simple basics that I have been addressing in this essay have gotten lost. David Collier (1991) has provided an assessment of the issues of comparative method debated in the last twenty years. Since Collier's coverage is excellent, it is highly telling that the control purpose of comparing is nowhere covered. Yes, our sophistication has grown – but at the expense of an increasingly missing core. As is shown by growing numbers of comparativists (in name) who never compare anything, not even "implicitly," thus forsaking standardized labels, common yardsticks, and shared parameters. Let us squarely face it: normal science is not doing well. A field defined by its method – comparing – cannot prosper without a core method. My critique does not imply, to be sure, that good, even excellent comparative work is no longer under way. But even the current good comparative work underachieves on account of our having lost sight of what comparing *is for*, distinctively *for*.

Notes

* Originally published as Giovanni Sartori (1991) "Comparing and Miscomparing," *Journal of Theoretical Politics* 3 (3): 243–57.

1 As Sigelman and Gadbois correctly put it, "Comparison presupposes multiple objects of analysis . . . one compares something to or with something else" (1983: 281).

2 Indeed, comparative politics is the one field of political science that defines itself by "a methodological instead of substantive label" (Lijphart 1971: 682). Similarly, in Holt and Turner (1970: 5), "the common-sense meaning of the term comparative . . . refers to a method of study and not to a body of substantive knowledge."

3 It is not often the case, as one can easily infer from skimming the bibliographies. Most single-nation studies plainly and wholeheartedly ignore the comparative frameworks and literature that bear on their topics.

4 Note that even "explanation" appears too strong a requirement to Cantori. In his appraisal, "comparative politics is more inclined towards interpretation than explanation," the difference between the two being that explanation "seeks to *demonstrate* the validity of its conclusion," whereas interpretation "seeks to *convince* only by means of persuasion" (Cantori and Ziegler 1988: 418).

5 It should be understood that the point bears on the normal science. In authors of the stature of Tocqueville, Durkheim, or Max Weber, the comparative component of their work is part and parcel of the richness of their thinking. As all my examples indicate, I am not speaking to "grand schemes" but to the single generalizations (causal-like hypotheses) that authors would "normally" formulate in pursuing their subject matter.

6 I say "presumably" to account for the counterarguments of Frendreis (1983: 258), and especially of Ragin (1987: 15–16), who contends that "the comparative method is superior to the statistical method in several important respects."

7 Lijphart and Smelser take a different view as to whether the experimental statistical and comparative methods are distinct methods (Lijphart), or simply different implementations of a same comparative logic (Smelser 1976: 158). Since the methods in question are not equivalent, in my opinion their distinctiveness matters more than their similarity.

8 Of course, in some instances one may statistically control both across a relatively small and a relatively large number of cases. Let the hypothesis be: party cohesion is a direct function of the degree of inter-party competition (and, thus, the lesser the competition, the higher the degree of infra-party fractionism). Here, comparative checking will help refine the hypothesis, so that a statistical control may subsequently become correctly applicable.

9 Entity stands here for whole systems, sub-systemic "segments" (vigorously upheld by LaPalombara 1970: 123ff), processes, or even, at the limit, for a single property or characteristic of a universe.

10 The point is made by Kalleberg (1966: 77–78) as follows: "Truly comparative concepts . . . can only be developed after classification has been completed. Classification is a matter of 'either-or'; comparison is a matter of more or less." I concur up until the last sentence. But why must comparisons be a matter of more-or-less? Kalleberg may have in mind, here, intra-class (not inter-class) comparing.

11 To specify, the first group of countries are predominant party systems that belong to a competitive setting (Sartori 1976; 192–201); Mexico is a hegemonic party polity that "licenses" a limited competition (230–38); and the third group is (was) one-party proper, in that it impedes competition and any other party (221–30).

12 While I quote from Smelser's more recent writing, one should also look into Smelser (1966 and 1967, *passim*).

13 It is open to question whether the most different systems design differs from the most similar one, in that the former consists of multilevel analysis and must observe "behavior at a level lower than that of systems" (as its proponents hold, p. 34). The point remains that seeking contrast and seeking similarity are different approaches.

14 Both strategies are discussed and illustrated at some length in Sartori (1986: 48–50 and *passim*). Take the "rule" that says: "a plurality system will produce . . . a two-party system . . . under two conditions: first, when the party system is structured, and, second, if the electorate which is refractory to whatever pressure of the electoral system happens to be dispersed in below-plurality proportions throughout the constituencies" (1986: 59).

Here, the first condition enters a necessary condition, and the second one actually incorporates in the law the exceptions resulting from above-plurality or above quotient distributions of incoercible minorities.

15 My argument is confined to "rule disconfirmation." Generally, and in principle, a theory T is falsified and, thus, rejected "if and only if another theory, T', has been proposed with the following characteristics: (1) T' has excess empirical content over T . . ., (2) T' explains the previous success of T . . . and (3) some of the excess content of T' is corroborated" (Lakatos 1970: 116).

16 These are the labels employed by Eckstein (1975: 80ff). Lijphart (1971: 691–93) also discusses the various uses and types of case studies. By combining the wordings of the two authors, one can distinguish among the following five kinds of case study: (1) configurative-idiographic (Eckstein), (2) interpretative (Lijphart), (3) hypothesis-generating (Lijphart), (4) crucial (Eckstein), that is, theory-confirming or disconfirming (Lijphart), and (5) deviant (Lijphart). An outstanding instance of the latter is Lipset et al.'s *Union Democracy* (1956), in which the International Typographical Union is systematically studied as a "deviation" from Michels's iron law of oligarchy.

17 Note that my distinction between case study and comparison does not imply in the least that the latter is a superior form of inquiry. If, as Eckstein (1975: 88) holds, "The quintessential end of theorizing is to arrive at *statements of regularity*," then the distinctive claim of the comparative method is not the discovery of "rulefulness" but its testing. There are many paths, not only the comparative one, that lead to discovery of law-like regularities.

18 This extreme view is drawn from Feyerabend (1975), whose epistemological stance is that: (1) theory determines concepts, and (2) data themselves are a function of theory, so that data described in terms of theory A cannot be "compared" to data stated in terms of theory B. For a rebuttal to which I subscribe, see Lane (1987).

19 Even so, it cannot be handled, I believe, by assuming, as Przeworski and Teune (1970: 12) do, that "most problems of uniqueness versus universality can be redefined as problems of measurement."

References

Cantori, J.L. and Ziegler, A.H. (eds.) (1988) *Comparative Politics in the Post-behavioral Era*, Boulder, CO: Lynne Rienner.

Collier, D. (1991) "The Comparative Method: Two Decades of Change," in D.A. Rustow and K.P. Erickson (eds.), *Comparative Political Dynamics: Global Research Perspectives*, New York: Harper & Row.

Dogan, M. and Pelassy, D. (1984) *How to Compare Nations: Strategies in Comparative Politics*, Chatham: Chatham House.

Eckstein, H. (1975) "Case Study and Theory in Political Science," in F.I. Greenstein and N.W. Polsby (eds.), *Handbook of Political Science*, vol. 7, Chapter 3, Reading, MA: Addison-Wesley.

Feyerabend, P. (1975) *Against Method*, London: Verso.

Frendreis, J.P. (1983) "Explanation of Variation and Detection of Covariation: The Purpose and Logic of Comparative Analysis," *Comparative Political Studies* 16: 255–72.

Holt, R.T. and Turner, J.E. (eds.) (1970) *The Methodology of Comparative Research*, New York: Free Press.

Huntington, S.P. and More, C.H. (eds.) (1970) *Authoritarian Politics in Modern Society*, New York: Basic Books.

Kalleberg, A.L. (1966) "The Logic of Comparison: A Methodological Note on the Comparative Study of Political Systems," *World Politics* 19: 69–82.

Lakatos, I. (1970) "Falsification and the Methodology of Scientific Research Programmes," in I. Lakatos and A. Musgrave (eds.), *Criticism and the Growth of Knowledge*, Cambridge: Cambridge University Press.

Lane, J.-E. (1987) "Against Theoreticism," *International Review of Sociology* 3: 149–85.

LaPalombara, J. (1970) "Parsimony and Empiricism in Comparative Politics," in R.T. Holt and J.E. Turner (eds.), *The Methodology of Comparative Research*, New York: Free Press.

Lijphart, A. (1971) "Comparative Politics and the Comparative Method," *American Political Science Review* 65: 682–93.

Lipset, S.M., Trove, M., and Coleman, J.S. (1956) *Union Democracy*, Glencoe, IL: Free Press.

Macridis, R.C. (1953) "Research in Comparative Politics," Report of the Social Science Seminar on Comparative Politics, *American Political Science Review* 47: 641–75.

Macridis, R.C. (1955) *The Study of Comparative Government*, New York: Random House.

Mayer, L.C. (1989) *Redefining Comparative Politics*, Newbury Park, CA: Sage.

Osgood, C.E. (1967) "On the Strategy of Cross-national Research into Subjective Culture," *Social Science Information* 6 (1): 5–37.

Przeworski, A. (1987) "Methods of Cross-national Research, 1970–83: An Overview," in M. Dierkes, H.N. Weiler, and A. Berthoin Antal (eds.), *Comparative Policy Research: Learning from Experience*, New York: St. Martin's Press.

Przeworski, A. and Teune, H. (1970) *The Logic of Comparative Social Inquiry*, New York: Wiley.

Ragin, C.C. (1987) *The Comparative Method: Moving Beyond Qualitative and Quantitative Strategies*, Berkeley: University of California Press.

Riker, W.H. (1982) "Two-party System and Duverger's Law," *American Political Science Review* 76: 753–66.

Sartori, G. (1970) "Concept Misformation in Comparative Politics," *American Political Science Review* 64 (4): 1033–53.

Sartori, G. (1976) *Parties and Party Systems: A Framework for Analysis*, New York: Cambridge University Press.

Sartori, G. (1984) "Guidelines for Concept Analysis," in G. Sartori (ed.), *Social Science Concepts: A Systematic Analysis*, London: Sage.

Sartori, G. (1986) "The Influence of Electoral Systems: Faulty Laws or Faulty Method?," in B. Grofman and A. Lijphart (eds.), *Electoral Laws and their Political Consequences*, New York: Agathon Press.

Sartori, G., Riggs, F.W., and Teune, H. (eds.) (1975) *Tower of Babel: On the Definition and Analysis of Concepts in the Social Sciences*, Pittsburgh: University of Pittsburgh, Occasional Paper 6: 7–37.

Sigelman, L. and Gadbois, G.H. (1983) "Contemporary Comparative Politics: An Inventory and Assessment," *Comparative Political Studies* 16 (3): 275–305.

Smelser, N.J. (1966) "Notes on the Methodology of Comparative Analysis of Economic Activity," *Transactions of the Sixth World Congress of Sociology*, vol. 2, pp. 101–17. Evian: International Sociological Association.

Smelser, N.J. (1967) "Sociology and the Other Social Sciences," in P.F. Lazarsfeld et al. (eds.), *The Uses of Sociology*, New York: Basic Books.

Smelser, N.J. (1976) *Comparative Methods in the Social Sciences*, Englewood Cliffs, NJ: Prentice Hall.

Somit, A. and Tanenhaus, J. (1964) *American Political Science: Profile of a Discipline*, New York: Atherton.

Sundquist, J.L. (1988) "Needed: A Political Theory for the New Era of Coalition Government in the United States," *Political Science Quarterly* 103: 613–35.

Verba, S. (1967) "Some Dilemmas in Comparative Research," *World Politics* 20: 112–27.

6 Further observations on concepts, definitions, and models

Giovanni Sartori

Democracy: "what is" vs. "how much"

A definition must embrace the whole of what it defines, but no more. Thus to define is, first of all, to assign limits, to delimit. An undefined concept is, by the same token, a boundless concept. The standard manner of delimiting a concept is to define it *a contrario*, by contrast, i.e., by establishing its opposite, contrary, or contradictory. Hence, in order to establish what democracy *is*, we must also establish what a democracy is *not*, that is, what is the opposite of democracy.

Generally, definitions *a contrario* are the easiest. What is white? It is the contrary of black. What is good? It is the contrary of bad. And so forth. The problem simply is to find – when seeking to delimit a concept – a "good opposite." But while most terms have antonyms, a good oppositeness of meaning may not be found easily. For example, when we attempt to define politics, we often say that politics is neither economics nor ethics, thus revealing that the concept of politics has no established opposite. The main point to note, however, is that the logical status of two contrasting terms may be of two sorts: they may either be or not be contradictories. In what follows I use *opposite* as the generic term for when the specification is unnecessary, i.e., for both cases; *contrary* for opposites that are not contradictories; and *contradictory* for two terms that are not only mutually exclusive but also exhaustively exclusive. The logical point is this: the principle of the excluded middle applies to the contradictories – not to contraries. It is only with contradictories that *tertium non datur*, that no third possibility exists (e.g., either one is alive or dead, married or single, two-legged or quadruped). Contraries are mutually exclusive but not exhaustively so; they admit, therefore, third, intermediate possibilities (e.g., neither big nor small, neither hot nor cold, neither rich nor poor).

While the mishandling of contraries and contradictories is a contributing factor, the major difficulties in determining what democracy *is not* currently stem from the methodological orientation promoted by the quantitative bent of the social sciences. Under the quantitative impetus, we are no longer prompted to ask *what is* (or is not) a democracy; we are, instead, required to ask *to what degree*, if any, a political system is a democracy. Does the second question supersede the first one? Is it a better question? This appears to be the prevailing view. I argue, instead, that both are equally legitimate and, indeed, mutually complementing questions.

Let us assess first the logical status of asking: *What is* democracy? Under this formulation, democracy is construed as an entity, as an object concept, and, more precisely, as a specific *class* (type) of political system. Therefore, the logical treatment entailed is classificatory – that is, a binary, dichotomous, or disjunctive treatment: we are required to decide whether a given polity is *either* democratic *or* not. This also entails that the differences sorted out by such treatment are of *kind* rather than of degree. And since we are dealing with a logical treatment, it is no objection at all to object that "what is" questions are vitiated by ontological and essentialist assumptions. If people misconstrue a logical treatment, this is a fault in its users, not of the logic that they misemploy.

When the question is, "To what degree is a polity *more* or *less* democratic?," we are no longer identifying an entity but rather *predicating* something about it. This is the same as saying that "democracy" is now conceived as a property concept, as a property (characteristic, attribute) of political objects. Under this formulation, the logical treatment is no longer binary (yes-no), but continuous (greater-lesser), usually described as the transformation of dichotomous (discrete) characteristics into continuous characteristics. It also follows – logically, not ontologically – that under this treatment, differences are of *degree*. It must be noted, however, that "how much?" questions can be formulated in two fundamentally different ways. In the case at hand, we may either ask to what extent a *democracy* is democratic, or ask to what extent *any polity* is democratic. If the first question is being asked, we shall see that the problem is easily handled. The difficulties arise with the second question, as I shall immediately explain.

When we predicate that a political system is democratic to some extent or degree, the preliminary question is: democratic with respect to which characteristic(s)? For instance, Douglas Rae (1971) selects the property "majority rule"; but democracy is majority rule *cum* minority rights – quite a different thing. Felix Oppenheim (1971) selects the characteristic "participation"; but this concept by now is so ill-defined that it might even lead to the finding that (on participation measure) the fullest democracy ever to exist was China at the time of its so-called cultural revolution. At least three difficulties arise along this path. First, hosts of characteristics or properties are eligible for selection – not only majority rule and participation, but also equality, freedom, consensus, coercion, competition, pluralism, constitutional rule, and more. Second, these characteristics are so interrelated that any single measure of any selected category is likely to produce highly erratic rank orderings. Third, and to my mind foremost, if we start (as we in effect do) from conceptual morass, operationalizations (remember that we presumably are seeking measures) can only add extravaganza to fuzziness.[1] But let us assume, for the sake of the argument, that all these difficulties have been overcome. We still have to confront the question of the heuristic value of this approach.

We are asking, let it be recalled, how much (or little) of a given democratic characteristic, or of a set (index) of democratic characteristics, can be found *across all political systems*. It is very unlikely that any measure of any category would ever yield a zero value, i.e., indicate a total absence of the characteristic being measured. If so, we would have to conclude that all existing political systems are democracies, albeit to a lesser and lesser degree; or, conversely, that all existing polities are non-democracies, except that, say, Cambodia or Albania are more non-democratic than Britain. Quite aside from the stultifying nature of such conclusions, what is completely missed by this kind of degreeism, or continuism, is that political systems are *systems*. That is, they are bounded wholes characterized by constitutive mechanisms and principles that are either present (albeit imperfectly) or absent (albeit imperfectly). Could Stalin or Hitler have been ousted from power by a free election? No. Can a President of the United States be impeached? Yes. Do parties (in the plural) compete among themselves in the Soviet Union? No. Do they compete in West Germany? Yes.

It can now be easily seen why the question, "To what degree is a *democracy* democratic?" is altogether a different question. When this is the query, the scholar assumes – even if unconsciously – a prior classificatory breakdown. If so, there is no incompatibility between the classificatory and the degree treatments. Within democracy as a *class* (type), one can assess as many variations *in degree* (of more-and-less democracy) as one sees fit.

The point that plagues our discussions bears, then, on the sloganistic abuse of the phrase "*All* differences are differences in degree." If one held today that all differences are in kind, most people would consider this a logical stupidity. Yet the first maxim is just as stupid as the second one. There is nothing in the intrinsic nature of human artifacts that establishes that all differences are of degree, just as there is nothing in the intrinsic nature of things that establishes that they are *of kind*. Differences are of degree if so treated (logically). Similarly, differences are of kind under the classificatory (*per genus et differentiam*) treatment. Whether differences are qualitative or quantitative, in kind or degree, discontinuous or continuous, is a matter of logical treatment and, therefore, a matter of deciding which logical treatment is appropriate for what purpose.

In my view, both "*What is* (democracy)?" and "*How much* (democracy)?" are rightful and complementary, not mutually exclusive, questions. It is also my view that they should be asked in that order. This is so because without establishing first what a thing *is* (and is not), we cannot establish its *degree* of being whatever it is declared to be. My stand is, thus, that variations within democracy or *of* democracy (relating to more and less democracy) require that we first establish to what they apply – that is, that we first decide what is, and what is not, a democracy. Only sloppy logic can dispose of all problems by declaring that everything is a matter of "more and less." This sloppy logic has prompted, in turn, the neglect of *a contrario* definitions, a neglect that needs to be redressed. Real people do live under regimes and political forms that they either wish to escape or long to enter. Indeed, in recent times, millions of people have fled their homelands at the risk of their lives. They have not done so for mere increment, for a lesser or greater "degree" of what they already had. Rather, they have sought what they did *not* have.

From classification to measurement

There are, conceivably, at least three ways of being displeased with my conceptual analysis. One is the classic objection that classes and types are only abstractions.

The second is the argument that classes and types are static, "locational" concepts, while we are in need of dynamic, "process" concepts. The third and major criticism is expressed, in brief, by the thesis that the logic of classification is superseded by measurement. These objections are not unrelated but are best confronted separately.

The first objection is as old as it is unconvincing. Aside from the fact that all scientific knowledge deals with generalizations and that all generalization implies abstraction, the Achilles heel of this objection is that it offers – as it stands – no alternative. Granted that classifications cannot follow the shades of reality, that they draw arbitrary cuts, it does not follow that we can dispense with classificatory mappings. The world of nature is surely as much a blend as is the world of man. Yet could a botanist or a zoologist master his field without having recourse to classificatory systems? Actually, the main difference between a zoologist and a social scientist is that the latter needs to be concerned with, and alerted to, classifications much more than the former. The social scientist needs them just as much, but he – unlike the zoologist – cannot be happy with his classifications once and for all: his world being extremely dynamic, he must reclassify, and classify anew, all of the time.

The second objection is as follows: I have been concerned, in the main, with locational concepts, not with process concepts. This can readily be acknowledged, but not without prior qualifications. First, locational concepts also allow for some dynamics, since the concrete cases can and do move from one box to another. However, some dynamics may not be enough dynamics. For instance, an analysis based on locational concepts – such as structural configurations – suits the nations that are built, but is ill suited for grasping the nation-building process. This has indeed been my view in dealing with the fluid polities, for my warning that classifications can be, in volatile contexts, very misleading, goes to support the view that developmental analysis needs broadly conceived process concepts (see Kothari 1967). On the other hand, process concepts also need a frame of reference that must be held constant. Therefore, after we have recognized the difference, and the different appropriateness, of locational vis-à-vis process concepts, the question remains: can we grasp dynamics regardless of, or without reference to, statics? This is what I do not believe, and there is something here that we can learn from our philosopher ancestors.

Until Kant, philosophy was largely static. Kant himself was a most meticulous constructor of logical filing systems. Then dynamics followed: Romanticism, classic idealism, and existentialism. With Fichte, Schelling, Hegel, and their descendants, we leap from photography to cinematography, from statics to kinetics. Dialectic, fluidity, *Aufhebung*, incessant change, action – for a century these have been the key words in European philosophy. The result has been unintelligible chaos. A reconstruction *ab imis* was necessary, analytic philosophy came to the fore, and most, if not all, of what had preceded was declared meaningless. The reaction of logical positivism, and especially of early logical positivism, was excessive, but vis-à-vis the philosophy of idealism and existentialism, the mark was well hit. The dialectical merging of all and any distinction – indeed, of analysis itself – was banned, and statics was restored.

Where does the analogy come in? It seems to me that a mood of "romantic dialectics" has been creeping into the social sciences. The current recommendations of avoiding dichotomies and logical polarizations, of concentrating on process, change, and the like, have a familiar ring. This is, in fact, the kind of logic that explains why liberty and coercion cannot be distinguished, why freedom is inseparable from oppression, and so forth. Anybody having passed through the experience of Hegelian dialectics, or of its Marxist follow-up, knows where this leads. Soft-pedaling of analytical thinking is dangerously close to confused (and confusing) thinking, just as "process logic" is dangerously conducive to dialectical obscurity. There is one thing that we should learn from what happened to philosophy: how to avoid the same pitfalls. Process concepts and process logic (or dialectics) yield returns, but only under the condition that we do not rush headlong into the Hegelian night in which all the cows appear black. The real world cannot be viewed only as a process – *becoming* – but also, at any point in time, as a state – *being*. With due respect to dynamics, "location" should not be downgraded. And to indict taxonomies for impeding the understanding of "process" is, in principle, no less absurd than to indict a globe or geological charts for obstructing traveling.

While I am not impressed by the first two objections, the real problem centers on the following query: how does the "qualitative science" dealing with *what is* questions relate to the "quantitative science" dealing with *how much* questions? Bluntly put, how do differences in *kind* relate to differences in *degree*? Or, viewed from the other end, how does pre-measurement relate to measurement? Along this itinerary, which is indeed a long itinerary, it is useful to distinguish among three steps, or phases. First, there is the classificatory treatment of concepts which is, logically, an *either-or* treatment: this *is*, or *is not*, that. If this mode of analysis is called the logic of classification, then the second step can appropriately be identified as a "logic of gradation"[2] consisting of a *more-or-less* (degree) treatment. This second stage is somewhat ambivalent. In no small part, the logic of gradation brings about a "quantitative idiom," which is nothing but an idiom largely exposed to abuse (Kaplan 1964: 13). This was well exemplified by the facile dictum that *all* differences are *only* differences in degree. At the same time, a more-or-less logical treatment is conducive to actual *measurement*, i.e., to attaching numerical values to items. But this is only the beginning of a quantitative science. The third step consists, then, in empowering numbers with their mathematical properties – that is, in bringing our measures under the concepts and the theories of mathematics. At this stage, the *quantitative* science is transformed into a *mathematical* science whose ultimate ideal is to discover and express general laws in the form of functional relationships between measured items.

There is no question that this program should be pursued. Thus, any researcher must weigh the opportunity of transforming the dichotomous characteristics drawn by the logic of classification into the continuous characteristics demanded by the logic of gradation. Nobody in his right mind can deny that the more we measure, the better. As for the mathematization of political science, what is subject to questioning is neither the desirability nor the enormous potentialities of this development, but rather whether the mathematics in use suits our problems. The point of divergence does not bear, then, on the program, but on its execution; and more exactly, on how the first step, i.e., the either-or (binary) treatment of the logic of classification, relates to the second step, i.e., the more-or-less (continuous) treatment of the logic of gradation. It is here that the issue is joined.

Over the past twenty years, the prevalent mood has been to do away with the *per genus et differentiam* mode of analysis under the assumption that the logic of classification was obstructive of, if not inimical to, the quantitative turn of the discipline. Not only was the quantitative science deemed capable of proceeding *without*, or outside of, the qualitative science; it was further assumed that the quantitative science, as expressed by the logic of gradation, required the actual dismantling and the positive rejection of the classificatory mode of analysis. In my view, these are grievous misunderstandings. The first assumption is simply untrue to our actual deeds, as is obvious if one pauses to consider that in the domain of politics, the qualitative science includes the quasi-totality of our theory. The second assumption has resulted – in the wake of the recommendation of dismissing the logic of classification – in our building a giant with feet of clay.

Lest my emphasis on the modes of concept formation (classificatory or other) be suspected of privileging the theoretical over the empirical side of the coin, let me take up the question at its data end. Data are "facts" as perceived and dissected by our tools of inquiry, i.e., by the observational concepts of a science. This is the same as saying that data are information processed by, and distributed in, *conceptual containers*. More exactly, data are observations collected and arranged according to how the concepts are shaped and defined by the fact seeker. Therefore, concepts are not only the units of thinking; concepts (observational concepts) are also, and just as much, *data containers*. If so, the crucial question is: what turns a concept into a valid *fact-finding container*?

Without delving into minutiae, let me simply note that the data base of a science is all the more satisfactory the more its data containers (concepts) are (i) *standardized* and endowed with (ii) high to maximal *discriminating power*. If they are not standardized, the information is not cumulative. But standardization is self-defeating unless the data containers are discriminating enough to allow for multipurpose utilization, thereby including utilizations as yet unforeseen. How can these two crucial requirements be met? Here is the rub: because I know of no other technique for meeting both requirements jointly, aside from the classificatory technique. Standardization and sharpening proceed hand in hand if and only if a general class (concept) is "unpacked" per *genus et differentiam* into mutually disjoined (either-or) classes that become, as we descend systematically the ladder of abstraction, always more specific – i.e., qualified by larger sets of attributes – and thereby more discriminating.

The point is, then, that research is infinitely wasteful unless it branches out from, and is brought back to, some common backbone. This backbone has long been provided by the logic of classification and the logical discipline thus resulting. If this discipline is relaxed and replaced by undisciplined checklists, each study becomes a fishing expedition that employs different nets and catches different fish. This may be pleasing for the ego of the researcher, but it leaves the science with haphazard, heterogeneous, and overlapping findings that add up to almost nothing as they are pooled together. On the other hand, we are hardly better off in turning to the other side of the ledger, for here we are left with "omnibus" data containers that hopelessly lack discrimination. Think of our standard categories and variables – social class, occupation, industrialization, literacy, modernization, participation, mobilization, integration, and the like. It is pretty certain that these variables do not measure, across the world, common underlying phenomena, and this is quite aside from the reliability of the data-gathering agencies. The point is, now, that the poorer the discrimination of our data containers, the more the facts are *misgathered* and, therefore, the greater the *misinformation*.

Some years ago, the saying was that we were theory rich and data poor. One could equally say, today, that we are theory poor and data cheated. Data cheated – I have said – because our data base is in bad shape. But why theory poor? Can this indictment be imputed to the same cause?

As we revert from the empirical to the theoretical concern, the issue is, in a nutshell, whether our knowledge still needs the logic of classification as a point of departure, or whether this first step blocks the others and should, therefore, be ostracized. The dilemma must be faced squarely. Either we take the view that the either-or treatment cannot be bypassed, or we must boldly reverse the itinerary and adopt the neo-Baconian optics: from the data back to science.[3] This is the dilemma, for the second step cannot possibly sustain the burden of being a founding, initial step. Degrees or quantities *of what*? Clearly, we cannot measure until we know what it is that we are measuring. *How much* questions – no matter how far they will subsequently lead us – can sensibly be asked only of things and events that belong (with respect to a given property) to the *same class*. The logic of gradation leads to sheer confusion unless a classificatory treatment is presupposed.

As for the neo-Baconian option, if it is true that data are nothing but information and observations sorted out and processed by ad hoc, conceptual containers, then the itinerary "from the data back to science" sounds very much like adding clay to clay. Quite aside from the monumental naiveté of the neo-Baconian epistemology, the facts of the matter are (i) that increasing amounts of research and survey data are matched by their equally increasing lack of comparability and cumulability and (ii) that most of the cheap and dirty data provided by statistical agencies despairingly lack discriminating power. Hence, the state of the data base points, if anything, to the vital necessity of improving the quality of the data *at the source*. Computer cleaning is no remedy for hopelessly vague and hopelessly overlapping categories.

Yet the neo-Baconian adept has nothing to say on how the fact finder should perform in finding the facts. He apparently is content with re-manipulating "masses of data" – just more of the same mess. The retort is, of course, that we now possess powerful statistical techniques that, from the data end, can do what formerly had to be done at the conceptual end: detect errors and shape or reshape the resulting theory. But statistical controls only control the variables in use; multiple regression analysis does not discover for us the variables that might account – once discovered – for the observed correlations. Likewise, only the indicators that we put in the computer are factored or clustered for relevant dimensions. In short, computer and statistical technology cannot surrogate what an atrophied formation of concepts does not provide (see Sartori 1975).

All in all, it seems to me that in the execution of our program, we are throwing away the baby and replacing it with dirty water. A checklist is only a poor substitute for a classification, and gradations without prior classification give to imprecision the appearance of precision. On the other hand, the limits of classifications can always be corrected by transforming dichotomies into continuous characteristics. However, the initial damage resulting from classificatory neglect and sloppiness remains, and is often amplified, throughout the subsequent transformations. Let it be repeated, therefore, that our understanding always and necessarily begins with *what is* questions. If such questions are not refined by a systematic logical treatment, we shall only have the worse of two worlds: a bad qualitative science that reflects itself into a bad quantitative science. The proof of the pudding is in the eating, and the eating that has resulted from taxonomic negligence is dismal.

By this, I do not intend in the least to contribute to the bad relationships between the nominal and the quantitative science.[4] Quite to the contrary, my intent has been to show how much both camps have to gain by implementing one another. The qualitative science largely remains with the hypotheses it generates, and badly needs measures that both refine and test these hypotheses. On the other hand, we must beware of a precision that is nothing but an operational artifact. In particular, measures are all the more useful and necessary the more we have first identified the problems, mapped the cases, and suggested causal explanations – that is, the more they are entered under well-circumscribed sets of nominal qualifications and assumptions. Words *alone* beat numbers alone. Words *with* numbers beat words alone. And numbers make sense, or much greater sense, *within* verbal theory.

Politics as collectivized decisions

Let me immediately begin by distinguishing between four kinds of decisions: (a) individual; (b) group; (c) collective; and (d) collectivized (Sartori 1987: 214–16).

Individual decisions are taken by each individual for himself, regardless of whether he is inner- or outer-directed. *Group decisions* imply that decisions are taken by a concrete group, that is, face-to-face, interacting individuals who mean- ingfully partake in the making of such decisions. *Collective decisions* are hardly amenable to a precise definition. Generally, they are understood to mean decisions taken by "the many." Contrasted (as my distinction implies) to group decisions, collective decisions assume a large body that does not and cannot perform – on account of its size – as concrete groups do. It should also be underscored that a col- lective decision should not be confused with a collective preference; the former need not generate the latter, to wit, an outcome that meaningfully expresses the social preference.

We then have *collectivized decisions*. Collective and collectivized decisions may be said to share the property of not being, in any meaningful sense, individual decisions. Even so, collectivized decisions are very different from all the other kinds. Individual, group, and collective decisions all make reference to a subject who makes the decisions. Collectivized decisions are, instead, decisions that apply to, and are enforced on, a collectivity, regardless of whether they are taken by the one, the few, or the many. The defining criterion no longer is *who* makes the decisions, but rather their scope: whoever does the deciding, *decides for all.*[5]

The notion of collectivized decisions permits, to begin with, the assertion that *politics consists of collectivized decisions.*[6] Note that collective and collectivized decisions correspond to one another only when the universe issuing the decisions coincides with the universe receiving them. This coinciding is of great theoretical interest and may occur. It occurs less and less, however, as the size of political units increases. At the macro level, therefore, it can be said that politics ultimately consists of enacted decisions that are removed from the competence of each individual and are *made by somebody for someone else*. This does not imply in the least that a collectivized decision is also a decision on behalf of its addressees; this may or may not be the case. The deciders decide for all only in the sense that their deciding falls on everybody's head.

Naturally, while all the decisions of a political nature are collectivized decisions, the obverse is not true: not all collectivized decisions are political. For instance, when we speak of economic power, we again refer to collectivized decisions, to the fact that somebody (the capitalist, the corporation, etc.) takes decisions for, and imposes them upon, wage earners and consumer publics. The difference among political power, economic power, and other powers as well, cannot be found in the notion of collectivized decisions. Rather, their difference is hierarchical. That is to say, collectivized decisions are political in that they are (a) sovereign; (b) without exit; and (c) sanctionable.[7] They are sovereign in the sense that they can overrule any other rule; without exit, as Hirschman would put it, because they reach out to the frontiers that territorially define citizenship; and sanctionable in the sense that they are sustained by the legal monopoly of force.

If politics is perceived as consisting of those collectivized decisions that are both overarching and of greater consequence to the well-being (or ill) of each and all, it is appropriate to begin with the libertarian ideal of Marx or with the anarchist's question: why have politics at all? This question is not trivial. After all, why should we like decisions made for us (in our place) *by others*, especially when – as in the case of politics – they can affect life and liberty? The answer has been given thousands of times, but another time will not hurt. In a hypothetical state of nature, all decisions are individual decisions. On the other hand, any organized collectivity submits to rules of collectivization, at least in the sense that it accepts collectivized decisions – this being the condition of its organization. Yet the respective ambits of individual versus collectivized decisions vary enormously across contemporary societies, even under equal technological and environmental conditions. For instance, the area of collectivized decisions is incommensurably greater in socialist (communist) than in non-socialist countries. The basic reason for this difference is ideological and need not be labored upon. Let us make sure, however, that the point on the ideological factor is made in a meaningful way.

It is often said that we are confronted with two ideologies – one individualistic and one collectivistic – and, thereby, with two intractables that must be left at that.

However, this way of disposing of the problem overstates the deadlock. The so-called ideology of individualism largely yields to collectivization whenever the utility or necessity of the latter is reasonably demonstrated. The obverse is not true. The ideology of collectivization is unyielding, for it perceives private or individual decisions as intrinsic evils – both because individualism is bad in itself and because it entails private property, private capital accumulation, and all the wrongs thus resulting. The "two ideologies" argument applies, then, to only one of the two. This allows us to distinguish between the "ideology" and the "utility" of collectivizing decisions, and to note that aside from ideological dogmatisms, the matter can and is in fact assessed in cost–benefit terms. The reasons given for collectivizing decisions formerly left to individual choice are generally related to technological imperatives and to the service and collective good needs of contemporary societies. In a number of cases, however, it is an open question whether the benefits of collectivizing a given decisional area (schooling, housing, transportation, utilities, and so forth) are not offset by the costs, at least in the longer run and in terms of cumulative effects. Hence, it is both useful and important to ask: *when* is it either necessary or convenient to collectivize an area of decisions? The ulterior and related question is: *how* should we proceed in collectivizing decisions?

What is a model?

What is a model? The issue is investigated in the philosophy of science literature, but the requirements set forth by the methodologist (versed in *logos*) generally are ignored by political scientists.[8] We may contend that we are entitled to decide for ourselves what we mean. Perhaps. But what do we mean? In his survey (with Laura Roselle) of "Model Fitting in Communism Studies" (1990: 66–116), Almond indicates that the term is "used generically to refer to explanatory mental constructs" (67). But aside from elemental look-and-see terms, most mental constructs are, to a lesser or greater extent, explanatory. Almond also notes that models "must be matched against reality," and that "the model-matching process is the way to get at the shape of reality" (67). But again, very few mental constructs (e.g., hopeless invisibles such as soul and God) are not matched against reality. Further, why the "shape" of reality? It is structure, not shape, that matters in this context. Be all of that as it may, it should be conceded that we may be unable to define something and yet understand it. Let us look, then, at the actual understanding.

In reviewing the literature, Almond draws a distinction between models and frameworks. In his account, "totalitarianism, developmental theories of communist systems, the various treatments . . . in terms of pluralism, interest group theory, bureaucratic politics, and patron–client relations, are applications of *explanatory models*." However, he goes on to note that "communism studies have also been influenced by *theoretical frameworks* such as structural-functionalism, decision process theory, modernization theory" (67–68).[9] Why are the first models and the latter frameworks? For instance, why is developmental theory a model and modernization theory a framework? What is the difference? If the distinction between models and frameworks carries a difference, it cannot be inferred from the above.

Perhaps the retort will be, "Who cares?" What matters is what we actually do, and in practice the "use of the model concept is relatively clear-cut. An interest group explanation of Soviet or Chinese politics seeks to explain the political process and its outputs by the actions and interaction of groups defined in some way" (Almond 1990: 68). But this is definitely not how the model concept is actually used. The account entirely misses that "model" embodies an overriding explanatory claim. Model is our *eureka*; whoever proposes a model proclaims, "I have found it!" Model is a prized word precisely because it is not an ordinary mental construct: it is a *key* – a key that opens hitherto closed doors. Models do more than ordinary concepts, more than humble variables: they unveil, they cut through the fog, they decipher. However, in order to have a key we must know how to make one; and in order to make one, we must know what a key is. So far, we have not moved an inch beyond verbal boasting. We boast about having a *clue*, a decisive clue; but we have no clue as to what that clue might be.

So, the question, What is a model?, cannot be circumvented. Let me give it another try from another end. Assuming that a model stands among concepts like an elephant stands among animals in general, do we recognize an elephant when we see it? Assuming that we do, let the question be: is there any construct that we all unquestionably recognize as a model? Yes. For instance, "equilibrium" is certainly a model. Equally, the "organic analogy" may be construed as a model. Deutsch proposed a model when he adapted cybernetics to politics. Likewise, Easton's elaboration of "system" provides a systemic model. It will also be generally acknowledged that rational choice theory has recourse to models, and that we are entitled to speak of game-theoretic models. Finally, I submit that the Downsian model of party competition does qualify for model status. While some of the aforesaid elephants are much bigger than others, even the small ones are still identifiable as elephants.

It is apparent, then, that models (proper) do exist. And if we keep in mind these models of "model," we can begin to extract sense out of nonsense. To begin with – and following Hempel's fundamental distinction (1965: 173ff) – all our examples definitely bear on "theoretical terms," not on observational terms.[10] But, of course, not all theoretical terms are models. In order to be what they claim to be, models are required, as I was saying, to provide a deciphering key: to bring out the underlying "nerves," skeleton, structure, or interplay (the mechanics) of something.[11]

Allow me to stop here, for my concern is only to make sure that we are able to distinguish between models and other constructs with a reasonable modicum of approximation. Concepts are all equally concepts, but they are not all alike. If we seek an eagle (a high-ranking concept), we shall not find one in a parrot. A theoretical term is not an observational (empirical) term; a model is not a framework, nor an approach, nor a mere focus; a typological construct is not a class construct.[12] These are not "nominal" differences, but differences of very great consequence. If model is a misnomer (as it is for much of the profession), then it misconstrues. Model-verbiage is not harmless; it is harmful. Therefore, it is of great substantive importance to establish – reverting to the matter at hand – that neither totalitarianism nor any of its "successor concepts" are models. If one has a model, good for him or her – and do tell me what it is. Still, there is life before models and without models.

Notes

* "Democracy: 'What is' vs. 'how much'" is excerpted from Giovanni Sartori (1987) *The Theory of Democracy Revisited*, Chatham, NJ: Chatham House, pp. 182–85.

"From classification to measurement" is excerpted from Giovanni Sartori (1976) *Parties and Party Systems: A Framework for Analysis*, New York: Cambridge University Press, pp. 293–98, 318–19.

"Politics as a collectivized decision" is excerpted from Giovanni Sartori (1987) *The Theory of Democracy Revisited*, Chatham, NJ: Chatham House, pp. 214–16.

"What is a model?" is excerpted from Giovanni Sartori (1993) "Totalitarianism, Model Mania, and Learning from Error," *Journal of Theoretical Politics* 5 (1): 5–22.

1 An extreme but telling illustration of the arbitrariness that can enter this transformation is the following operationalization of party "competition" by Przeworski and Sprague (1971: 208 and *passim*): "A knock at the door by a party voter."
2 I deliberately say "logic of gradation" instead of "logic of comparison." The latter denomination leans on the authority of Hempel (1952: 54–58) and is picked up by Kallberg (1966) and Oppenheim (1975), among others. Nonetheless, it is a misnomer, for also the logic of classification "compares" (this is how differences and similarities are sorted out).
3 See, on the point, the perceptive discussion by Holt and Richardson (1970: 58–69) of what they describe as "atheoretic approaches to theory development."
4 This final paragraph is taken from Sartori (1976: 318–19).
5 The distinction between collective and collectivized decisions is generally missed by the political economy and/or the public choice literature. Two good surveys of the aforesaid literature are Mueller (1979) and Frohlich and Oppenheimer (1978).
6 This is but one characteristic, not an exhaustive definition. For a detailed analysis, see Sartori (1973).
7 The hierarchical difference between political and economic power assumes market-type conditions. In a state-owned, centrally planned economy, the difference becomes minimal for, in practice, the wage earner does not have an exit option. Furthermore, the economic sanction (being left to starve) is even more formidable, in and by itself, than most politically enforced sanctions.
8 For Brodbeck (1959: 374, 376 and *passim*), the first requirement is "structural isomorphism": the model and what it stands for must have the "same form" (structure). A lesser requirement is for "model" to be linked to "covering law" (e.g., Moe 1979). For a general appraisal, see Bruschi (1971).
9 Later, at pp. 72–73, Almond distinguishes between (i) "modeling metaphor," (ii) mapping or heuristic devices (e.g., system theory, structural-functionalism, decision theory, and political culture), which facilitate description and comparison but are not "in themselves explanatory," (iii) "conceptual frameworks," which are the same as the former, but now "enable us to do the job of explanation systematically and rigorously," and (iv) patron–client model, interest group model, and bureaucratic politics model, "which are of a different order." I cannot make sense of this even greater haze.
10 The distinction admits a middle ground between the two, but is clear-cut in principle: theoretical terms have no denotation, and it is only their theoretical function (for the theory to which they belong) that establishes their meaning.

11 This entails, inter alia, that models do not grow "old." They can be discarded on a number of grounds and indeed replaced by different and better ones. But to say that a model is obsolete, that it has been outdated by the events, quite simply indicates that we are not dealing with a model (proper).

12 In particular, if what is intended by model is only an ideal type, then this understanding should be explicitly stated and the latter notion must be qualified.

References

Almond, G. (1990) *A Discipline Divided: Schools and Sects in Political Science*, Newbury Park, CA: Sage.

Brodbeck, M. (1959) "Models, Meaning and Theories," in L. Gross (ed.), *Symposium on Sociological Theory*, New York: Harper & Row.

Bruschi, A. (1971) *La Teoria dei Modelli nelle Scienze Sociali*, Bologna: Il Mulino.

Frohlich, N. and Oppenheimer, J.A. (1978) *Modern Political Economy*, Englewood Cliffs, NJ: Prentice Hall.

Hempel, C. (1952) *Fundamentals of Concept Formation in Empirical Science*, Chicago: University of Chicago Press.

Hempel, C. (1965) *Aspects of Scientific Explanation*, New York: Free Press.

Holt, R.T. and Richardson, J.M. (1970) "Competing Paradigms in Comparative Politics," in R.T. Holt and J.E. Turner (eds.), *The Methodology of Comparative Research*, New York: Free Press.

Kallberg, A.L. (1966) "The Logic of Comparison," *World Politics*, 19 (1): 69–82.

Kaplan, A. (1964) *The Conduct of Enquiry*, San Francisco: Chandler Publishing Co.

Kothari, R. (1967) "Implications of Nation-building for the Typology of Political Systems," paper presented at the International Political Science Association Congress, Brussels.

Moe, T.M. (1979) "On the Scientific Status of Rational Models," *American Journal of Political Science* 23 (1): 215–43.

Mueller, D.C. (1979) *Public Choice*, Cambridge: Cambridge University Press.

Oppenheim, F.E. (1971) "Democracy: Characteristics Included and Excluded," *The Monist* 55 (1): 29–50.

Oppenheim, F.E. (1975) "The Language of Political Enquiry," in F.I. Greenstein and N.W. Polsby (eds.), *Handbook of Political Science*, Reading, MA: Addison-Wesley.

Przeworski, A. and Sprague, J. (1971) "Concepts in Search of Explicit Formulation: A Study in Measurement," *Midwest Journal of Political Science*, 15 (2): 183–218.

Rae, D. (1971) "Political Democracy as a Property of Political Institutions," *American Political Science Review* 65 (1): 111–19.

Sartori, G. (1973) "What Is Politics," *Political Theory* 1 (1): 5–26.

Sartori, G. (1975) "The Tower of Babel," in G. Sartori, F.W. Riggs, and H. Teune (eds.), *Tower of Babel: On the Definition and Analysis of Concepts in the Social Sciences*, Pittsburgh: International Studies Association, University of Pittsburgh, Occasional Paper 6: 7–37.

Sartori, G. (1976) *Parties and Party Systems: A Framework for Analysis*, New York: Cambridge University Press.

Sartori, G. (1987) *The Theory of Democracy Revisited*, Chatham, NJ: Chatham House.

Part II
Extending the Sartori tradition

7 Point of departure

Intension and extension[1]

Gary Goertz

There are few articles in political science that deserve the predicate "classic," but Sartori's "Concept Misformation in Comparative Politics" certainly merits the label. Thirty-plus years since its appearance in the *American Political Science Review* (1970), it shows up regularly on qualitative and research methods syllabi.[2] Sartori and Collier form a league of their own when it comes to the literature on concepts. In many ways, Collier's work is a natural extension of Sartori's and as such will receive substantial attention in this chapter.

One of Sartori's major contributions to the literature on concepts is perhaps his idea of the ladder of generality.[3] He was concerned with how the extension (i.e., empirical coverage) of a concept varied with its intension (i.e., the concept itself). Loosening the concept results in "conceptual stretching," whereby a concept would become applicable to more cases, but would be potentially stretched beyond recognition. In my framework, Sartori was thinking about what happens when one adds or subtracts secondary-level dimensions (i.e., attributes and defining characteristics), and its impact on the empirical coverage of the concept. Often this addition or subtraction is done via adjectives. As a result, I will talk about "concepts +/– adjectives" as a shorthand for what happens when one changes intension by changing the number of secondary-level dimensions and the downstream consequences of this on the number of observations in the category (i.e., extension).

Ideal types fit into this discussion because in general, they have zero extension, i.e., there are no actual examples of the ideal type. When ideal types of this sort are used, they raise a set of issues regarding the underlying basic concept and how to structure the secondary-level ones. It is quite surprising, given the frequency with which scholars refer to ideal types, that there exists little methodological analysis of them.

Finally, I end with a brief analysis of the gendered welfare state. Typically, with concepts +/– adjectives, the adjective points to a new or underappreciated secondary-level dimension, e.g., gender. Over the last ten to fifteen years, scholars have investigated this previously unexplored facet of the welfare state (see Pierson 2000 or Orloff 1996 for reviews). Because scholars have looked at a new dimension to the welfare state, they have produced a new series of analyses. To add gender dimensions to the classic welfare state concept means examining new hypotheses about it. Gender is an important new dimension because it is closely linked to causal hypotheses about the causes and effects of the welfare state.

The ladder of generality and concept extension

Sartori is probably best known for his discussion of conceptual stretching and the ladder of generality. Sartori never makes explicit his view on concept structure, i.e., how defining attributes and dimensions are aggregated, probably because it was not considered problematic at the time. Since Aristotle's time, concepts are defined via necessary and sufficient conditions. Of course, we now know that it is not necessarily so; for example, Collier and Mahon (1993) analyze radial concepts and Goertz (2006) discusses at length family resemblance concepts. In this section, I explore concept structures and their relationship to Sartori's claims about conceptual stretching and the ladder of generality. First, I analyze the basic principle of the ladder of generality in terms of extension, intension, and concept structures. I then proceed to illustrate how the basic mathematical and logical principles work themselves out using the literature and quantitative data on concepts such as peasant, (social) revolution, and welfare state.

While Sartori did not hide the source of the basic ideas he used in his classic *American Political Science Review* (1970) article, he did not really elaborate on their origins either. His view on concepts comes quite directly from philosophical logic, the use of which is quite overt in Sartori et al. (1975). It would be hard to find a philosophical logic textbook (starting with J. S. Mill) that does not have a chapter on definition and concepts. All these textbooks see concepts as defined via necessary and sufficient conditions. Sartori does not really say this explicitly, but one can go to a classic philosophical logic textbook of the 1930s and 1940s by Cohen and Nagel, who are more explicit about it:[4]

> "A definition," according to Aristotle, "is a phrase signifying a thing's essence." By the essence of a thing he understood the set of fundamental attributes which are the necessary and sufficient conditions for any concrete thing to be a thing of that type. It approximates to what we have called the conventional intension of a term.
>
> (1934: 235)

Gerring, in his book on concepts and methodology, gives a brief genealogy which ends with Sartori (see also, Adcock and Collier 2001):

> The classical approach to concept formation [necessary and sufficient conditions] may be traced back to Aristotle and the scholastic philosophers of the Middle Ages. For later variants, see Chapin (1939), Cohen and Nagel (1934), DiRenzo (1966), Dumont and Wilson (1967), Hempel (1952, 1965a, 1965b, 1966), Landau (1972), Lasswell and Kaplan (1950), Lazarsfeld (1966), Meehan (1971), Stinchcombe (1968, 1978), Zannoni (1978) and most important Sartori (1970, 1984), and Sartori et al. (1975).
>
> (2001: 66 n.1)

The methodological problem that motivated Sartori was one of comparative politics. If we have a fine-grained, multidimensional concept that applies well to one or two cases, then it might not "travel" well when applied to other cultures, countries, or time periods. Sartori suggests that in order to make the concept more general – i.e., applicable to more observations – one can "stretch" the concept by reducing its attributes (i.e., number of dimensions).

Sartori thus refers to the relationship between intension and extension. Basically, the intension is the concept while the extension is the cases that fall under the concept. For example, for Theda Skocpol, "social revolutions are rapid, basic transformations of a society's state and class structures; and they are accompanied and in part carried through by class-based revolts from below" (1979: 4–5). The extension, within her scope conditions, consists of Russia 1917, China 1950, and France 1789. Within larger scope conditions, Foran (1997) has added other cases such as Iran 1979 and Mexico 1910.

In principle, it is the intension that determines the extension. In good social science, theory should drive the choice of cases. It is the theory of social revolution that should determine which cases are selected, not necessarily the everyday use of the term "revolution" or the informal ideas about which cases fit. However, in practice, scholars often generate general concepts based on one or two cases (e.g., the Netherlands for Lijphart or Austria and Switzerland for Katzenstein) and then generalize to other countries that seem similar.

If one increases the number of secondary-level attributes in the intension *and* if – this is the big "if" that Sartori does not mention – one uses the necessary and sufficient condition structure, then there is an inverse relationship between intension and extension:

> The law of inverse variation must, therefore, be stated as follows: *If a series of terms is arranged in order of increasing intension, the denotation of the terms [extension] will either remain the same or diminish.*
>
> (Cohen and Nagel 1934: 33; italics original)

In short, we can increase the coverage (i.e., extension) of a concept by reducing its intension (i.e., number of attributes). More specifically and more accurately, we can increase the extension by reducing the number of necessary attributes in the intension. "Conceptual stretching" thus means, in operational terms, eliminating necessary dimensions. This makes the concept more general and simultaneously increases the distance it can travel.

Table 7.1 illustrates Sartori's conceptual stretching principle. Here the concept under discussion is "peasant," for which there are five potential characteristics or dimensions that have been applied to define a peasant. Notice that as the number of characteristics increases, the extension decreases. Kurtz writes, "Obviously, the more properties in the definition (the more specific it is), the fewer real-world 'peasants' it would tend to cover" (2000: 98). He then links this claim in a footnote to Sartori's idea that extension is inversely related to intension.

The fly in the ointment is that this all depends on the necessary and sufficient condition structure. As we shall shortly see, if one uses the family resemblance structure one can get the opposite relationship: extension increases with intension.

Table 7.1 The ladder of abstraction: dimensions underlying various concepts of peasants.

Intension	Minimalist	Anthropological	Moral economy	Marxian	Weberian
Rural cultivators	Yes	Yes	Yes		
Peasant villages characterized by distinct cultural practices		Yes	Yes		
High levels of rural social subordination			Yes	Yes	Yes
Peasants control/own land				Yes	Yes
Extension	*Very Large*	*Large*	*Moderate*	*Moderate*	*Very Small*
Examples	Popkin (1979) Lichbach (1994) Bates (1988)	Redfield (1955) Kroeber (1948) Banfield (1958)	Scott (1976) Managna (1991)	Wolf (1969) Paige (1975)	Moore (1966) Shanin (1971)

Source: Adapted from Kurtz (2000: 96; Chapter 11 in this volume).

This becomes pretty clear once one begins to think about the mathematical operations that typify the necessary and sufficient condition structure in contrast with the family resemblance one. Since Sartori uses logic as his preferred mathematics, we can contrast the necessary and sufficient condition AND with the family resemblance OR. The logical AND typifies the necessary condition structure while the logical OR does the same for family resemblance structures. More formally, necessary condition structures have the form X_1 AND X_2 AND X_3, while family resemblance structures take the form X_1 OR X_2 OR X_3. Clearly, if we add attributes with AND, the extension can only go down (or remain the same in exceptional circumstances). However, if we use OR to add dimensions, then the extension almost certainly goes up. This is visible if one imagines Venn diagrams: the intersection of two sets (representing two attributes) is almost always smaller than either set individually. In contrast, the union is almost always larger than the individual sets. In practice, the family resemblance approach does not use the union per se. Typically, two observations are considered members of the same family if they share *enough* characteristics, an application of the m-of-n rule; an observation falls under the concept if it has at least m of the n defining characteristics.

To show that the ladder of generality does not work for family resemblance concepts, we can revert to what is called an existence proof: give an example where intension increases extension. Suppose that the family resemblance rule is "if more than two of four dimensions are present then the country is a welfare state." We can contrast that situation with an increase in intension to six dimensions while keeping the rule that a country is a welfare state if it has more than half the total number of dimensions. Assume that the cases follow the binomial theorem, e.g., one can toss four or six coins to decide whether the country has a welfare state.

According to the binomial formula, the percentage of welfare states increases from 31 percent of the total with four dimensions to 34 percent with six. This calculation assumes that each dimension occurs with 0.5 probability. The more likely a country is to code positively on each dimension, the bigger the difference becomes, although modestly so. For example, with a 0.75 probability of each dimension occurring, we now get 83 percent of the cases as welfare states on the more-than-half rule with six dimensions, with 74 percent on the four-dimension concept. In summary, the claim about the inverse relationship between extension and intension does not hold for concepts in general. In fact, for the family resemblance school of concepts there can be a positive relationship between intension and extension.

To see how this can work, I use Hicks's (1999) data on the formation of welfare states in developed countries in the early twentieth century. In his analysis of welfare state formation, Hicks considered that a welfare state had formed in 1920 if it provided at least three of four classic services of welfare states: (1) old age pensions, (2) workers accident compensation, (3) health care, and (4) unemployment insurance. To examine how the ladder of generality can work in the opposite direction, we can contrast two family resemblance rules: (a) a welfare state exists if it has at least one of two services or (b) a welfare state exists if it has at least two of four services. In short, I use the m-of-n rule of one-half: in one case it is "at least one of two" and in the second it is "at least two of four."

Using Hicks's data (1999: 51) for when his fifteen developed countries established these various programs, we find the following results.[5] Using only two dimensions to conceptualize the welfare state means that we have six possible ways to define a welfare state from a total of four dimensions. With two dimensions, we get the following number of welfare states:

> Workers compensation, Unemployment compensation = 14 welfare states
> Pensions, Workers compensation = 14 welfare states
> Pensions, Health = 13 welfare states
> Health, Unemployment compensation = 11 welfare states
> Pensions, Unemployment compensation = 10 welfare states
> Health, Workers compensation = 10 welfare states

With four dimensions the result is:

> At least two of four dimensions present = 13 welfare states

Using real data, we can see that by increasing intension from two dimensions to four, we increase extension half the time from 10 or 11 welfare states to the 13 welfare states that result from the application of the "at least two out of four" rule.

Concepts +/– adjectives

The ladder of generality focuses on what happens in terms of extension when the dimensions of the concept are added or removed. Perhaps the most common way to add and subtract dimensions is by attaching adjectives to the concept. More generally, we have the linguistic and semantic fact that we often attach adjectives to concepts. For example, a bewildering array of adjectives has been used to modify the basic-level concept of democracy. Corporatism has been modified by "liberal," "societal," or "democratic," among others. What is not clear is how adding an adjective modifies the three-level structure of concepts. I suggest that the adjective is usually a secondary-level dimension. What I call the "classical" operation (following Collier and Levitsky, this volume, Chapter 13) means that the adjective is a new dimension that is "added" to the existing ones, i.e., "concepts plus adjectives," increasing the number of secondary-level dimensions or defining attributes by one. Collier and Levitsky (1997) brought to scholars' attention another use of adjectives that they called "diminished subtypes." This second, nonstandard use is for the adjective to refer to a concept with the value on a secondary-level dimension changed from one to zero, i.e., "concepts minus adjectives." Hence, one is not reducing the number of defining dimensions, but rather changing the values on some of the existing dimensions. I use the term "concepts +/– adjectives" to suggest that we need to consider what the adjective means when dealing with secondary-level dimensions.

The classical approach to concepts, as we have seen, is a necessary and sufficient condition one. Concept plus adjective then means we are adding a new dimension to the existing one. For example, "presidential" when modifying democracy adds a new attribute to those already existing for democracy. Since classical concepts use the necessary condition operation as their structural principle, we use AND to conjoin the attribute presidential to the concept democracy. The basic principle is that "all noun modifiers are to be treated via conjunction" (Lakoff 1987: 14). For example, Stepan and Skach write the following on parliamentary and presidential democracy:

> A pure parliamentary regime in a democracy is a system of mutual dependence: (1) The chief executive power must be supported by a majority in the legislature and can fall if it receives a vote of no confidence. (2) The executive power (normally in conjunction with the head of state) has the capacity to dissolve the legislature and call for elections. A pure presidential regime in a democracy is a system of mutual independence: (1) the legislative power has a fixed electoral mandate that is its own source of legitimacy. (2) The chief executive power has a fixed electoral mandate that is its own source of legitimacy. These necessary and sufficient characteristics are more than classificatory.
>
> (1993: 3–4)

Notice that the intension of both definitions is limited by democracy, e.g., "A pure parliamentary regime *in a democracy*." At the end, the authors explicitly see the "parliamentary" adjective as adding two necessary conditions that are jointly sufficient (for example, see Figure 7.1).

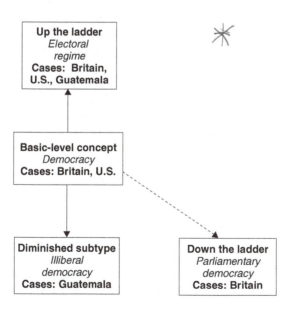

Figure 7.1 Diminished subtypes and the ladder of generality.

Source: Collier and Levitsky (1997, Figure 2).

As Goertz (2006) discusses at length, the fuzzy logic of necessary conditions uses the minimum to score a case with multiple necessary condition dimensions, i.e., $Y = \min(X_1, X_2, X_3)$. So a fuzzy logic concept plus adjective would be interpreted in that fashion:

> They [Osherson and Smith 1982, a classic article] now consider three concepts: *apple*, *striped*, and *striped apple*. They correctly observe that within classical fuzzy set theory there is only one way to derive the complex category *striped apple* from the categories *apple* and *striped*, namely, by intersection of fuzzy sets – which is defined by taking the minimum of the membership values in the two component fuzzy sets.
>
> (Lakoff 1987: 140)

In the classic sense, concept plus adjective invokes the subsetting operation. Notice in particular that within the classic conception, adjectives do not take away characteristics but can only add dimensions. Hence, within the classic theory, the extension of a concept plus adjective must always be smaller.

As we have seen in the previous section, the ladder of generality is all about adding and subtracting dimensions. Since we have a classic necessary and sufficient condition concept, the ladder of generality says that by adding an adjective, we then reduce the extension of the concept. When students of comparative politics compare parliamentary to presidential democracies, they are contrasting *within* the population of democracies.

It is important to understand that this serves as the baseline, default interpretation of a concept plus adjective. However, actual semantic, linguistic practice does not always conform to the canons of logic.[6] I examine some ways in which this can happen. I will leave the most obvious variation until the next section, where the adjective signals that one is removing attributes, hence concepts minus adjectives. But first I will briefly discuss another problem that can arise when the basic concept is not fixed. Since it is not fixed, adjectives become necessary to assign a certain interpretation to the concept. The example I shall use is the concept of revolution.

Table 7.2 gives a modified survey of the concept of revolution taken from Sartori's anthology on concepts (Kotowski 1984 – see Chapter 8 this volume). The names that appear on this list constitute many of the key contributors to the literature on revolution over the years before 1984. Kotowski is quite explicit about the fact that the characteristics listed in the table are necessary conditions for a revolution.[7]

Clearly, Moore and Skocpol have the most restrictive concept of revolution since theirs contains the most necessary conditions. By the ladder of generality principle, their concepts will have the least extension of any of those in the table. The first thing that any knowledgeable reader of Skocpol will exclaim is that her book is not about revolutions per se but about *social* revolutions. Voilà. We see that the adjective "social" has been added to the concept of revolution.

If we subtract two attributes, (1) changes in systems of stratification and (2) major political structural change, we arrive at Huntington's, Davies's, and

Table 7.2 Concepts with adjectives: unstable basic-level concept of revolution.

Scholar	Violence	Popular involvement	Change in governing body	Minor political structural change	Major political structural change	Stratification changes
Social revolution						
Skocpol	Y	Y	Y	Y	Y	Y
Moore	Y	Y	Y	Y	Y	Y
Political revolution						
Huntington	Y	Y	Y	Y	N	N
Johnson	Y	Y	Y	Y	N	N
Davies	Y	Y	Y	Y	N	N
Rebellion						
Gurr	Y	Y	N	N	N	N

Source: Adapted from Kotowski (1984: 422; Chapter 8 in this volume).

Johnson's concepts of revolution. We have subtracted the adjectives, if you will, that deal with system-wide changes, the "social" part of Skocpol's definition. We now have what for Skocpol and Moore would be *political* revolutions, e.g., the American Revolution. Here, again, we see an adjective appearing.

If we continue to remove dimensions, those dealing with (1) minor political structural change and (2) change of governing body, we arrive at the concept of Gurr. Taking the lead from the title of his book, we might call them "rebellions," since they do not necessarily involve social or political change.

Because the attributes used to define revolution can vary so widely, one needs adjectives to fix the meaning of the concept for the author. Skocpol had to affix "social" or some other term to revolution because she had to distinguish her dependent variable from other common uses of the term revolution. So whether it is concepts +/– adjectives depends on what is taken as the basic-level concept. From Skocpol's perspective, "political revolution" subtracts the system-wide and societal dimensions from the social revolution concept. From the other side, "social revolution" works classically by adding new attributes to the view of revolution as working only on government structures.

Collier and Levitsky specifically deal with what happens when you "subtract" an attribute from a concept, i.e., concepts minus adjectives, as well as adding an attribute. Of particular importance is their concept of a "diminished subtype." It is worth citing them at length:

> An alternative strategy of conceptual innovation, that of creating "diminished" subtypes, can contribute both to achieving differentiation and to avoiding conceptual stretching. It is a strategy widely used in the literature on recent democratization. Two points are crucial for understanding diminished subtypes.

First, in contrast to the classical subtypes discussed above, diminished subtypes are not full instances of the root [basic-level] definition of "democracy" employed by the author who presents the subtype. For example, "limited-suffrage democracy" and "tutelary democracy" are understood as less than complete instances of democracy because they lack one or more of its defining attributes. Consequently, in using these subtypes the analyst makes a more modest claim about the extent of democratization and is therefore less vulnerable to conceptual stretching.

The second point concerns differentiation. Because diminished subtypes represent an incomplete form of democracy, they might be seen as having fewer defining attributes, with the consequence that they would be higher on the ladder of generality and would therefore provide less, rather than more, differentiation. However, the distinctive feature of diminished subtypes is that they generally identify specific attributes of democracy that are missing, thereby establishing the diminished character of the subtype, at the same time that they identify other attributes of democracy that are present. Because they specify missing attributes, they also increase differentiation, and the diminished subtype in fact refers to a different set of cases than does the root definition of democracy.

(Collier and Levitsky 1997: 437–38)

The key principle that Collier and Levitsky note is that, with a diminished subtype, certain attributes of democracy are missing. For example, the government does not respect civil liberties, making it an illiberal state. The difference between concepts plus adjectives and concepts minus adjectives appears to be that the concept plus adjectives concept adds *new* characteristics or dimensions while the concept minus adjective form changes the value from one to zero on an *existing* dimension. To formulize slightly, let's assume the concept of democracy has three defining attributes or dimensions, X_1, X_2, and X_3, and, for simplicity, that these are necessary and sufficient conditions for a country to be considered a democracy (this is not essential, as I discuss below). Concepts plus adjectives, or what Collier and Levitsky call the "classical subtype," means adding a new dimension, X_4, to the concept via the adjective, as in the example of parliamentary democracy.

To be considered a democracy or a parliamentary democracy means that $X_1 = 1$, $X_2 = 1$, $X_3 = 1$, and $X_4 = 1$ (assuming still the necessary and sufficient condition concept structure). The diminished subtype or concepts minus adjectives means, in contrast, $X_1 = 1$, $X_2 = 1$, $X_3 = 0$. The diminished subtype is thus missing a core attribute of democracy: the subtraction is not of dimensions themselves but the changing of values on existing dimensions to zero.

Within my framework, then, to change a value on an existing dimension from one to zero is to move left along the authoritarianism–democracy continuum. Figure 7.2 represents how things look from the perspective of my concept framework. As we change attributes from one to zero – create diminished subtypes – we have regimes that are less and less democratic. Movement is horizontal from democracy to authoritarianism.

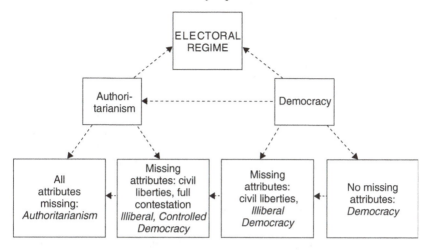

Figure 7.2 Concepts +/– adjectives and the authoritarian-democracy continuum.

Note: The arrows in this figure are used in the sense of Collier and Levitsky.

It is worth noting that this view of diminished subtypes works from the authoritarian end of the spectrum as well. One can start with cases where $X_1 = 0$, $X_2 = 0$, $X_3 = 0$, i.e., a perfectly authoritarian regime, and have a diminished subtype where $X_1 = 0$, $X_2 = 0$, $X_3 = 1$, for example, a liberal authoritarian state, perhaps an authoritarian state that respects civil liberties but has no elections.

So what does all this mean for the topic of this chapter, intension versus extension? The answer is nothing. In this formulation, the intension-extension question becomes: is the extension greater (or less) in the diminished subtype $X_1 = 1$, $X_2 = 1$, $X_3 = 0$ than the full concept $X_1 = 1$, $X_2 = 1$, $X_3 = 1$? The answer is that the extension can go up or can go down. It all depends on the relative number of cases of $X_3 = 1$ versus $X_3 = 0$ (I encourage the reader to do a few Venn diagrams to convince herself).

I have suggested that concepts plus adjectives involve adding a new attribute to an existing set, while concepts minus adjectives involves changing the value on an already existing dimension. Collier and his colleagues have made a major contribution to clearing up significant confusion on this key point of concept building. They have made it clear that when one sees a concept with an adjective in the literature, one cannot assume the classical operation of creating subsets, whereby the adjective adds a new dimension to the concept. Often, the scholar is focusing on a configuration of the concept *with zero on some existing attribute.*

Ideal types: zero extension

One concept-building strategy known to most social scientists uses the "ideal type" construction. This chapter focuses on concepts and their extensions; an ideal type usually has the empty set as its extension. It is an *ideal* type because it never or rarely can be found in practice. In practice, the principle meaning of ideal type is that the concept has zero extension.

The ideal type concept traces its historical origins back to Max Weber (1949). Burger describes Weber's view: "Ideal types are statements of general form asserting the existence of certain constellations of elements which are empirically only approximated by the instances of the class of phenomena to which each type refers" (Burger 1987: 133–34). There has developed a small literature devoted to Weber and his methodology, including the ideal type. Unfortunately, these analyses and debates about Weber are conducted in a very abstract and philosophical way (e.g., Heckman 1983). There is very little in the way of guidelines that permits one to evaluate what a good or bad ideal type looks like, and hence, little guidance on how to construct an ideal type concept.[8]

More useful than the controversial subject of what Weber said about ideal types is what sociologists and political scientists have done when they have created ideal types. My analysis may not capture what Weber thought, but I hope to be faithful to common practice of scholars who create and use ideal types.

An ideal type in my framework would mean those cases that score one (i.e., the maximum) on all the secondary-level dimensions. In many ways, I think this is the best way to think about ideal types. Inherent in the notion of an ideal type is that it lies at the extreme, usually positive, pole of the continuum. There can be nothing, conceptually at least, which is more ideal. It is useful to think of ideal types in geometric terms. The ideal type (like the ideal point in spatial utility models) is the point where all dimensions are at the maximum. One can contrast, that is, measure the distance between any given empirical object and that ideal point (Gärdenfors 2000).

What seems to typify ideal types in practice is that while they do not necessarily differ from ordinary concepts on intension, they do differ from them on extension. Typically, when a scholar proposes an ideal type, she is thinking that the extension of the ideal type is likely to be zero or very small: "I shall take it that a distinguishing characteristic of ideal type concepts is that they have no instances" (Papineau 1976: 137). The ideal generally is one that cannot be attained in practice. George W. Bush may aspire to being a man without sin, but he is unlikely to achieve his ideals. This certainly lies behind Weber's use of the term. Ideal types were useful as a means – really a standard – for thinking about a less-than-ideal reality.

An important part of concept design is whether one can find actual cases with the maximum or minimum values on the scale of the basic-level concept. The advice to the concept-builder is to think seriously about this issue. One might want to stretch out the scale so that there are very few (if any) cases at either extreme. The underlying idea is that if there are large clumps of cases at either extreme, then in reality the end points are not the ideal types and one could go further in either direction.

I would like to consider an example of ideal type concepts that I think brings out many of the important questions that need to be answered in making an ideal type concept. Robert Dahl's concept of democracy and polyarchy is an excellent example, and it is an ideal type in action which clearly uses a necessary and sufficient condition structure.

Robert Dahl's conceptualization of democracy is perhaps one of the most famous ideal types in the literature.[9] Dahl has developed the same basic view of democracy over forty years (1956, 1971, 1989, 1998). He is interesting because he clearly distinguishes between the ideal type "democracy," which no country has ever achieved, and "polyarchy," the term he prefers for those states that are closest to the democracy ideal. Dahl is quite unusual in separating so clearly the ideal type from the lower levels. By contrast, most scholars prefer to keep the same word for the ideal type and those phenomena that come close. He quite clearly expresses his views on democracy in terms of ideal types:

> In this book I should like to reserve the term "democracy" for a political system one of the characteristics of which is the quality of being completely or almost completely responsive to all its citizens. Whether such a system actually exists, has existed, or can exist need not concern us for the moment. Surely one can conceive a hypothetical system of this kind; such a conception has served as an ideal, or part of an ideal, for many people. As a hypothetical system, one end of a scale, or a limiting state of affairs, it can (like a perfect vacuum) serve as the basis for estimating the degree to which various systems appropriate this theoretical limit.
>
> (1971: 2)

Here we see most of the typical features of an ideal type. The extension of the concept may well be zero or near zero. The usefulness of the ideal type is as a standard against which one can compare existing objects.

It is worth noting that Dahl views democracy in a multilevel fashion typical of complex concepts (1971):[10]

I. Formulate preferences
   A. Freedom to form and join organizations
   B. Freedom of expression
   C. Right to vote
   D. Right of political leaders to compete for support
   E. Alternative sources of information

II. Signify preferences
   A. Freedom to form and join organizations
   B. Freedom of expression
   C. Right to vote
   D. Eligibility for public office
   E. Right of political leaders to compete for support
   F. Alternative sources of information
   G. Free and fair elections

III. Have preferences weighted equally in conduct of government
   A. Freedom to form and join organizations
   B. Freedom of expression

C. Right to vote

D. Eligibility for public office

E. Right of political leaders to compete for support

F. Alternative sources of information

G. Free and fair elections

H. Institutions for making government policies depend on votes and other expressions of preference

One way to build into the concept that its extension is likely to be zero is to use the necessary and sufficient condition structure for the concept. Dahl quite clearly uses AND at both levels of his concept of democracy. Everything at all levels is connected via AND. This makes it very difficult to find any real world phenomenon that satisfies such exigent conditions. To make things even more difficult, Dahl says that the above structure is necessary, but *not* sufficient: "These, [secondary-level dimensions] appear to me to be three necessary conditions for a democracy, though they are probably not sufficient" (Dahl 1971: 2).[11]

In short, democracy remains a pretty unattainable ideal: "Polyarchy is one of the most extraordinary of all human artifacts. Yet it unquestionably falls well short of achieving the democratic process" (Dahl 1989: 223). Polyarchy describes well those states that have made significant progress. "Democracy" is an ideal for which we should strive but which we are unlikely to achieve.

It is not hard to find others with a similar take on ideal types. For example, in the context of concepts of political parties:

> It is important to note that the models of political parties that we describe below are ideal types, in the strictest Weberian sense of that term. As such, they are heuristically useful insofar as they give easily understandable labels that will help the reader more easily comprehend otherwise complex, multidimensional concepts. Moreover, they facilitate analysis insofar as they serve as baselines for comparisons involving real-world cases, or as extreme endpoints of evolutionary processes that might never be fully attained. As with all ideal types, however, one should not expect that real-world political parties fully conform to all of the criteria that define each party model; similarly, some parties may include elements of more than one ideal type. Perhaps most importantly, individual parties may evolve over time, such that they may have most closely approximated one party type in an earlier period, but shift in the direction of a different type later on.
>
> (Gunther and Diamond 2003: 172)

Within my framework for concept construction, thinking in terms of ideal types provides no additional benefits. The positive and negative extremes or poles almost by definition provide a standard of comparison. In reality, when most scholars use the term "ideal type," all they really mean is that the extension is zero at the pole. Whether or not the extension is large or small near these poles is an empirical puzzle that calls for a causal explanation. For example, there are good causal reasons why it is hard to achieve absolute zero temperature. The existence of few or zero cases *anywhere* along the continuum from the negative pole to the positive – for example, in the gray zone between democracy and authoritarianism – generally poses questions worth examination.

Theoretical implications of concepts +/– adjectives: gender and the welfare state

Much of my analysis of concepts +/– adjectives has been devoted to clarifying issues of concept structure and its relationship to empirical extension. It could appear that the mundane maneuver of adding or subtracting adjectives has little in the way of upstream or downstream ramifications on theory. In this concluding section, I will illustrate that the addition of a dimension can have widespread and very important implications for theory and how we view the phenomenon described by the concept.

A major new development in the literature on the welfare state over the last decade has involved the analysis of the gender bias both in the welfare state itself and in the scholarly literature on it which has reproduced that bias. In these few pages, I cannot even begin to cover all the ramifications of the gender critique of the welfare state literature (for reviews, see Orloff 1996 and Pierson 2000). Of direct concern to me is how gender issues modify our concept of the welfare state and the implications for both theory and methodology in terms of both the concept itself and its links to theories about the welfare state.

The classic idea of a welfare state at its core involves the provision of goods and services to some large part of the population. One can reasonably ask (independent of gender, really): (1) Who are the main target populations? (2) What kinds of goods and services get delivered? Virtually all social welfare programs targeted male workers in nonagricultural occupations, typically industrial employees. Implicit in welfare state policies was a typical recipient who was male, married, and head of a household with children. Clearly, the wife/mother provided (unpaid, of course) childcare, health care, and often services to aged parents, in addition to basic household duties.

If you examine the list of services typically included in the operationalization of the welfare state and which faithfully reflect the concept, almost all deal with problems of the workingman. What happens if there is an accident on the job? What happens when he is unemployed? What happens when he gets old? Using the previously discussed example of Hicks, we can see that his four dimensions of the welfare state deal with these kinds of services. The goods and services for the household/family thus are funneled through the principal (male) wage earner.

One can then ask what kinds of goods and services would be appropriate for a female head of household to keep her alive and well. In addition to worker compensation, she would need maternity leave. To maintain her income (i.e., remain employed), she would need childcare. She would need a pension plan tied not just to the income of her spouse (not just survivor benefits). Thus, to really take into account the concerns of women in the population, particularly as (single) heads of households, we need to reconceptualize the welfare state.

Orloff (1993) provides a nice example of what this means. She takes Esping-Andersen's (1990) very influential view of the welfare state and asks what would have to be "added" to incorporate the concerns of women. She starts with the three dimensions or defining attributes of the welfare state according to Esping-Andersen. The first dimension involves the extent to which the welfare state provides services in contrast to the use of some market mechanism:

> A fundamental dimension that varies across welfare states concerns the "range, or domain, of human needs that are satisfied by social policy" instead of by the market (Esping-Andersen and Korpi 1987: 41), that is, "how state activities are interlocked with the market's and the family's role in social provision" (Esping-Andersen 1990: 21). . . . Thus, there will be class-influenced debates over the content of social policy and over the relative roles of markets and policies in determining welfare outcomes.
>
> (Orloff 1993: 310)

The second dimension for Esping-Andersen deals with "stratification," or how welfare states get involved with redistribution of income and problems of income inequality:

> A second dimension of policy regimes is stratification. . . . [P]ower resources analysts [e.g., Esping-Andersen] argue that systems of social provision have stratifying effects: some policies may promote equality, cross-class solidarity, or minimize economic differences, while others may promote social dualism or maintain or strengthen class, status, or occupational differentiation.
>
> (ibid.: 311)

This is the question about who benefits from the policies of the welfare state. Do these policies reinforce or mitigate inequalities generated by the market or other mechanisms?

Finally, the third dimension deals with the extent to which the welfare state creates "citizenship rights" and results in the "decommodification" of goods and services. The first dimension already talked about the state versus the market in terms of the delivery of services. The third dimension reinforces this by saying that some goods are decommodified because of welfare state policies:

> The third dimension of the welfare state concerns the character of social rights of citizenship. Some benefits are *universal*, that is, they are available to all citizens of a certain age or condition (e.g., sickness, unemployment, parenthood); some benefits depend on *labor market participation and financial contributions*; and some benefits are *income-tested*, that is, they are available only to those with income assets below a certain level. . . . Esping-Andersen argued that the extent to which the rights embodied in social programs promote or

circumscribe decommodification of labor is a critical dimension that varies across welfare states.

(ibid.)

Orloff argues that to take into account gender, one must *add* two dimensions to the Esping-Andersen concept of the welfare state. The first dimension requires that in addition to maintaining the basic wage of (male) workers, the strength of a welfare state should depend on the degree to which it supports paid labor by women:

> Thus, the decommodification dimension must be supplemented with a *new* analytic dimension that taps into the extent to which states promote or discourage women's paid employment – the right to be commodified. I call this fourth dimension of welfare-state regimes *access to paid work*. . . . Thus, I contend that the extent to which the state ensures access to paid work for different groups and the mechanisms that guarantee jobs (e.g., reliance on private employment, creation of tax incentives, legal regulation of private employment, or public jobs programs) are dimensions of all policy regimes.

(ibid.: 318)

The second new gender dimension argues that in addition to including the degree to which state policies encourage paid work for women, one needs to extend the range of concerns from individual men or women to the household and family. Most dramatically, the group of people most excluded from the traditional model was single-mother families. In the traditional system, all monies and services to the family, wife/mother, and children, were funneled through the working father. One thus needs to think about what services would be appropriate to keep a *household* going that might be headed by a single woman:

> If decommodification is important because it frees wage earners from the compulsion of participating in the market, a parallel dimension is needed to indicate the ability of those who do most of the domestic and caring work – almost all women – to form and maintain autonomous households, that is, to survive and support their children without having to marry to gain access to breadwinners' income.

(ibid.: 319)

If we conceive of the welfare state along these new lines, then there are important downstream implications for measures of the welfare state, as traditionally defined. Most quantitative studies of the welfare state use spending data (usually from the International Labor Organization [ILO]) for programs typically part of the male welfare state.[12] ILO spending data (1949–present) do cover "family allowances" and hence, in part, include programs that form part of Orloff's two additional dimensions. But Orloff argues that we also need to include all spending categories for programs that support (1) paid women's work and (2) women's capacity to maintain an autonomous household.

Beyond this, a gendered analysis of the welfare state suggests a more radical reconceptualization of the welfare state along with common quantitative measures. With rare exceptions, all post–World War II analyses of the welfare state use spending data. However, the gender analysis of the welfare state often focuses quite explicitly on *rights*. For example, O'Connor et al.'s (1999) analysis of Australia, Canada, the United States, and the United Kingdom includes abortion rights as a central dimension of comparison. Rights to divorce, contraception, and abortion are absolutely fundamental to women's welfare. In addition to the spending dimensions of the welfare state, one could certainly add a series of rights as new dimensions to the concept of the welfare state.

I have argued throughout this chapter that how we conceptualize a phenomenon has deep and intimate links with basic-level causal theories. One of the important, if not the most important, signs of this in welfare state literature is how gendered analyses have moved the welfare state variable from the dependent variable side of the equation to the independent variable side. Before the "nonsilent revolution" in the literature of the 1990s, the welfare state often appeared as the dependent variable: one explained the causes of its origin or expansion. In contrast, much of the gender literature looks at the impact (or not) of the welfare state on women's quality of life. A core question is the influence of the welfare state, not its causes. Not surprisingly, this is one area where rights play a key role. For women, it is not just spending, but control over their bodies that determines many aspects of their well-being. We add new secondary-level dimensions to the concept of the welfare state because we now know that they have important causal powers in the lives of women (and, of course, men). We add these new dimensions to the concept because we cannot understand how the welfare state works for 50 percent of the population without them.

A gender analysis of the welfare state illustrates what I mean by an ontological, realist, and structural analysis of concepts. It is not really about definitions as much as about analyzing how welfare policies work. You cannot make gender analysis go away by saying, "This is what I mean by the welfare state" (the Red Queen strategy). The concept of the welfare state matters because it is embedded in important theories about the welfare state and its impact on individuals. It is not surprising that when the welfare state was viewed through the male model, one of the key independent variables was labor union strength. Because we see the dependent variable now in a new light, we can then look to new kinds of independent variables. Given this new perspective on the welfare state, we can ask causal questions about its impact on women's lives (e.g., Skocpol 1992). Using a chemical metaphor, finding out about the nuclear structure of copper means we can better understand the properties of copper. Now that we better understand the gendered character of the welfare state, we can better understand its policies, their causes and effects.

Conclusion

The act of adding or subtracting secondary-level dimensions, i.e., concepts +/– adjectives, has tremendous repercussions on the theory and methodology of concepts. The issues surrounding conceptual stretching are really about how empirical extension varies depending on changes in the concept structure (intension). The most striking distinguishing characteristic of an ideal type concept involves a claim about its empirical extension. As Collier and his colleagues have noted, to use adjectives does not always mean adding a secondary-level dimension but sometimes changing the value on an existing dimension from one to zero.

To analyze effectively all of these kinds of questions requires a clear notion of concept structure. Once we have the three-level framework in hand and once we are clear about the character of the necessary and sufficient condition and family resemblance structures, we can begin to gain a clear understanding of the relationship between intension and extension. For example, the well-known claim that extension is inversely related to intension holds in general only for necessary and sufficient condition concepts. For family resemblance concepts, the relationship can go in the other direction.

Much remains to be done on the concepts +/– adjectives front. It is not at all clear that concepts +/– adjectives always work as I have described them here. A big class of examples is gendered concepts. If we were to follow the standard (necessary and sufficient condition) procedure, "women's (social) movement" is a subset of the class of all social movements. It is not clear that many working in the area would agree with this (e.g., Mazur and Stetson 2003). If the literature on cognitive psychology is any guide, the use of necessary and sufficient conditions is rare in natural social settings. There are good reasons why philosophers and social scientists continue to use the necessary and sufficient condition concept, but it might well be the case that when one uses concepts +/– adjectives, the end result is something quite different from what one would predict using the procedures discussed in this chapter.

The gendered welfare state literature illustrates that adding new characteristics can generate whole new research agendas. By including dimensions of special relevance to women and by putting the welfare state on the independent variable side of the equation, we gain dramatic new insights into the workings and nature of public policy in developed countries. By including these dimensions on the dependent variable side, we begin to think differently about the role of groups like labor unions in the creation of the welfare state. Here, again, we see the core and intimate relationship between causal theories and concepts. To include a new dimension in a concept is to see a new cause or a new effect.

Notes

* Adapted from Gary Goertz (2006) *Social Science Concepts: A User's Guide*, Princeton: Princeton University Press, Chapter 3.

1 Editors' note: As indicated in the Introduction to this volume, this chapter reviews and extends some of the arguments presented in the chapters below – specifically those by Kotowski, Kurtz, and Collier and Levitsky. Correspondingly, Table 7.1 is a very slight adaptation of Table 11.1 below (Chapter 11 by Kurtz); Table 7.2 is adapted from Table 8.1 (Chapter 8 by Kotowski); and Figure 7.1 is taken from an earlier published version

of Chapter 10 (Collier and Levitsky). To maintain the completeness of the present chapter by Goertz, these tables and figures are included here, as published in his original text.

2　A sample of the syllabi on the qualitative methods site – http://www.asu.edu/clas/polisci/cqrm/ – would reveal this (accessed January 15, 2008).

3　Sartori's term was "ladder of abstraction," but following Collier and Mahon (1993), I use "ladder of generality," since that is a more accurate term.

4　One can find the same basic presentation in contemporary philosophical logic textbooks, e.g., Copi and Cohen (1990).

5　I use Hicks's "binding or extensive" data.

6　There is a large cognitive psychology literature on concepts +/– adjectives. It is clear that the ordinary person's manipulation of concepts and adjectives does not conform to classic necessary and sufficient condition logic. For a good review, see Murphy (2002).

7　In fact, however, in some cases it is not clear that the author really thinks they are necessary: recall that within Sartori's framework the necessary condition structure is a given.

8　It is striking how often ideal types are used, and how little they are discussed in methodology texts.

9　Max Weber's ideal type analysis of bureaucracy is another very famous example.

10　See Dahl (1989: 222) for a different three-level model of democracy.

11　Schmitter and Karl adopt the Dahl list of prerequisites and add two more necessary conditions: "Popularly elected officials must be able to exercise their constitutional powers without being subjected to overriding (albeit informal) opposition from unelected officials [e.g., army]. . . . The polity must be self-governing; it must be able to act independently of constraints imposed by some other overarching political system" (1991: 81).

12　Welfare spending is defined by the ILO as government spending related to schemes, transfers, or services that (1) grant curative or preventive medical care, maintain income in case of involuntary diminution of earning, or grant supplementary income to persons with family responsibilities, (2) are legislatively sanctioned, and (3) are administered publicly or semi-publicly.

References

Adcock, R. and Collier, D. (2001) "Measurement Validity: A Shared Standard for Qualitative and Quantitative Research," *American Political Science Review* 95: 529–46.

Burger, T. (1987) *Max Weber's Theory of Concept Formation: History, Laws, and Ideal Types*, Durham, NC: Duke University Press.

Chapin, F. (1939) "Definition of Definitions of Concepts," *Social Forces* 18: 153–60.

Cohen, M., and Nagel, E. (1934) *An Introduction to Logic and Scientific Method*, New York: Harcourt, Brace.

Collier, D. and Levitsky, S. (1997) "Democracy with Adjectives: Conceptual Innovation in Comparative Research," *World Politics* 49: 430–51.

Collier, D. and Mahon, J.E., Jr. (1993) "Conceptual 'Stretching' Revisited: Adapting Categories in Comparative Analysis," *American Political Science Review* 87: 845–55.

Copi, I. and Cohen, C. (1990) *Introduction to Logic*, 8th edn, London: Macmillan.

Dahl, R. (1956) *A Preface to Democratic Theory*, Chicago: University of Chicago Press.

Dahl, R. (1971) *Polyarchy: Participation and Opposition*, New Haven, CT: Yale University Press.

Dahl, R. (1989) *Democracy and Its Critics*, New Haven, CT: Yale University Press.

Dahl, R. (1998) *On Democracy*, New Haven, CT: Yale University Press.

DiRenzo, G. (1966) "Conceptual Definition in the Behavioral Sciences," in G. DiRenzo (ed.), *Concepts, Theory, and Explanation in the Behavioral Sciences*, New York: Random House.

Dumont, R. and Wilson, W. (1967) "Aspects of Concept Formation, Explication, and Theory Construction in Sociology," *American Sociological Review* 32: 985–95.

Esping-Andersen, G. (1990) *The Three Worlds of Welfare Capitalism*, Cambridge: Polity Press.

Esping-Andersen, G. and Korpi, W. (1987) "From Poor Relief to Institutional Welfare States: The Development of Scandinavian Social Policy," in R. Erikson et al. (eds.), *The Scandinavian Model: Welfare States and Welfare Research*, Armonk, NY: M.E. Sharpe.

Foran, J. (1997) "The Comparative-Historical Sociology of Third World Social Revolutions: Why a Few Succeed, Why Most Fail," in J. Foran (ed.), *Theorizing Revolution*, London: Routledge.

Gärdenfors, P. (2000) *Conceptual Spaces: The Geometry of Thought*, Cambridge, MA: MIT Press.

Gerring, J. (2001) *Social Science Methodology: A Criterial Framework*, Cambridge: Cambridge University Press.

Gunther, R. and Diamond, L. (2003) "Species of Political Parties: A New Typology," *Party Politics* 9: 167–99.

Heckman, S. (1983) *Weber, the Ideal Type, and Contemporary Social Theory*, Notre Dame, IN: University of Notre Dame Press.

Hempel, C. (1952) *Fundamentals of Concept Formation in Empirical Science*, International Encyclopedia of Unified Science, vol. 2, no. 7, Chicago: University of Chicago Press.

Hempel, C. (1965a) "Typological methods in the natural and social sciences," in C. Hempel (ed.), *Aspects of Scientific Explanation*, New York: Free Press.

Hempel, C. (1965b) *Aspects of Scientific Explanation and Other Essays in the Philosophy of Science*, New York: Free Press.

Hempel, C. (1966) *Philosophy of Natural Science*, Englewood Cliffs, NJ: Prentice Hall.

Hicks, A. (1999) *Social Democracy and Welfare Capitalism: A Century of Income Security Politics*, Ithaca, NY: Cornell University Press.

International Labor Organization (1949–present) *The Cost of Social Security*, Geneva: ILO.

Kotowski, C. (1984) "Revolution," in G. Sartori (ed.), *Social Science Concepts: A Systematic Analysis*, Beverly Hills, CA: Sage.

Kurtz, M. (2000) "Understanding Peasant Revolution: From Concept to Theory and Case," *Theory and Society* 29: 93–124.

Lakoff, G. (1987) *Women, Fire and Dangerous Things: What Categories Reveal about the Mind*, Chicago: University of Chicago Press.

Landau, M. (1972) *Political Theory and Political Science: Studies in the Methodology of Political Inquiry*, New York: Macmillan.

Lasswell, H. and Kaplan, A. (1950) *Power and Society: A Framework for Political Inquiry*, New Haven, CT: Yale University Press.

Lazarsfeld, P. (1966) "Concept Formation and Measurement in the Behavioral Sciences: Some Historical Observations," in G. DiRenzo (ed.), *Concepts, Theory, and Explanation in the Behavioral Sciences*, New York: Random House.

Mazur, A. and Stetson, D. (2003) "Quantifying Complex Concepts: The Case of the Women's Movement in the RNGS Project," *APSA-CP Newsletter* 14: 11–14.

Meehan, E. (1971) *The Foundations of Political Analysis: Empirical and Normative*, Homewood, AL: Dorsey Press.

Murphy, G. (2002) *The Big Book of Concepts*, Cambridge, MA: MIT Press.

O'Connor, J., Orloff, A., and Shaver, S. (1999) *States, Markets, Families: Gender, Liberalism, and Social Policy in Australia, Canada, Great Britain, and the United States*, Cambridge: Cambridge University Press.

Orloff, A. (1993) "Gender and the Social Rights of Citizenship: The Comparative Analysis of Gender Relations and Welfare States," *American Sociological Review* 58: 303–28.

Orloff, A. (1996) "Gender in the Welfare State," *Annual Review of Sociology* 22: 51–78.

Papineau, D. (1976) "Ideal Types and Empirical Theories," *British Journal for the Philosophy of Science* 27: 137–46.

Pierson, P. (2000) "Three Worlds of Welfare State Research," *Comparative Political Studies* 33: 791–821.

Sartori, G. (1970) "Concept Misformation in Comparative Politics," *American Political Science Review* 64 (4): 1033–53.

Sartori, G. (1984) "Guidelines for Concept Analysis," in G. Sartori (ed.), *Social Science Concepts: A Systematic Analysis*, London: Sage.

Sartori, G., Riggs, F., and Teune, H. (1975) *Tower of Babel: On the Definition and Analysis of Concepts in the Social Sciences*, Pittsburgh: International Studies Association, University of Pittsburgh, Occasional Paper 6: 7–37.

Schmitter, P. and Karl, T. (1991) "What Democracy Is . . . and Is Not," *Journal of Democracy* 2: 75–88.

Skocpol, T. (1979) *States and Social Revolutions: A Comparative Analysis of France, Russia, and China*, Cambridge: Cambridge University Press.

Skocpol, T. (1992) *Protecting Soldiers and Mothers: The Political Origins of Social Policy in the United States*, Cambridge, MA: Harvard University Press.

Stepan, A. and Skach, C. (1993) "Constitutional Frameworks and Democratic Consolidation: Parliamentarism versus Presidentialism," *World Politics* 46: 1–22.

Stinchcombe, A. (1968) *Constructing Social Theories*, New York: Harcourt, Brace & World.

Stinchcombe, A. (1978) *Theoretical Methods in Social History*, New York: Academic Press.

Weber, M. (1949) *Max Weber on the Methodology of the Social Sciences*, trans. and ed. E.A. Shils and H.A. Finsh, Glencoe, IL: Free Press.

Zannoni, P. (1978) "The Concept of Elite," *European Journal of Political Research* 6: 1–30.

8 Revolution

Untangling alternative meanings

Christoph Kotowski

There are two major reasons for scholarly confusion about the term "revolution." First, there is widespread disagreement about which phenomena are to be included among the referents of the term; and second, scholars characterize revolutions differently, thus attaching different connotations to the term which consequently give it different meanings. Previous conceptual analyses have primarily attacked the former source of confusion, the "boundary problem." Most of these attempts simply have declared that revolution is an umbrella term covering any kind of violent change of the governing body (Amann 1962; Calvert 1970; Laquer 1968). By stipulating that a revolution is any event in which violence coincides with a change of the governing body, these authors have avoided making the difficult distinctions between revolutions, coups, secessions, "palace revolutions," and so on.

This mode of conceptual analysis leads to the formulation of a relatively clear and well-bounded concept of revolution, but it nevertheless must be rejected for two reasons. First, most scholars who study actual revolutions and theorize about them deliberately state that they are not interested in mere coups or seizures of power, but in a very special phenomenon. Thus, the aforesaid stipulation bears little relevance to actual investigation of revolution in the social sciences. Second, the approach is incomplete in that it deals only with the boundary problem: no effort is made to analyze how the term's connotation affects the formulation of the concept. Consequently, its whole meaning is never captured.

This conceptual analysis will attempt to improve on previous efforts. First, I will show how various authors demarcate the boundaries of the referents by discussing the characteristics commonly attributed to revolutions. Then, by examining disciplinary and theoretical contexts, I will differentiate between three major meanings commonly imputed to the term. Not surprisingly, at present there exists no single formulation of the concept applicable to the study of revolution in all the different fields and theoretical traditions in the social sciences.

Controversies in the social sciences

The apparent confusion over the concept of revolution results from social scientists' practice of defining and redefining the term to meet their research needs.

Researchers are interested in different phenomena, but maintain the word revolution for the events that they are studying. Thus, there are great – probably irresolvable – controversies among scholars about which events are to be included among the referents. For example, Theda Skocpol (1979) considers herself to be a "class analyst"; political events are to be explained fundamentally by the relationships between social classes. Her research interests lie in the dynamics of class conflict and how these conflicts are resolved in the political arena. Not surprisingly, she retains the term revolution to refer only to rare and dramatic types of class conflict and social change.[1]

In contrast to Skocpol, Ted R. Gurr (1978: 304) tells us that his classic book *Why Men Rebel* (1970) "is about political violence, not revolution." However, when discussing the concept of revolution (1973) he adamantly argues that one should not define revolution in terms of social change: to do so would be question begging since it fails to deal with such questions as, "When does social change become revolutionary?" Social changes are effects of revolutions to be assessed empirically; if one wishes to retain the term revolution for changes, then one should use terms like "political revolution" (in which governmental power changes hands) or "revolutionary change" (in which social transformation takes place). Thus, Gurr has one criterion for revolution – massive violence. Consequently, revolution becomes a broad term referring to a wide array of violent confrontations.

Skocpol and Gurr are on the extremes of the controversy about the defining attributes of the term revolution. The former posits one of the smallest sets of attributes; the latter, one of the largest. However, their dispute is by no means unique. In looking through Appendix I, one immediately spots many differences in the intension of the various definitions of revolution. Huntington requires political structural change, but Brinton does not; Johnson requires violence, but Tilly does not; and so forth. In short, there is no general agreement on the necessary and sufficient characteristics of revolution, and therefore no agreement on which events are to be subsumed under the category.

Disputes about the intension of the concept can be understood in terms of three broad groupings of theorists. For the first group, revolution is seen as a form of violence. Gurr (1973: 359), for example, uses phrases like "revolutions and lesser forms of violence," and at one point explicitly states that, "the properties and processes that distinguish a riot from a revolution are substantively and theoretically interesting . . . but at a general level of analysis they seem to be differences of degree, not kind" (Gurr 1970: 5). James C. Davies (1962), Harry Eckstein (1965), David V. J. Bell (1973) and Mostafa Rejai (1977) characterize revolutions in much the same way. Eckstein goes so far as to suggest that we stop using the term revolution altogether and replace it with the term "internal war."

A second group of theorists characterizes revolutions as a breakdown of the political and/or social system. Lynford P. Edwards (1970 [1927]: 5) stated this point of view succinctly over fifty years ago: "Revolution involves the disintegration of society." Crane Brinton (1965 [1938]), Chalmers Johnson (1966), and Samuel P. Huntington (1968) see revolutions in much the same light. Brinton and Johnson see revolutions as a kind of pathology afflicting the social organism.

Huntington, focusing on political factors, views them as a breakdown of the political system due to insufficient institutionalization.

Finally, a third group of theorists views revolution as a sudden transformation of the society and polity that makes possible a higher form of human existence. This characterization is most often associated with Marx and Marxists who argue that "revolution is the driving force of history" (Marx 1972 [1846]), that "revolutions are the locomotives of history" (Marx, cited in Skocpol 1979: 3), or that "revolutions are the mad inspiration of history" (Trotsky, cited in Friedrich 1966: 4). Even neo-Marxists who have discarded some of the most cumbersome and problematic ideological baggage of Marxism, such as Skocpol and her mentor Barrington Moore, have maintained largely the same notion of revolution. However, this "progressive" conception of revolution is not necessarily tied to Marxism. Hannah Arendt (1965 [1963]), for example, characterizes revolutions fundamentally as a striving for freedom. All of these theorists realize that revolutions also involve violence and the destruction of the old order, but they view it mainly in terms of the creation of a new and better order.

To summarize, we find three major ways of characterizing revolutions and any number of ways to delimit the corresponding attributes. It should not surprise us that revolution is often used in an unclear or confused manner. Few if any of the definitions in Appendix I are satisfactory. Most of the definitions are a mere listing of equally weighted characteristics, without pointing to the general category to which the term belongs and without isolating its most crucial characteristics. Compounding the confusion, writers at times skip from one characterization of revolution to another. Johnson, for example, tells us on the first page of *Revolutionary Change* that, "Revolutions are social changes"; yet we are told only a few pages later that revolutions should be studied as "a form of violence" (1966: 1, 7).

Rejai commits the same error: first he argues that revolutions should be viewed as "a fundamental transformation of an existing society/polity by mass violent means," but later he defines revolution as "abrupt, illegal mass violence aimed at the overthrow of the political regime as a step to overall social change" (1977: v, 8). The latter cannot be seen as an improved or sharpened version of the former; it is a wholly new definition. There is a major difference between the assertion that revolution is a type of change that relies on violence, and the assertion that revolution is a type of violence that aims at change. While the intensional characteristics may be the same in both cases, in the former revolution is characterized as a form of change while in the latter it is seen as a form of violence.

Similarly, Jean Baechler's *Revolution* (1970) is a *tour de force* of different meanings and characterizations of revolution. First, he argues that revolutions, narrowly defined, are "the illegal seizure[s] of power" (xi). Next we are told that revolution is a type of social "mutation" (20–21). A few pages later he declares that, "revolutions are defined as ways of challenging the social order, they obviously rely on conflict" (24). Then he claims that revolution "is a conflict" (30). Finally he adds, "I must remind the reader that by 'revolutions' I mean protest movements that manage to seize power" (91). Thus, in less than a hundred pages the concept has changed its meaning from a type of political change, to a social change, to a challenge relying on conflict, to a type of conflict, and finally to a successful challenge of political power by a "protest movement."

Previous conceptual analyses

All previous conceptual analyses with which I am familiar have sought to eliminate the confusion about the term revolution by formulating a single new concept. This can be done either through a historical examination of the term or through stipulation. The former method seeks to return to the original meaning of the term by examining its *Geistesgeschichte*. However, while this may be a valuable strategy in many cases, it cannot be used to explicate the modern concept of revolution. As Arendt (1965 [1963]: 41–47) points out, revolution was originally an astronomical term, referring to the lawfully revolving motion of the stars. When first applied to human affairs, the term carried the implication of a swinging back to a preordained order; revolution actually meant "restoration." She concludes that, "nothing could be farther removed from the original meaning of the word 'revolution' than the idea of which all revolutionary actors have been possessed and obsessed, namely, that they are agents in a process which spells the definite end of an old order and brings about the birth of a new world" (ibid.: 42).

Peter Calvert (1970: 132–36) posits nine different historical uses of the term revolution: defiance of authority, social dissolution, overthrow of rulers, revulsion against misused authority, constitutional change, reordering of society, inevitable stage of development, permanent attribute of an ideal order, and psychological outlet. However, he argues that most of these formulations are "mystical" with little practical applicability to politics and political science. Thus, he opts for the second mode of forming a single concept, stipulating that the term revolution should apply to "all forms of violent change of the government or regime" (ibid.: 140–41). The referents of the term are thus relatively well demarcated. Any event marked by the coincidence of two characteristics, violence and governmental change, is declared to be a revolution.[2]

Other conceptual analysts have sought to resolve the confusion about revolution in much the same manner. George Pettee (1966: 15–16), for example, terms the following kinds of violent political change as "revolutions": (1) *private palace revolutions*, which are the quiet replacement of top officials by some elicit means (his example for this type of revolution is Macbeth's succession after murdering Duncan); (2) *public palace revolutions*, which replace top officials after some kind of minor public battle for power; (3) *secession*,[3] which is "the rebellion of one area against the rule of another country"; (4) *great national revolutions*, which are mass phenomena and change both political and social structures (e.g., the French and Russian Revolutions); and (5) *systematic revolutions*, in which not just one state but an entire civilization is transformed (e.g., the fall of the Roman Empire). Thus, Pettee treats revolution as an umbrella term; any kind of violent or illicit transfer of political power is labeled a "revolution."

Peter Amann (1962) argues that the defining characteristic of revolution is the competition between "power blocs" for political power, and that the revolution is completed when a new "power bloc" has achieved a monopoly of power. While he does not explicitly state that violence is a defining characteristic of revolution, this is strongly implied by the use of the term "power bloc." If he had intended to include nonviolent competition for political power, terms like "contender" or "alternate authorities" would have been more appropriate. As it is, we are left with the imagery of a violent confrontation between power blocs. Amann proudly points to the fact that this definition avoids the "fine distinction" between revolution and *coup d'etat*. This leads us to conclude that revolution is a broad term that applies to all kinds of violent political change.

Charles Tilly (1975) conceives of revolution in much the same manner as Amann. He defines the concept in terms of "multiple sovereignty." A revolution is characterized by the mobilization of "contenders" who challenge the authority of the existing government. When one of these contenders manages to secure a commitment from some significant portion of the population, a state of "multiple sovereignty" exists; this state may also be called a "revolutionary situation." If one of the contenders actually manages to seize full political power, the result is a "revolutionary outcome." Tilly never defines the term "revolution," but it is clear that he takes it to be synonymous with "revolutionary outcome." Unlike Amann, however, Tilly explicitly states that violence is not a necessary characteristic. Thus, Tilly's conceptualization is even broader than that of other conceptual analysts; any kind of unconstitutional change of government is a "revolution."[4]

Each of these conceptual analyses attempts to formulate a well-bounded concept of revolution. However, these formulations are objectionable on two counts. First, the "clarity" of their relatively well-bounded conceptualization is achieved by stipulations that are not arbitrary – for violence and change of government are generally recognized characteristics – but still deviate substantially from much scholarly use of the term. Most, although admittedly not all, theorists of revolution are interested in studying rare and dramatic phenomena, whereas the definitions proposed by the authors that we have just reviewed "seize" referents (e.g., coups, secessions, etc.) of lesser interest, not to say of a different kind.

Second, the aforesaid conceptual analyses are inadequate because they are incomplete. They attack only the boundary problem and make little effort to analyze the intension of the term. This omission is difficult to understand in the analysis of a term so rich in connotation. We can demonstrate the importance of the connotation of the term. Everyone would agree that the French Revolution was a true revolution, but different authors will characterize the event as either the birth of a new order or as the "breakdown" of a system. Clearly, in this case, differences in the intension of the concept are much more important than those about the extension, because they do not result in a different slicing of cases.

A complete analysis of the concept of revolution must cover both the intension and the extension of the term. That, in brief, is the project of this article. First, I will examine further and explicate five defining characteristics commonly attributed to revolution. Second, I will organize these characteristics in a table with nine authors (Tilly, Gurr, Brinton, Davies, Johnson, Huntington, Marx, Moore, and Skocpol) in order to show how they demarcate the referents of the term. Third, I shall examine these authors' actual sorting of cases, to see whether it is consistent with their abstract formulation of the concept. Finally, I will show how disciplinary and theoretical contexts affect the characterization of the concept.

The necessary characteristics

Revolutions are complex phenomena. They may be accompanied by numerous events, and they may produce any number of changes. In this section, however, I shall discuss only those characteristics that some (although not all) authors hold to be necessary characteristics. I will, in a sense, be offering a "mini" conceptual analysis of the following proposed defining characteristics of revolution: (1) *violence*, (2) *popular involvement*, (3) *change of the governing body*, (4) *structural political change*, and (5) *changes in the systems of social stratification*. At present, I intend only to explicate these characteristics, not to assess any author's conceptualization of revolution. I will refer to the authors listed above, but only to clarify the characteristics.

Before doing this, however, I would like to point out one peculiarity of the concept of revolution; namely, that all but one of the authors mentioned above conceive of revolution as an *extended process*.[5] That is, many of the events leading up to the occurrences of 1688, 1789, 1917, 1949, and so on, and many of the events following them all are considered part of the process of revolution. For example, Gurr and Davies view revolution as a type of aggression, and aggression is necessarily (in their view) linked to frustration, and frustration is necessarily linked to deprivation. Thus, the concept of revolution cannot be separated from the deprivation–frustration–aggression syndrome. Similarly, those who see revolution as the breakdown of a social order (Edwards; Johnson) or of a political system (Brinton; Huntington) cannot separate the concept of revolution from the whole process of breakdown. The same is of course doubly true for Marxists and neo-Marxists, who define revolution in terms of the solution of ongoing historical contradictions. Thus, virtually all major theorists of revolutions see them as extended processes, not merely as events. The consequences of this are that many events that would ordinarily be considered causes and/or effects are "swallowed" into the concept as defining characteristics. This makes revolution a very complex concept.

Violence

Are revolutions, by definition, violent? Would a phenomenon manifesting all the other characteristics of revolution still be considered a revolution if it were not violent? For example, had Allende managed to transform Chile into a Cuban-style society/polity, would this too have been a revolution? On this point, aside from Tilly, our authors agree: violence is a necessary characteristic of revolution.

However, in and of itself, the statement that violence is a necessary characteristic of revolution is not very helpful since violence itself has been conceived of in many different ways. Scholars generally assume that there is a consensus about the meaning of violence, that the word is virtually self-explanatory. This, unfortunately, is not the case. As Tilly notes (somewhat overstating the case), "at the present state of knowledge and theory concerning violence any definition will be arbitrary in some regards and debatable in many others" (Tilly 1975: 513, 1978: 176). Perhaps the problem is not that hopeless. In the current social science literature, I find three main formulations of the concept: (1) violence as any kind of antisocial or harmful behavior; (2) violence as "brute harm," and (3) violence as harm done in violation of pre-established social norms. Of these, I find only the third formulation acceptable. As we shall see, the first formulation is not in keeping with most accepted usage of the term "violence" and is also useless in empirical research; the second formulation is more suitable to research but, after some examination, it turns out to be conceptually troublesome.

Chalmers Johnson is among the authors who conceive of violence in a broad manner to include almost any type of antisocial behavior. He defines violence as "either behavior which is impossible for others to orient themselves to or behavior which is deliberately intended to prevent orientation and the development of stable expectations with regard to it" (1966: 8). He prefers this Parsonian sociological formulation because it makes the concept easier to incorporate into a social-systemic theory of revolution. However, in addition to simply being too obscure, we must reject this formulation because it is far too broad. Johnson himself admits that this conception of violence includes such minor incidents as insults, "lunatic acts," and politically motivated fasts as well as full-fledged mass violence as in civil war (1966: 10). Johan Galtung (1969: 168) has an even broader conception of violence. He claims that, "violence is present when human beings are influenced so that their somatic and mental realizations are below their potential realizations." Threats, lies, and even indoctrination are thus included as acts of violence. Another author goes so far as to include the "silent violence: famine and inequality" in his concept of violence (Spitz 1978).

These formulations make the term violence a virtual synonym for "undesirable." If we were to accept them, empirical research would be severely hobbled. If insults count as a form of violence, then violence is a regular part of the proceedings in every Western parliament. Surely we must make a qualitative distinction between a heated debate on the floor of the House of Commons and an outright civil war in Lebanon, rather than simply lumping both together as "violent." For this reason, many scholars have come to rely on what Terry Nardin (1972: 115) calls the "brute harm" concept of violence.

Ted Gurr (1973: 360), for example, defines violence as the "deliberate use of force to injure or destroy physically, not some more general category of coercive actions or policies, and not institutional arrangements that demean or frustrate their members." This definition is relatively well suited to "seizing the objects" that Gurr wants to examine, but comes short of capturing his own full meaning of the concept. When examining Gurr's work, it is important to realize that he uses the terms *violence* and *aggression* as virtual synonyms. He defines the latter as "behavior designed to injure, physically or otherwise, those toward whom it is directed" (1970: 33). Thus, the two concepts differ only in that aggression includes nonphysical (presumably psychological) damage; in empirical research and at the operational level, however, the two are virtually indistinguishable. Violence is conceived of as a non-rational outburst of aggression, although Gurr admits that on rare occasions it may have mainly purposive aims.[6]

Hannah Arendt, also broadly within the "brute harm" school of thought, takes precisely the opposite approach from Gurr. While she never defines violence in *On Violence*, she does argue that violence is distinguished by its instrumental character and its use of implements (1970 [1969]: 46). Thus, we may surmise from her text that violence is the use of implements for the destruction of persons or property in the pursuit of some greater goal.

Both Gurr and Arendt are excessively restrictive in their formulation of the concept of violence. It is always difficult to determine with any certainty the intention (motive) behind an act. In any case, both non-rational and purposive acts should count as violent. However, while Arendt and Gurr disagree about the intention (motive) that lies behind an act of violence, both agree that the act must be done with intent. This intent has two components. First, the act must be deliberate (as opposed to accidental). Second, it must be designed to do damage. Introducing intent into the concept does not rob it of its usefulness in empirical research; such intent is generally empirically ascertainable. While there may be questionable cases, there is undeniably intent behind such acts as joining a guerilla group, storming a government building, or the police's opening fire on a crowd of demonstrators. These actions may be motivated by any number of good or bad intentions, but intent is clearly present in each case. So let us provisionally posit the following "brute harm" definition of violence: violence consists of *actions intended to do physical harm to persons or property*.

The problem with such a definition, as Nardin points out (1972: 118), is that, "persons" and "property" are not natural facts but social institutions. "Persons" are social institutions in the sense that not all living (physically defined) human beings are necessarily included into the notion of person. For instance, slaves were not considered "persons"; the same is true in caste-type societies for the lower castes. And "property" certainly is, in a roundabout fashion, a social institution. Granted that persons and property are not social institutions to the same extent and manner, it can still be said with reference to both that it is not just intended "brute harm" that constitutes violence but "brute harm" done in violation of certain social sanctions of some widely recognized social norm.

Charles Tilly attempts to avoid these problems in his "brute harm" formulation of the concept by defining violence as "any observable interaction in which persons or objects are seized or physically damaged over resistance" (1975: 513; see also 1978: 176). Presumably, the interaction in question would not meet resistance to the destruction of objects that were not somehow conceived of as property of some kind, nor would the interaction continue over resistance if it were doing damage accidentally. However, the "over resistance" clause creates more problems than it solves. Violence may be purely one-sided, and not resisted. Under Tilly's definition, shooting an unsuspecting passerby in the back would not be considered an act of violence. Surely we wish to retain such events within the term "violence."

Thus, we must retain Nardin's notion that violence involves the violation of norms as well as doing harm. Indeed, as Henry Bienen (1968: 4) notes, "violence carries overtones of 'violating.'" Such a formulation is consistent with most scholarly uses of the term. Elizabeth Converse's (1968: 482) extensive review of the first twelve years of the *Journal of Conflict Resolution* concludes that scholars generally use the term "violence" only to denote the illegitimate use of force and "acts not legitimated by a government's law." Thus, I will ultimately define violence as *illegal actions to do physical harm to persons or property – in violation of recognized social norms.*[7]

This definition specifically excludes acts intended to do *psychological* damage. A definition including psychological damage would involve too much conceptual stretching; it packs too much into the concept of violence. A Marxist, for example, might argue that the teaching of religion or of "bourgeois" history, philosophy, or economics constitutes psychological damage. Conversely, others might argue that, during the Soviet period, the Soviet schools were psychologically damaging the youth with indoctrination. If we include such phenomena as a form of violence then we will soon be to the point where we cannot say or do anything without "doing violence" to someone. The category of psychological harm is better covered by such concepts as mind control, intimidation, and the intentional infliction of emotional distress.

Note that my own formulation of the concept of violence is a relatively narrow one: it includes acts of bloodshed only if accompanied by the violation of accepted norms. Still, even with the concept so narrowly formulated, most of our authors would agree that violence is a necessary characteristic of revolution. Gurr and Davies, who analyze revolution with an "aggregate psychological" theory, conceive of revolution as a type of violence or aggression. Social and political "breakdown" theorists (Edwards, Brinton, and Johnson) see violence as an inevitable result of the crumbling of governmental authority. Johnson in particular argues that widespread "disorientation" may lead many members of a society to be easily swayed into wholly senseless violence. Huntington argues that even if the institutions of the old order are feeble, it will take violence to overthrow them. Marx, Moore, and Skocpol would argue along similar lines. Even when the accession of a new ruling class is imminent and obvious, the old ruling class never simply steps aside politely; it must be overthrown. Thus, there is general consensus that violence is a necessary characteristic of revolution. Among the authors surveyed, only Tilly does not make it a defining characteristic.

Popular involvement

Do revolutions necessarily entail some kind of popular involvement in the revolutionary process? We find less scholarly disagreement on this point than on whether violence is a defining characteristic. But before discussing which authors hold widespread involvement to be a necessary characteristic, I will explain why I say "popular involvement" rather than popular participation or mass mobilization.

On the one hand, "popular participation" may refer to the self-activation and organization of some significant percentage of a society's population. For example, when the Czarist regime collapsed in 1917, the peasants did not have to be activated by others to seize the land or establish peasant councils, nor were the urban councils the conscious creation of revolutionary parties. Until late in the game, Lenin was at best wary of the councils precisely because they were autonomously created.

On the other hand, "mass mobilization" may be used to characterize the activation of a significant portion of the population by an elite in a consciously directed manner. In revolutions this may happen in one of two ways. First, the mass may be mobilized by revolutionary elites in order to seize power. Perhaps the best example of this is the Chinese Revolution in which Mao and the Chinese communists slowly built their organization and a mass following. Second, the revolutionaries may mobilize people after they are already in formal control of the government, in order to carry through a social transformation. Such mobilization took place after 1917 and after 1945 (in Eastern Europe), but perhaps the single best example of this kind of revolutionary mass mobilization is the Nazi revolution. Not only did the Nazis perpetually hold rallies to bolster their support, but the National Socialist *Gleichschaltung* also brought every group of any importance under direct Nazi control and made them instruments of the national socialist transformation.

Thus, by "popular involvement" I mean both popular participation and mass mobilization. I do not wish to address the dispute about whether popular involvement is elite directed, or instead spontaneous and autonomous. By saying that an event is marked by popular involvement I only wish to imply that it is not exclusively an affair within the elite. It is, of course, impossible to demarcate precisely at what point "popular involvement" begins. Does it involve at least 10 percent of the population? 25 percent? 50 percent? However, when looking at concrete events, we can usually distinguish between exclusively elite affairs and those marked by popular involvement. There are borderline cases – for example, a military takeover brought on by widespread unrest and resistance, as in Pakistan in 1977. Yet usually it is easy to establish whether the seizure of power was accomplished by a few highly placed military officials (as in most Latin American and African coups) or whether many non-elites were also involved (as in Iran or Vietnam).

Most of the authors examined in this analysis do make popular involvement a necessary characteristic of revolution. The formulations of the concept by Gurr, Davies, and Johnson require the inclusion of popular involvement since their theories of revolution are based on arguments about how widespread revolutionary discontent is created. Gurr and Davies argue that revolution is the result of a certain kind and quantity of widespread "relative deprivation," while Johnson accounts for revolution by pointing to widespread social "disorientation." Huntington's conception must include popular involvement since he views revolutions as the result of too much participation for the existing institutions to accommodate. On different grounds, Moore and Skocpol incorporate popular involvement into their definitions of revolution (see Appendix I).

On the other hand, Tilly's concept of revolution requires only the unconstitutional transfer of power; thus, popular involvement is not a necessary characteristic. Brinton's definition requires only the violent (or at least forceful) transfer of power; popular involvement is seen as a characteristic only of certain "great revolutions." Finally, and interestingly, Marx is ambivalent as to whether popular involvement is a necessary characteristic. The proletarian revolution would, of course, be a large popular movement, but revolutions of the past had been fought between competing upper classes. For example, the "bourgeois revolutions" are seen as contests between the nobility and the bourgeoisie. The lower classes were not necessarily involved (see for example, Marx and Engels 1972 [1848]).

Unconstitutional change of governing body

There is a general consensus that a minimally necessary characteristic of revolution is sonic wholesale and unconstitutional replacement of the governing body. Agreement on this point is so widespread that few authors ever consider the matter in detail. However, while the characteristic is relatively self-explanatory, a few underpinnings are in order.

First, by "governing body" I mean the whole set of several hundred or several thousand top decision makers, not just the presidency or a few top posts. That is to say, the revolutionaries must take control of all the important ministries – interior, defense, foreign, economic, and education. All top-level administrators in each of these ministries must be replaced so that the revolutionaries have firm control over the whole governmental apparatus.

Second, while there is widespread agreement that the unconstitutional change of the governing body is a necessary characteristic of revolution, the importance attributed to this characteristic varies greatly from author to author. Tilly (as noted earlier) defines revolution as a period of "multiple sovereignty" followed by the accession to power of a new group of leaders. Thus, what I have called the "unconstitutional change of the governing body" is in his view the only necessary characteristic of revolution; it is a necessary and sufficient characteristic.

In contrast to this position is the view that the change of the governing body is a necessary characteristic, but one of only secondary or minor importance. Marx, Moore, and Skocpol all clearly think that a revolution will entail some kind of wholesale change of leadership, but this is not a sufficient condition, nor even one of major importance. These authors focus on social, economic, and political *structures* – not on persons. Old leaders at the head of new structures are much more revolutionary than new leaders at the head of old structures. In fact, Moore (1966: 228–313, 433–52) suggests that in "revolutions from above," a large part of the old elite remains in place. He points out that the National Socialists in Germany coalesced with large elements of the old ruling class, leaving many old elites in their former positions (although under increased Nazi control). Nevertheless, the changes in political structures under the Nazis make this a revolution. Thus, while it generally is agreed that revolutions involve some wholesale change of the governing body, the theoretical cleavages between Tilly on the one extreme and Moore on the other are quite apparent.

Finally, we must look at the puzzling case of Ted Gurr's formulation of the concept of revolution. As noted earlier, he is firmly resistant to the idea of defining revolution in terms of change of any kind. Thus, theoretically, a change of the governing body should not be considered a necessary characteristic. However, as we shall see below, Gurr uses the term exclusively for events in which a change of the governing body has in fact occurred (see Appendix II and "The extension"). Let us say, then, that Gurr oscillates as to whether change of the governing body is a necessary characteristic.

Structural political change

Up to this point, we have noted that there is a general consensus on some necessary characteristics of revolution: almost all authors require violence, popular involvement, and a change of the governing body. On the question of whether revolution necessarily entails structural political change, there is, instead, divergence. Tilly, Gurr, and Brinton do not make structural change of any kind a necessary condition for revolution. Davis, Johnson, and Huntington require at least some change of political structures. Marx, Moore, and Skocpol argue that there must be a fundamental change of political structures.

However, while all the authors are clear about whether they consider structural political change a necessary characteristic, few are clear about what structural political change entails. Johnson claims that revolutions change the "constitution"; Marx says the "superstructure" is transformed; Moore speaks of a "new order"; and Skocpol argues that "state structures" are transformed (see Appendix I). All of the foregoing arguments clearly point to changes above and beyond the mere replacement of the governing body, but it is hard to pin down the additional elements.

To be sure, efforts have been made to elucidate the concept of "political structure." David Easton (1959: 228–29), for example, points to three "levels or foci around which support is typically mobilized in every political system." The first "level" is the government, the "political leaders and associated administrative organization" (what I earlier called the governing body). Second is the regime or "constitutional order," namely, the fundamental rules of the game that regulate political participation. Easton lists as examples the distinction between democracy and dictatorship, a presidential system and a parliamentary system, and monarchy versus republic. Finally, there is the level of political community, "the most inclusive aggregate of persons who identify with each other as a group, and who are prepared to regulate their differences by means of decisions accepted as binding because they are made in accordance with shared political norms and structures." To illustrate this "level," Easton argues that Frenchmen may feel no particular loyalty to the Fifth Republic but they do maintain a loyalty to the existence of France as a political community.

Chalmers Johnson adapts this scheme to analyze the changes that a revolution may yield. He argues that change may happen at one of three levels:

> *Change of government* – "the formal political and administrative institutions that make and execute decisions for a society. . . . Resorts to violence in order to

cause change at this level will be simple rebellions; they seek to replace persons who are believed to be occupying various positions of authority illegitimately.

Regime change – "the fundamental rules of the political game in a society: democracy, dictatorship, monarchy, oligarchy, federalism, constitutionalism, and the like."

Change of community – "the broadest level of social organization and consciousness, the level where fundamental values cohere with cardinal demands of environment adaptation. It is here that we speak of, for example, 'peasant society' combined with 'subsistence polyculture.'"

(Johnson 1966: 140–41)

Easton's and Johnson's analysis of the levels of a political system is a useful starting point for assessing the concept of political structure, but we must make two modifications. First, the typology mixes the concepts of political and social structure in a confusing manner. I shall treat social structural change separately in the following section. Second, the concept of "regime" is too inclusive. The difference between dictatorship and democracy is on a different level than the difference between presidentialism and parliamentarism.

Thus, in reconstructing the concept of change in political structure, we should distinguish between two general types of change. I will call these "minor" and "major" structural political change. "Minor" structural political change refers to structural adjustments of the political system that maintain the same basic kind of political system; there is a change in the "rules of the game" but one is still playing the same game. For example, in 1958 France changed from a parliamentary system to a presidential system, but both were essentially democracies. "Major" structural political change is a fundamental change of the system; the "game" is entirely different. It is at this level that we speak of changes from monarchy to republic or from dictatorship to democracy. These are profound changes in which the principles of political participation and decision making are altered. For example, the Russian Revolution transformed a feudal-monarchic polity into a "dictatorship of the proletariat"; the Nazi revolution transformed the German political system from a parliamentary (if malfunctioning) democracy into a totalitarian single-party/state system. These are radical changes in the type of rule, not merely adjustments of institutions.

Changes in the systems of social stratification

Many writers, particularly writers in the Marxist tradition, have argued that changes in the systems of social stratification (class and status) are a fundamental cause of revolutions. At present, I wish to ask whether revolutions necessarily (by definition) cause some further change in these systems of stratification. This question goes beyond asking whether a revolution enfranchises or disenfranchises a given class or status group. The questions here are the following: do revolutions change the relationships between classes and status groups? Do they ultimately cause or lead up to the creation and destruction of classes and status groups?

Classes and status groups are created gradually. They may, however, be destroyed relatively rapidly. Sometimes such a destruction may be a prerequisite for the development of a new class or status group; it certainly would change the relationships between the remaining classes and status groups. The destruction of such social strata can come about in one of two ways. The first is outright liquidation – the old ruling class may be summarily executed almost to a man. The "Cambodian revolution" (if one can refer to it as a revolution) is the most extreme example of this approach, although it was also used in less drastic form in the French and Russian Revolutions. The second mode is less ruthless and traumatic. The old ruling class is deprived of its political and economic power, thus losing the ability to preserve itself as a distinct entity. The members of the old ruling class are not liquidated; rather, they are slowly absorbed into other classes. The Glorious Revolution is perhaps the most extreme example of this. It marked the point of no return in the British aristocracy's fall from power. The revolution substantially weakened the aristocracy politically, and slowly – in the course of the next two centuries – its power eroded to the point at which it ceased to function as a class of major importance.

The case of the German landed aristocracy provides another example. During the 1918–19 revolution, the *Junkers* had to give up their exclusive claim to political power. Top officials were to be elected but the aristocracy still was disproportionately powerful because the *Reichswehr* and much of the civil service was either drawn from or remained loyal to the aristocracy. When Hitler came to power, he was careful not to harm the Junkers' interests (e.g., he gave subsidies to Prussian landowners), but he further diluted their political power by establishing firm control over the civil service and at least some control over the military. After World War II, almost all of the aristocracy's power base was eroded and it has since ceased to exist as a separate class or estate.

Is a change in the social systems of stratification as described above a necessary characteristic of revolution? All consensus breaks down on this point. Only the "class analysts" – such as Marx, Moore, and Skocpol – unequivocally require such changes as a necessary characteristic. Huntington's definition is problematic. It mentions a change in "social structure" (although he does not explain what he means by the term), yet he focuses overwhelmingly on political changes (see particularly 1968: 308–15). None of the other theorists make changes in the systems of stratification a necessary characteristic. Johnson (1966: 140–41) argues that far-reaching social changes rarely are achieved by revolutions; most revolutions stop at what he calls the level of "regime change." Brinton and Davies make no mention of social changes as defining characteristics of revolution, and Gurr and Tilly strongly argue against the notion that social changes are by definition a part of revolution.

More on the intension

Now that each of the major characteristics of revolution has been explicated to some degree, I can organize the intension of the various formulations of the concept, as in Table 8.1. This table shows which authors posit which characteristics

Table 8.1 The necessary characteristics of revolution

	Tilly	Gurr	Brinton	Davies	Johnson	Huntington	Marx[b]	Moore	Skocpol
Violence	N	Y	Y	Y	Y	Y	Y	Y	Y
Popular involvement	N	Y	N	Y	Y	Y	?	Y	Y
Change of governing body	N/Y[a]	?	Y	Y	Y	Y	Y	Y	Y
"Minor" political structural change	N	N	N	Y	Y	Y	Y	Y	Y
"Major" political structural change	N	N	N	N	N	N	Y	Y	Y
Changes in systems of stratification	N	N	N	N	N	N	Y	Y	Y

Notes

Y = Yes; N = No; ? = Uncertain.

a   See note 4

b   I take Marx to be representative of the whole Marxist school of thought including Engels, Lenin, Trotsky, and Luxemburg.

as necessary or defining characteristics of revolution. All theorists – including those like Gurr and Tilly, who have broad formulations – would of course agree that a revolution *may* be accompanied by any or all of the characteristics discussed above. The table indicates, however, whether or not the characteristic in question is a *necessary element* of the concept of revolution.

Note that there is substantial agreement on three defining characteristics of revolution: violence, change of the governing body, and, to a lesser extent, popular involvement. Thus, we could at this point formulate a *minimal intensional definition*: revolution is a phenomenon marked by the coincidence of violence, popular involvement, and a change in the governing body. However, this definition would not satisfy most of the theorists under consideration. It is perhaps a reasonable synthesis of Tilly's, Gurr's, and Brinton's formulations, but all other theorists require at least one additional element: Davies, Johnson, and Huntington do not require "major" structural political change, but insist that there must at least be structural political change of some kind. Thus, we may posit a second definition: revolution is a phenomenon marked by the coincidence of violence, popular involvement, change of the governing body, and at least some degree of structural political change.

But even this definition would not satisfy all the theorists. In addition to these characteristics, Marx (and Marxists in general), Moore, and Skocpol require that there be "major" structural political change and that there be a change in the systems of social stratification. We thus obtain a third definition: revolution is a phenomenon marked by the coincidence of violence, popular involvement, change of the governing body, "major" structural political change, and a change in the systems of social stratification.

Note that Table 8.1 is arranged so that the authors to the left have the broadest, most inclusive formulation of the concept. As we move to the right, the referents are narrowed down until, with Marx, Moore, and Skocpol, the term revolution refers only to rare phenomena. Thus, as we can see, the intension of the concept varies depending on one's theoretical and research interests, and it seems to me that it would be arbitrary to select any single bounding as the "correct" one.

Finally, one point about Marx, Moore, and Skocpol: with the exception of Marx's indeterminacy about popular involvement, the three authors all posit the same characteristics of revolution. Should I not have grouped them all together as "Marxists" or under some other label? I could have done so. However, I have chosen to put each theorist in a separate column to illustrate that while each theorist has a different theory of revolution and while Marx is separated from the others by over a century, there has been remarkable consistency and cumulativeness in their formulations.[8]

The extension

Do the abstract formulations that we have just surveyed match each author's actual use of the term? Appendix II lists all the events that the authors under discussion call revolution in the works examined. These lists are not exhaustive of all the events a particular author would consider a revolution; none of the authors offer such a list. Nonetheless, we have enough to assess whether their actual use of the term is consistent with their abstract formulations of the concept. In Appendix II, I have listed the authors in the same order as in Table 8.1 – going from the most inclusive formulation of the concept to the most restrictive, from Tilly to Skocpol.

The results of the test are mixed. There is basic consistency, but in most of the lists a few items fit oddly. For example, Tilly's use of the term revolution in *From Mobilization to Revolution* (1978) generally is in line with what one would expect given his loose formulation of the concept. He applies the term not only to spectacular events like the French and Russian Revolutions, but also to comparatively minor occurrences like "Latin American revolutions" (e.g., coup*s*) and the "Burmese Revolution" of 1954. We might ask, however, where was the "displacement of one set of power holders by another" in the "Russian Revolution" of 1905, which never got beyond the state of "multiple sovereignty"? The old regime was in crisis, but there was no transfer of power.[9]

Gurr's use of the term revolution never contradicts his formulation of the concept, but he does lead us to think that revolution might ultimately have to be characterized by some kind of political change. Gurr, it will be recalled, strongly opposed the idea of incorporating the characteristic of change into the concept of revolution; revolution is defined exclusively as a form of violence. However, he actually employs the term only to refer to events in which political and/or social changes did in fact occur. Gurr uses other terms to describe events marked by the same kind of violence as any of the "revolutions" that he mentions but which are not marked by the same kinds of change. For example, Gurr speaks of the Nigerian "civil war," the "uprising" in the Dominican Republic in 1965, and the "massive violence" in China from 1966 to 1969, to mention just a few examples. Given his formulation of the concept, should not all of these also be "revolutions"?

Crane Brinton is at times loose in his use of the term. He speaks of the "American Negro Revolution," the Polish "Revolution . . . from outside," and the "MacArthur Revolution" in Japan. Perhaps these characterizations are excusable because they are often meant in a metaphorical sense and occasionally qualified by putting the word revolution in quotation marks. Still, such loose usage can only lead to further confusion.

James C. Davies, on the other hand, seems to be rather careful. He uses the term revolution sparingly to refer only to major events. The shortness of his list of events termed revolution is perhaps due to the fact that his works are much shorter than those of the other authors. Nevertheless, the only questionable item on his list is, once again, the "Russian Revolution of 1905." Conversely, Chalmers Johnson is less than careful. Recall that Johnson requires at least some "minor" political structural change (in his terms, some degree of *regime* change) as a necessary characteristic of revolution. Yet he freely uses the term revolution without qualification or quotation marks to refer to the "Hungarian Revolution" of 1956, the "Santo Domingo Revolution" of 1965, and even the "Berkeley Revolution" of 1964 and the CIA-sponsored "Revolution at the Bay of Pigs" (the quotation marks are mine).

Finally, Huntington, Marx, Moore, and Skocpol all are relatively consistent. One might dispute Moore's characterization of the American Civil War as a "capitalist revolution" or the events in Germany and Japan as "revolutions from above," but Moore is careful to explain why he uses these terms. More importantly, his use of the term in these cases is in keeping with his formulation of the concept. Although both Moore and Skocpol refer to the "Russian Revolution of 1905," they usually are careful to qualify unsuccessful revolutions as "failed" or "abortive." Skocpol's characterization as revolutions of the events in Angola, Bolivia, and Guinea Bissau certainly is questionable, but the inclusion of these borderline cases is a relatively minor sin compared to the frequently gross misuse of the term.

My reconstruction might simply conclude at this point that revolution is an elastic concept, expanded or contracted to be more or less inclusive. Some scholars include coups, secessions, and rebellions, while others include only the "great revolutions." However, this conclusion would be unsatisfactory because we cannot yet coherently arrange the semantic field of revolution. This is so largely because all definitions up to now have been stated in terms of coexistent characteristics that are equally weighted. This makes it virtually impossible to determine how the term revolution is related to its neighboring terms in the semantic field. For example, let us say that we define revolution as the "coincidence" of violence, popular involvement, and a change of the governing body. How do we place the term in a semantic field? Do we say that revolution is a type of violence, and thus set it in the field *types of violence*? Or do we say that it is one kind of political change and hence arrange it in the field *types of political change*? None of these questions can be answered as long as we merely define revolution as the "coincidence" of a sheer enumeration of characteristics.

To solve these problems, we must delve further into the meaning of the concept. As we will see, the extension will aid us greatly in arranging the semantic field. But in order to explicate and analyze the extension, we will have to examine the disciplinary and theoretical contexts of the concept of revolution.

Alternative theories and meanings of the concept

Disciplinary slicing

One might at first glance think that a disciplinary slicing would not be of much help in examining the intension of our concept. Tilly, Brinton, and Moore are historians. Gurr, Davies, Johnson, and Huntington are political scientists. Skocpol is a sociologist. And how shall we classify Marx? As a philosopher? A political economist? It hardly seems to matter, as none of these disciplinary titles appears to have any influence on the formulation of the concept. However, if we look at which discipline's theoretical tools are employed by the aforesaid theorists, then we find that they break down into two groups. In the first group are Davies and Gurr, who employ psychological frustration-aggression theory to explain revolutions. The seven other theorists all abide by what might loosely be termed "political sociology": they explain a political phenomenon – revolution – by pointing to its social roots and organizational dynamics. This is a salient disciplinary cleavage because the psychological approach individualizes and then aggregates the characteristics of and phenomena related to revolution. The political sociologist examines the society/polity as a unit, not as an aggregate of individuals. This difference, as we will see, greatly affects the meaning of the concept.

The aggregate-psychological formulation

Psychological analysis of revolutions is not new. However, the early psychological analysis of Le Bon, Pareto, and Freud focused on the dynamics of crowd or mass behavior; the "mass" was the unit of analysis. Modern psychological analysis of revolution focuses on individuals and then aggregates their psychic states and behavior. The groundbreaking work in this research tradition was James C. Davies's now seminal article, "Toward a Theory of Revolution," first published in 1962. In this work, Davies unveils the famous "J-Curve" and begins a school of thought that explains revolutions in terms of what has since been called "relative deprivation" – the gap between what people want and what they get.

Davies views his theory as a synthesis of the "Marxian notion that revolutions occur after progressive degradation and the de Tocqueville notion that they occur when conditions are improving" (ibid.: 17). This synthesis produces the theory that "revolutions are most likely to occur when a prolonged period of objective economic growth and social development is followed by a short period of sharp reversal" (Davies 1962: 6). This sharp reversal causes revolution because it creates an "intolerable gap" between "actual need satisfaction" and "expected need satisfaction," as Davies depicts graphically (as in Figure 8.1).

However, in this early article the causal link between relative deprivation and revolution is not clearly spelled out. At some points, he portrays the revolutionary impulse as a purposive response to real or perceived threats to basic needs. Elsewhere, he leads us to think that the revolutionary impulse is merely an aggressive outburst brought on by frustration. This uncertainty is illustrated by the fact that in the 1962 work, Davies does not cite the classic study on *Frustration and Aggression* by Dollard et al. (1939) even though much of the argument is phrased

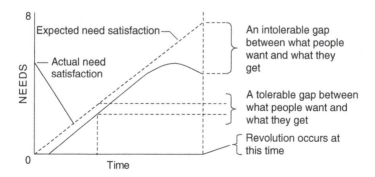

Figure 8.1 Need satisfaction and revolution.

in the idiom of the frustration–aggression school. Such uncertainty creates difficulties in analyzing his formulation of the concept. If revolutions are seen as aggressive outbursts, then we would subsume the concept under the general heading of "collective violence"; if they are seen as purposive responses to threats, another heading might be more appropriate.

In subsequent works, this uncertainty was resolved (see Davies 1969, 1971). By the late 1960s, Davies and several other scholars began to explicitly base their theories of revolution on the Dollard et al. (1939: 1) thesis that, "aggression is always a consequence of frustration. More specifically, the proposition is that the occurrence of aggressive behavior always presupposes the existence of frustration and, contrariwise, that the existence of frustration always leads to some form of aggression."

Perhaps the greatest work to come out of this school of thought is Ted Gurr's book *Why Men Rebel*. This book is a masterful application of this theory to the problem of rebellions and revolutions. However, in his rigor he takes the psychologizing of political concepts to something of an extreme. An incredible variety of political phenomena are explained in terms of relative deprivation and the frustration–aggression syndrome, even if, at times, the phenomena in question fit the conceptualization oddly. For example, ideologies (insofar as Gurr considers them as at all significant) are not examined as promoters of group cohesion and solidarity, nor as tools of mobilization, and certainly not as any kind of analysis of the political situation. Gurr assesses them only in terms of their ability to increase the expectations of the masses (Gurr 1970: 194–200). He also doubts that political groups have important instrumental functions; he argues that their emotive functions are much more important (ibid.: 310–16). Even the essentially political concept of democracy is psychologized. Rather than arguing that revolutions are less likely in democracies because people already have influence in the political system or because democracies are more adaptive, Gurr argues that revolutions are less likely because democracies have "channels for expressive protest" (ibid.: 304–10).

The psychologizing of political concepts greatly curtails their intension. Psychologizing individualizes the formulation of the concept; that is, the individual is the unit to be observed. In the case of revolution, violence then becomes the central characteristic because if the unit of observation is an individual in a crowd, it is the only observable characteristic. One cannot observe a single individual in a great mass carrying out a fraction of a social or political change; one can only observe him being violent. Thus, the storming of the Bastille is characterized as an instance of mass violence, not as part of the crumbling of the Old Regime. The Russian Civil War is seen as organized collective violence and not as a conflict between two political organizations and the constituencies they represent.

Since the aggregate-psychological school views revolution as a kind of violence, it cogently follows that the semantic field is to be arranged by relating it to other forms of collective violence. Gurr (1970: 11, 334–38; see also Gurr 1968), following Eckstein, proposes the following typology of collective violence:

(1) *Turmoil*, which is relatively spontaneous and unorganized collective violence such as in localized rebellions, riots and some violent political strikes.

Gurr argues that turmoil occurs when the masses are affected by relative deprivation but the elite is not; hence, there is no disenchanted elite to organize and channel the aggressive energy of the masses.

(2) *Conspiracy*, in which some sector of the elite is affected by relative deprivation, but the masses are not. Thus, the elite engages in conspiratorial activity – for example, coup d'etat or small-scale terrorism.

(3) *Internal war*, which occurs when both the masses and some sector of the elite are affected by relative deprivation. This category includes major guerilla wars, large-scale rebellions, and revolutions.

This is a good arrangement but for one fault: the category of "internal war" is too inclusive. We are thus advised to distinguish between rebellions and revolutions. Davies (1969: 549) argues that while revolutions may differ from rebellions in any number of ways (e.g., duration, the intensity of violence), the fundamental difference is that revolutions remove the established government. Gurr never explicitly makes such a distinction, but (as noted earlier) he uses the term revolution only in cases where there was some political change, at least a change of the governing body. Thus, we may incorporate Davies's distinction into our reconstruction of the semantic field, as in Figure 8.2.

In summary, the aggregate-psychological school of thought views revolution primarily as a type of violence. Revolutions are also marked by popular involvement, a change of the governing body, and, depending on the author, at least some degree of political structural change. However, because revolutions are conceived of primarily as outbursts of aggressive energy, neither "major" structural political change nor a change in the social systems of stratification are considered necessary characteristics.

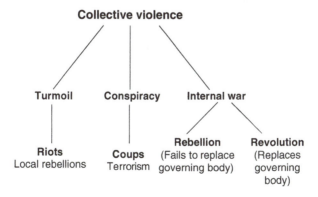

Figure 8.2 The semantic field of revolution in aggregate psychological formulation.

Theoretical context slicing

We are left with a rather unwieldy conglomeration of theorists that I earlier termed "political sociologists." There are many differences among them. Tilly's theory focuses on organizational factors. Brinton, Huntington, and Skocpol focus on the old regime. Johnson looks at social systemic factors, Moore at a wide variety of historical data, and Marx explains revolutions mainly by pointing to economic factors. However, regarding their conceptions of revolution, the overriding theoretical cleavage is between Marxists and theorists in the Marxist tradition on the one hand, and theorists outside of or opposed to that theoretical tradition on the other. Marx, Moore, and Skocpol belong to the former group; Tilly, Brinton, Johnson, and Huntington to the latter.

The difference *between* these thinkers is not so much that they attribute different characteristics to the concept of revolution. Rather, the most important differences concern the characterization of revolution. There are two main aspects to these differences. First, Marxists and Marxist-inspired writers characterize revolutions as a type of structural development of the society/polity, while non-Marxist social scientists tend to characterize them as a pathology of the system. Johnson, for example, specifically states that revolution in a social system is analogous to disease in an organism (1966: 3). Brinton likens revolution to a fever in a diseased organism (1965 [1938]: 16–17). Huntington is less taken by such biological analogies but he clearly views revolutions as the breakdown of a political order. Marxist and Marxist-inspired writers, on the other hand, view revolutions as a necessary form of rapid development. Thus, revolutions are analogous to rapid, traumatic physical changes that an organism undergoes during the process of growth (e.g., birth and puberty). These changes may be painful, but they are a natural and normal part of development; they are hardly a "pathology." One occasionally finds biological analogies in Marx's writings.[10] Contemporary writers are less prone to make such analogies explicitly – they discuss revolution in terms of the resolution of "structural contradictions" in society – but the analogy generally holds.

Second, Marxists and Marxist-inspired writers characterize revolutions as inherently progressive. The other writers will admit that revolutions may, on occasion, contribute to human progress, but they do not incorporate this notion into their concept of revolution. This is a fundamental difference. The Marxist and Marxist-inspired formulation is organized around the notion of progress; revolutions are seen as essential to historical progress. Thus, I will label this formulation the "progressive" concept of revolution.[11]

The progressive formulation

The "progressive" concept of revolution is rooted in the Enlightenment's conception of history. Contemporary Western society, as Charles Frankel (1967) notes, conceives of change differently than most of humankind has. In the past and in many non-Western societies today, historical changes – insofar as people were at all aware of them – were conceived of as cyclical at best. With the advent of modern science, however, it became patent that scientific truths were cumulative – that human knowledge would grow. This conception set the groundwork for the eighteenth-century Enlightenment, which posited a social and moral progress as well. History had a directional flow. This intellectual tradition was Marx's starting point. However, he found past formulations of the concept of progress too abstract.

Marx argued that history had progressed through a number of stages identified as "modes of production": primitive communism, a slave-based city-state system, manor-based feudalism, industrial capitalism, and finally socialism and communism. At each stage, mankind's lot as a whole was improved. Revolutions are crucial to this progressive drive. Indeed, the function of revolutions is to make historical progress possible. If a given event had all the other characteristics of revolution but did not somehow add to this crescendo of history, it would not have been a revolution. However, past revolutions had not transformed the mode of production directly. Rather, revolutions transformed the old and outmoded political, legal, and ideological superstucture. Revolutions "unfettered" the "forces of production" to expand and develop further in a new "mode of production" under a new "superstructure."

In non-Marxian terms, revolutions remove the political, legal, institutional, and social barriers to further economic and social development. Thus, the French Revolution was not a "bourgeois revolution" in the sense that it was the armed movement of the bourgeoisie to wrest power from the aristocracy. While the bourgeoisie was active in the revolution, it was a bourgeois revolution mainly in the sense that it established the legal, political, administrative, and ideological structures necessary for the further development of bourgeois society.[12] The socialist revolution, however, would differ from all other revolutions in that it would be a conscious transformation of society in which economic structures would be changed directly.

This conception of revolution – revolution as the sweeping away of outmoded political and ideological constraints – has been a consistent and stable formulation in the European Marxist tradition. Rosa Luxemburg, for example, described the capitalist superstructure as a "wall" that stood between capitalist and socialist society. Only the "hammer blow" of revolution could break this wall down (Luxemburg 1971 [1891]: 84–85). In 1905, Trotsky argued that the Russian bourgeois revolution "attempts to free bourgeois society from the shackles and fetters of absolutism and feudal property" (1963 [1905]: 54–55). Modern Marxist scholars do not speak of "walls" or "shackles" of history that must be broken, but the fundamental idea remains the same (see, for example, Balibar's definition in Appendix I).

Beginning in the 1960s, however, a number of scholars started using many of Marx's insights and analytical tools while ostensibly distancing themselves from most of the trappings of traditional Marxism. The most prominent of these scholars is Barrington Moore, whose analysis has a Marxian flavor in that he uses "class analysis," yet does not retain Marx's teleological assumptions or his vocabulary. Moore does not posit a single sequence of historical development, nor does he project some ultimate winner in the class struggle. He restricts himself to uncovering the dynamics and class struggles underlying the transformations that already have occurred. His analysis examines only one kind of transition – that from traditional agrarian societies to modern industrial ones. He summarizes his argument in the following manner:

> There are . . . three routes to the modern world. The earliest one combined capitalism and parliamentary democracy after a series of revolutions: the Puritan Revolution, the French Revolution and the American Civil War. . . . I have called this the route of bourgeois revolution. . . . The second path was also a capitalist one, but, in the absence of a revolutionary surge, it passed through reactionary political forms culminating in fascism. It is worth emphasizing that, through revolution from above, industry did manage to grow and flourish in Germany and Japan. The third route of course is the communist one.
>
> (Moore 1966: 413)

Note that unlike most Marxists, Moore does not view fascism as a "counter-revolution." Rather, because fascism too played a modernizing role in establishing a political framework compatible with the needs of a modern society and economy, it is classified as a type of revolution. Again, as with traditional Marxists, revolution is defined in terms of breaking down political barriers that stand in the way of further social and economic development.

Theda Skocpol retains the same formulation of the concept of revolution and builds on Moore's analysis to suggest the dynamics behind the collapse of the outmoded "superstructures." She argues that,

> revolutionary political crises, culminating in administrative and military breakdown, emerged because imperial states became caught in the cross-pressures between intensified military competition or intrusions from abroad and constraints imposed on monarchical responses by the existing agrarian class structures and political institutions. The old-regime states were prone to such revolutionary crises because their existing structures made it impossible for them to meet the particular international military exigencies that each had to face in the modern era.
>
> (Skocpol 1979: 285)

This, again, is the familiar image of revolution as, in Marx's terms, a "gigantic broom" that sweeps away outmoded legal and political structures.[13] Thus, Marxists and neo-Marxists alike view revolutions fundamentally as a particular kind of historical transformation. Violence is always present in revolutions, but they should be characterized as a type of change, not as a type of violence. It follows that in arranging the semantic field, we now must relate revolution to other kinds of historical transformations, as in Figure 8.3.

Historical transformations may be either progressive or reactionary. By "reactionary" I simply mean that the change in question hinders or reverses the "advance" of history as posited by the theory under consideration. "Progress" can be made in one of three ways:

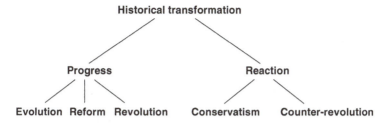

Figure 8.3 The semantic field of revolution in the "progressive" formulation.

- By *evolution*, which is the unconscious and gradual transformation of economic, political, and social structures.
- By *reform,* which is gradual but conscious change ("reform" generally applies only to political and economic institutions, while social relations generally are transformed either by evolution or revolution).[14]
- By *revolution*, which is conscious, wholesale change.

In the past, "bourgeois revolutions" have mainly transformed political structures; "socialist revolutions" change political, social, and economic structures. Conversely, reaction involves either conservatism or counter-revolution. The former is an attempt to slow down both evolution and reform and to avoid revolution altogether. Counter-revolution is used in two senses. First, as any movement or event that attempts to suppress a revolution. Second, as any movement that attempts to "roll back the wheel of history"; that is, any movement that seeks to reverse the directional flow of history.[15]

The breakdown formulation

In contrast to the foregoing Marxian and neo-Marxian concept of revolution, which I have called the "progressive formulation," the other writers whom I have labeled "political sociologists" posit what might best be called a *breakdown* concept of revolution. The notion that revolution is a kind of breakdown of the society/polity is perhaps the oldest formulation of the concept (dating back at least to Aristotle's concept of *stasis*) and it remains to this day the most prominent formulation of the concept among non-Marxist social scientists.

Lynford P. Edwards and, later, Crane Brinton paint a gloomy picture of revolution as the disintegration of a society and its political system. They portray it as a feverish and painful process that does not accomplish anything that could not have been achieved by other means. The process begins with an old regime that is torn by a striking excess of social tensions, structural political and economic blockages, and (more often than not) a government that is rotten with corruption. The first symptom of imminent revolution is the "transfer of the allegiance of intellectuals" from the old order to new ideals and new men. Then comes the first revolutionary government, a moderate government functioning under the banner of *liberte, egalite, et fraternite.* These moderates, however, cannot restrain the more radical revolutionaries; thus the extremists come to power and carry out a reign of terror. Finally, after the exhaustion of revolutionary energies, the extremists are ousted in the "thermidore" and the society returns to normal political, social, and economic processes.

What has the society gained from this feverish and delirious process? Brinton admits that revolution may have some curative effects – the new regime may be more efficient and less corrupt than the old. However, he argues, the day-to-day life of the average man is changed little because "the behavior of men changes with a slowness comparable to the kind of changes the geologist studies" (Brinton 1965 [1938]: 244).

Edwards's and Brinton's works are masterful applications of organismic and functional theory to the problem of revolution. After Talcott Parsons's systems theory supplanted the earlier functional analysis, the theory and concept of revolution had to be adjusted. Chalmers Johnson's book *Revolutionary Change* stands as the authoritative application of Parsonian theory to the study of revolution.

Johnson argues that revolutions are caused by a "disequilibrium" in the social system. A society is in disequilibrium when the values of the society are not synchronized with its social structure. The people become rootless and "disoriented," more prone to demagogy, and easily led to violence. At this point even a minor event – an "accelerator" – may trigger full-fledged revolution (Johnson 1966: 59–118, see especially 106). What changes does a revolution bring about? Much like Edwards and Brinton, Johnson argues that revolutions only rarely produce great social changes. There may be some minor changes in the political structure of society, but changes in the day-to-day life of the average man – what Johnson calls changes of the "community" – are very rare (139–41). Whatever change does occur comes at a high cost. All revolutions, Johnson argues, are "immensely damaging to the values of the particular social system" (xiv). Moreover, revolutions accomplish nothing that could not be accomplished otherwise. "Creative political action is the specific antidote for revolutionary conditions" (166). In short, Johnson views revolutions as the result of a political malfunction. They are a breakdown of the political and social system.

Huntington (1968) also posits a kind of "breakdown" theory of revolution; however, his breakdown is caused by "overload" rather than "disequilibriation." Revolutions occur when new groups become politically active while the existing institutions are insufficient to process all the new inputs. Thus, the political system overloads and breaks down. The revolutionaries may build a new set of stable political institutions, but revolution is primarily conceived of as a violent collapse of the old ones. (See also Huntington 1965.)

To summarize, non-Marxist political sociologists see revolutions mainly as a form of political change. This change, to be sure, is marked by violence and it may bring progressive change, but these authors would not characterize revolution as a type of violence or as a type of progressive transformation. Therefore, in arranging the semantic field, we must relate the term revolution to other kinds of political change, as in Figure 8.4.

Political change may be legal or illegal. Legal change is, almost by definition, nonviolent. Illegal change must be broken up into two categories – violent and

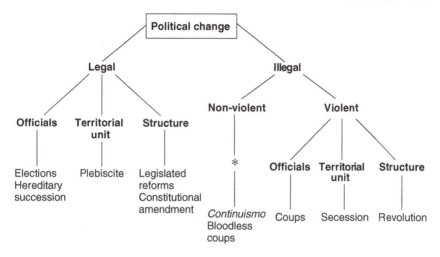

Figure 8.4 The semantic field of revolution in the "breakdown" formulation.

* Indicates that at present we lack a term for this kind of change.

nonviolent. We do not have any good terms for illegal, nonviolent changes, although such changes do take place. The best single example would be De Gaulle's assumption of power in 1958 and his subsequent formation of the Fifth Republic. The other prime example of this mode of political change is what Latin Americans refer to as a *continuismo*, in which an elected leader abrogates the constitution and does not stand for re-election. Illegal and violent political change may change officials (the governing body), the political unit, or the political structure. The first is called coup d'etat; the second, secession; and the third, revolution. Note that unlike the arrangement of the semantic field of the "progressive" conception of revolution, here there is a legal and nonviolent counterpart for every kind of illegal and violent change: officials may be changed by elections or hereditary secessions, the territorial unit by plebiscite, and political structure by legislated reform, constitutional amendment, or referendum. Hence, this formulation of the concept implies that revolutions cannot achieve anything that legal methods cannot also achieve.

Tilly, we might note, is an exception among this group of non-Marxists. It will be recalled that Tilly conceives of revolution as any period of "multiple sovereignty" followed by the displacement of one set of power holders by another. This definition includes even a coup d'etat in which the period of multiple sovereignty would have to be measured with a stopwatch. Thus, as violence is also not a characteristic of revolution, we could summarize Tilly's formulation of the concept by saying that in his view the entire right-hand side of Figure 8.4 comes under the heading of revolution; *continuismo*, secession, "great revolutions," and so on are all types of revolution. Tilly, however, represents a minority view. All other theorists, as we have seen, would not make revolution as all-inclusive as does Tilly.

Conclusion

This reconstruction of revolution has shown that the extension or denotation of the concept has been expanded and contracted by scholars to suit their research needs. The term revolution covers a wide range of referents, and these are bounded differently from author to author. In examining the intension of the concept, we find three relatively clear and distinct meanings: (1) revolution as a violent outburst, (2) revolution as a progressive historical transformation, and (3) revolution as an illegal and violent political change.

Does this conclusion mean that we must abandon Sartori's contention that the semantic projection of a term is the key to its meaning? That "the beginning is the word"? No. It is not difficult to trace the roots of the divergence on the concept of revolution. Most succinctly put, revolution is a "loaded word." Among major social science concepts, it has perhaps the strongest evaluative connotation, both positive and negative. If one sees revolution as a step toward human progress and if one has a theory that posits the necessity of revolution for such progress, then one will hardly be satisfied with a definition of revolution that stops at violence. Contrariwise, if one attaches a negative value to the term and one has a theory that revolution is caused by a malfunction in the political and/or social system, then there is a great temptation to put into the category of "contingent characteristics" everything that happens after the shooting stops.

Ideally, this reconstruction might serve as a foundation for the formulation of a single, improved concept that all social scientists could use. However, in the case of the concept of revolution, I doubt that such consensus is possible. Each of the three intensions of the concept is coherently formulated; each makes significant distinctions between the term revolution and the other terms in the semantic field; and each is formulated consistently enough within its research tradition to promote further inquiry and debate within that tradition. This indeterminate conclusion should not, however, make us despair. Perhaps consensus on the concept of revolution is beyond our reach, but clarity and consistency never is. If scholars do not all attach the same meaning to the concept of revolution, they can at least specify which "meaning" they "mean."

Appendix I: Definitions of revolution

Peter Amann (1962: 39): "revolution prevails when a state's monopoly of power is effectively challenged and persists until a monopoly is reestablished."

Hannah Arendt (1965 [1963]: 39): "only where change occurs in the sense of a new beginning, where violence is used to constitute an altogether different form of government, where the liberation from oppression aims at least at the constitution of freedom can we speak of revolution."

Etienne Balibar (Althusser and Balibar 1979: 203): "The antagonisms between productive forces and the relations of production have the effect of a revolutionary rupture, and it is this effect which determines the transition from one mode of production to another ('progressive epochs in the economic formation of society'), and thereby the transformation of the whole social formation."

David V. J. Bell (1973: 9–10): "the most appropriate [definition] for our purposes views revolution as a form of internal war. In this book, the two terms will be used interchangeably . . . internal war, or revolution, represents the 'polar case' of resistance. It occurs when resistance aimed at changing the entire system has become highly organized, violent and widespread in participation."

Crane Brinton (1965 [1938]: 4, 16–17): (1) "[Revolution is a] . . . drastic, sudden substitution of one group in charge of running a territorial entity by another group hitherto not running that government. There is one further implication: the revolutionary substitution, if not made by actual violent uprising, is made by *coup d'etat*, *Putsch*, or some other kind of skullduggery." (2) "We shall regard revolutions as a kind of fever . . . in the old regime, there will be signs of the coming disturbance. . . . Then comes a time when the full symptoms disclose themselves, and when we can say the fever of revolution has begun. This works up, not regularly but with advances and retreats, to a crisis, frequently accompanied by delerium. . . . Finally the fever is over, and the patient is himself again."

Peter Calvert (1970: 141): "[Political scientists should] . . . retain the term 'revolution' itself as a political term covering all forms of violent change of government or regime originating internally."

James C. Davies (1962: 6): "Revolutions are here defined as violent civil disturbances that cause the displacement of one ruling group by another that has a wider base of support."

Lynford P. Edwards (1970 [1927]: 2): "[Revolutions are] a change brought about not necessarily by force and violence, whereby one system of legality is terminated and another is originated."

Carl J. Friedrich (1966: 5): "[Revolution is] . . . a sudden and violent overthrow of an established political order."

Great Soviet Encyclopedia (Prokhov [ed.] 1978): "a profound qualitative change in the development of a phenomenon of nature, society, or knowledge, for example the geological revolution, the industrial revolution, the scientific and technological revolution, the cultural revolution, and the revolution of physics and philosophy. The concept of revolution is most frequently used in describing social development. . . . The concept is an integral aspect of the dialectical conception of development. It reveals the internal mechanism of the law of the transformation of quantitative into qualitative changes. Revolution means a break in gradualness, a qualitative leap in development. It differs from evolution – the gradual development of a process – and also from reform. Between revolution and reform there exists a complex correlation determined by the concrete historical content of the revolution and the reform."

Mark N. Hagopian (1975: 1): "A revolution is an acute, prolonged crisis in one or more of the traditional systems of stratification (class, status, power) of a political community, which involves a purposive, elite-directed attempt to abolish or recon-struct one or more of said systems by means of an intensification of political power and a recourse to violence."

E. J. Hobsbawm (1962: 46): "To call this process the Industrial Revolution is both logical and in line with established tradition. . . . If the sudden, qualitative and fun-damental transformation, which happened in or about the 1770s, was not a revolu-tion then the word has no common sense meaning."

Samuel P. Huntington (1968: 264): "A revolution is a rapid, fundamental, and vio-lent domestic change in the dominant values and myths of a society, in its political institutions, social structure, leadership and government activity and policies."

Chalmers Johnson (1966: 1): "Revolutions are social changes. Sometimes they succeed; often they fail. Revolutionary change is a special kind of social change, one that involves the intrusion of violence into civil social relations. And revolu-tion, both as a form of behavior and as a concept, concerns the most basic level of man's communal existence – its constitution, in the Aristotelian sense of the prin-ciples of distributive justice prevailing in a particular society."

Eugene Kamenka (1966: 124): "Revolution is a sharp, sudden change in the social location of political power, expressing itself in the radical transformation of the process of government, of the official foundations of sovereignty or legitimacy and of the conception of the social order."

Walter Laquer (1968: 501): "Revolution in its most common sense is an attempt to make a radical change in the system of government. This often involves the infringement of prevailing constitutional arrangements and the use of force."

C. B. Macpherson (1966: 140): "Revolution is . . . a transfer of state power by means involving the use or threat of organized unauthorized force, and the subse-quent consolidation of that transferred power, with a view of bringing about funda-mental change in social, economic and political institutions."

Karl Marx (1972 [1859]): "Then begins an epoch of social revolution. With a change of the economic foundation the entire immense superstructure is more or less rapidly transformed."

Barrington Moore, Jr. (1972 [1970]: 169–70): "it is necessary to be clear about what we mean by revolution. Angry uprisings by segments of the lower classes stretch back at least as far as the slave revolts of antiquity. . . . These revolts, on the other hand, either lacked altogether or displayed only to a very minimal degree one element crucial to modern revolutions, the idea of somehow using the anger of the lower classes not only to destroy the prevailing social order, but also to create a new and different one in which the traditional forms of oppression would cease."

William H. Overholt (1977: 493): "A revolution occurs when a domestic insurgent group displaces the government of a society by means which are illegitimate according to the values of the existing regime, and when fundamental political institutions are destroyed or transformed and fundamental values of the system are dramatically changed."

Mostafa Rejai (1977: v, 8): (1) "'Revolution' is provisionally viewed as a fundamental transformation of an existing society/polity by mass violent means." (2) "Political revolution refers to abrupt, illegal mass violence aimed at the overthrow of the political regime as a step to overall social change."

Theda Skocpol (1979: 4): "Social revolutions are rapid, basic transformations of a society's state and class structures; they are accompanied and in part carried through by class-based revolts from below. Social revolutions are set apart from other sorts of conflict and transformative processes above all by the combination of two coincidences: the coincidence of societal structural change with class upheaval; and the coincidence of political with social transformation. . . . Political revolutions transform state structures but not social structures, and they are not necessarily accomplished through class conflict."

Charles Tilly (1978: 193): "A revolutionary outcome is the displacement of one set of powerholders by another. . . . Provisionally, let us take power over government as our reference point. A revolutionary outcome is the displacement of one set of members of the polity by another set."

Appendix II: Events termed "revolution"

Below are listed all the events that the theorists examined in this essay called "revolution," either in the text or in the index of the various works cited. Thus, these should not be seen as exhaustive lists, but only as partial lists of sets of events that are definitely considered to be referents of the term revolution. I have once again ordered the theorists from the broadest to the narrowest formulations of the concept.

Charles Tilly: *From Mobilization to Revolution* (1978)
Algerian Revolution
American Revolution
Burmese Revolution (1954)
Chinese Revolution
Cuban Revolution
Egyptian Revolution (1952)
English Revolution (1640)
European Revolution (1848)
French Revolution (1789)
French Revolution (1830)
French Revolution (1848)
French Revolution (1870)
German Revolution (1848)
German Revolution (1918–19)
Italian Revolution (1848)

Latin American Revolutions
Mexican Revolution
Russian Revolution (1905)
Russian Revolution (1917)
Spanish Revolution (nineteenth century)
Turkish Revolution (1919)
Vietnamese Revolution

Ted Robert Gurr: *Why Men Rebel* (1970)
American Revolution
Bolivian Revolution (1952)
Chinese "Cultural Revolution"
Costa Rican Revolution (1948)
Cuban Revolution
Egyptian Revolution (1952)
French Revolution (1789)
French Revolution (1830)
French Revolution (1848)
French Revolution (1871)
Indonesian Revolution (1947)
Mexican Revolution
Nazi Revolution
Puritan Revolution
Russian Revolution
Spanish Revolution (1931)
Sudanese Revolution (1964)
Turkish Revolution
Zanzibar Revolution (1963)

(Gurr also speaks of "Hungarian Revolutionaries," but he calls the events of 1956 an "uprising," and of "revolutionary activity" in France in May of 1968, but calls these events a "riot and general strike.")

Crane Brinton: *The Anatomy of Revolution* (1938)
Algerian Revolution
American Revolution
American Civil Rights Movement
Athenian Revolution (411 B.C.)
Chinese Revolution
Cuban Revolution
English Revolution
French Revolution
Ghandian Revolution in India
Haitian Slave Revolution
Hungarian Revolution (1849)
Hungarian Revolution (1956)

Irish Revolution (1916–21)
"Latin American Revolution"
MacArthur Revolution (Japan, 1945)
Meiji Revolution (Japan, 1868)
Mexican Revolution
Nazi Revolution
Polish "Revolution . . . from outside" (1945)
Russian Revolution

(Brinton also speaks of "revolutionary measures" taken by Mustapha Kemal, but only to contrast it with changes brought by revolutions such as in Russia. He also uses the term "Industrial Revolution" but immediately adds that this is loose usage.)

James C. Davies: "Toward a Theory of Revolution" (1962), and *When Men Revolt and Why* (1971)
American Revolution
Chinese Revolution
Egyptian Revolution
French Revolution
Nazi Revolution
Russian Revolution (1905)
Russian Revolution (1917)

Chalmers Johnson: *Revolutionary Change* (1966)
Algerian Revolution
American Revolution
Berkeley Revolution (1964)
Central Intelligence Agency's sponsored Revolution at the Bay of Pigs
Chinese Revolution
Cuban Revolution
French Revolution (1789)
French Revolution (1871)
German Revolution (1918)
Hungarian Revolution (1918)
Hungarian Revolution (1956)
Revolution of 1848
Russian Revolution (1905)
Russian Revolution (1917)
Santo Domingo Revolution (1965)
Turkish Revolution

Samuel P. Huntington: *Political Order in Changing Societies* (1968)
Algerian Revolution
American Revolution
Bolivian Revolution

Chinese Revolution
Cuban Revolution
English Revolution
French Revolution
Guatemalan Revolution
Mexican Revolution
Russian Revolution
Turkish Revolution
Vietnamese Revolution
Yugoslav Revolution

Karl Marx: "German Ideology," "The Eighteenth Brumaire of Louis Bonaparte,"
and "The Civil War in France," and Marx and Engels, "The Communist Manifesto"
(all in Tucker 1972)
(European) Revolution of 1848–49
French Revolution (1789)
French Revolution (1830)
French Revolution (1848)
French Revolution (1871)

Barrington Moore, Jr.: *Social Origins of Dictatorship and Democracy* (1966)
American Civil War: The Last Capitalist Revolution
Chinese Revolution
French Revolution (1789)
French Revolution (1830)
Abortive German Revolution of 1848
German Revolution "From Above"
Glorious Revolution
Japanese Revolution "From Above"
Puritan Revolution
Russian Revolution (1905)
Russian Revolution (1917)

Theda Skocpol: *States and Social Revolutions* (1979)
Algerian Revolution
Angolan Revolution
Bolivian Revolution
Chinese Revolution
Cuban Revolution
English Revolution of 1640–89 (a "political revolution")
Ethiopian Revolution
French Revolution
Failed German Revolution of 1848–50
Guinea Bissau Revolution
Meiji Restoration as "Political Revolution"

Mexican Revolution
Mozambiquan Revolution
Abortive Russian Revolution (1905)
Russian Revolution (1917)
Vietnamese Revolution
Yugoslav Revolution

Notes

* Originally published as Christoph M. Kotowski (1984) "Revolution," in G. Sartori (ed.), *Social Science Concepts: A Systematic Analysis*, Beverly Hills, CA: Sage, Chapter 8.

1 Note her definition in Appendix I and her sparing use of the term in Appendix II.
2 I use the qualified expression "relatively well defined" because Calvert does not analyze either the concept of violence or governmental change. Consequently, the concept is not as clearly bounded as it might be.
3 The term "secession" is mine; Pettee offers no label for this type of "revolution."
4 Tilly's formulation of the concept of revolution changed between 1975 and 1978. In the earlier work, which is largely a literature review and conceptual analysis, Tilly argues that the only defining characteristic of revolution is a state of "multiple sovereignty." In the later work, Tilly reformulates his conception to include only those cases in which political power has changed hands.
5 Tilly is the exception.
6 Gurr (1970: 36) asserts that, "the primary source of the human capacity for violence appears to be the frustration–aggression mechanism." See pp. 210–33 for his discussion of the possible utility of violence.
7 Unfortunately, I see no way around qualifying the "brute harm" definitions with the admittedly relativistic clause "in violation of recognized social norms." Without such a qualifier, we would have to include acts of legal punishment, self-defense, parental discipline, and the like as types of "violence."
8 By arguing that the Marxist study of revolution is cumulative, I do not mean that it is slowly approaching the "truth" about revolutions or that it is superior to non-Marxist study. I only mean that Marxists have an authoritative framework which, at least in the West, is constantly being updated and refined.
9 However, given the widespread use of the expression "the Revolution of 1905," Tilly's usage here is understandable.
10 In the "Communist Manifesto," for example, Marx and Engels say that, "modern bourgeois society has sprouted from the ruins of feudal society" (Marx and Engels 1972 [1848]: 474). In the "Critique of the Gotha Program," Marx speaks of the "birth pangs" to be endured when communist society emerges from capitalist society (1972 [1875]: 531).
11 I resist the temptation to simply label this formulation the "Marxist" concept of revolution because one need not be a Marxist to characterize revolutions in this manner. Moore and Skocpol, in any case, would spurn this label.
12 Marx's view of revolutions is most succinctly summarized in his analysis of the French Revolution: "The centralized state power, with its ubiquitous organs of standing army, police, bureaucracy, clergy and judicature . . . originates from the days of absolute monarchy, serving the nascent middle-class society as a mighty weapon against feudalism. Still, its development remained clogged by all manner of medieval rubbish, seignoral rights, local privileges, municipal and guild monopolies and provincial constitutions. The gigantic broom of the French Revolution swept away all these relics of bygone times, thus clearing simultaneously the social soil of its last hindrances to the superstructure of the

modern state edifice" (quoted in Skocpol 1979: 174). Another aspect of the notion that revolutions set up the political and social framework for a coming society is examined in Burke (1981). He examines Marx's claim at the end of Part I of the "German Ideology" that revolution is necessary, as an educational experience, so that the proletariat can rid itself of "the muck of ages and become fitted to found society anew."

13   Regarding the French Revolution, for example, Skocpol argues, "Thus, despite the fact that they had not caused the revolution, or suddenly been furthered by it, the capitalist relations of production could gradually but steadily expand in the relatively favorable legal and administrative framework crystallized by the revolution. . . . Indeed, the revolution is best understood as a 'gigantic broom' that swept away the 'Medieval rubbish' of seigneuralism and particularistic privilege – freeing the peasantry, private wealth holders, and the state alike from the encumbrances of the old regime" (Skocpol 1979: 205).

14   Few Marxists would claim that reform can produce the same kinds of change that revolution can produce. This does not mean, however, that they view reform as unprogressive. This case is best made by Luxemburg (1971 [1889]).

15   For an expanded discussion of the Marxian concept of counter-revolution, see Bronstein (1981).

References

Althusser, L. and Balibar, E. (1979) *Reading Capital*, trans. B. Brewster, London: Verso.
Amann, P. (1962) "Revolution: A Redefinition," *Political Science Quarterly* 77: 36–53.
Arendt, H. (1965 [1963]) *On Revolution*, New York: Viking.
Arendt, H. (1970 [1969]) *On Violence*, New York: Harcourt Brace Jovanovitch.
Beachler, J. (1975) *Revolution*, trans. J. Vickers, Oxford: Basil Blackwell and Mott Ltd.
Bell, D.V.J. (1973) *Resistance and Revolution*, Boston: Houghton Mifflin.
Bienen, H. (1968) *Violence and Social Change*, Chicago: University of Chicago Press.
Brinton, C. (1965 [1938]) *The Anatomy of Revolution*, New York: Vintage Books.
Bronstein, L. (1981) "The Concept of Counterrevolution in Marxian Theory," *Studies in Soviet Thought* 22: 175–92.
Burke, J.P. (1981) "The Necessity of Revolution," in J.P. Burke et al. (eds.), *Marxism and the Good Society*, New York: Cambridge University Press.
Calvert, P. (1970) *Revolution*, New York: Praeger.
Converse, E. (1968) "The War of All Against All: A Review of the *Journal of Conflict Resolution*," *Journal of Conflict Resolution* 12: 471–532.
Davies, J.C. (ed.) (1962) "Toward a Theory of Revolution," *American Sociological Review* 27: 5–19.
Davies, J.C. (1969) "The J-curve of Rising Expectations and Declining Satisfaction as a Cause of Some Great Revolutions and Contained Rebellions," in H.D. Graham and T.R. Gurr (eds.), *Violence in America*, Washington, DC: United States Government Printing Office.
Davies, J.C. (ed.) (1971) *When Men Revolt and Why*, New York: Free Press.
Dollard, J., Doob, L., Miller, N.E., Mowrer, O.H., and Sears, R. (1939) *Frustration and Aggression*, New Haven, CT: Yale University Press.
Easton, D. (1959) "Political Anthropology," in B.J. Siegal (ed.), *Biennial Review of Anthropology*, Stanford: Stanford University Press.
Eckstein, H. (1965) "On the Etiology of Internal Wars," *History and Theory* 4: 133–63.
Edwards, L.P. (1970 [1927]), *The Natural History of Revolutions*, Chicago: University of Chicago Press.
Frankel, C. (1967) "The Idea of Progress," in P. Edwards (ed.), *The Encyclopedia of Philosophy*, vol. 6, New York: Macmillan.

Friedrich, C.J. (1966) "An Introductory Note on Revolution," in C.J. Friedrich (ed.), *Revolution*, NOMOS VIII, New York: Atherton Press.

Galtung, J. (1969) "Violence, Peace and Peace Research," *Journal of Peace Research* 3: 167–91.

Gurr, T.R. (1968) "Psychological Factors in Civil Violence," *World Politics* 17: 386–430.

Gurr, T.R. (1970) *Why Men Rebel*, Princeton: Princeton University Press.

Gurr, T.R. (1973) "The Revolution–Social Change Nexus," *Comparative Politics* 5 (3): 359–92.

Gurr, T.R. (1978) "Burke and the Modern Theory of Revolution, A Reply to Freeman," *Political Theory* 6 (3): 299–311.

Hagopian, M.N. (1975) *The Phenomenon of Revolution*, New York: Dodd, Mead.

Hobsbawm, E. (1962) *The Age of Revolution: Europe 1789–1848*, London: Weidenfeld and Nicolson.

Huntington, S.P. (1965) "Political Development and Political Decay," *World Politics* 17 (3): 386–430.

Huntington, S.P. (1968) *Political Order in Changing Societies*, New Haven, CT: Yale University Press.

Johnson, C. (1966) *Revolutionary Change*, Boston: Little, Brown.

Kamenka, E. (1966) "The Concept of Political Revolution," in C.J. Friedrich (ed.), *Revolution*, NOMOS VII, New York: Atherton Press.

Laquer, W. (1968) "Revolution," D.L. Sills (ed.), *The Encyclopedia of Philosophy*, vol. 13, New York: Crowell-Collier and Macmillan.

Luxemburg, R. (1971 [1899]) "Social Reform or Revolution," in D. Howard (ed.), *Selected Political Writings of Rosa Luxemburg*, New York: Monthly Review Press.

MacPherson, C.B. (1966) "Revolution and Ideology in the Late Twentieth Century," in C.J. Friedrich (ed.), *Revolution*, NOMOS VII, New York: Atherton Press.

Marx, K. (1972 [1846]) "The German Ideology," in R.C. Tucker (ed.), *The Marx-Engels Reader*, New York: Norton.

Marx, K. (1972 [1859]) "Preface to a Contribution to the Critique of Political Economy," in R.C. Tucker (ed.), *The Marx-Engels Reader*, New York: Norton.

Marx, K. (1972 [1875]) "Critique of the Gotha Program," in R.C. Tucker (ed.), *The Marx-Engels Reader*, New York: Norton.

Marx, K. and Engels, F. (1972 [1848]) "Communist Manifesto," in R.C. Tucker (ed.), *The Marx-Engels Reader*, New York: Norton.

Moore, B., Jr. (1966) *Social Origins of Dictatorship and Democracy: Lord and Peasant in the Making of the Modern World*, Boston: Beacon Press.

Moore, B., Jr. (1972 [1970]) *Reflections on the Causes of Human Misery*, Boston: Beacon Press.

Nardin, T. (1972) "Conflicting Perceptions of Political Violence," in C.P. Cotter (ed.), *Political Science Annual*, vol. 4, Indianapolis: Bobbs-Merril.

Overholt, W.H. (1977) "An Organizational Theory of Revolution," *American Behavioral Scientist* 20 (4): 493–520.

Pettee, G. (1966) "Revolution – Typology and Process," in C.J. Friedrich (ed.), *Revolution*, NOMOS VII, New York: Atherton Press.

Prokhov, A.M. (ed.) (1978) *Great Soviet Encyclopedia*, vol. 21, New York: Macmillan.

Rejai, M. (1977) *The Comparative Study of Revolutionary Strategy*, New York: David McKay.

Skocpol, T. (1979) *States and Social Revolutions*, New York: Cambridge University Press.

Spitz, P. (1978) "The Silent Violence: Famine and Inequality," *International Social Science Journal* 4: 867–92.

Tilly, C. (1975) "Revolutions and Collective Violence," in F. Greenstein and N. Polsby (eds.), *Handbook of Political Science*, vol. 3, Reading, MA: Addison-Wesley.
Tilly, C. (1978) *From Mobilization to Revolution*, Reading, MA: Addison-Wesley.
Trotsky, L. (1963 [1905]) "The Motive Force of the Russian Revolution," in I. Howe (ed.), *The Basic Writings of Trotsky*, New York: Schrocken Books.
Tucker, R.C. (ed.) (1972) *The Marx-Engels Reader*, New York: Norton.

9 Culture

Joining minimal definitions and ideal types

John Gerring and Paul A. Barresi

Decades after Giovanni Sartori's path-breaking work, and a century after the linguistic turn in philosophy, the process of concept formation in the social sciences is still an ad hoc, largely intuitive affair. Although scholars are aware of the importance of defining key terms and using those terms in a consistent manner, few of them have sought to specify the grounds on which one should prefer one term over another, or one definition over another. Are all stipulative definitions equally sound as long as they are clearly defined and consistently employed?

Scholars usually resolve this question by an appeal to context, but this appeal is itself highly ambiguous. Which context or contexts are relevant, and which aspects of that context or contexts are determinative? At some level, *all* semantic questions appeal to context. What is clear, however, is that appeals to the proximate context of a work are insufficient to resolve questions of definition, for key terms are embedded in a linguistic context that is much broader than the work itself. A term may be employed clearly and consistently within a given work but remain ambiguous in the corresponding field or subfield because it is used differently in other language areas. If we are to avoid definitional solipsisms, then we must think about concept formation as a discipline-wide problem, not a problem limited to particular authors or research contexts.

For some time, it has been a standard complaint that the social science vocabulary lacks the clarity and consistency of the natural science vocabulary (e.g., Wilson 1998: 198). Disturbingly, we find that key words in the social science lexicon often are defined in different ways (polysemy); that different terms often mean approximately the same thing (synonymy); and that these terms and meanings undergo continual revision. As a result, knowledge accumulation – or even productive argumentation – is difficult. Indeed, lexical confusion may be regarded as both a primary cause of the ongoing fragmentation of the social sciences at the turn of the twenty-first century, and a principal medium through which that fragmentation occurs. Because we cannot achieve a basic level of agreement on the terms by which we analyze the social world, agreement on conclusions is impossible.

Regrettably, social scientists have paid little attention to concept formation. This lack of attention is all the more remarkable given the resurgence of interest in questions of research design and qualitative methodology (King et al. 1994). One reason for this neglect is the relatively un-integrated state of concept research. Most work on the subject relates to particular fields, concepts, or conceptual problems. The relevance of this methodological spadework, although potentially great, has been easy to ignore. Synthetic approaches to concept formation are often difficult to interpret and, more importantly, are at odds with one another. Too often, research on concepts has mirrored the very fragmentation that we observe in its subject matter, the social science lexicon.

Building on earlier studies (Gerring 1997, 1999, 2001), we attempt a synthesis of work on concept formation as it relates to definition. Our argument hinges on a fundamental distinction between general and contextual definitions – the former pertaining to broad linguistic contexts, the latter to particular research contexts. Observing this distinction, we then elaborate a method of deriving a general definition that relies on the conjoined use of minimal and ideal-type definitions – a "min-max" strategy. We then illustrate this strategy by defining the keyword "culture," a term which has plagued the social sciences for over a century. Finally, we discuss the utility of a general definition in stipulating contextual definitions and in resolving conceptual ambiguity in the social sciences.

Putting ordinary language to work: the importance of general definitions

Whatever its ambiguities, the world of natural language is not random. Indeed, norms embedded in everyday usage may be looked upon as a source of regularity, if not always logic. Rather than endeavoring to "straighten out" natural language, philosophers in the ordinary language tradition suggest that we figure it out. Natural language makes sense to its users, they reason; why should it not make sense to academics? It is clear, writes Wittgenstein,

> that every sentence in our language is "in order as it is." That is to say, we are not *striving after* an ideal, as if our ordinary vague sentences had not yet got a quite unexceptional sense, and a perfect language awaited construction by us. On the other hand, it seems clear that where there is sense there must be perfect order. So there must be perfect order even in the vaguest sentence.
>
> (Quoted in Oppenheim 1981: 178)

Wittgenstein's critique of logical positivism is strongly stated and is itself susceptible to criticism. He fails to define "perfect order," for example. Yet, the ordinary language critique seems a useful corrective to the enthusiasms of various reconstructive efforts, from Wittgenstein's own early work (the aptly titled *Tractatus logico philosophicus*) to the classificatory approaches embraced by Oppenheim (1981), Sartori (1984), and others.

It is less clear, however, what ordinary language philosophy portends for the practice of the social sciences. What would it mean to practice a social science rooted in ordinary language? Would it entail a social science limited to *natural* language? Or would it mean respecting terms and definitions as understood within specialized language regions (e.g., within subfields of a particular social science)?

Once we have engaged in an ordinary language analysis of key terms, how should we define those terms? This last question is crucial, for the strength of ordinary language analysis has been in elucidating the complexity of terms, not in bringing order to that complexity. As Pitkin (1967: 8) notes, "the problem is not to state the correct meaning of the word, but to specify all the varieties of its application to various contexts." Ordinary language analysis, as pioneered by John Austin and others, is usually an exercise in "splitting," not "lumping." Definitions are collected, usages reviewed, and meanings parsed, but Humpty Dumpty is left on the ground.

If ordinary language analysis is to facilitate empirical analysis by elucidating usable concepts, then we must make an effort to put Humpty Dumpty back together again. Our lexicon must respect the normal usage of key terms, such that the meanings we give them not only resonate with the ordinary meanings of those terms, but also elucidate their meanings in a manner concise enough to restore a greater sense of stability and focus to the social science lexicon. It also must move beyond the extreme polysemy offered by standard lexical treatments of a word, such as those found in dictionaries or in more extensive analyses of usage, such as ordinary language studies. It must take into account the fact that reportive or customary lexical definitions are not definitions per se but rather sets of definitional options.

Our approach to improving the utility of the social science lexicon is situated between the classificatory (Sartori) and ordinary language (Wittgenstein) camps. It seeks to employ the insights and techniques of ordinary language philosophy in the service of social science analysis. It seeks, in other words, to put ordinary language to work in social science settings.

Our point of departure is the distinction between *general* and *contextual* definitions.[1] The first sort of definition seeks to determine what a term means within a general context of usage – usually, a language or language region – while making few judgments about the correctness of any particular definition or definitions, except when required by general patterns of usage. General definition is thus a refinement of standard lexical (i.e., dictionary) and ordinary language approaches to definition.

Contextual definition, in contrast, asks what a term means or should mean within a narrower context, perhaps a specific research site or research problem. It reaches beyond the myriad semantic possibilities offered in a general definition towards a particular resolution of attributes and referents. A contextual definition may be single-purpose or multi-purpose but is never all-purpose. It is the sort of definition that we are likely to find in studies of particular subjects and is sometimes referred to as a stipulative definition or definition-in-use (Robinson 1954).

Granted, the difference between general and contextual definitions is not always clear-cut. While general definitions aim to be of use in particular research contexts, contextual definitions strive for general status. Both sorts of definition are liable to general criteria of concept formation (Gerring 2001: Chapter 3). Nonetheless, the distinction between a definition that is crafted for general use and one that is crafted for use in a specific context is essential.

To understand why this is so, consider that the contextual range and empirical utility of concepts tend to vary inversely. General definitions maximize the former;

contextual definitions maximize the latter. Because of its specific empirical content, a contextual definition will travel awkwardly outside its home turf. Because of its grand purview, a general definition will usually require some specification when applied to a particular empirical task.

Social scientists may be tempted to see general definitions as merely definitional – which is to say, of no empirical value. Yet, we must know what a word generally is understood to mean before we can define it contextually. Concepts that cause the most trouble in the social sciences – e.g., "justice," "democracy," "power," and "ideology" – are problematic because we do not know what they mean generally, not because we lack contextual definitions. Indeed, there are hundreds if not thousands of contextual definitions circulating for each of these terms. Many are quite specific. But this specificity has not clarified matters. Indeed, it has clouded the situation. Insofar as empirical work on justice employs different definitions of the term or different labels for the same general concept (in order to escape ambiguities that have crept into the term), it is impossible to integrate work on this subject. This semantic confusion and disciplinary parochialism is the sort that *we* want to avoid.

Concepts, like theories, are best approached from a wide-angle perspective. If we do not take into account the many definitional options available for a term, we risk constraining our understanding of a phenomenon. We also risk ending up with a highly idiosyncratic definition – one that will not travel to other research sites, that will not cumulate with other work on the subject, and that, for both of these reasons, will not advance the field.

A min-max strategy of general definition

How, then, shall we go about crafting a general definition for a multivalent concept? This task may be broken down into three steps, as specified in Table 9.1: (1) sampling usages; (2) typologizing attributes; and (3) constructing minimal and ideal-type definitions. The goal is not only to interrogate usage norms but also to integrate them into a coherent, concise, and unified framework.

The first step is relatively unproblematic, having precedent in ordinary language analysis and most conceptual analysis (e.g., Sartori 1984). It involves obtaining a representative sample of formal definitions and usages of a chosen term from relevant fields or subfields and from natural language. Usages may bring to light meanings that are not contained in formal definitions, perhaps because they are so obvious, and may clarify meaning when formal definitions are vague. Usage also

Table 9.1 The process of min-max definition

1. Sample (sample representative usages and definitions within a linguistic context)
2. Typologize (arrange non-idiosyncratic attributes in a single typology)
3. Define
    (a) Minimal (identify those few attributes that all non-idiosyncratic uses of the term have in common)
    (b) Ideal-type (identify those attributes that define a term in its purest, most "ideal" form)

entails discussion of the referents of a concept, which cannot reasonably be segregated from its definition.

Wherever different senses of a word are radically disparate and seemingly unrelated – e.g., "pen" (writing instrument) and "pen" (enclosure) – we must restrict our survey of definitions and usages to one or the other. Of course, homonymy (of which the two radically different meanings of "pen" are an example) and polysemy (where a word invokes a number of closely related meanings) is sometimes a matter of degree. In borderline cases, the analyst will have to judge which sense should be split off, and considered to be an independent concept, and which should be retained, so as to create a concept or concepts of maximum coherence.

Representativeness in the sampling process is achieved by searching for whatever variation in usage and formal definition might exist within a language region, and by keeping track of the frequency of these various usages and definitions. Thus, if it is suspected that a word is used differently in a particular subfield, then the hunt ought to extend to that subfield. In the near future, one may be able to employ digitized texts in random sampling of language regions, enabling one to reach a more exact measurement of the frequency of usage and definitional variation. Yet, mechanized sampling probably will not alter our understanding of key terms significantly, for language is extraordinarily regular. Moreover, our intent is to discard only idiosyncratic usages and definitions. As long as the sample is sufficiently large and reasonably well balanced, we are likely to encounter all common usages. The principle of redundancy may serve as an indicator of sufficiency – when we reach a point where new definitional attributes and usages begin to repeat those that we have already encountered, then we may call off the hunt.

The issue of scope – how many language regions to survey – is also crucial. Here, the twin criteria of contextual range and coherence must guide our decisions. A sampling is better if it covers more language regions – perhaps extending to related languages, related fields, and even the etymology of a term. Yet, if this broad search reveals significant differences in meaning – differences that correspond to different language regions – then the analyst may restrict the scope of the investigation in order to preserve the coherence of the concept. Any sampling is likely to have a home turf – perhaps a particular field of social science – that is extensively canvassed and other areas that are surveyed more superficially. In any case, the scope of the survey will determine the scope of the resulting definition. As long as the scope of the survey is specified, this aspect of the definitional process should not cause confusion.

The construction of a typology rests on the assumption that although definitions for a given term are, in principle, infinite (because attributes can be combined in an infinite number of ways), most definitions juggle and re-juggle the same set of attributes. By combining near-synonyms and by organizing them along different dimensions, we ought to be able to reduce this definitional profusion into a single table of attributes. We may regard this table as a term's lexical definition because it merely reports the many meanings of the term extant in a broad linguistic context.[2]

To stop here, however, is to leave the term relatively undefined. If the term is ambiguous in normal usage, then this ambiguity will be reflected in the typology. A term may even possess blatantly contradictory attributes, as with "ideology" (Gerring 1997). Thus, in order to restore a semblance of coherence – so as to create a usable concept – we shall have to go further. This step, we argue – the step from lexical definition to general definition – is the critical step in establishing clarity and consistency in the social science lexicon. It involves two complementary definitional strategies, *minimal* and *ideal-type*.

Minimal definitions identify the bare essentials of a concept which are sufficient to bound it extensionally while maintaining all non-idiosyncratic meanings associated with the term. Minimal definitions embody all definitional attributes that are necessary and, therefore, are always present. Sufficiency, as we shall see, cannot be determined outside of a particular context and is best ignored in the min-max strategy of general definition. The resulting minimal definition should be capable of substituting for all non-idiosyncratic uses of the term and should be fairly parsimonious.[3]

Ideal-type definitions, in contrast, aim for a collection of attributes that is "maximal" in that it includes all non-idiosyncratic characteristics that together define the concept in its purest, most "ideal" form. As Weber describes it, "an ideal-type is formed . . . by the synthesis of a great many diffuse, discrete, more or less present and occasionally absent *concrete individual* phenomena, which are arranged according to those one-sidedly emphasized viewpoints into a unified *analytical* construct" (1949 [1905]: 90; see also Burger 1976). Ideal types, as the term suggests, need not have a real empirical referent, although they always have an ideal one.

Minimal definitions are minimal in their attributes but maximal in their phenomenal range, while ideal-type definitions are maximal in their attributes but minimal in their phenomenal range. By combining these two definitional strategies, we invoke a well-known feature of concept formation – the inverse correlation that exists between intension and extension. Over a century ago, Stanley Jevons (1958 [1877]: 26) pointed out that when the definitional attributes of a word are expanded (e.g., when "war" becomes "foreign war"), its empirical breadth generally is narrowed. Otherwise put, more focused definitions encompass fewer phenomena. Weber also noticed that "concepts with ever wider scope [have] ever smaller content" (quoted in Burger 1976: 72).[4] The relationship is illustrated in Figure 9.1.

Although intension is inversely correlated with extension, the same relationship does not necessarily exist between the number of attributes encompassed by a definition and its empirical range. The empirical range of a short definition can be very constricted, depending on the attributes that are included in it. It is the identity of those attributes, and not merely their number, that determines the extension of a concept. Perhaps the inverse relationship between intension and extension is best understood not as a function of the length of a definition, but rather as a product of the different goals of minimal and ideal-type definitions. Ideal-type definitions aim to identify the ideal properties of a concept (and thus its smallest extensional range), whereas minimal definitions aim to identify the minimal properties of a concept (and thus its greatest extensional range).

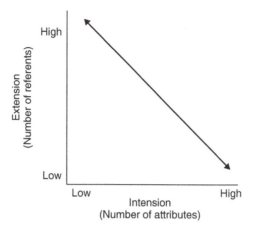

Figure 9.1 Intension and extension.

Adapted from Collier and Mahon (1993: 846).

Culture

To illustrate the application of the min-max strategy of general definition, we offer a min-max definition of culture. Social scientists have been concerned with the concept of culture since the nineteenth century and continue to be so today. Among the many scholarly works on culture, one stands out as comprehensive and authoritative. Kroeber and Kluckholm's *Culture: A Critical Review of Concepts and Definitions* (1963), which appeared originally in 1952, has been cited repeatedly as a primary source for discussions about the meaning of that term. Regrettably, it is also somewhat dated. Thus, we supplement this survey with an examination of a wide variety of more recent discussions of the concept in the social sciences (see, e.g., Freilich 1989; Harrison and Huntington 2000; Münch and Smelser 1992; Shweder and LeVine 1984). From each of these sources, we culled not only definitions of culture ("Culture is . . .") but also uses of the term.

Based on this analysis, we argue that culture can be understood along three dimensions: (1) how it is produced and transmitted; (2) the characteristics that it exhibits; and (3) the functions that it performs.

Each of these dimensions offers several definitional options (attributes), as listed in Table 9.2. The minimal definition, of course, specifies only those attributes that are common to (or at least implied by) all non-idiosyncratic definitions and usages. The ideal-type definition includes all attributes belonging to the concept in its purest, most "ideal" form.

We argue that culture, minimally defined, is any phenomenon that is social, ideational or symbolic, patterned and shared by the members of a social group. Culture as an ideal type includes all minimal attributes and many more besides. It is social, human, ideational or symbolic, patterned, shared, enduring, cumulative, coherent, differentiated, comprehensive, holistic, non-interest-based, implicit, causal, and

Table 9.2 "Culture": min-max definitions

Minimal attributes	
Production and transmission:	Social
Characteristics:	Ideational or symbolic
	Patterned
	Shared
Ideal type attributes	
Production and transmission:	Social
	Human
Characteristics:	Ideational or symbolic
	Patterned
	Shared
	Enduring
	Cumulative
	Coherent
	Differentiated
	Comprehensive
	Holistic
	Non-interest-based
	Implicit
Functions:	Causal
	Constitutive

constitutive. These contrasting definitions – one narrow, the other capacious – delimit the usage range of this vast and protean concept in the contemporary social sciences.

Several cognate and usage distinctions must be clarified before we continue. The minimal definition refers to culture without a modifier. If we speak of specific cultures (*a* culture or *the* culture), we must add an additional feature to the definition – *differentiation*. Culture may be universal, but *a* culture must be distinct from other cultures. The minimal definition focuses on the first, more general usage of culture; the ideal-type definition encompasses both usages.

The term culture sometimes is used to refer to mere evidence of culture or of a culture, such as a stone found at an archaeological dig. As with mere manifestations of culture, the cultural-ness of mere evidence of culture is derived from its relationship to a larger set of phenomena deemed to be cultural. Thus, this usage is parasitic on the general definition.

Neither the minimal definition nor the ideal-type definition of culture encompasses cognates such as "cultured" and "cultivated" (in the sense of civilized) or "cultivation" and "cultivating" (in the sense of growing or tending). These meanings are sufficiently distinct to be regarded as separate concepts.

Minimal attributes

Social

Social scientists generally agree that culture is a social product (Almond and Powell 1978: 25; D'Andrade 1984: 91–92; Patterson 2000: 208; Spiro 1984: 323).

As such, it is also "extragenetic," "extrasomatic," "outside-the-skin," or "extrinsic" to the human organism (Geertz 1973: 44, 52, 92). Indeed, perhaps the most important point of departure for modern conceptions of culture is the nature/nurture distinction. Unfortunately, few scholars agree on how we should parse this complex dichotomy. Presumably, the more we learn about the human genome, the more we will learn about how genetics conditions thought and behavior and, thus, about the nature/nurture divide. If we reach a point in history where humans begin modifying their own genotypes or the genotypes of their offspring – as seems increasingly likely – then we will create a reciprocal relationship between nature and nurture that will destroy the distinction between them. Be that as it may, "culture" – according to its current usage – refers only to beliefs or behaviors that are produced socially and, thus, are non-natural.

In a related vein, social scientists also agree that culture is something that is transmitted socially or "learned" (Barnes 1988: 18; D'Andrade 1995: 212; Goodenough 1989: 94; Greif 1994: 915; Kroeber 1948: 253; Patterson 2000: 208; Schein 1985: 9; Verba 1965: 550). Accordingly, they often describe culture as the product of "socialization," "education," "media exposure," or "social transmission" (Almond 1990: 144; Spiro 1984: 323; Verba 1965: 551); as something that is "taught" to or internalized by individuals (Almond and Verba 1989: 13; Freilich 1989: 10); or as a phenomenon into which individuals are "inducted" (Almond and Verba 1989: 13). Most writers view this learning process as a process of inheritance whereby a culture is passed down from generation to generation (Freilich 1989: 8; Geertz 1973: 89; Lewis 1961: xxiv; Patterson 2000: 209; Pye 1965: 7; Richerson and Boyd 1989: 121; Shweder 2000: 163; Verba 1965: 551). This attribute of culture has led some writers to speak of culture as a "heritage" or "tradition" (D'Andrade 1995: 212; Freilich 1989: 9; Spiro 1984: 323).

Ideational or symbolic

All definitions and usages of culture assume that it has an ideational or symbolic component, even if only implicitly. Social scientists consider ideas and symbols to be cultural by themselves (Dittmer 1977: 557; Freilich 1989: 8; Geertz 2000 [1972]: 198, 201) but consider rules, behavior, and material objects to be cultural only when they signify something other than merely themselves (Benedict 1934: 53). Berger (1995: 9) captures this distinction when he writes: "Not all of the facts of social life are 'cultural,' but some are . . . meanings, many of which inhabit a quasi-sacred realm, revealed and conveyed by custom, utterance, and other symbolic evocations." Other scholars have drawn a similar distinction (Eagleton 1991: 28).

The distinction between culture and institutions is the hardest to discern, for these two terms often are used to refer to identical or overlapping phenomena. Institutions usually are understood to include formal rules, norms, and patterns of behavior (Peters 1999). These formal rules, norms, and patterns of behavior are socially generated, patterned, and learned. It is no surprise, then, that culturalists and institutionalists often claim the same phenomena as their own. The only clear point of difference between cultures and institutions is that cultures have an ideational or symbolic component and need not include formal rules or behavior patterns. Thus, as the emphasis of a topic shifts from informal to formal rules, and from ideas to behavior, it likely will shift from the realm of culture to the realm of institutions. The line is not clear and bright, but it is the only line that we can draw.

Thus, the minimal definition of culture does not exclude material objects, behavior, rules, or institutions from its realm. It simply indicates that these subjects must have ideational or symbolic significance in order to qualify as cultural. Despite widespread disagreement among social scientists about how to define culture, general agreement does exist about its essentially ideational or symbolic nature. Ideas and symbols can stand on their own as cultural phenomena (provided that they meet the other criteria of the minimal definition) but other phenomena must have ideational or symbolic significance in order to qualify as cultural. Behavior, as such, is not culture.

Patterned

Social scientists generally agree that cultures are patterned (Almond and Powell 1966: 50; Dawson and Prewitt 1969: 27; Fagen 1969: 5; Verba 1965: 520), an attribute that they also capture by near-synonyms such as "ordered" or "organized" or when they describe culture as a "system" (Alexander 1992: 295; Freilich 1989: 9; Geertz 1973: 92, 363). Ruth Benedict (1934: 53), for example, observes that

> a culture, like an individual, is a more or less consistent pattern of thought and action. Within each culture there comes into being characteristic purposes not necessarily shared by other types of society. In obedience to these purposes, each people further and further consolidates its experience, and in proportion to the urgency of these drives the heterogeneous items of behavior take more and more congruous shape.

For structuralists such as Lévi-Strauss (1963), the patterned quality of culture is its dominant feature. For interpretivists such as Geertz (1973), it is less important. For post-structuralists such as Clifford (1988), it is even less so. Nevertheless, all social scientists seem to agree that it lies somewhere in between pure voluntarism and pure structure. It exhibits a chosen-ness, insofar as cultures are humanly created and undergoing continual change, as well as a given-ness, insofar as humans are born into a culture and thus inherit (rather than choose) its rules, obligations, and understandings. The given-ness of culture imposes a degree of order upon an otherwise random assemblage of traits.

Consider Oscar Lewis's (1961: xxiv) presentation of the idea of a culture of poverty:

> In anthropological usage the term culture implies, essentially, a design for living which is passed down from generation to generation. In applying this concept of culture to the understanding of poverty, I want to draw attention to

the fact that poverty in modern nations is not only a state of economic depriva-tion, of disorganization, or of the absence *of* something. It is also something positive in the sense that it has a structure, a rationale, and defense mechanisms without which the poor could hardly carry on. In short, it is a way of life, remarkably stable and persistent, passed down from generation to generation along family lines. The culture of poverty has its own modalities and distinc-tive social and psychological consequences for its members. It is a dynamic factor which affects participation in the larger national culture and becomes a subculture of its own.

Lewis conceives of poverty not as an inchoate and entirely reactive phenomenon, but as one with an underlying structure. He also believes, however, that poor people have volition. Other social scientists have made similar observations (Berger 1995: 15–16; Freilich 1989: 10).

To be sure, cultural patterns are not always obvious, and are not always evident to the individuals who are adherents of a particular culture. "Etic" analysis may be necessary to elucidate an underlying pattern (Pike 1967: 38). For present purposes, what is relevant is that the existence of a pattern qualifies a behavior or idea as cul-tural. According to standard usage of the term, randomly occurring phenomena – whether ideational or non-ideational – do not qualify as cultural.

Shared by the members of a social group

Social scientists recognize that culture is something shared by the members of a social group (Barnes 1988: 2; Goodenough 1989: 93; Jackman and Miller 1996: 635; Kluckholm 1951: 86; Lane 1992: 364; LeVine 1984: 67; Macridis 1961: 40; Schein 1985: 7; Shweder 2000: 163; Sil 2000: 358; Thompson et al. 1990: 1; Wildavsky 1987: 5). For Elkins and Simeon (1979: 129), for example, "[p]olitical culture is the property of a collectivity – nation, region, class, ethnic community, formal organization, party, or whatever." Individuals do not have cultures, although they partake of culture and, hence, are carriers of culture. Nations are the social groups with which the culture concept is most commonly associated (Almond and Verba 1989: 13; Brown 1977: 1; Dogan and Pelassy 1984: 58), although it also is frequently applied to subnational groups. Thus, social scientists write of Navajo culture or American culture but also of woodworker culture, Yankee culture, or law student culture. Increasingly, social scientists recognize a "world" culture (Jepperson et al. 1996: 34).

Ideal-type attributes

Having discussed the minimal attributes of culture, we now proceed to those addi-tional attributes that define culture in its ideal-type form. Minimal and ideal-type definitions differ not only in the number of attributes that they encompass but also in another important respect. Minimal definitions have relatively clear borders and, thus, delineate relatively crisp concepts. Ideal-type definitions are much fuzzier.

Because ideal-type definitions are not necessarily a function of phenomena that exist in the real world, membership in the conceptual universe described by an ideal-type definition is a matter of degree.

Human

Social scientists generally consider culture to be a distinctly human phenomenon (Benedict 1934: 53; Freilich 1989: 8; Goodenough 1989: 95). To be sure, the sacrosanct distinction between humans and higher mammals has broken down in recent years, largely due to the work of biological anthropologists (de Waal 1996, 2001; Whiten et al. 1999). Even so, culture is *quintessentially* a human creation.

Enduring

Implicit in the learned, patterned, and shared attributes of culture is its enduring quality. As Barnes (1988: 16) notes: "Unless populations are physically eliminated, cultures are seldom created or destroyed by political power. It is true that powerholders are important interpreters and manipulators of culture . . . but . . . cultures resist manipulation; people defend their assumptions." To be sure, cultures are often in flux, changing over time as the social groups that bear them adapt them to new circumstances (Freilich 1989: 9; Goodenough 1989: 96; Keesing 1974: 75–76; Kroeber 1948: 253; Verba 1965: 520). Nevertheless, one thinks of a strongly "cultural" phenomenon as one that endures the onslaughts of time (Geertz 1973: 408; Inglehart 1988: 1203; Jackman and Miller 1996: 635; Wildavsky 1989: 61).

Cumulative

Social scientists sometimes define culture as cumulative. Geertz (1973: 46, 363), for example, defines it as "the accumulated totality" of "organized systems of significant symbols." For him (ibid.: 408), "[c]ulture moves rather like an octopus – not all at once . . . but by disjointed movements of this part, then that, and now the other which somehow cumulate to directional change." Indeed, the cumulative nature of culture is implied by its patterned quality. Cumulation is what happens when the center of gravity and boundaries of this pattern change over time.

Coherent

Social scientists frequently remark on the coherence of culture (Geertz 1973: 17; Jackman and Miller 1996: 634–45; Pye 1965: 7). Culture is "logically interconnected" (Freilich 1980) or "interlocking" (Spiro 1984: 323), attributes which are implied by the patterned quality of culture, already discussed. To reiterate the argument quoted above, Ruth Benedict (1934: 53) observes that,

> cultural behavior . . . tends . . . to be integrated. A culture, like an individual, is a more or less consistent pattern of thought and action. Within each culture

there come into being characteristic purposes not necessarily shared by other types of society. In obedience to these purposes, each people further and further consolidates its experience, and in proportion to the urgency of these drives the heterogeneous items of behavior to take a more and more congruous shape.

As a symbolic phenomenon, a culture must "make sense." The sense-making may be imposed from within – by the members of the social group that bears the culture – or from without – by an ethnographer. Of course, sense may be reconstructed for a congeries of ideas and actions in different ways – too many ways, some might argue. Of the world of anthropology, LeVine (1984: 72) remarks:

No ethnographer who has followed Malinowski's (now standard) program for intensive fieldwork has failed to find increasing connectedness and coherence in customs – particularly in their ideational dimension – as he or she becomes better acquainted with their meanings in vernacular discourse and practice. There is controversy about the degree and kind of coherence – claims that cultures are deductive systems, pervasive configurations, seamless webs, have been repeatedly made and just as often disputed – but even those most skeptical of cultural coherence would not return to the earlier view of customs as discrete traits.

Frequently, the coherence of a culture is simply assumed without being proven. Even so, the assumption of coherence lies just below the surface of any assertion about culture. Ideas, practices, and symbols that are coherent are more cultural for being so.

Differentiated

Cultures often are assumed to be differentiated from one another and, thus, unique to particular social groups (Inglehart 1988: 1203; Kluckholm 1951: 86; Schein 1985: 7, 9; Schneider 1976: 206; Shweder 2000: 163). This external differentiation is the flip side of internal coherence. If cultures are internally coherent, then they must be distinct from other internally coherent cultures. "[C]onflict among cultures is a precondition of cultural identity," Wildavsky (1987: 7) writes. "It is the differences and distances from others that define one's own cultural identity."

To be sure, different cultures may have elements in common. Indeed, to the extent that we compare cultures at all, we do so with a common vocabulary that reflects the minimal and ideal-type definitions of culture, implying that any given culture can be described by reference to the same set of attributes. If two sets of beliefs and practices are to be described as distinct cultures, then any common elements either must be combined with other elements that the putative cultures do not have in common or must themselves either be put together in different ways or possessed to different degrees.

Comprehensive

Social scientists generally consider culture to be more or less comprehensive (Boas 1930: 75; D'Andrade 1995: 212; Pye 1965: 7; Williams 1981: 11). If a putative culture were to encompass beliefs and behaviors of relevance to only one or two issues – e.g., abortion, or abortion and taxes – then it would not be a culture but merely an issue-position or -positions. A culture, in contrast to an issue-position, encompasses beliefs and practices of relevance to a wider swath of experience. D'Andrade (1995: 212), for example, defines culture as "the entire social heritage of a group, including material culture and external structures, learned actions, and mental representations of many kinds." Indeed, the greater the range, the greater the confidence that a putatively cultural phenomenon qualifies as a culture. To be sure, cultures may be borne by sub-societal groups and individuals may belong to more than one culture-bearing social group – hence, "woodworking" culture, "railroad" culture, and "Wall Street" culture. Yet, each of these cultures qualifies as such only because its beliefs and practices are of relevance to a broader array of topics than the activity at its core – shaping wood, running railroad cars, or buying and selling securities.

Holistic

Some social scientists characterize culture as holistic, a quality consistent with its more or less comprehensive nature. Dittmer (1977: 555), for example, observes that, "political culture should be conceptualized as an emergent variable, whose properties transcend the sum of its members' belief- and value-systems." Other social scientists have made similar points (Benedict 1934: 53).

Non-interest-based

To say that a belief or behavior is cultural is to imply – at least within the context of an ideal-type definition – that this belief or behavior is not merely a function of self-interest (Wildavsky 1987: 4–5). To be sure, "self-interest" can be interpreted in many ways. Some scholars would claim that self-interest is itself a culturally contingent fact (Citrin and Green 1990; Kingdon 1993; Mansbridge 1983). Nevertheless, to the extent that social scientists are able to identify beliefs and behaviors as interest-based, they are less likely to consider them as cultural.

Implicit

Social scientists sometimes define culture as non-formalized thought or behavior. Barnes (1988: 15), for example, asserts that culture

> *at a minimum . . .* suggests the "easy" behavior. That is, cultural patterns provide the routine, largely unexamined options followed by most people most of the time. In programming language, culture provides the "default option," followed when there are no particular reasons for choosing another pattern of behavior.

Other social scientists have made similar points (Elkins and Simeon 1979: 128), sometimes describing culture as "taken-for-granted" or as a "background" phenomenon (Goldstone 1991: 434). The distinction between a purely formal rule and an informal cultural norm highlights the implicitness of culture, as does the distinction between the formal ideology of a political party (as expressed, for example, in its platform or constitution) and that party's political culture (Freeman 1986).

Causal

Social scientists frequently observe that culture constrains or influences human action (Almond and Powell 1978: 25; Barnes 1988: 112; Dogan and Pelassy 1984: 58; Inglehart 1988: 1203; Jackman and Miller 1996: 635; Kluckholm and Kelly 1945: 97; Kroeber and Parsons 1958: 583; Laitin 1986: 171; Levy 1984: 232; Parsons 1951: 87; Pye 1965: 7; Rosenbaum 1975: 121; Spiro 1984: 323, 324, 328; Verba 1965: 517). Culture is said to exert a bounding influence, setting limits on the range of possible behaviors that are considered to be acceptable (Elkins and Simeon 1979: 128, 131; Goodenough 1989: 95). Ian Lustick (1997: 12), for example, defines culture as "the array of symbols, shared expectations, and interactive patterns that limit and stabilize the boundaries of variation observable within groups as individuals within those groups perform life functions." Other social scientists look upon culture as "integrative," binding members of a community together and establishing separate roles and identities (Schein 1985: 9). Indeed, it would be difficult to conceive of any pattern of ideational or symbolic activity that was shared by the members of a social group but had no effect on any other aspect of the group's life. Culture is not merely inert; it does things.

Constitutive

For some social scientists, culture performs not only a causal function but a constitutive one as well (Wendt 1999). It not only constrains human behavior as a more or less mechanical matter of cause and effect but also infuses human beings or their experiences with an essence that helps to make them what they are. Talcott Parsons (1951: 34), for example, observes that, "culture is not merely 'situational' relative to action but becomes directly constitutive of personalities as such." Similarly, Wildavsky (1987: 17) emphasizes that, "cultures constitute our political selves." Still other social scientists note the constitutive role that culture plays in shaping human thoughts, beliefs, and emotions, as well as the ways of life to which individuals are deeply attached (Shweder 2000: 163; Spiro 1984: 324, 328; Williams 1981: 11).

Reflections on the min-max strategy of general definition

Having elucidated from the social science literature minimal and ideal-type definitions of "culture," we may now reflect on some of the general properties of the min-max strategy of general definition. Our observations fall into five categories: (1) the replicability of the strategy; (2) the resonance of definitions produced by the strategy; (3) the implications of the min-max strategy of general definition for cluster strategies of definition; (4) the consistency of the min-max strategy with the results of recent research on language cognition; and (5) the implications of min-max definitions for contextual definitions.

Replication

First of all, it should be emphasized that the min-max strategy is just that – a strategy, not a formula. Different researchers applying the min-max strategy to the same term are likely to produce different minimal and ideal-type definitions. Ideal-type definitions are especially likely to vary. In elucidating an ideal-type definition of "culture" from the social science literature, for example, we have been forced to make many choices along the way – e.g., how to group near-synonyms into coherent and comprehensible categories, what to label these categories when a parcel of near-synonyms are more or less interchangeable, and so forth. Nevertheless, the definitional peculiarities produced by these choices are likely to be minor. They do not mitigate the viability of the min-max strategy as a way of reducing semantic plenitude down to manageable proportions and of creating "bounding" definitions. Indeed, the variation that we might expect to find among different min-max definitions is probably less than the variation found among dictionary and ordinary language definitions, and is much less than that found among social scientific definitions in works on a given subject (see later discussion). In sum, the min-max strategy of general definition can be replicated (to the degree that any qualitative work in the social sciences can be replicated).

Resonance

The first virtue of the min-max strategy is that it trespasses lightly on ordinary usage. Min-max definitions resonate with natural language and, more importantly, within the lexicon of the social science community. In contrast, stipulative definitions often fail to resonate with either, thus creating a well-known problem in social science discourse – idiosyncrasy.

To be sure, departures from commonly used terms and definitions are justified when no existing term or definition captures a concept for which a term or definition is sorely needed. Nevertheless, these situations are relatively rare in the social sciences. More typically, neologisms result from a failure to adequately survey the existing field of terms and definitions. Thus, Geertz (1973: 220) identifies "maps of problematic social reality and matrices for the creation of collective conscience" with the term "ideology" rather than culture – an odd choice given the normal understandings of these two terms. Merelman (1969), Mullins (1972), and Wilson (1992) make similar choices, which we would prefer to call errors. Min-max definitions based on general surveys of usage preclude, or at least discourage, this sort of nonsense-making, identifying the boundaries that rightly constrain all sensible definitions.

Of course, min-max definitions are not merely reiterations of standard usage. If they were, then we would halt the process of definition after constructing a typology of definitional attributes, thus approximating the approach of lexical definitions and ordinary language analysis. The min-max strategy is "reconstructive," but minimally so. As we have suggested, it is probably best understood as a marriage of the ordinary language and classificatory approaches.

Readers might wonder whether the min-max strategy adequately preserves the plenitude of meanings contained in ordinary usage. Are all social science concepts two-dimensional? Wittgenstein (1953) points out that family-resemblance concepts have no attributes common to all usages, or at least none that would be considered sufficient to define a concept, even in a minimal sense. Collier and Mahon (1993) offer the example of "mother," noting that a genetic mother, birth mother, nurturing mother, and stepmother share only one attribute in common – being female. Clearly, a minimal definition of mother must consist of more than simply being human and female (Taylor 1995: Chapter 3). This objection might be damaging to the min-max strategy if "mother" were a key social science term. It is not, however. In general, concrete terms like "mother" are more likely to suffer from definitional ambiguity than the more abstract terms that are the staple of social science discourse. The abstract nature of the latter reduces – but does not eliminate – the problem of multiple usages without shared attributes. "Culture," for example, has no nominative attributes that could be included in a minimal definition. Yet, we were able to identify three adjectival attributes – ideational or symbolic, patterned and shared – that were sufficient to bound the culture concept extensionally and thus to provide a minimal definition. Other social science terms probably could be handled in a similar manner.

Abstract concepts pose a different sort of problem, however. Consider "justice," which may be interpreted as a matter of rights, needs, or deserts; as aggregative or distributive; as equality, variously understood; or as an action that benefits the least advantaged (there are, of course, many other options). Concepts of such great complexity do not seem to map neatly into two-dimensional space. Yet, despite its multiple meanings, we may construe a minimal definition for this complex term. Justice is "treating equals equally" and "to each his due." These Aristotelian maxims are consistent with all definitions of justice and all non-idiosyncratic uses of the term. We might also construct an ideal-type definition by combining all or most of those qualities traditionally attributed to acts of justice, with a paradigmatic example of justice-in-action serving as a model. Saving Holocaust victims presumably satisfies every possible definition of justice. It thus offers an exemplar of justice in its most "ideal" form, from which we might extract a set of ideal-type attributes.

Other concepts also could be subjected to this accordion-like definitional strategy.[5] "Equality," for example, might be defined minimally as "a relationship which obtains among persons or things which have been measured and found to be identical by reference to such standards of comparison as are deemed relevant to the inquiry at hand" (Westen 1990: 181). Maximally, equality presumably would refer to "pure" or "absolute" equality, a state in which all things that matter are enjoyed equally. "Political party" could be defined minimally as an organization that nominates individuals for elective or non-elective office. An ideal-type definition presumably would encompass many other attributes, including a shared ideology, an organizational apparatus, a well-defined membership, and endurance over time. "Democracy" could be defined minimally as rule by the people, and maximally by all the attributes traditionally associated with this word, including the social, polit-ical, and civil dimensions of democracy.

We should note that many apparent deviations from normal usage are best char-acterized as commentaries on normal usage. As commentaries, these deviations retain the connotations normally associated with a term, even while they stretch the concept to which the term refers to fit new contexts. Schaffer (1998a: 2) reports that "democracy" is sometimes used in contexts far removed from politics, and hence departs from the minimal definition of "rule by the people." Affordable gourmet ice cream, one columnist writes, is "street-corner democracy in action: for five gooey mouthfuls, a secretary could eat as well as Donald Trump" (quoted in Schaffer 1998a: 2). Despite the non-political context, "democracy" as used to describe gour-met ice cream recalls the general definition – "rule by the people." Indeed, this usage of "democracy" is intentionally ironic and, as with all ironic comments, its sense depends on the "straight" reading of the word.

Min-max and cluster strategies

The min-max strategy of general definition initially seems quite different from a "cluster" strategy. The latter seeks to break down complex words into their compo-nent parts, with separate usages that demonstrate a higher degree of internal coher-ence than the concept signified by the complex word itself, and which are well differentiated from each other. For example, David Miller (1976) employs a clus-ter strategy of definition in arguing that social justice is really three concepts mis-leadingly packed into one, according to whether one considers the question from the perspective of rights, needs, or deserts. Similarly, Hanna Pitkin (1967) argues that representation contains at least three dimensions: (1) descriptive; (2) symbolic; and (3) substantive. Collier and Levitsky (1997) discuss different kinds of democ-racy, including social democracy, parliamentary democracy, and illiberal democ-racy. One could perform a similar analysis on most abstract terms in the social science lexicon.

The crucial question is: how distinct are the multiple usages of each of these terms? If they are sufficiently distinct – if there is little overlap between social jus-tice as "rights" and social justice as "needs," for example – then we are justified in considering these meaning-clusters as separate concepts. These separate concepts, in turn, might be analyzed according to the min-max strategy of general definition. If, however, the meanings of these multiple usages turn out to be similar once they are disaggregated into their basic attributes or if the separate usages are not well established, then we might be justified in treating them all as parts of a single con-cept. The question of whether multiple usages of a term signifies a single concept or multiple concepts is an empirical one. For example, if we were trying to define the word "case," then we would want to distinguish between separate concepts signified by the usages of the term that differ radically from one another. When used as a synonym for "circumstance" (e.g., "in the first case"), "case" means something quite different from what it means in methodological contexts, where it is used to refer to an observation that provides evidence for a proposition (Gerring 2001: Chapter 8). Accordingly, "case" signifies a cluster of at least two distinct concepts. Alternatively, we could treat these multiple meanings as "subtypes" that revolve around a single general definition. This alternate strategy would be easier if these sub-concepts could be distinguished from one another and from the general definition by separate terms – e.g., "social democracy," "liberal democracy," and so forth (Collier and Levitsky 1997). In any case, cluster strategies of definition are not viable substitutes for the min-max strategy of general definition but may be viewed as complementary to it.

The min-max strategy and language cognition

The lexicon of the social sciences is not autonomous from natural language. Indeed, virtually all of the key terms of the social sciences are adapted from natural language (Mahon 1998; Schaffer 1998b). Moreover, the process of concept formation in the social sciences, while not identical to concept formation in ordinary language, is still liable to cognitive constraints. Thus, it is important to consider the extent to which the min-max strategy of general definition conforms to recent research on language cognition (D'Andrade 1995; Lakoff 1987; Rosch et al. 1976; Taylor 1995).

One of the most important discoveries in this fast-developing field is the role of the prototype in imposing conceptual order on the infinite complexities of empirical reality (Rosch 1975). In a series of early experiments, Rosch and her colleagues explored common nouns like "bird" in order to discern the extent to which different pictorial representations of this family accorded with respondents' ideal notions of what a bird should look like. Respondents strongly embraced certain birds, such as the robin, over others, such as the penguin, which exhibited fewer of the qualities of "birdness" (Rosch et al. 1976). The general conclusion drawn from this research is that human beings perceive the world through filters in the form of idealized cognitive models (ICMs) rather than through abstract "definitions."

What is striking about this research is how closely the workings of the prototype mirror the workings of ideal-type definitions. Although our emphasis has been on the formal definitional attributes of the ideal-type, these attributes often are drawn from real exemplars. We can hardly conceive of "fascism" without conjuring up images of Nazi Germany. Nor can we conceptualize "justice" without some putatively real examples of justice-in-action. Many other social science concepts have exemplars or paradigm cases around which their definitions revolve. Idealized cognitive models may or may not exist in the real world but they are always ideal-typical. Again, the workings of natural language and the social sciences seem to be in tandem. A Lockean/Platonic circularity underlies the use of key concepts in both. We apprehend the real in terms of the ideal, and the ideal in terms of the real.

Minimal definitions are both more austere and more abstract than ideal-type definitions or prototypes. Yet, minimal definitions also have a direct parallel in cognitive linguistics. Langacker (1987: 373) considers that words are learned through a process of association and definitional adjustment, in which one instance of a concept (e.g., "free") is associated with another, and another, until a single abstract concept – or "schema" – encompassing all such instances is formed. The contrast between a prototype and a schema reproduces many of the elements of min-max definitions. Langacker (ibid.: 371) explains:

> A prototype is a typical instance of a category, and other elements are assimilated to the category on the basis of their perceived resemblance to the prototype; there are degrees of membership based on degrees of similarity. A schema, by contrast, is an abstract characterization that is fully compatible with all the members of the category it defines (so membership is not a matter of degree); it is an integrated structure that embodies the commonality of its members, which are conceptions of greater specificity and detail that elaborate the schema in contrasting ways.

Social science speech and ordinary speech are not identical. Sartori (1984) is correct to point out that the social science lexicon does not, and need not, reproduce ordinary language. As cognitive research has revealed, however, some versions of social science concept formation are more compatible with natural language than others. *Ceteris paribus*, we ought to prefer the version that is more "natural."

Min-max and contextual definitions

Properly constructed, minimal and ideal-type definitions travel comfortably across contextual borders. They are hardy. Minimal definitions are travel-worthy because they are highly inclusive. Ideal-type definitions travel easily because they eschew the hard-and-fast boundaries of minimal definitions. They take a more permissive attitude to the task of operationalization; entities fall *more or less* into the semantic realm of a concept.

Contextual definitions, by contrast, are not as broadly applicable. The distinction between the two seems obvious enough once it has been pointed out. Yet, the failure to recognize such a distinction underlies a good deal of unproductive argumentation in the social sciences. It is as if Adam were to begin associating a given set of personality traits with an individual named Eve, and thereafter to consider it a breach of conceptual validity to call other persons by that name. "Eve" (Adam's wife) is a contextual definition of a more general concept with the same name. Much the same could be said for many abstract concepts in the social sciences today. Every author seems to have a pet referent with which he or she associates a set of defining characteristics and uses in a particular research context, while giving little thought to other referents and contexts that might require other definitions. Each purports to be authoritative (Culture is . . . . The state is . . . . Justice is . . . .); each is militant in defense of his or her key word and definition. They are jousting knights with definitional banners. Thus is semantic confusion born and conceptual disarray propounded.

Consider in this light the list of definitions of culture provided in Kroeber and Kluckholm's exhaustive compendium (1963 [1952]). We are not arguing that any of these definitions are wrong. Rather, they are partial. They bring to light certain aspects of the culture concept while excluding or downplaying others. They are, in this sense, stipulative and arbitrary – but only if understood as general definitions. If, instead, we look upon these definitions as contextual, then it becomes possible to reconcile the profusion and prolixity of "culture" with a central, enduring core meaning – which we hope to have provided here.

Concluding thoughts

A min-max general definition specifies the parameters of a concept, both a minimum and a maximum of attributes and entities. In this way, the min-max definition defines the frame within which contextual definitions should fall, a handy way of identifying the attribute and entity space of a concept. The minimal definition of a term offers a short set of attributes to which others may be appended, while the ideal-type offers a long list of attributes from which attributes may be subtracted. Somewhere in between lies the terrain of non-idiosyncratic contextual definitions. For scholars working on culture, Table 9.2 offers a concise yet comprehensive set of definitional options. We ought to be able to construct similar typologies for all social science concepts and thereby vastly reduce the time and effort that now are required to find the right term for a given research context, and the right definition for a given term in a given research context. When all concepts are so considered, the min-max strategy of general definition outlined here provides a terminological scaffolding upon which the welter of terms and meanings in the social sciences can be organized in a reasonably stable and well-organized manner.

This scaffolding is not a classificatory one, in which terms are arranged in a hierarchical fashion, defined by always-and-only attributes that establish a one-to-one correlation between words and things. Rather than a pyramid of terms, the min-max strategy establishes an irregularly structured two-dimensional space in which terms inhabit more or less fixed locations. Meanings overlap but are never perfectly synonymous. Meanings for a single term are plural but not infinite. Thus, although we cannot dispense with the twin problems of polysemy and synonymy, we can manage their ambiguities.

The two-dimensional space is mapped by minimal and ideal-type definitions – the former establishing an outer ring, and the latter establishing an inner ring, for each concept. Between these two extremes, a concept's interpretation fluctuates but without losing its essential meaning. These meanings continue to resonate even when a term is defined contextually. So understood, the signposts provided by min-max general definitions should allow us to navigate through semantic space without getting lost in our words.[6]

Let us consider, in this light, the oft-discussed problem of culture's "residual" status. The concept of culture, according to most culturalists (e.g., Thompson et al.

1990: 217–18), is like a scarce species threatened by well-armed poachers. The attributes and referents of this defenseless concept are being appropriated by neighboring terms (e.g., "structures," "institutions"), leaving culture bare and unadorned, which is to say, meaningless. To be sure, there are many imperialisms at work in the fields of culture, structure, and institutions. If economists are keen to claim cultural ground for their own, then so are culturalists eager to make excursions into enemy territory – into the world of "self-interest" and "rationality." Thus do we play musical chairs with words, defining our opponents out of existence (Sartori 1975: 9; see also Sartori 1984: 38, 52–53). Practitioners in any field of inquiry are apt to privilege terms and definitions that allocate the greatest and theoretically most important semantic ground to themselves.

This unseemly scramble for semantic *Lebensraum* confirms the relativist's view of the social sciences – mutually incompatible and incommensurable paradigms competing in a violent turf battle over what is sense and what is non-sense. The victor is that group of social scientists who struggle most aggressively to redefine the conceptual universe in a power-grab for meaning. To the extent that this view accurately describes the history and current state of the social sciences, it is a withering indictment. Where are we to look for an alternative to the incessant and apparently unproductive lexical battles that plague the social sciences?

There are many possibilities – epistemological, ontological, and methodological – but only one that is sufficiently grounded in common sense and common practice to be mutually acceptable to all parties. This option, we have argued, is the ordinary language approach to concept formation, as structured by the min-max strategy of general definition.

Of course, there always will be conceptual frontiers in the social sciences and these frontiers always will be susceptible to border skirmishes among neighboring terms. Yet, the question of which among a set of neighboring terms "owns" particular attributes or entities is not entirely up for grabs. Some borders are more defensible than others. Minimal definitions establish the outer boundaries of a concept and, thus, are likely to overlap with the minimal definitions of neighboring concepts. Ideal-type definitions, in contrast, are the highest walls of the strongest castle, nestled deep in the interior of a concept's conceptual realm. Ideal-type definitions encompass fewer phenomena than do minimal definitions, but the ownership of these phenomena is less in doubt.

The min-max strategy of general definition should help us to define key concepts more easily, to define the range of those concepts (differentiating between general and contextual definitions), and to avoid sterile debates that are purely "semantic" – where language gets in the way of understanding. It is often said that the social sciences lack for having a common language, a common lexicon by which to conduct research, arbitrate disputes, and cumulate discoveries. The min-max strategy of general definition can help to create that common language.

We do not mean to suggest that minimal and ideal-type definitions are permanent or fixed. Indeed, general definitions undergo continual revision. As social scientists suggest new attributes for a concept, our conception of the concept changes. These changes are incremental, however, occurring over many decades, and exhibit a high degree of subsequent stability. They do not challenge the utility of minimal and ideal-type definitions as bounding (and hence defining) devices.

Indeed, any progress in the social sciences is likely to be reflected in conceptual development; a stagnant lexicon is rarely a useful lexicon. The intention of the min-max strategy of general definition is to structure the ongoing debates over terms and meanings so that they can proceed more productively. We hope that we have demonstrated the utility of this strategy by narrowing the scope of contention with respect to one especially recalcitrant concept – "culture." We now know what it is that we are talking about, at least in a general way, when we employ this complex and multivalent term. We also know where to go for a more precise meaning – the contextual definition – serviceable in a particular research setting.

Notes

* Originally published as John Gerring and Paul A. Barresi (2003) "Putting Ordinary Language to Work: A Min-Max Strategy of Concept-Formation in the Social Sciences," *Journal of Theoretical Politics* 15 (2): 201–32.

1 This distinction is similar but not identical to the "two-level" approach associated with the work of Manfred Bierwisch (1981; see also Bierwisch and Schreuder 1992). See also discussion in Taylor (1995: Chapter 14).
2 We should note that the choice of labels for each of the primary attributes of a term is almost always arbitrary because a number of near-synonyms generally vie for our attention. Thus, in the illustration of the min-max strategy of general definition that follows, we have said that "culture" is social; but we might also have said that it is "learned" or "non-natural" or that it is a "heritage" or "tradition." Each of these near-synonyms expresses the sense in which culture is created and passed on, and makes clear that it is not merely instinctive or reactive.
3 Definitional strategies similar to the "minimal" strategy have been employed by various writers, although not always by this name. See, e.g., Debnam (1984) on "power," Freeden (1994: 146) on "ineliminable" attributes, Hamilton (1987) on "ideology," Pitkin (1967: 10–11) on "basic meaning," and Murphey (1994: 23–24). Sartori endorses minimal definition in early work (1975: 34–35; 1976: 61) but drops the matter in his classic work on concept formation (1984). It should be noted that minimal definition is similar, though not identical, to a "procedural minimum" definition (Collier and Levitsky 1997). In the latter, the search is for an operationalization that satisfies all definitional requirements of a concept.
4 See also Angeles (1981: 141), Cohen and Nagel (1934: 33), Collier and Mahon (1993), Frege, quoted in Passmore (1967 [1961]: 184), and the now-classic treatment, Sartori (1970: 1041).
5 We are indebted to David Waldner for suggesting this metaphor.
6 This metaphor is a slight revision of Kaplan's. Concepts, he writes, "mark out the paths by which we may move most freely in logical space" (1964: 52).

References

Alexander, J. (1992) "The Promise of a Cultural Sociology," in R. Münch and N.J. Smelser (eds.), *Theory of Culture*, Berkeley: University of California Press.
Almond, G.A. (1990) "The Study of Political Culture," in G.A. Almond (ed.), *A Discipline Divided: Schools and Sects in Political Science*, Newbury Park, CA: Sage.
Almond, G.A. and Powell, G.B., Jr. (eds.) (1966) *Comparative Politics Today: A Development Approach*, Boston, MA: Little, Brown.

Almond, G.A. and Powell, G.B., Jr. (eds.) (1978) *Comparative Politics: Systems, Processes, and Policy*, 2nd edn., Boston: Little, Brown.

Almond, G.A. and Verba, S. (1989) *The Civic Culture: Political Attitudes and Democracy in Five Nations*, Newbury Park, CA: Sage.

Angeles, P.A. (1981) *Dictionary of Philosophy*, New York: Barnes and Noble.

Barnes, S.H. (1988) *Politics and Culture*, Ann Arbor: University of Michigan Institute for Social Research, Center for Political Studies.

Benedict, R. (1934) *Patterns of Culture*, New York: Mentor.

Berger, B.M. (1995) *An Essay on Culture: Symbolic Structure and Social Structure*, Berkeley: University of California Press.

Bierwisch, M. (1981) "Basic Issues in the Development of Word Meaning," in W. Deutsch (ed.), *The Child's Construction of Language*, London: Academic Press.

Bierwisch, M. and Schreuder, R. (1992) "From Concepts to Lexical Items," *Cognition* 42: 23–60.

Boas, F. (1930) *Anthropology: Encyclopedia of the Social Sciences*, vol. 2, New York: Macmillan.

Brown, A. (1977) "Introduction," in A. Brown and J. Gray (eds.), *Political Culture and Political Change in Communist States*, New York: Holmes and Meier.

Burger, T. (1976) *Max Weber's Theory of Concept Formation: History, Laws, and Ideal Types*, Durham, NC: Duke University Press.

Citrin, J. and Green, D.P. (1990) "The Self-interest Motive in American Public Opinion," *Research in Micropolitics* 3: 1–27.

Clifford, J. (1988) *The Predicament of Culture: Twentieth-century Ethnography, Literature, and Art*, Cambridge, MA: Harvard University Press.

Cohen, M.R. and Nagel, E. (1934) *An Introduction to Logic and Scientific Method*, New York: Harcourt, Brace and Company.

Collier, D. and Mahon, J.E., Jr. (1993) "Conceptual 'Stretching' Revisited: Adapting Categories in Comparative Analysis," *American Political Science Review* 87: 845–55.

Collier, D. and Levitsky, S. (1997) "Democracy with Adjectives: Conceptual Innovation in Comparative Research," *World Politics* 49: 430–51.

D'Andrade, R. (1984) "Culture Meaning Systems," in R.A. Shweder and R.A. LeVine (eds.), *Culture Theory: Essays on Mind, Self, and Emotion*, Cambridge: Cambridge University Press.

D'Andrade, R. (1995) *The Development of Cognitive Anthropology*, Cambridge: Cambridge University Press.

Dawson, R.E. and Prewitt, K. (1969) *Political Socialization*, Boston: Little, Brown.

de Waal, F. (1996) *Good Natured: The Origins of Right and Wrong in Humans and Other Animals*, Cambridge, MA: Harvard University Press.

de Waal, F. (2001) *The Ape and the Sushi Master*, New York: Basic Books.

Debnam, G. (1984) *The Analysis of Power: Core Elements and Structure*, New York: St. Martin's Press.

Dittmer, L. (1977) "Political Culture and Political Symbolism: Toward a Theoretical Synthesis," *World Politics* 29: 552–83.

Dogan, M. and Pelassy, D. (1984) *How to Compare Nations*, Chatham, NJ: Chatham House.

Eagleton, T. (1991) *Ideology: An Introduction*, New York: Verso.

Elkins, D.J. and Simeon, R.E.B. (1979) "A Cause in Search of Its Effect, or What Does Political Culture Explain?," *Comparative Politics* 11: 127–45.

Fagen, R.R. (1969) *The Transformation of Political Culture in Cuba*, Stanford: Stanford University Press.

Freeden, M. (1994) "Political Concepts and Ideological Morphology," *Journal of Political Philosophy* 21: 140–64.

Freeman, J. (1986) "The Political Culture of the Democratic and Republican Parties," *Political Science Quarterly* 101: 327–56.

Freilich, M. (1980) "Culture Is 'Proper' Not 'Smart': A Conceptualization Which Makes a Difference," paper presented at the American Anthropological Association annual meeting, Washington, DC.

Freilich, M. (1989) "Introduction: Is Culture Still Relevant?," in M. Freilich (ed.), *The Relevance of Culture*, New York: Bergin and Garvey.

Geertz, C. (2000 [1972]) "Deep Play: Notes on the Balinese Cockfight," in L. Crothers and C. Lockhart (eds.), *Culture and Politics: A Reader*, New York: St. Martin's Press.

Geertz, C. (1973) *The Interpretation of Cultures*, New York: Basic Books.

Gerring, J. (1997) "Ideology: A Definitional Analysis," *Political Research Quarterly* 50 (4): 957–94.

Gerring, J. (1999) "What Makes a Concept Good? An Integrated Framework for Understanding Concept Formation in the Social Sciences," *Polity* 31: 357–93.

Gerring, J. (2001) *Social Science Methodology: A Criterial Framework*, Cambridge: Cambridge University Press.

Goodenough, W.H. (1989) "Culture: Concept and Phenomenon," in M. Freilich (ed.), *The Relevance of Culture*, New York: Bergin and Garvey.

Goldstone, J.A. (1991) "Ideology, Cultural Frameworks, and the Process of Revolution," *Theory and Society* 20: 405–53.

Greif, A. (1994) "Cultural Beliefs and the Organization of Society: A Historical and Theoretical Reflection on Collectivist and Individualist Societies," *Journal of Political Economy* 102: 912–50.

Hamilton, M.B. (1987) "The Elements of the Concept of Ideology," *Political Studies* 35: 18–38.

Harrison, L.E. and Huntington, S.P. (eds.) (2000) *Culture Matters*, New York: Basic Books.

Inglehart, R. (1988) "The Renaissance of Political Culture," *American Political Science Review* 82: 1203–30.

Jackman, R.W. and Miller, R.A. (1996) "A Renaissance of Political Culture?," *American Journal of Political Science* 40: 632–59.

Jepperson, R.L., Wendt, A., and Katzenstein, P.J. (1996) "Norms, Identity, and Culture in National Security," in P.J. Katzenstein (ed.), *The Culture of National Security*, New York: Columbia University Press.

Jevons, W.S. (1958 [1877]) *The Principles of Science*, New York: Dover.

Kaplan, A. (1964) *The Conduct of Inquiry: Methodology for Behavioral Science*, San Francisco: Chandler.

Keesing, R.M. (1974) "Theories of Culture," *Annual Review of Anthropology* 3: 73–97.

King, G., Keohane, R.O., and Verba, S. (1994) *Designing Social Inquiry: Scientific Inference in Qualitative Research*, Princeton, NJ: Princeton University Press.

Kingdon, J.W. (1993) "Politicians, Self-interest, and Ideas," in G.E. Marcus and R. Hanson (eds.), *Reconsidering the Democratic Public*, University Park: Pennsylvania State University Press.

Kluckholm, C. (1951) "The Concept of Culture," in D. Lerner and H.D. Lasswell (eds.), *The Policy Sciences*, Stanford, CA: Stanford University Press.

Kluckholm, C. and Kelly, W.H. (1945) "The Concept of Culture," in R. Linton (ed.), *The Science of Man in the World Crisis*, New York: Columbia University Press.

Kroeber, A.L. (1948) *Anthropology*, New York: Harcourt, Brace.

Kroeber, A.L. and Kluckholm, C. (1963 [1952]) *Culture: A Critical Review of Concepts and Definitions*, New York: Vintage/Random House.

Kroeber, A.L. and Parsons, T. (1958) "The Concepts of Culture and of Social System," *American Sociological Review* 23: 582–83.

Laitin, D. (1986) *Hegemony and Culture*, Chicago: University of Chicago Press.

Lakoff, G. (1987) *Women, Fire, and Dangerous Things: What Categories Reveal About the Mind*, Chicago: University of Chicago Press.

Lane, R. (1992) "Political Culture: Residual Category or General Theory?," *Comparative Political Studies* 25: 362–87.

Langacker, R.W. (1987) *Foundations of Cognitive Grammar: Theoretical Prerequisites*, Stanford: Stanford University Press.

LeVine, R.A. (1984) "Properties of Culture An Ethnographic View," in R.A. Shweder and R.A. LeVine (eds.), *Culture Theory: Essays of Mind, Self, and Emotion*, New York: Cambridge University Press.

Levy, R.I. (1984) "Emotion, Knowing, and Culture," in R.A. Shweder and R.A. LeVine (eds.), *Culture Theory: Essays of Mind, Self, and Emotion*, New York: Cambridge University Press.

Lustick, I.S. (1997) "Culture and the Wager of Rational Choice," *ASPA-CP Newsletter* 8 (2): 11–14.

Lévi-Strauss, C. (1963) *Structural Anthropology*, New York: Doubleday.

Lewis, O. (1961) *The Children of Sanchez: Autobiography of a Mexican Family*, New York: Vintage Books.

Macridis, R. (1961) "Interest Groups in Comparative Analysis," *Journal of Politics* 23: 25–45.

Mahon, J.E., Jr. (1998) "Political Science and Ordinary Language: Why Don't We Have Conferences on 'The Transition to Polyarchy'?," paper presented to the International Social Science Council Committee on Conceptual and Terminological Analysis, 14th World Congress of Sociology, Montreal.

Mansbridge, J. (1983) *Beyond Adversarial Democracy*, Chicago: University of Chicago Press.

Merelman, R.M. (1969) "The Development of Political Ideology: A Framework for the Analysis of Political Socialization," *American Political Science Review* 63: 750–67.

Miller, D. (1976) *Social Justice*, Oxford: Clarendon Press.

Mullins, W.A. (1972) "On the Concept of Ideology in Political Science," *American Political Science Review* 66: 498–510.

Münch, R. and Smelser, N.J. (eds.) (1992) *Theory of Culture*, Berkeley: University of California Press.

Murphey, M.G. (1994) *Philosophical Foundations of Historical Knowledge*, Albany, NY: SUNY Press.

Oppenheim, F.E. (1981) *Political Concept: A Reconstruction*, Chicago: University of Chicago Press.

Parsons, T. (1951) *The Social System*, New York: Free Press.

Passmore, J. (1967 [1961]) "Arguments to Meaninglessness: Excluded Opposites and Paradigm Cases," in R. Rorty (ed.), *The Linguistic Turn: Recent Essays in Philosophical Method*, Chicago: University of Chicago Press.

Patterson, O. (2000) "Taking Culture Seriously: A Framework and an Afro-American Illustration," in L.E. Harrison and S.P. Huntington (eds.), *Culture Matters*, New York: Basic Books.

Peters, B.G. (1999) *Institutional Theory in Political Science: The "New Institutionalism,"* London: Pinter.

Pike, K. (1967) *Language in Relation to a Unified Theory of the Structure of Human Behavior*, 2nd edn., The Hague: Mouton.

Pitkin, H.F. (1967) *Representation*, Berkeley: University of California Press.

Pye, L.W. (1965) "Introduction: Political Culture and Political Development," in L.W. Pye and S. Verba (eds.), *Political Culture and Political Development*, Princeton: Princeton University Press.

Richerson, P.J. and Boyd, R. (1989) "A Darwinian Theory for the Evolution of Symbolic Cultural Traits," in M. Freilich (ed.), *The Relevance of Culture*, New York: Bergin and Garvey.

Robinson, R. (1954) *Definition*, Oxford: Clarendon Press.

Rosch, E. (1975) "Cognitive Representations of Semantic Categories," *Journal of Experimental Psychology: General* 104: 192–233.

Rosch, E., Mervis, C., Gray, W., Johnson, D., and Boyes-Braem, P. (1976) "Basic Objects in Natural Categories," *Cognitive Psychology* 8: 382–439.

Rosenbaum, W.A. (1975) *Political Culture*, New York: Praeger.

Sartori, G. (1970) "Concept Misformation in Comparative Politics," *American Political Science Review* 64 (4): 1033–53.

Sartori, G. (1975) "The Tower of Babel," in G. Sartori, F.W. Riggs, and H. Teune (eds.), *Tower of Babel: On the Definition and Analysis of Concepts in the Social Sciences*, Pittsburgh: International Studies Association, Occasional Paper no. 6: 7–37.

Sartori, G. (1976) *Parties and the Party System*, Cambridge: Cambridge University Press.

Sartori, G. (1984) "Guidelines for Concept Analysis," in G. Sartori (ed.), *Social Science Concepts: A Systematic Analysis*, Beverly Hills, CA: Sage.

Schaffer, F.C. (1998a) *Democracy in Translation: Understanding Politics in an Unfamiliar Culture*, Ithaca, NY: Cornell University Press.

Sartori, G. (1998b) "Why Don't Political Scientists Coin More New Terms?," paper presented at the annual meeting of the American Political Science Association, Boston.

Schein, E. (1985) *Organizational Culture and Leadership*, San Francisco: Jossey-Bass.

Schneider, D. (1976) "Notes Toward a Theory of Culture," in K. Basso and H. Selby (eds.), *Meaning in Anthropology*, Albuquerque: University of New Mexico Press.

Shweder, R.A. (2000) "Moral Maps, 'First World' Conceits, and the New Evangelists," in L.E. Harrison and S.P. Huntington (eds.), *Culture Matters*, New York: Basic Books.

Shweder, R.A. and R.A. LeVine (eds.) (1984) *Culture Theory: Essays on Mind, Self, and Emotion*, New York: Cambridge University Press.

Sil, R. (2000) "The Foundations of Eclecticism: The Epistemological Status of Agency, Culture, and Structure in Social Theory," *Journal of Theoretical Politics* 12: 353–87.

Spiro, M.E. (1984) "Some Reflections on Cultural Determinism and Relativism with Special Reference to Emotion and Reason," in R.A. Shweder and R.A. LeVine (eds.), *Culture Theory: Essays on Mind, Self, and Emotion*, New York: Cambridge University Press.

Taylor, J.R. (1995) *Linguistic Categorization: Prototypes in Linguistic Theory*, 2nd edn., Oxford: Clarendon Press.

Thompson, M., Ellis, R., and Wildavsky, A. (1990) *Cultural Theory*, San Francisco: Westview Press.

Verba, S. (1965) "Comparative Political Culture," in L.W. Pye and S. Verba (eds.), *Political Culture and Political Development*, Princeton: Princeton University Press.

Weber, M. (1949 [1905]) *The Methodology of the Social Sciences*, New York: Free Press.

Wendt, A. (1999) *The Social Theory of International Politics*, Cambridge: Cambridge University Press.

Westen, P. (1990) *Speaking of Equality*, Princeton: Princeton University Press.

Whiten, A., Goodall, J., McGrew, W.C., Nishida, T., Reynolds, V., Sugiyama, Y., Tutin, C.E.G., Wrangham, R.W., and Boesch, C. (1999) "Cultures in Chimpanzees," *Nature* 399: 682–85.

Wildavsky, A. (1987) "Choosing Preferences by Constructing Institutions: A Cultural Theory of Preference Formation," *American Political Science Review* 81: 3–21.

Wildavsky, A. (1989) "Frames of Reference Come from Cultures: A Predictive Theory," in M. Freilich (ed.), *The Relevance of Culture*, New York: Bergin and Garvey.

Williams, R. (1981) *The Sociology of Culture*, New York: Schocken.

Wilson, E.O. (1998) *Consilience: The Unity of Knowledge*, New York: Alfred A. Knopf.

Wilson, R.W. (1992) *Compliance Ideologies: Rethinking Political Culture*, Cambridge: Cambridge University Press.

Wittgenstein, L. (1953) *Philosophical Investigations*, New York: Macmillan.

10 Democracy

Conceptual hierarchies in comparative research[1]

David Collier and Steven Levitsky

The global wave of democratization in the final decades of the twentieth century presented scholars with the challenge of conceptualizing a diverse array of post-authoritarian regimes. The national political regimes in Latin America, Africa, Asia, and the former communist world that emerged in the democratic third wave (Huntington 1991) exhibited important attributes of democracy. Yet these regimes differed profoundly both from each other and from the democratic regimes of advanced industrial countries. Indeed, scholars considered many not to be fully democratic.[2]

This chapter argues that researchers responded to this challenge by pursuing two potentially contradictory goals. On the one hand, they attempted to increase *analytic differentiation* in order to capture the diverse regimes that had emerged. On the other hand, they sought to avoid the *conceptual stretching* that may occur when the concept of democracy is applied to cases for which, by relevant scholarly standards, it is not appropriate (Collier and Mahon 1993; Sartori 1970). The result was a proliferation of alternative conceptual forms, including a surprising number of subtypes involving democracy with adjectives.[3] Examples from among the hundreds of subtypes that appeared in the scholarly literature were neo-patrimonial, illiberal, delegative, managed, and low-intensity democracy.

This proliferation of subtypes occurred despite efforts by leading analysts to standardize usage on the basis of procedural definitions of democracy in the tradition of Joseph Schumpeter (1947) and Robert A. Dahl (1971). This standardization succeeded in important respects. Yet as democratization continued and attention focused on an increasingly diverse set of cases, scholars introduced even more subtypes and additional conceptual innovations. The resulting conceptual confusion served as a strong reminder that tools for understanding and clarifying concepts are crucial to the social science enterprise.

We seek to refine available tools for concept analysis, focusing on the concepts employed in studies of democracy at the level of national political regimes, with particular attention to work on Latin America. Our goal is to examine the strategies of conceptual innovation that emerged and to explore trade-offs among them.

This chapter first introduces a new framework for analyzing two forms of conceptual hierarchy that are central to these strategies – the *kind hierarchy* associated with *classical subtypes* of democracy, and the *part–whole hierarchy* associated with *diminished subtypes* of democracy. We then address the *root concept* of democracy in this literature, and go on to examine specific forms of conceptual innovation: moving up and down a kind hierarchy, moving down a part–whole hierarchy, shifting the overarching concept in a kind hierarchy, and *precising* the definition of democracy itself so as to make explicit features of democracy that might otherwise be taken for granted.

A central objective of the chapter is to encourage more careful definition and use of concepts. This is an important goal, given that the diverse conceptual forms examined here typically were central to the researchers' main substantive arguments. These concepts served as the data containers that conveyed the most salient facts about the regimes under discussion (Sartori 1970: 1039). In order adequately to describe these newly formed regimes, these data containers had to be employed with care.

Improved description, in turn, is essential for assessing the causes and consequences of democracy – a central goal in this literature. Many studies have treated democracy as an outcome to be explained, including major works of comparative-historical analysis and studies of the "social requisites" of different regime types.[4] Other analyses have looked at the impact of democracy – and specific types of democracy – on economic growth, income distribution, economic liberalization and adjustment, and international conflict.[5] In these studies, the results of causal assessment can be strongly influenced by the definition and meaning of democracy employed.[6] We hope that the present discussion serves as a step toward greater consistency and clarity of meaning, which in turn will provide a more adequate basis for assessing causal relationships.

Kind hierarchies and part–whole hierarchies

Conceptual hierarchies have long played a key role in comparative research. Giovanni Sartori's classic work reshaped thinking about comparison by formulating the idea of a *ladder of abstraction*.[7] This ladder or hierarchy – which posits a vertical array of concepts – has been crucial in efforts to pursue the two-fold goal of increasing analytic differentiation and avoiding conceptual stretching (Collier 1995; Collier and Mahon 1993; Sartori 1970).

The present analysis focuses on kind hierarchies and part–whole hierarchies. This approach provides more self-explanatory labels for the two forms of conceptual structure examined here, as well as linking this discussion to a wider literature on concepts and conceptual change.[8]

Kind hierarchies

A *kind hierarchy* is a nested set of concepts in which the subordinate concepts or subtypes are a *kind of* in relation to the superordinate concepts. An example is Sartori's (1970: 1042) discussion of conceptual choices in the field of comparative administration, which in important respects draws on Weber. Taking as a point of

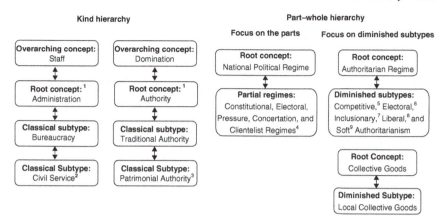

[1]Authority and administration are treated here as the root concepts. See discussion in the accompanying text; [2]Sartori (1970: 1042); [3]Weber (1978: 212–254); [4]Schmitter (1992: 426–430); [5]Levitsky and Way (2002); [6]Schedler (2006); [7]Bagley (1984: 125); [8]Jowitt (1999: 225); [9]Means (1996).

Figure 10.1 Kind hierarchy and part-whole hierarchy.

departure the concept of administration, we may argue that bureaucracy is a kind of administration, and civil service is a kind of bureaucracy. Looking up the hierarchy, administration is in turn a specific kind of staff[9] (Figure 10.1). Collier and Mahon (1993: 846) also suggest an example from Weber: taking the concept of authority as a point of departure, they observe that traditional authority is a kind of authority, and patrimonial authority is a kind of traditional authority. Again, looking up the hierarchy, authority is a specific type of domination (i.e., it is legitimate domination). Yet another example is found in the literature on corporatism: corporatism and pluralism are seen as specific types in relation to an overall system of interest intermediation (Collier 1995: 143; Schmitter 1974).

In discussing a kind hierarchy, it is helpful to distinguish the root concept, the overarching concept, and subtypes. The root concept is the level in a conceptual hierarchy that is the initial point of reference in a given study or line of analysis.[10] Thus, in the literature cited above on corporatism, the root concept is corporatism. In relation to this root concept, the system of interest intermediation is the overarching concept, in that corporatism is a *kind of* in relation to this overarching idea. Specific subtypes of corporatism – for example, liberal corporatism – are a *kind of* in relation to the root concept of corporatism.

Three points about kind hierarchies should be underscored here – points that converge with the standard understanding of Sartori's ladder. (1) The subordinate concepts at a lower level in the hierarchy routinely are understood as *classical subtypes* (Lakoff 1987: *passim*; Taylor 2003: Chapter 2). This is another way of saying that each subordinate concept has the attributes of the superordinate concept *plus* attributes that differentiate it – i.e., the relationship of *genus et differentia*. In

Weber, for example, authority is distinguished from domination by the further differentiating attribute of legitimacy. (2) The relationship among levels is characterized by a pattern of inverse variation.[11] Further down the hierarchy, the concepts have more defining attributes – i.e., greater *intension* – and encompass fewer instances – i.e., more limited *extension*. By contrast, further up the hierarchy, concepts have fewer defining attributes and encompass more instances – i.e., more limited intension and greater extension. (3) Correspondingly, we find the familiar trade-off between avoiding conceptual stretching and achieving more fine-grained analytic differentiation. For instance, designating a particular form of rule as domination would avoid the conceptual stretching that could arise from inappropriately calling it a system of authority (i.e., legitimate domination). At the same time, designating it as a system of domination provides less analytic differentiation than does the designation of authority.

Part–whole hierarchies

Part–whole hierarchies build on the idea that we can meaningfully identify *parts of* many phenomena and entities. Just as a tree has branches as component parts, so – in Schmitter's (1992) analysis of partial regimes – a national political regime has five parts: the constitutional, electoral, pressure, concertation, and clientelist regimes (Figure 10.1).

The idea of part–whole hierarchies is crucial in the present analysis because it is the basis for understanding what we call *diminished subtypes*. Here, the focus is not on the specific parts of a given phenomenon taken separately, but rather on instances in which one (or potentially a few) of these parts is missing or only partially present – yet all (or most) of the other parts are present. Here again we can use the idea of the root concept and the subtype. In this instance, the subtype encompasses many features of the root concept, yet some are missing. For example, we find many diminished subtypes of authoritarianism, as with competitive, electoral, inclusionary, liberal, and soft authoritarianism. Another example is Desposato's (2001: 126) analysis of *public goods*, i.e., goods that have the defining attributes of being non-rival and non-exclusive. Desposato focuses on what he calls *local* public goods, for which their distinctively local character attenuates – but definitely does not eliminate – the attribute of non-exclusivity. Hence, this is a diminished subtype of public goods.[12]

An observation should be added about the role of well-bounded concepts in part–whole hierarchies and diminished subtypes. At various points in the present volume, we find the argument, formulated by Sartori (e.g., 1970: 1036–40), that before turning to the question of degrees and partial instances, analysts should specify when a phenomenon is present or absent. This approach is essential in developing diminished subtypes. Thus, the question of "diminished in relation to what?" is crucial.[13]

We now explore how these two forms of conceptual hierarchy were employed in the literature on the third wave of democracy. To do so, we first introduce the root concept of democracy that was the point of departure for this literature.

Defining the root concept of democracy

In his famous analysis of essentially contested concepts, W. B. Gallie argues that democracy is "*the* appraisive political concept *par excellence*."[14] Correspondingly, one finds recurring disputes over appropriate meaning and definition. However, the goal of Gallie's analysis was not simply to underscore the importance of such disputes, but to show that recognition of the contested status of a given concept opens the possibility of understanding each meaning within its own framework.

The root concept of democracy in the literature on the third wave was anchored in a *procedural minimum* definition. This definition focused on democratic *procedures*, rather than on substantive policies or other outcomes that might be viewed as democratic. It was *minimal* in that it deliberately focused on the smallest possible number of attributes that still were seen as producing a viable standard for democracy. Not surprisingly, there was some disagreement about which attributes are needed for the definition to be appropriate. For example, most (but not all) of these scholars differentiated what they viewed as the more specifically political features of the regime from characteristics of the society and economy. They argued that the latter were more appropriately analyzed as potential causes or consequences of democracy, rather than as features of democracy itself (Karl 1990).

The procedural minimum definition most widely used in this literature presumes genuinely contested elections with full suffrage and the absence of massive fraud, combined with effective guarantees of civil liberties, including freedom of speech, assembly, and association.[15] However, some variants on this definition were also important. Certain scholars, for example, created an *expanded* procedural minimum definition by adding (and in a sense making explicit) the criterion that elected governments must, to a reasonable degree, have effective power to govern vis-à-vis the military and other powerful, non-elected actors. As we will see below, this was a crucial issue in some countries.

Strategies of conceptual innovation

We turn now to specific strategies of innovation found in this literature. These strategies employ the kind hierarchy and classical subtypes; the part–whole hierarchy and diminished subtypes; shifting the overarching concept within a kind hierarchy; and refining (or precising) the definition of democracy to encompass features that are not stipulated in a particular definition, but that are critical to the wider understanding of democracy.

Working with classical subtypes in a kind hierarchy

As argued in the introduction, key analytic goals in the literature on the third wave were to achieve analytic differentiation among the diverse forms of democracy that emerged, while at the same time avoiding conceptual stretching in analyzing these regimes.

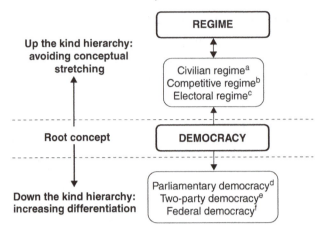

[a]Booth (1989: 26); [b]Collier and Collier (1991: 354); [c]Petras and Leiva (1994: 89); [d]Linz (1994: 3); [e]Gasiorowski (1990: 113); [f]Gastil 1990: 35.

Figure 10.2 The kind hierarchy: increasing differentiation versus avoiding conceptual stretching.

In the tradition of Sartori, greater analytic differentiation that captured these diverse forms of democracy could be achieved by moving *down* a kind hierarchy to classical subtypes that had more defining attributes and fit a narrower range of cases. These subtypes provide more fine-grained distinctions that often are invaluable to the researcher. A standard example would be parliamentary democracy (Figure 10.2).

However, subtypes formed in this manner may leave analysts more vulnerable to conceptual stretching. They presume that the cases under discussion definitely are democracies and, as can be seen in the figure, these subtypes may incorporate further differentiating attributes inappropriate to the cases under analysis. One standard approach to avoiding this problem is to move up the kind hierarchy to concepts that have fewer defining attributes and correspondingly fit a broader range of cases. In the present context, this could be accomplished by working with concepts located *above* the root concept of democracy within the kind hierarchy. Scholars commonly viewed democracy as a specific type in relation to the overarching concept of regime. Hence, if they had misgivings as to whether a particular case was really a *democratic* regime, they could move up the hierarchy and simply call it a regime.

An obvious trade-off arises here. Shifting to a concept as general as regime entailed a loss of analytic differentiation. Scholars therefore typically moved to an intermediate level (Figure 10.2), adding adjectives to the term regime and thereby generating classical subtypes to differentiate specific *types* of regime. The resulting subtypes remained more general than the concept of democracy, encompassing not only democracies but also some non-democracies. Examples included *civilian regime, competitive regime,* and *electoral regime.* While scholars thus achieved some analytic differentiation in relation to regime, they did not specifically commit themselves to the claim that the case under discussion was a democracy. A similar pattern was followed when scholars used a synonym for regime, such as *civilian rule* or *competitive polity* (Karl 1986; Wilson 1993).

Although climbing the hierarchy in this way helped to avoid conceptual stretching, it had an important drawback: it produced a sharp loss of analytic differentiation. These two strategies of moving down and up the kind hierarchy could advance one or the other of these goals, but not both at once.

Working with diminished subtypes in a part–whole hierarchy

An alternative strategy of conceptual innovation, widely employed in this literature, was to use diminished subtypes within a part–whole hierarchy. This approach had the merit of simultaneously avoiding conceptual stretching and increasing analytic differentiation. Examples included *limited suffrage democracy* and *tutelary democracy.* Unlike classical subtypes in a kind hierarchy, diminished subtypes achieved both goals discussed here. First, because these subtypes served to designate partial democracies, analysts were less vulnerable to conceptual stretching in that they made a more modest claim about the extent of democratization. The second point concerned differentiation. The distinctive feature of diminished subtypes is that they generally identify specific attributes of democracy that are missing, thereby establishing the diminished character of the subtype. At the same time, they stipulate other attributes of democracy that are still present. Given this focus on specific combinations of attributes, these subtypes increase differentiation.

Table 10.1 presents examples of the numerous diminished subtypes that were generated in relation to the root concept of democracy noted above. For the purpose of illustration, we focus on examples in which the author was reasonably careful in isolating a single missing attribute.

The subtypes in the first group (1a) refer to cases where the missing attribute was full suffrage. Here, we find terms such as *male* or *oligarchical democracy,* which were used to distinguish contemporary cases from historical cases prior to the advent of universal suffrage. Where the attribute of full contestation was missing (1b), as when important parties are banned from electoral competition, we find terms such as *controlled* and *restrictive democracy.* Where civil liberties were incomplete (1c), scholars used terms such as *electoral* and *illiberal democracy.*

The subtypes in the final group (2) are those introduced by the scholars who created the expanded procedural minimum definition – which as noted above added the defining attribute that, to a reasonable degree, the elected government had effective power to govern. From that point of departure, these scholars introduced diminished subtypes for which this attribute was missing. Examples that referred to cases where the military was seen as having an inordinate degree of ongoing political power included *protected democracy* and *tutelary democracy.*

Table 10.1 Part-whole hierarchy: examples of diminished subtypes

1. Diminished from procedural minimum definition

(1a) **Missing attribute: Full suffrage**	(1b) **Missing attribute: Full contestation**	(1c) **Missing attribute: Civil liberties**
Limited democracy[a]	Controlled democracy[d]	Electoral democracy[g]
Male democracy[b]	De facto one-party democracy[e]	Hard democracy[h]
Oligarchical democracy[c]	Restrictive democracy[f]	Illiberal democracy[i]

2. Diminished from expanded procedural minimum definition

Missing attribute: Elected government has effective power to govern
Guarded democracy[j]
Protected democracy[k]
Tutelary democracy[l]

Notes
a Archer (1995: 166); b Sorensen (1993: 20); c Hartlyn and Valenzuela (1994: 99); d Bagley (1984: 125); e Leftwich (1993: 613); f Waisman (1989: 69); g Hadenius (1994: 69); h O'Donnell and Schmitter (1986: 9); i Emmerson (1995); j Torres Rivas (1994: 27); k Loveman (1994: 108–11); l Przeworski (1988: 60–61).

Diminished subtypes, then, were a useful means to avoid conceptual stretching in cases that were less than fully democratic. They also provided new analytic differentiation. Various scholars have pointed to the need for moving beyond a dichotomous conceptualization of authoritarianism and democracy, and have recognized the *hybrid* or *mixed* character of many post-authoritarian regimes.[16] Diminished subtypes can bring into focus the diverse features of these hybrid regimes.

However, for countries considered less than fully democratic, the question arose as to whether it would be better to avoid identifying them as subtypes of democracy – for example, in cases of gross violations of civil liberties and/or severe restrictions on electoral competition. An instance of such questioning was Bruce Bagley's rejection of the numerous diminished subtypes of democracy that had been applied to the National Front period in Colombia (1958–74). These subtypes included *restricted, controlled, limited, oligarchical, elitist,* and *elitist-pluralist* democracy. Bagley instead characterized Colombia as a diminished subtype of authoritarianism: *inclusionary authoritarian regime* (Bagley 1984: 125–27). A parallel use of a diminished subtype is Levitsky and Way's (2002: 52–58) characterization of Russia under Putin and Peru under Fujimori. These are treated not as partial democracies but instead as competitive authoritarianism regimes.

Shifting the overarching concept

A further strategy of conceptual innovation involved a different approach to modifying kind hierarchies. In this case, scholars shifted the overarching concept, in relation to which democracy was seen as a specific instance. This shift in the over-arching concept changed the meaning of the root concept, i.e., of democracy. In this sense it may be seen as a more drastic modification, compared with the two strate-gies just discussed.

Scholars in this literature most commonly understood democracy in relation to the overarching concept *regime*, and the procedural criteria for democracy dis-cussed above were features of the regime. Yet some analysts came to view democ-racy as a root concept in relation to other overarching concepts, such as democratic *government* or democratic *state*. Hence, when a given country was labeled *demo-cratic*, the meaning was modified according to the alternative overarching concept.

Scholars used the strategy of shifting the overarching concept in order to create a standard that could be either less or more demanding for classifying cases as dem-ocratic. These alternatives may be illustrated with examples from the analysis of Brazil (Table 10.2). Some scholars found that in the immediate post-1985 period, Brazilian politics was so poorly institutionalized that it appeared inappropriate to use the overarching label regime, yet they felt it was unreasonable to insist that Brazil was not democratic. They thereby lowered the standard for labeling it a democracy by referring to a democratic situation.[17] Other scholars, out of a similar concern with the implications of regime, shifted the overarching concept by using the terms democratic government or democratic moment.[18] The idea of a democratic *government*, for example, served to suggest that, although a particular government[19] had been elected democratically, the sustainability of democratic procedures remained in doubt.

Alternatively, by shifting the overarching concept from regime to state, O'Donnell established a more demanding standard for labeling a particular country as a democracy. Brazil's presidential election of 1989 led some scholars – previ-ously skeptical about Brazilian democracy – to accept the idea that Brazil had a democratic regime. In this context, O'Donnell went on to pose questions about

Table 10.2 Shifting the overarching concept: post-1985 Brazil

Author	Lowering the standard		Point of departure	Raising the standard
	Democratic situation	Democratic government	Democratic regime	Democratic state
Duncan, Baretta and Markoff[a]	Yes		No	
Hagopian and Mainwaring[b]		Yes	No	
O'Donnell[c]		Yes	No	
O'Donnell[d]			Yes	No

Notes
a Duncan, Baretta and Markoff (1987: 62); b Hagopian and Mainwaring (1987: 485); c O'Donnell (1988: 281); d O'Donnell (1993: 1360).

the democratic character of the state in Brazil. He observed that, in the context of widespread neofeudalized and sometimes sultanistic political relationships in some regions of the country, the national state did not protect basic rights of citizenship within the framework of law (1993: 1359; *passim*, 2001). This failure might not directly influence the functioning of the regime, in the sense of affecting the elections and associated civil liberties that were core features of the procedural understanding of a democratic regime. However, O'Donnell argued that this failure of the legal and bureaucratic institutions of the state was a crucial feature of Brazilian politics, as well as politics in several other Latin American countries. Although he recognized that Brazil had a democratic regime, he excluded it from the set of countries which he considered to have democratic states.

To summarize, shifting the overarching concept within the kind hierarchy served to introduce finer differentiation. When this strategy lowered the standard for declaring a given case a democracy, it also helped avoid stretching the concept. When the strategy raised the standard, it typically was acknowledged that the cases of concern were in fact democratic regimes.[20] Hence, the motivating concern was not the problem of conceptual stretching. Rather, this innovation provided additional analytic differentiation by pointing to respects in which the countries might be considered non-democratic.

Precising the definition

A final strategy consisted of *precising* the definition of democracy itself by adding defining attributes.[21] This approach thereby changed the root concept in relation to which both the kind hierarchies and the part–whole hierarchies were structured. As the concept of democracy was extended to new settings, researchers sometimes confronted a particular case that was classified as a democracy on the basis of a commonly accepted definition. Yet such a case might not have been seen as fully democratic in light of a larger shared understanding of the concept.[22] This mismatch between the case and the formal definition sometimes led analysts to make explicit one or more criteria that were implicitly understood as part of the overall meaning of democracy, but that were not included in the prior definition. The result was a new definition intended to change how a particular case was classified. This new definition increased analytic differentiation by fine-tuning the cut-point between democracy and non-democracy. Simultaneously, precising the definition avoided conceptual stretching by not including cases that did not fit the new conception of democracy.

One example of precising the definition was the emergence of the expanded procedural minimum definition, noted above. In several Central American countries, as well as in South American cases such as Chile and Paraguay, one legacy of authoritarian rule was the persistence of reserved domains of military power over which elected governments had little or no authority (Valenzuela 1992: 70). Hence, despite free or relatively free elections, civilian governments in these countries were seen by some analysts as lacking effective power to govern.

Given these authoritarian legacies, and often in reaction to claims that these countries were democratic because they had held free elections, some scholars modified the procedural minimum definition by explicitly specifying that the elected government must to a reasonable degree have effective power to rule. With this revised definition, countries such as Chile, El Salvador, and Paraguay were excluded by some scholars from the set of cases classified as democracies, even though they had held relatively free elections.[23] These scholars thereby modified the definition by including an attribute that was taken for granted in studies of advanced industrial democracies, yet was absent in these particular Latin American cases. This revised definition was widely accepted, though some disagreement continued about the classification of specific cases.[24]

In this instance, precising the definition sharpened analytic differentiation by fine-tuning the cut-point between democracy and non-democracy. It also avoided conceptual stretching in the sense of not including cases that did not fit this larger conception of democracy. However, because precising the definition introduced changes in the entire constellation of meanings connected with the idea of democracy, it was the most drastic among the strategies discussed here.

Correspondingly, other initiatives to precise the definition received less acceptance and served to illustrate pitfalls of this strategy. A second example illustrates the problem of what might be called a Tocquevillean definition, which encompassed a focus on selected aspects of social relations. In analyzing post-authoritarian Brazil, scholars such as Francisco Weffort and Guillermo O'Donnell were struck by the degree to which rights of citizenship were undermined by the pervasive semi-feudal and authoritarian social relations that persisted in some regions of the country. In light of this concern, they precised the definition of democracy so as to exclude Brazil. Thus, Weffort added the definitional requirement of "some level of social equality" for a country to be considered a democracy, and O'Donnell introduced a similar stipulation.[25] In adopting the Tocquevillean view, these authors basically saw themselves as remaining within the procedural framework. However, introducing issues of social relations nonetheless represented a sharp departure from earlier procedural definitions, and this approach was not widely followed.[26]

A third effort at precising, which likewise was not widely accepted, arose from a concern that, in many new democracies in Latin America and former communist countries, some elected presidents made extensive use of decree power, circumvented democratic institutions such as the legislature and political parties, and governed in a plebiscitary manner that had strong authoritarian undercurrents. In the Latin American context, prominent examples of this failure of horizontal accountability[27] included Carlos Menem in Argentina, Fernando Collor de Mello in Brazil, and, in the most extreme case, Alberto Fujimori in Peru. The concern with these authoritarian tendencies led some authors to include checks on executive power in their procedural criteria for democracy, thus excluding cases of unconstrained presidentialism.[28] However, this innovation was likewise not widely adopted.

Precising the definition can serve both to introduce finer differentiation and to avoid conceptual stretching. Yet caution is in order. Among alternative strategies of conceptual innovation examined here, precising introduced the most drastic change by modifying the definition of democracy itself. More generally, if an innovation based on precising is widely accepted, it changes the definitional point of departure for all the other strategies, thereby unsettling the *semantic field*.[29] By contrast, the introduction of a new subtype does not pose this problem. For literatures in which conceptual confusion is a recurring problem, the analytic gains from precising the definition must be weighed against this cost.

A related concern is the problem of definitional gerrymandering, in the sense that scholars might introduce a new definition as an ad hoc means of dealing with an anomalous case.[30] However, the contrast between the first example of precising (adding the criterion of effective power to govern) and the third example (adding horizontal accountability) shows that scholars may in fact impose constructive limits on this type of innovation. In the first example, the inability of elected governments to exercise effective power was seen as invalidating their democratic character. By contrast, the third example involved heavy-handed assertions of power by the president, and a crucial point was that these presidents *were* elected leaders. Hence, it might be argued that it was appropriate to treat these regimes as meeting a minimal standard for democracy and to avoid precising, as long as they maintained presidential elections, the legislature continued to enjoy some autonomy, and a general respect for civil liberties was maintained.[31]

Concluding observations

We have discussed strategies of conceptual innovation employed by scholars as they addressed a two-fold challenge in characterizing the diverse regimes that emerged in the third wave of democracy: increasing analytic differentiation, while simultaneously avoiding conceptual stretching. Our goal has been to examine the structure of these alternative strategies and to evaluate their strengths and weaknesses. Even when these analysts proceeded intuitively, rather than self-consciously, they tended to operate within these hierarchical structures. However, in the interest of conceptual and analytic clarity, it was far more desirable for scholars to proceed self-consciously, with full awareness of the trade-offs among the strategies.

The strategies employed in addressing these analytic challenges are summarized in Figure 10.3. Conceptual innovation occurred at three levels: the root concept of democracy itself, the subtypes, and the overarching concept. We observed that the strategies of (1) moving down the kind hierarchy to classical subtypes of democracy and (2) moving up that hierarchy to classical subtypes of regime could usefully serve either to increase differentiation or to avoid conceptual stretching, but they could not do both simultaneously. By contrast, these two goals could simultaneously be achieved by (3) creating diminished subtypes within the framework of a part–whole hierarchy and (4a) shifting the overarching concept as a means of lowering the standard. By contrast, (4b) shifting the overarching concept

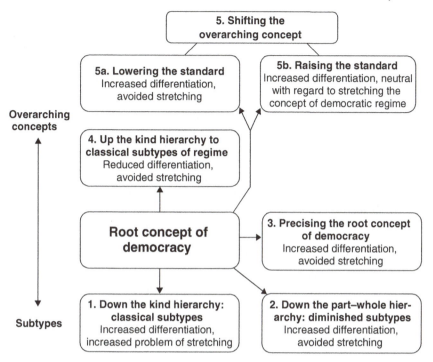

Figure 10.3 Evaluating the strategies: differentiation and avoiding stretching.

to raise the standard for democracy introduced finer differentiation but did not avoid stretching.

The fifth strategy – i.e., (5) precising the definition of democracy by adding defining attributes – had the merit of contributing both to avoiding stretching (vis-à-vis a larger understanding of democracy) and to achieving finer differentiation. However, as with shifting the overarching concept, it was a more drastic approach in that it shifted the meaning of other concepts in the hierarchy.

We have also underscored distinctive issues that arose with particular strategies. Diminished subtypes were useful for characterizing hybrid regimes, but raised the issue of whether these regimes should be treated as subtypes of democracy, rather than subtypes of authoritarianism or some other regime type. Shifting the overarching concept with the goal of raising the standard was not relevant to the problem of conceptual stretching. However, it allowed scholars to introduce new analytic issues without abandoning a procedural definition of democracy. Finally, the strategy of precising the definition was subject to the perennial problem of scholarly disputes over definitions of democracy, as well as to the need to impose limits on definitional gerrymandering.

The diverse strategies summarized in Figure 10.3 also point to a broader problem. This literature on the third wave of democracy – as in many areas of the social sciences – faced a major dilemma in the proliferation of literally hundreds of subtypes, many of which meant approximately the same thing. The consequence could too readily be scholarly confusion, as well as undermining the theory-building enterprise. Although new types were created in part because scholars were pursuing these goals of differentiation and avoiding conceptual stretching, they also were introduced with the goal of developing compelling labels that drew attention to novel forms of democracy. In the larger literature on national political regimes, important analytic innovations have periodically been introduced in conjunction with the creation and/or systematization of concepts that vividly capture important constellations of phenomena: e.g., authoritarianism, polyarchy, bureaucratic authoritarianism, corporatism, and consociational democracy. The invention of additional concepts that play this same role is an important goal in the ongoing study of regimes. However, if research on political phenomena such as democracy were to degenerate into a competition over who can produce the next famous concept or subtype, the comparative study of regimes would be in serious trouble.

Hence, we propose another major objective of concept usage – one that introduces a further trade-off vis-à-vis the two goals of achieving analytic differentiation and avoiding conceptual stretching. Scholars should aim for parsimony and avoid excessive proliferation of new terms and concepts. Coordinating scholarly inquiry around carefully developed concepts will facilitate constructive dialogue and theory-building. Otherwise, the advantages that may derive from the conceptual refinements analyzed here will be overridden by the resulting conceptual confusion.

Notes

* Extensively revised version of David Collier and Steven Levitsky (1997) "Democracy with Adjectives: Conceptual Innovation in Comparative Research," *World Politics* 49 (3): 430–51.

1 This chapter is a substantially revised version of David Collier and Steven Levitsky (1997) "Democracy with Adjectives: Conceptual Innovation in Comparative Research," *World Politics* 49 (3): 430–51. We acknowledge the valuable comments on this new version provided by Robert Adcock, Nora Archambeau, Mauricio Benítez, Taylor Boas, Christopher Chambers-Ju, John Gerring, Fernando Daniel Hidalgo Maiah Jaskoski, Jody LaPorte, James Mahoney, Josephine Marks, Sebastián Mazzuca, and Miranda Yaver.

2 Schedler (2002) writes of the "foggy zone" with regard to regime types. See also the other articles in the April 2002 issue of the *Journal of Democracy* on hybrid regimes.

3 A parallel expression, "democracy without adjectives," appeared in debates in Latin America among observers concerned with the persistence of incomplete and qualified forms of democracy (see, for instance, Krauze 1986).

4 Lipset (1959, 1994), Londregan and Poole (1996), Luebbert (1991), Moore (1966), Przeworski and Limongi (1997), and Rueschemeyer et al. (1992).

5 Bollen and Jackman (1985), Brown et al. (1996), Linz and Valenzuela (1994), O'Donnell (1994), Przeworski and Limongi (1993), Remmer (1986), Russett (1993), Sirowy and Inkeles (1990), Stallings and Kaufman (1989), and Stepan and Skach (1993).

6 Bollen and Jackman (1989: 613–16), Russett (1993: 15–16), and Paxton (2000).

7 The distinction between Sartori's ladder of abstraction and Collier and Mahon's (1993) idea of a ladder of generality should be noted. The concepts further up on Sartori's ladder of abstraction have fewer defining attributes. With these concepts fewer differentiating criteria are employed in making empirical observations, which by standard usage is what is meant by abstract. The limiting case of an abstract concept is one located in a theoretical system and has no empirical referents at all. Collier and Mahon later sought to elaborate Sartori's focus by speaking of a *ladder of generality*. The characteristic of greater generality is a concomitant of the greater degree of abstraction: with fewer defining attributes, the concepts are more general. We now view the notion of a kind hierarchy as a more self-explanatory framing that encompasses both of these two understandings of ladders.

8 In linguistics, a kind hierarchy is called a hyponomy, and a part–whole hierarchy a meronymy (Cruse 2004: 148–54). For a discussion of how these two forms of hierarchy play a role in the conceptual change associated with scientific revolutions, see Thaggard (1990, 1992).

9 That is, staff in Weber's sense, as with the immediate set of employees who support the work of a given leader or executive.

10 Rather than referring to the root concept, Goertz (2006: *passim*) writes of the *basic level*. We prefer the idea of root concept because to us it suggests more directly that the level at which the root concept is located may vary according to the context of analysis. This focus of the context of meaning – and, correspondingly, the contrasting levels on a hierarchy that are appropriate – is parallel to Cruse's (1977) arguments on *lexical specificity* (see also Cruse 2004: 368).

11 This pattern of inverse variation is a standard feature of conceptual structure, and for present purposes it is a basic and valuable point of reference. However, in some contexts this inverse pattern does not hold (Copi and Cohen 2002: 116).

12 Diminished subtypes do not necessarily take the form of the root concept plus an adjective. In Skocpol's (1979: 4) study, the focus is on social revolutions, which in her analysis encompassed the transformation of both social structure and political structure. By contrast, in her usage, political revolutions involve only political transformation. For her, political revolution is therefore a diminished subtype vis-à-vis her overall concept of social revolution: one element is missing.

13 The centrality of this question is evident in Table 10.1 below, where the diminished subtypes take on distinct meanings according to the definition of the root concept.

14 Gallie (1956: 184, italics in the original); see also Collier et al. (2006).

15 Diamond et al. (1989: xvi), Di Palma (1990: 16), and O'Donnell and Schmitter (1986: 8); see also Linz (1978: 5).

16 Conaghan and Espinal (1990: 555), Hartlyn (1994: 93–96), Karl (1995), Malloy (1987: 256–57), Weffort (1992b: 89–90), and Levitsky and Way (forthcoming).

17 This distinction followed the example of Juan Linz's (1973) analysis of Brazil during the earlier post-1964 authoritarian period: Linz introduced the concept of an *authoritarian situation* to take into account the weak institutionalization of national political structures.

18 Malloy (1987: 236) used the expression democratic *moment* to convey basically the same idea as democratic *government*.

19 Government is understood here as the head of state and the immediate political leadership that surrounds the head of state.

20 For example, O'Donnell (1993: 1355), in his discussion of the democratic state, was quite explicit in saying that the countries under discussion had democratic regimes.

21 Copi and Cohen (2002: 106–09) and Sartori (1984: 81).

22 This distinction between the commonly accepted definition of democracy and the larger understanding of the concept is parallel to the contrast between the systematized concept and the background concept discussed by Adcock and Collier (2001).

23 Karl (1990: 2), Loveman (1994), and Valenzuela (1992); see also Rubin (1990).

24 For example, in analyzing Chile in the post-1990 period, Rhoda Rabkin took exception to the usage adopted by scholars who introduced the expanded procedural minimum definition. She argued that the problem of civilian control of the military did not represent a sufficient challenge to the democratically elected government to justify calling Chile a *borderline* democracy, as she put it (Rabkin 1992–93: 165).
25 O'Donnell (1988: 297–98, 1992: 48–49) and Weffort (1992a: 18, 1992b: 100–01).
26 As we saw above, O'Donnell subsequently opted for shifting the overarching concept as an alternative means of incorporating this set of concerns.
27 Authors who employed horizontal accountability in their definitions included Ball (1994: 45–46) and Schmitter and Karl (1991: 76, 87). O'Donnell and Schmitter (1986: 8) actually include it in their formal definition, but it appears to play no role in their subsequent analysis.
28 Fish (2001: 54) later wrote of superpresidentialism.
29 On the problem of unsettling the semantic field, see Sartori (1984: 51–54).
30 Jennifer Widner suggested this term.
31 For Peru under Fujimori and Venezuela under Chávez, the regime clearly failed to meet a minimum standard due to violations of civil liberties.

References

Adcock, R. and Collier, D. (2001) "Measurement Validity: A Shared Standard for Qualitative and Quantitative Research," *American Political Science Review* 95 (3): 529–46.
Archer, R.P. (1995) "Party Strength and Weakness in Colombia's Besieged Democracy," in S. Mainwaring and T.R. Scully (eds.), *Building Democratic Institutions: Party Systems in Latin America*, Stanford: Stanford University Press.
Bagley, B.M. (1984) "Colombia: National Front and Economic Development," in R. Wesson (ed.), *Politics, Policies, and Economic Development in Latin America*, Stanford: Hoover Institution Press.
Ball, A.R. (1994) *Modern Politics and Government*, 5th edn., Chatham, NJ: Chatham House.
Bollen, K.A. and Jackman, R.W. (1985) "Political Democracy and the Size Distribution of Income," *American Sociological Review* 50 (4): 438–57.
Bollen, K.A. and Jackman, R.W. (1989) "Democracy, Stability, and Dichotomies," *American Sociological Review* 54 (4): 612–21.
Booth, J.A. (1989) "Framework for Analysis," in J.A. Booth and M.A. Seligson (eds.), *Elections and Democracy in Central America*, Chapel Hill: University of North Carolina Press.
Brown, M.E., Lynn-Jones, S.M., and Miller, S.E. (eds.) (1996) *Debating the Democratic Peace: An International Security Reader*, Cambridge, MA: MIT Press.
Collier, D. (1995) "Trajectory of a Concept: 'Corporatism' in the Study of Latin American Politics," in P.H. Smith (ed.), *Latin America in Comparative Perspective: New Approaches to Method and Analysis*, Boulder, CO: Westview Press.
Collier, D. and Levitsky, S. (1997) "Democracy with Adjectives: Conceptual Innovation in Comparative Research," *World Politics* 49 (3): 430–51.
Collier, D. and Mahon, J.E., Jr. (1993) "Conceptual 'Stretching' Revisited: Adapting Categories in Comparative Analysis," *American Political Science Review* 87 (4): 845–55.
Collier, D., Hidalgo, F.D., and Maciuceanu, A.O. (2006) "Essentially Contested Concepts: Debates and Applications," *Journal of Political Ideologies* 11 (3): 211–46.
Collier, R.B. and Collier, D. (1991) *Shaping the Political Arena: Critical Junctures, the Labor Movement, and Regime Dynamics in Latin America*, Princeton: Princeton University Press.

Conaghan, C.M. and Espinal, R. (1990) "Unlikely Transitions to Uncertain Regimes? Democracy without Compromise in the Dominican Republic and Ecuador," *Journal of Latin American Studies* 22 (3): 553–74.

Copi, I.M. and Cohen, C. (2002) *Introduction to Logic*, 11th edn., Upper Saddle River, NJ: Prentice Hall.

Cruse, D.A. (1977) "The Pragmatics of Lexical Specificity," *Journal of Linguistics* 13 (2): 153–64.

Cruse, D.A. (2004) *Meaning and Language: An Introduction to Semantics and Pragmatics*, Oxford: Oxford University Press.

Dahl, R.A. (1971) *Polyarchy: Participation and Opposition*, New Haven, CT: Yale University Press.

Desposato, S. (2001) "Institutional Theories, Social Realities, and Party Politics in Brazil," Doctoral Dissertation, Department of Political Science, University of California, Los Angeles.

Diamond, L., Linz, J.J., and Lipset, S.M. (1989) "Preface," in J.J. Linz, L. Diamond, and S.M. Lipset (eds.), *Democracy in Developing Countries: Latin America*, Boulder, CO: Lynne Rienner.

Di Palma, G. (1990) *To Craft Democracies: An Essay on Democratic Transitions*, Berkeley: University of California Press.

Duncan Baretta, S. and Markoff, J. (1987) "Brazil's Abertura: Transition to What?," in J.M. Malloy and M.A. Seligson (eds.), *Authoritarians and Democrats: Regime Transition in Latin America*, Pittsburgh: University of Pittsburgh Press.

Emmerson, D. (1995) "Region and Recalcitrance: Rethinking Democracy through Southeast Asia," *Pacific Review* 8 (2): 223–48.

Fish, M.S. (2001) "The Dynamics of Democratic Erosion," in R. Anderson, Jr., M.S. Fish, S.E. Hanson, and P.G. Roeder (eds.), *Postcommunism and the Theory of Democracy*, Princeton: Princeton University Press.

Gallie, W.B. (1956) "Essentially Contested Concepts," *Proceedings of the Aristotelian Society* 56: 167–98.

Gasiorowski, M.J. (1990) "The Political Regimes Project," *Studies in Comparative International Development* 25 (1): 109–25.

Gastil, R.D. (1990) "The Comparative Survey of Freedom: Experiences and Suggestions," *Studies in Comparative International Development* 25 (1): 25–50.

Goertz, G. (2006) *Social Science Concepts*, Princeton: Princeton University Press.

Hadenius, A. (1994) "The Duration of Democracy: Institutional vs. Socio-economic Factors," in D. Beetha (ed.), *Defining and Measuring Democracy*, London: Sage.

Hagopian, F. and Mainwaring, S. (1987) "Democracy in Brazil: Problems and Prospects," *World Policy Journal* 4: 485–514.

Hartlyn, J. (1994) "Crisis-ridden Elections (Again) in the Dominican Republic: Neopatrimonialism, Presidentialism, and Weak Electoral Oversight," *Journal of Interamerican Studies and World Affairs* 36 (4): 91–144.

Hartlyn, J. and Valenzuela, A. (1994) "Democracy in Latin America since 1930," in L. Bethell (ed.), *The Cambridge History of Latin America*, vol. 6, Cambridge: Cambridge University Press.

Huntington, S.P. (1991) *The Third Wave: Democratization in the Late Twentieth Century*, Norman: University of Oklahoma Press.

Jowitt, K. (1999) "The Leninist Legacy," in V. Tismaneanu (ed.), *The Revolutions of 1989*, New York: Routledge, Chapter 11.

Karl, T.L. (1986) "Democracy by Design: The Christian Democratic Party in El Salvador," in G. Di Palma and L. Whitehead (eds.), *The Central American Impasse*, London: Croom Helm.

Karl, T.L. (1990) "Dilemmas of Democratization in Latin America," *Comparative Politics* 23 (1): 1–21.

Karl, T.L. (1995) "The Hybrid Regimes of Central America," *Journal of Democracy* 6: 72–86.

Krauze, E. (1986) *Por una democracia sin adjetivos*, Mexico City: Joaquín Mortiz/ Planeta.

Lakoff, G. (1987) *Women, Fire, and Dangerous Things: What Categories Reveal about the Mind*, Chicago: University of Chicago Press.

Leftwich, A. (1993) "Governance, Democracy, and Development in the Third World," *Third World Quarterly* 14 (3): 605–24.

Levitsky, S. and Way, L. (2002) "The Rise of Competitive Authoritarianism," *Journal of Democracy* 13: 51–66.

Levitsky, S., and Way, L. (forthcoming) *Competitive Authoritarianism: International Linkage, Organizational Power, and the Fate of Hybrid Regimes*, New York: Cambridge University Press.

Linz, J.J. (1973) "The Future of an Authoritarian Situation or the Institutionalization of an Authoritarian Regime: The Case of Brazil," in A. Stepan (ed.), *Authoritarian Brazil: Origins, Policies, Future*, New Haven, CT: Yale University Press.

Linz, J.J. (1978) *The Breakdown of Democratic Regimes: Crisis, Breakdown, and Reequilibriation*, Baltimore, MD: Johns Hopkins University Press.

Linz, J.J. (1994) "Presidential or Parliamentary Democracy: Does It Make a Difference?," in J.J. Linz and A. Valenzuela (eds.), *The Failure of Presidential Democracy*, Baltimore, MD: Johns Hopkins University Press.

Linz, J.J. and Valenzuela, A. (eds.) (1994) *The Failure of Presidential Democracy*, Baltimore, MD: Johns Hopkins University Press.

Lipset, S.M. (1959) "Some Social Requisites of Democracy: Economic Development and Political Legitimacy," *American Political Science Review* 53 (1): 69–105.

Lipset, S.M. (1994) "The Social Requisites of Democracy Revisited," *American Sociological Review* 59 (1): 1–22.

Londregan, J.B. and Poole, K.T. (1996) "Does High Income Promote Democracy?," *World Politics* 49: 1–30.

Loveman, B. (1994) "'Protected Democracies' and Military Guardianship: Political Transitions in Latin America, 1978–1993," *Journal of Interamerican Studies and World Affairs* 36 (2): 105–89.

Luebbert, G.M. (1991) *Liberalism, Fascism, or Social Democracy: Social Classes and the Political Origins of Regimes in Interwar Europe*, New York: Oxford University Press.

Means, G. (1996) "Soft Authoritarianism in Malaysia and Singapore," *Journal of Democracy* 7 (4): 103–17.

Malloy, J.M. (1987) "The Politics of Transition in Latin America," in J.M. Malloy and M.A. Seligson (eds.), *Authoritarians and Democrats: Regime Transition in Latin America*, Pittsburgh: University of Pittsburgh Press.

Moore, B., Jr. (1966) *Social Origins of Dictatorship and Democracy: Lord and Peasant in the Making of the Modern World*, Boston: Beacon Press.

O'Donnell, G. (1973) *Modernization and Bureaucratic-Authoritarianism: Studies in South American Politics*, Institute of International Studies, Politics of Modernization Series no. 9, Berkeley: University of California.

O'Donnell, G. (1988) "Challenges to Democratization in Brazil," *World Policy Journal* 5: 281–300.

O'Donnell, G. (1992) "Transitions, Continuities, and Paradoxes," in S. Mainwaring, G. O'Donnell, and J.S. Valenzuela (eds.), *Issues in Democratic Consolidation: The New South American Democracies in Comparative Perspective*, Notre Dame, IN: University of Notre Dame Press.

O'Donnell, G. (1993) "On the State, Democratization and Some Conceptual Problems: A Latin American View with Glances at Some Postcommunist Countries," *World Development* 21 (8): 1355–69.

O'Donnell, G. (1994) "Delegative Democracy," *Journal of Democracy* 5 (1): 55–69.

O'Donnell, G. (2001) "Democracy, Law, and Comparative Politics," *Studies in Comparative International Development* 36 (1): 7–36.

O'Donnell, G. and Schmitter, P.C. (1986) *Transitions from Authoritarian Rule: Tentative Conclusions about Uncertain Democracies*, Baltimore, MD: Johns Hopkins University Press.

Paxton, P. (2000) "Women's Suffrage in the Measurement of Democracy: Problems of Operationalization," *Studies in Comparative International Development* 35 (3): 92–111.

Petras, J. and Leiva, F.I. (1994) *Democracy and Poverty in Chile: The Limits to Electoral Politics*, Boulder, CO: Westview Press.

Przeworski, A. (1988) "Democracy as a Contingent Outcome of Conflicts," in J. Elster and R. Slagstad (eds.), *Constitutionalism and Democracy*, Cambridge: Cambridge University Press.

Przeworski, A. and Limongi, F. (1993) "Political Regimes and Economic Growth," *Journal of Economic Perspectives* 7 (3): 51–69.

Przeworski, A. and Limongi, F. (1997) "Modernization: Theories and Facts," *World Politics* 49 (2): 155–83.

Rabkin, R. (1992–93) "The Aylwin Government and 'Tutelary' Democracy: A Concept in Search of a Case?," *Journal of Interamerican Studies and World Affairs* 34 (4): 119–94.

Remmer, K.L. (1986) "The Politics of Economic Stabilization: IMF Standby Programs in Latin America, 1954–1984," *Comparative Politics* 19 (1): 1–24.

Rubin, H. (1990) "Paraguay after Stroessner: One Step Away from Democracy," *Journal of Democracy* 1 (4): 59–61.

Rueschemeyer, D., Huber, E., and Stephens, J.D. (1992) *Capitalist Development and Democracy*, Chicago: University of Chicago Press.

Russett, B. (1993) *Grasping the Democratic Peace: Principles for a Post-Cold War World*, Princeton: Princeton University Press.

Sartori, G. (1970) "Concept Misformation in Comparative Politics," *American Political Science Review* 64 (4): 1033–53.

Sartori, G. (1984) "Guidelines for Concept Analysis," in G. Sartori (ed.), *Social Science Concepts: A Systematic Analysis*, Beverly Hills, CA; Sage.

Schedler, A. (2002) "The Menu of Manipulation," *Journal of Democracy* 13 (2): 36–50.

Schedler, A. (2006) *Electoral Authoritarianism: The Dynamics of Unfree Competition*, Boulder, CO: Lynne Rienner.

Schmitter, P.C. (1974) "Still the Century of Corporatism?," *Review of Politics* 36 (1): 85–131.

Schmitter, P.C. (1992) "The Consolidation of Democracy and Representation of Social Groups," *American Behavioral Scientist* 35 (4/5): 422–49.

Schmitter, P.C. and Karl, T.L. (1991) "What Democracy Is . . . and Is Not," *Journal of Democracy* 2 (3): 75–88.

Schumpeter, J.A. (1947) *Capitalism, Socialism and Democracy*, 2nd edn., New York: Harper & Brothers.

Sirowy, L. and Inkeles, A. (1990) "The Effects of Democracy on Economic Growth and Inequality: A Review," *Studies in Comparative International Development* 25: 126–57.

Skocpol, T. (1979) *States and Social Revolutions*, New York: Cambridge University Press.

Sorensen, G. (1993) *Democracy and Democratization: Process and Prospects in a Changing World*, Boulder, CO: Westview Press.

Stallings, B. and Kaufman, R. (eds.) (1989) *Debt and Democracy in Latin America*, Boulder, CO: Westview Press.

Stepan, A. and Skach, C. (1993) "Constitutional Frameworks and Democratic Consolidation: Parliamentarianism versus Presidentialism," *World Politics* 46 (1): 1–22.

Taylor, J.R. (2003) *Linguistic Categorization*, 3rd edn., Oxford: Oxford University Press.

Thagard, P. (1990) "Concepts and Conceptual Change," *Synthese* 82 (2): 255–74.

Thagard, P. (1992) *Conceptual Revolutions*, Princeton: Princeton University Press.

Torres Rivas, E. (1994) "La gobernabilidad centroamericana en los noventa," *América Latina Hoy* 2: 27–34.

Valenzuela, J.S. (1992) "Democratic Consolidation in Post-transitional Settings: Notion, Process, and Facilitating Conditions," in S. Mainwaring, G. O'Donnell, and J.S. Valenzuela (eds.), *Issues in Democratic Consolidation: The New South American Democracies in Comparative Perspective*, Notre Dame, IN: University of Notre Dame Press.

Waisman, C.H. (1989) "Argentina: Autarkic Industrialization and Illegitimacy," in L. Diamond, J.J. Linz, and S.M. Lipset (eds.), *Democracy in Developing Countries: Latin America*, Boulder, CO: Lynne Rienner.

Weber, M. (1978) "The Types of Legitimate Domination," in G. Roth and C. Wittich (eds.), *Economy and Society*, Berkeley: University of California Press.

Weffort, F. (1992a) "New Democracies, Which Democracies?," Working Paper no. 198, Latin American Program, Washington, DC: Woodrow Wilson International Center for Scholars.

Weffort, F. (1992b) *Qual democracia?*, São Paulo: Companhia das Letras.

Wilson, R. (1993) "Continued Counterinsurgency: Civilian Rule in Guatemala," in B. Gills, J. Rocamora, and R. Wilson (eds.), *Low Intensity Democracy: Political Power in the New World Order*, London: Pluto Press.

11 Peasant

Clarifying meaning and refining explanation

Marcus J. Kurtz

Over the past three decades, scholars have proposed a variety of competing explanations of peasant revolution (e.g., Migdal 1974; Paige 1975; Popkin 1979; Scott 1976; Skocpol 1979; Wolf 1969). Subsequent efforts at hypothesis refinement and testing, however, have only reproduced and expanded the scope of theoretical disagreements (see Bates 1984; Diskin 1996; Magagna 1991; Paige 1996; Seligson 1996; on empirical theory testing and refutation, see Anderson 1993; Anderson and Seligson 1994; Jenkins 1983). Much of this disputation arises from differences in the conceptualization of the key actor in most theories of revolution – the peasantry. These conceptual differences, in turn, profoundly affect the construction of theoretical arguments and the domains to which they can correctly be applied. Consequently, the regnant theoretical dissensus is unsurprising. Since conceptual differences are logically prior to the testing of theory, until they are resolved, progress through the empirical adjudication of competing explanations will be difficult.

How does a focus on conceptualization help? It helps to establish whether what *appear* to be rival explanations of peasant revolution employ a shared understanding of peasant, and hence whether they are, in fact, seeking to explain the same outcome. We can thereby avoid irresolvable debates, inappropriate claims of refutation (or confirmation), and a tendency to overstate the generality of theoretical claims. In the research design process, we will improve our attentiveness to how the concepts we employ should shape the cases we examine. It will not, however, solve all our problems. Even among scholars who share conceptual frameworks, important differences remain to be adjudicated on the basis of the empirical evidence. All theories of peasant revolution must establish their validity in the face of theoretical approaches focused on other causal agents (since these are not restricted to any particular notion of a peasantry).[1] Finally, by highlighting the links among conceptualization, theory construction, and case selection, I seek to emphasize the analytical payoffs from more serious attention to concepts in the construction of research designs more generally.

This chapter takes as its starting point the conceptual structure of the term peasant as it has developed in recent academic usage. Five definitions of the term emerge, each implying a different set of empirical cases that fall within the boundary of the concept. The consequence of these differences is quite serious.

Frequently, the empirical cases used to test the theoretical predictions of different scholars are not within the domain to which their respective theories apply. The confusion results from the use of the same term – peasant – for what are often quite different concepts. When this is the case, no hypothesis test can be employed, as "testing" a theory in a case to which it was not intended to apply is no test at all. To the extent that the empirical scope of different theories diverge entirely, they cannot be considered competing explanations. I make this case particularly in relationship to the debates among moral economy, political economy (rational choice), and structural explanations of social revolution.[2]

To unravel the relationship between concept formation and theory testing in the case of peasant revolution, I have identified four principal dimensions that are used in different combinations in defining the term. All scholars of revolution at a very minimum understand peasants to be rural cultivators. But many consider them to be *more* than this. Three additional attributes, or combinations of them, figure prominently in academic understandings of peasants. Alternatively, they (1) own or control the land they cultivate, and/or (2) are socially subordinate to a rural dominant class, and/or (3) are typified by distinctive community cultural practices. Based on these four attributes, we can identify five distinctive definitions of the peasantry. The *Weberian* conception considers peasants to be typified by all three attributes – land ownership, cultural, and social – in addition to being rural cultivators.[3] The *Marxian* tradition focuses on the combination of land ownership and social subordination (Paige 1975). The *anthropological* tradition centers its understanding on the cultural distinctiveness of peasant communities (Banfield 1958; Redfield 1955). The *moral economy* approach adds social subordination to this focus on the integrity of the peasant community (Scott 1976). Finally, a *minimalist* understanding of peasants, focusing only on their status as rural cultivators, can be found most prominently in rational-choice approaches to peasant revolution (Lichbach 1994; Popkin 1979). Given the divergent definitions of peasant, it is hardly surprising that scholars disagree about their role in social revolutions.

This chapter proceeds in two parts. First, I examine the differing usages of the concept peasant in the social sciences. Crucially, these conceptual differences demarcate distinct subgroups of rural cultivators that can properly (for each school of thought) be considered peasants. Second, I examine the implications of this conceptual murkiness for the construction and assessment of causal hypotheses. Two conclusions follow. First, the conceptualization that one employs has a powerful effect on the hypotheses one produces. Second, inattention to the scope conditions entailed by different conceptions of peasants undermines the empirical evaluation of theories of revolution. Although not all analyses suffer from this defect, much of the ongoing debate over the causes of revolution results from conceptual problems and thus only indirectly represents meaningful theoretical and empirical differences.

Imposing structure: five traditions of conceptualizing peasants

The "absence of an adequate conceptual framework for the study of the peasantry" was noted almost twenty years ago by Deere and De Janvry (1979: 601). The problem of divergent definitions periodically has resulted in calls for the abandonment of the concept altogether (see Chiñas 1972; Ennew et al. 1977; Isaacman 1993). But the existence of disagreements does not imply that there are no common features to all understandings of what a peasant is. The conceptualizations bear a structured relationship to each other; indeed, all begin with the same background assumptions. As different theoretical traditions add more properties to the definition of a peasant, the range of empirical cases to which it applies necessarily shrinks (Table 11.1).[4] It is in the differing domains entailed by each conceptualization that difficulties in theory testing emerge.

Any effort at conceptualization inherently involves simplifications of a complex underlying social reality. But for social science to begin to make sense of the world, reality must be rendered by means of these much more tractable abstractions. As Scott pointed out, similar simplifications are essential to the practice of administration and governance. Such simplifications are Janus-faced, however. They inherently ignore much local specificity that can produce severe unintended consequences for those acting on the basis of these conceptual abstractions. The point is that conceptualization matters, and that the trade-off between abstraction and specificity is anything but "purely definitional" (Scott 1998: Chapter 1).[5] For social scientists, it affects social theory; for political leaders, it affects societal outcomes.

The dimensions of the concept

What, then, is a peasant? Table 11.1 sets out the properties used to define differing conceptions of the peasantry, as well as the relative empirical scope entailed by each definition. Below, I set out the basic contours of meaning of each of the underlying attributes used in different conceptualizations of the peasantry. It is important to remember that these dimensions represent idealizations that are unlikely to be reflected in perfect fashion in any real-world example.

Rural cultivators

The *Oxford English Dictionary* defines a peasant simply as "one who lives in the country and works on the land." Peasants commonly are understood to be rural cultivators. Academic definitions of peasant all share this background condition and proceed to build their respective conceptions on top of it, based on various combinations of three additional attributes – landholding, social subordination, and cultural distinctiveness. In addition to being defining attributes for many conceptions of a peasantry, these attributes also demarcate the boundaries of most well-known and commonly used subtypes of rural cultivators.[6]

Community cultural distinctiveness

A cultivator community whose members adhere to deeply-held cultural practices and that has strong boundaries to community membership is used as a defining

Table 11.1 Conceptual dimensions: competing understandings of peasants

	Minimalist	Anthropological	Moral economy	Marxian	Weberian
1. Rural cultivators	Yes	Yes	Yes	Yes	Yes
2. Peasant communities characterized by distinct cultural practices		Yes	Yes	Yes	Yes
3. High levels of rural social subordination			Yes	Yes	Yes
4. Peasants control and/or own land				Yes	Yes
Range of cases covered	Very large	Large	Moderate	Moderate	Very small
Examples	Popkin (1979) Lichbach (1994) Bates (1984, 1988), and most rational choice theories	Redfield (1955) Kroeber (1948), also Banfield (1958)	Scott (1976) Magnana (1991) Kerkvliet (1977)	Wolf (1969)[a] Paige (1975)	Moore (1966) Shanin (1971)

Note

a While Wolf's conceptualization is Marxian, his theoretical argument is sometimes moral and economic in tone.

characteristic of a peasantry. Central to such integration are geographical proximity, limited intra-village class differentials, and traditional cultural practices that imply significant (though not necessarily symmetrical) reciprocity.

Social subordination

A third dimension is social subordination. A situation of high subordination is a direct relationship of surplus extraction from the cultivator to some other agrarian social actor (for example, moneylenders, landlords, the state, the general store, or religious elites). It also carries with it the connotation of low social standing, and often also of exploitation. A situation of low subordination, by contrast, could include production for a capitalist market as long as the market power (e.g., market monopolization, cartelization, or monopsony) of various other classes does not make for extensive and direct extraction.

Control or ownership of agricultural land

Because peasant societies predate modern notions of property, ownership and control of agricultural land must be considered together. Peasants may own the land upon which they grow crops and control the process of production (e.g., which crops to plant, how to do so, when to harvest, how to divide the labor). If they do not own it, they may still have high levels of control over day-to-day productive activity (for example, in various forms of tenancy and collective land ownership). The absence of control over production defines the subset of rural cultivators who are wage-laborers. In practice, however, these distinctions can be very difficult to tease out, as rural cultivators often derive their subsistence from complex combinations of owned land, tenancy, and wage labor.[7]

Alternative conceptions of peasant

The task now is to understand the empirical scope of the alternative sets of defining properties laid out in Table 11.1. By doing this, the conceptualizations can be ordered with respect to the number of properties they contain, and thus the range of real-world rural cultivators that would fall within their boundaries. Obviously, the more properties in the definition (the more specific it is), the fewer real-world peasants it would tend to cover.[8]

Minimalist

The minimalist conception – essentially that peasants are rural cultivators – is a major approach in the literature on revolution. It is most prominent among scholars such as Popkin and Bates, who emphasize that peasants are individual rational actors. Popkin (1979: 1) explicitly rejects the emphasis on the cultural distinctiveness of peasant villages, arguing that most of the world's peasants live in open villages. Initially, he suggests that tightly integrated corporate communities existed as a historical fact (ibid.: 35). But by the end of his book he seems to depart from this position, quoting Hinton's argument that "peasant society exhibits an all-pervading individualism engendered by the endless personal struggle to acquire a little land to beat out the other fellow in the market place" (ibid.: 251). The powerful assumption is thereby made that peasant society is characterized by individual cost–benefit calculation, and is not really a tightly integrated collectivity.

For Popkin, the other potential properties may be present in peasant society, but they are not definitional of it. For him, rural cultivators might be involved in diverse forms of land tenure (from rich peasant employers through sharecroppers and landless day laborers). Peasants may be socially subordinate, but they exist in such relationships to rural elites only insofar as free-rider problems inhibit collective negotiation of prices, rents, or wages. Thus, peasants are at their core simply rural cultivators – the broadest possible meaning (ibid.: 9, 27).

The minimalist conception of a peasantry includes a large number of individuals within the conceptual boundary of the term. Such a broad approach poses challenges and opportunities. It requires that scholars find analytically meaningful similarities among peasants in widely varying socio-cultural, geographic, and historical settings. Popkin and others have focused on a shared pattern of rational, individual decision making. In the face of earlier literature that considered peasants to be "backward" or "traditional," it has been the particular contribution of these scholars to propose that peasants may in fact *not* be different types of decisionmakers (see, e.g., Bates 1988: 504–07). To the extent to which this is convincing, however, it makes room for theories with broad empirical domains.

Anthropological

The next conception of peasant comes from what I have called the anthropological tradition. Perhaps the foundational figure in this tradition is Alfred Kroeber, who considered peasantries "part-societies with part-cultures" (1948: 284). That is, the characteristic feature of peasants is that they have a defined set of cultural practices that are distinct from the urban pattern. This could be embodied in the form of local dialects, patterns of dress, religious rituals, etc. Redfield goes further, claiming that peasant society and culture are not only distinct from urban culture, but share common features throughout the world (1987: 60). More specifically, the principal unit of organization and social meaning for peasants is the local village community, which exists in structured relationships with the larger society that surrounds it (Redfield 1955: 9–10). This conception also influenced the work of political scientist Edward Banfield (1958).

Moral economy

The moral economy approach got its start in the work of E. P. Thompson, who focused more broadly on the impoverished classes in eighteenth-century England – peasant and non-peasant alike (1971). He has two definitional foci: the norms and integration of communities, and the presence of subordination to local dominant classes. Thompson (ibid.: 78) argues that small towns contained within them a sense of "traditional rights or customs" of which all community members were aware. But, unlike the Marxists, there is no focus on landholding in his understanding of peasants, whom he considers merely "rural laborers." Scott follows the same line, seeing peasants as individuals that "live in small, relatively homogeneous villages where much of their life is governed by local custom" (1977b: 4). Peasants, in direct contrast to urban workers, have communal norms, beliefs, and histories that form the core of their identities (Scott 1979: 101). Magagna (1991: 13–15) adds that for peasants, spatial boundaries (i.e., villages) shape the very "nature and meaning of agrarian social structure." This is, however, an ideal type. Even traditional communities have substantial individualistic cultural characteristics. What is critical is whether village norms are important enough to be seen as guides to peasant behavior.

Cultural patterns such as reciprocity, forced generosity, and communal landholdings are typical ways in which, for Scott, peasants provide themselves with subsistence insurance for times of dearth (1976: 5). This is, however, only half of Scott's definition. The need for such mechanisms of minimum-subsistence insurance derives largely from the claims to peasant surplus made by outsiders – mainly landlords or the state. Thus, the peasantry is a culturally articulated community set in a subordinate structural position relative to outside social actors. The moral economy definition would include a moderate spectrum of cultivators under the rubric of peasant. Typical landholding peasants, sharecroppers, tenants, and agricultural wage laborers all would qualify. Farmers, tribespeople, and all poorly integrated community systems would be excluded.[9]

Scott's more recent work, while centrally concerned with peasant politics, is not about social revolution. Still, even in his work on everyday resistance, essential components of his understanding of a peasantry include social subordination and the presence of a "supportive subculture" that often implies a "venerable popular culture of resistance" (Scott 1985: 35). Later, in his work examining class relations through the prism of contrasting public discourses and the "hidden transcripts" of social subordinates, moral economic notions of economic domination and the cultural distinctiveness of subalterns remain present (Scott 1990: 18–21). When Scott turns his attention to the state, he argues that the misapprehensions (via abstraction, simplification, and ignorance) of the distinctiveness and specificity of the local norms and practices of peasants can have disastrous consequences (see, for example, the discussion of Soviet collectivization in Scott 1998: Chapter 6).

Marxian

The Marxian conception of peasant principally is derived from Marx's work on the French peasantry and also centers the definition of a peasant along two of the three axes. It claims that peasants are at once small-landowners and subordinate within the prevailing mode of production. For Marx, implicitly, agricultural wageworkers – the landless – would "really" be proletarians and not peasants. In Marx's discussion of France, peasants are seen as small landholders, isolated from each other, and engaged in competition in a way that inhibits collective action. However, "insofar as [they] ... live under economic conditions of existence that separate their mode of life, their interests, and their culture from those of other classes, and put them in hostile opposition to the latter, they form a class" (Marx 1987: 332). These cultivators are clearly in a subordinate relationship to other classes, but their individual landholding puts them in competition with each other; they are thus unable to become a "class for themselves." There is, for Marx, no peasantry without landholding or without subordination.

Paige, a contemporary neo-Marxist, has developed a theory of rural class conflict that focuses on "cultivating classes" as the central actors (in their relationship with non-cultivating dominant classes). His theoretical sweep thus extends beyond the peasantry to include rural workers. But while all cultivators are, for him, necessarily socially subordinate, only some are characterized by landholding. He reserves the term peasant for this group (Paige 1975: 27). This distinction is central for him, because it is only the wage-laboring cultivators and *not* the peasants who are potentially revolutionary (33–35).[10] Paige's recent work, while much more focused on the "class narratives" of the Central American coffee aristocracy, continues to utilize a Marxian notion of a peasant. They still are defined by landholding, and remain carefully distinguished from the migratory laborers and informal sectors who are, for him, the bearers of revolutionary crisis in the region (Paige 1997: 30–31, 81, 93–95). Deere and De Janvry, in their attempt to impose conceptual clarity on the term peasant, similarly focus on the social organization of landholding (production and reproduction on the peasant family farm) and subordination (1979: 602, 607).

Weberian

The most encompassing conception of the peasantry derives from Weber. For him, the peasant "was and remains a smallholder, furnished with land as compensation for subordination to his master. . . ." (Weber 1979: 179). Cultural norms are hierarchical and personalistic, rather than the individual and rational pattern that prevails in the cities. To be a true peasant in the Weberian conception, rural producers have to control (but not necessarily own) land, be subordinate, and culturally distinct from urban-dwellers.

Shanin follows this approach. He argues that a true peasant would be characterized by: (1) family farm-based production, (2) a farm economy of a low level of specialization, (3) a specific traditional culture related to the manner of living in small villages, and (4) a relationship of domination by outsiders, which could be enforced variously through land tenure, direct physical coercion, and abuse of market power (Shanin 1971: 289–300). Perhaps the clearest example of this usage in scholarship on revolution is in the work of Barrington Moore. In his discussion of peasants and revolution, Moore focuses on all three attributes: "the character of the link between peasant community and the overlord [subordination], property and class divisions within the peasantry [land tenure], and the degree of solidarity or cohesiveness displayed by the peasant community [culture]" (Moore 1966: 468).

Conceptualization and the construction of theories of peasant revolution

Scholars have long been aware of the disagreements among different conceptualizations of peasants. These disagreements routinely are noted in the opening paragraphs of works on revolution. However, seldom are their implications for the construction and testing of theories directly explored. The tendency is to be explicit about one's own conceptualization, and then to proceed with the explanatory argument without reference to the consequences that would derive from alternative conceptualizations.

Conceptual disagreements have affected the empirical study of peasant revolution in two ways. First, the type of theory one constructs is closely tied to the conceptualization one employs. Eric Wolf has recently taken this point still further, arguing that there are important connections between conceptualization and power itself, and that prevailing anthropological definitions of culture have obscured this nexus (Wolf 1999: 19–20). But if concepts guide our thinking, then differences between theoretical arguments may reflect differences in conceptualization rather than competing empirically testable propositions about a shared set of actors. Hempel makes this point directly: "In actual scientific practice the processes of framing a theoretical structure and interpreting it are not always sharply separated . . ." (1957: 32). Theory informs conceptualization, and the reverse. I contend that this issue has bedeviled theories of revolution, given the absence of conceptual uniformity. However, if conceptual differences are made explicit, the lack of conceptual uniformity could be a strength rather than a weakness, as the resulting theoretical pluralism may heighten creativity in dealing with a poorly understood and complex social phenomenon.

The second consequence is serious and arises from the empirical cases that are used to test competing arguments about peasant revolution. In some cases, debates are carried on between scholars who test competing theories in cases to which they were never meant to be applied. This occurs because different conceptualizations entail different universes of empirically relevant cases. Careful attention must be paid to whether the cases analyzed are within the scope of the theory being evaluated.

Walker and Cohen have pointed out that "scope statements" – explicit definitions of the class of cases to which a theory applies – are essential to its testing (1985: 291). My goal here is to show that the scope of a theory is linked to the conceptualization of its central causal variables, and that where conceptual consensus is absent, problems of miscommunication and theory misevaluation are rife.

Two recommendations follow. First, we must be much more self-conscious in our conceptualization (*and* in understanding the implicit and explicit conceptual boundaries used by others) in the process of hypothesis testing and refinement. Failure to do so will result in irresolvable debates, inappropriate claims of theory refutation, and a tendency to make theoretical claims at a broader level of generality than is appropriate. Second, we must carefully examine when theorists actually offer competing explanations of a single phenomenon. This must be distinguished from instances in which there are really two different theories designed to be applied to two different domains of cases that are established by contrasting definitions of peasant. The separation of theoretical domains does not fully solve the problem, for within each particular conceptualization of a peasantry there remains substantial theoretical and empirical disagreement. But recognizing conceptual differences should make it possible for scholars to focus their energies on areas where empirical analysis can render theoretical judgments.

Concept, theory, and a debate that is not: moral economy versus political economy

The process of theory construction does not proceed in a conceptual vacuum. If, as Laitin argues, "it is hard to think about the political world without them [concepts]," then differences in conceptualization must produce differences in how we explain politics (1995: 455). I attempt to show how wide divergences in the conceptualization of peasants have led to strongly contrasting theories of peasant revolution that are sometimes not truly contending explanations. Table 11.2 summarizes the theoretical position of three principal authors from the moral economy, political economy, and Marxian schools, and the areas to which extension of their theories would be problematic. In this section, I argue that the well-known debate between moral economy and political economy approaches to explaining revolutions is, in fact, best understood as involving conceptual differences that render the two theories largely incommensurable. In other cases, for example, debates between Marxian and political economy perspectives, conceptual differences have not undermined the clash of alternative explanations or the process of theory testing. A focus on conceptual underpinnings is required, however, if we are to recognize and avoid these potential pitfalls.

We saw above that moral economy approaches to revolution define peasants in terms of the cultural distinctiveness of their villages and the presence of social subordination. Political economy approaches had the greatest empirical sweep, requiring only the background condition that peasants be rural cultivators. Linked to at least Popkin's version of this approach, however, is the assumption that peasants are individual cost–benefit calculators. From this, each perspective develops an "image" of village life that forms the context of its theoretical arguments. For moral economy, villages are closed, tightly knit (but not egalitarian), and corporate. For political economy, they are open, stratified, and internally competitive. It is a small step from these assumptions for the former to develop a theory of *group* moral codes, and the latter a theory of the barriers to *individual* participation in collective action.

Obviously, the tightly integrated villages of moral economy theory are characterized by varying degrees of individualism as well. The empirical assumption built into Scott's theory is that strong collective norms are also present and guide behavior. He argues that peasants, by-and-large, live only a hair's breadth away from threats to their very physical survival. Out of this reality comes a "safety-first" behavioral principle "which lies behind a great many of the technical, social, and moral arrangements of a pre-capitalist agrarian order" (Scott 1976: 5). This is no

Table 11.2 Theories of peasant revolution and the conceptual limits on their extension

Author	Definition	Cases examined	Summary of argument	Cases to which theory extension may be inappropriate
Scott	Moral economy	Colonial Vietnam and Burma (through the Great Depression)	Traditional community structures define the culturally acceptable form of surplus extraction. If the penetration of markets or states changes the *form* of extraction in ways that undermine year-to-year collective food security, then the subsistence ethic is violated and revolt is likely.	Modern or highly individualized contexts. Where capitalist transition is consolidated. Where community structures are weak.
Popkin	Minimalist	Vietnam (principally 1940s–1950s)[a]	Free-rider problems are seen as the basic barrier to the mobilization of peasants. They can be successfully overcome through a combination of effective leadership, individual incentives, and the credibility of organizational entrepreneurs' promises of future benefits.	Where simple individual cost-benefit calculation is an inaccurate model of peasant decision making. Where free-rider problems do not structure collective action.
Paige	Marxian	Vietnam and Guatemala (1940–1980s)	Revolutionary and non-revolutionary outcomes are seen as products of differing agrarian class relations. In particular, landholding peasants are unlikely to produce revolution, which results from a combination of cultivators dependent on wages and elites dependent on land.	Where agrarian class structures are not well consolidated. Where export-oriented capitalist traditions are not complete.

Note

a While Popkin discusses Vietnamese social and political organization as far back as the pre-colonial era, the actual instances of peasant mobilization he examines principally date from the 1940s and 1950s.

primitive egalitarian utopia, however. Rather, such an agrarian order is shot through with struggle, inequality, and extraction by elites. What is critical for Scott is the *type* of extraction. The key change comes when "the growth of the colonial state and the commercialization of agriculture exposed an ever-widening sector of the peasantry to new market-based insecurities which increased the variability of their income above and beyond the traditional risk in yield fluctuations" (ibid.: 57).[11] The penetration of markets and states may modernize agriculture and raise rural incomes, but *if* it removes guarantees of minimum food security that village cultural and technological practices had formerly provided, then the morality of the subsistence ethic is violated and rebellion is likely. It is emphatically not exploitation that causes peasant revolt, nor is it capitalism; rather, revolt is caused by new or different forms of exploitation that bring with them increases in year-to-year food insecurity.

This theory is intimately associated with the conceptualization of peasantry that Scott employs. His focus on the social and moral customs that undergird village life makes sense only in the context of long-standing villages that have developed such practices to cope with centuries of living on the edge of subsistence. Risk aversion and the "safety-first" principle are simply responses to life in a pre-capitalist agrarian economy. They may very well *not* be likely or rational responses to life as a rural cultivator within a reasonably well-established capitalist economic order. And with the passage of time, fewer and fewer peasantries may meet the criteria of Scott's moral economy definition. It is in the passing of this traditional society – a dynamic state – that Scott's theory has empirical bite. His is an explanation of what sort of externally induced transformation will (or will not) engender potentially revolutionary peasant resistance.

Popkin's minimalist conceptualization of a peasantry, by contrast, has a large empirical scope. It is this fact that makes it difficult and essential, however, to ascertain the theoretically relevant similarities between all members of the peasant category. One of the ways to seek this homogeneity of peasants is by making an effort to challenge the more restrictive (lower range of cases) conceptual dimensions used by others, most particularly the moral economists. If he were successful in this endeavor, he would also be able to make those individuals whom Scott defined as peasants fit within his own conceptualization, and establish a basis for the comparative evaluation of theory.

I contend, however, that these authors and other contributors to the debate may not be talking about the same objects of study. Moral economists Scott and Kerkvliet are explicit that they are interested in *pre-capitalist* peasantries (Kerkvliet 1977: 17–25; Scott 1976: 9). To be sure, they analyze peasantries in transition under the influence of an expanding state or what Wolf has called "North Atlantic capitalism," but theirs is a theory of how a traditional peasantry reacts to change. Popkin, on the other hand, is careful to explain that for him peasants are self-interested *individual* decision-makers (1979: 30). The individuals that the moral economists consider peasants fall within Popkin's minimalist definition only if pre-capitalist peasants are individual decision-makers in the utility-maximizing sense. Popkin recognizes this and thus is careful to introduce a negative restriction on the minimalist definition of a peasant – they must *not* live in tightly integrated, culturally bounded communities that could induce collective forms of decision making. That is, he is considering a peasantry that has already succumbed to the forces of commercialization and modernization. And Popkin goes to great lengths to argue that this is true of Vietnam, his empirical case (1979: 38, 55, 99, 108).

Popkin takes great pains to try to show that Vietnamese peasants are best seen as *individuals* "seeking to stabilize and secure their own existence" (ibid.: 88). Even so, in his discussion of pre-colonial and colonial villages, while he demonstrates inegalitarian socio-economic patterns, he concedes that they contained important redistributive features, often had very sharp cultural boundaries, and were closed and corporate (88, 94, 99). He and Scott concur that the advent of French colonialism dramatically changed rural social structure and the terms of peasant existence (ibid.: Chapter 4). The problem is that the type of peasant analytically central to his theory of mobilization came about as a result of the transformations of the colonial era. As a consequence, his compelling empirical analysis of four peasant movements is temporally situated well *after* the period of time in which the type of peasants central to Scott's analysis existed.

The issue here, as Weber would be quick to point out, is that the type of individualistic and cost–benefit calculating behavior constructed in Popkin's theory is a decidedly modern phenomenon. It makes sense only where the transformation to commercial agriculture and market rationality is widespread and thoroughgoing (Alexander 1983: 35). The process of rationalization for Weber "is the deliberate substitution for the unthinking acceptance of ancient custom [e.g., the subsistence ethic of the moral economists], of deliberate adaptation to situations in terms of self interest" (1978: 30). Rationalization and the penetration of markets and bureaucracies are inextricably linked (71). But moral economists cast their theories about social contexts in which exactly such forms of production and their associated patterns of atomistic decision making have not fully penetrated. It is a separate claim to argue that rational, individual decision making predates capitalist transformation. Such an approach is considered below, and certainly is a fruitful line of exploration.

As presented, moral economy is a theory of the implications of market and state penetration *into* pre-capitalist communities.[12] Popkin's political economy is a theory about actors who operate in contexts in which market organization has already attained predominance. Understood in this way, there is no reason why the moral economy and political economy approaches could not *simultaneously* be correct (or incorrect). They may both refer to peasants, but they are not talking about the same social actors. I do not intend to make an empirical critique of either approach, and claim only that they are not competing explanations.

It is also critical to understand here that I do not intend a general indictment of rational-choice approaches as inapplicable to certain types of peasant society. Rather, I contend that without modification to account for some of the cultural and social aspects of pre-capitalist communities, Popkin's version of individual rationality is an incomplete description of the decision-making processes of the types of peasant central to moral economy approaches. That is, the peasants that meet Scott's definition would not easily be understood using Popkin's theoretical apparatus, *and* vice versa. This does not, however, mean that Popkin's theory is inadequate for the case to which he applied it, or a wide variety of more contemporary peasantries. Nor does it mean that a differently formulated rational-choice inspired theory would necessarily fail to be theoretically competitive with moral economy approaches in a different set of cases.

Understanding the problem

Desai and Eckstein think of these conceptual differences in terms of the dependent variable of revolution. For them, there are pre-modern and modern revolutions, the latter being characterized by the presence of a bureaucratic revolutionary organization. While this formulation recognizes the conceptual core of the problem, narrowing the dependent variable is perhaps not the appropriate solution. As they themselves put it, "not only is revolutionary organization a modern phenomenon, but it is *made possible* by modernity" (Desai and Eckstein 1990: 458; italics original). But since modernity here is essentially the penetration of modern market-rational social patterns into the peasantry, the conceptual issue is how the peasantry has changed, not how revolution has changed. That is, as what constitutes a peasant has changed, then the causes of peasant revolution also have changed, including in the twentieth century the centrality of an organized revolutionary party. This is part of the cause of modern revolution, not part of its definition.

Similarly, Somers and Goldfrank, in their trenchant critique of Paige's structural theory, hit on the centrality of the distinction between "traditional" subsistence economies and modern commercial enclaves (1979: 444). Their criticism of Paige, that he has "nothing to say about the effects of price fluctuations and the demand-induced conversion of lands formerly devoted to subsistence," applies to Popkin as well (451). But neither theorist should have much to say, because this important question asks about a set of social actors not consistent with their conceptualization – subsistence (i.e., traditional) peasants under pressure from encroaching markets. It is not an accident that Scott's theory, which employs a conceptualization fully consonant with such peasant actors, has much to say on the topic. The theoretical silence that Somers and Goldfrank detect speaks, however, to a problem of theoretical incommensurability rooted in conceptual differences, not to theoretical inadequacy in the work of Paige (or by extension, Popkin), taken in their appropriate empirical domains.

It is only Popkin's attempt to universalize his particular version of the logic of individual decision making, leading him inappropriately to project his theory into pre-capitalist settings, that weakens an otherwise compelling explanation. In the process of defining his perspective, he critiques the moral economists as arguing that, "social relations in precapitalist or noncapitalist settings are more moral than are relations in capitalist settings, and that the externally induced 'breakdown' of precapitalist institutions hurts peasant welfare" (Popkin 1979: 3). This is not quite Scott's point. Moral economy theory provides a basis for understanding what types of exploitation are not likely to threaten subsistence, and thus could be tolerated, and those that undermine the basic subsistence minimum, at least from time to time. It is important that the former may, over time, involve much more extraction than the latter. The penetration of market relations does not necessarily increase exploitation. Rather, it may be differently exploitative. It may create instabilities that threaten subsistence, even while returns improve on average. Scott's theory attempts to derive a basis for understanding what types of exploitation will be perceived as unjust. But recall that for Scott, all peasants are by definition subject to exploitation and subordination.

While the derivation of peasant moral economy – based in the subsistence ethic – is conceptualized as responsive to a "static" pattern of socio-economic organization, the theory of revolution is dynamic. Scott and other allied approaches analyze traditional peasantries in the process of transformation, either from encroaching states or the penetration of commercial forces.[13] In a similar vein, Hobsbawm's discussion of social banditry examines the dynamics of transformation, especially "disintegrating kinship society and the transition to agrarian capitalism" (1969: 14). Social banditry as a phenomenon ceases to exist once the transformation to fully commercial agriculture is complete (15). What is critical is that the dynamic of peasant mobilization is understood as a response to transformative processes within *traditional* (pre-capitalist) peasantries.

Popkin's alternative is rooted in the notion that peasants are individual utility maximizers much like anyone else. In this sense, it relies on a more static conceptualization of socio-economic organization. To be sure, in this world, modernization may proceed apace and society may be shot through with conflicts, but the rural economy is not seen as being in the throes of a "great transformation." Popkin's theory concerns the political dynamics of an already commercialized agrarian economy, rather than of the commercialization of agriculture.

From this perspective, decision making involves trade-offs between different sorts of short-run and long-run investments designed to improve their individual or familial subsistence level. The key issue from the perspective of mobilization and revolutionary activity involves the "conflicts between individual and group benefits" (Popkin 1979: 4). The problem is defined as a version of Olson's dilemma of collective action (1966). As Popkin puts it, "unless the expected [individual] benefits outweigh the costs, the villager can be presumed not to contribute to collective action" (1979: 24). In Vietnam, it was only the skilled leadership of Communist cadres or various religious movements that could provide the incentives necessary to support collective action. Leaders accomplished this by excluding non-participants from the benefits of collective action, coordinating their contributions, manipulating information, and breaking larger goals into smaller discrete subsets. In this fashion they could convince peasants that their participation would have an appreciable effect on outcomes, and overcome barriers to action (Popkin 1979: 257, 259). Popkin does not attempt to reinterpret, from his own theoretical perspective, the movements central to Scott. I contend this is because peasants of this earlier time period do not conform to the definition upon which Popkin's theory is founded.

A political economy perspective could be reformulated to fit pre-capitalist contexts, and might make moral economic predictions. For example, one could argue that free riding may be sanctioned through powerful community norms, and the *individual* costs of inaction are potentially enormous because general subsistence is threatened.[14] The marginal private share of a collective effort – even in a relatively large group – might well be critical even if one contributes only a small amount to the outcome and the impact is barely noticeable; one is, after all, on the very margin of physical survival. In addition, one cannot underestimate the enforcement power of community norms. Scott has discussed norms as individual incentives guiding peasant decision making (1979: 116). But as formulated, these are two different theories designed for two different contexts. To apply them to cases of "peasant revolution" in general overlooks the widely differing usages of the term peasant that each perspective employs. One theory cannot be tested against the other, because they do not compete. They lack an equivalent focus.

Lichbach extends Popkin's line of thinking, focusing on the importance of selective incentives in generating collective action. Again, he points out that collective action – here subtly redefined as "collective organization" – depends on the private distribution of benefits from group membership. His examples range from the Nature Conservancy to the American Political Science Association. But the minimalist conception of peasants that he employs leads him to consider this an adequate theoretical model for peasants across time and place.

A compelling case can be made that modern rural cultivators in free-market economies behave like environmentalists or political scientists, insofar as they face standard collective action dilemmas. But the universalization of this model to as wide a range of peasantries as Lichbach covers is problematic. Not all peasantries are modern, not all rural areas are heavily marketized, and not all peasant organization takes on the rational-legal/bureaucratic form identified by Lichbach (1994: 389). Rather, the minimalist conception of peasantry leads him, like Popkin, to the theoretical step of universalizing a particular version of the logic of collective action. Scott is quick to critique such moves, giving examples of movements that are difficult to explain by an appeal to strictly individual logic – including the Wellingsborough Diggers and Zapata's uprising in early twentieth-century Morelos (Scott 1977a: 232). Notably, these are not modern contexts, though they may well be modernizing. As a result of this conceptual issue, a compelling and plausible theory is stretched to cover cases where its assumptions and predictions are unconvincing. But this is not a falsification of the theory more generally.

More recently, Lichbach has noted that solutions to collective action dilemmas are contingent on the character of the groups acting and the institutional environment within which they act (1998: 411). Thus, different types of groups (in this case, types of peasants) could potentially solve the problem of collective action in different fashions. He thinks of these solutions (i.e., causes of mobilization) as falling into four broad types: markets, communities, contracts, and hierarchies (409–10). That is, rebellion can have different causes in different groups. Unfortunately, in his empirical work on peasant rebellion, he continues to assume that pre-capitalist and modern peasantries form a single homogeneous group. Pursuing this notion of causal heterogeneity among different peasant groups, however, would help make rationalist approaches more commensurable with moral economy ones.

Attempts at coping with conceptual problems

Bates takes an important stride forward in recognizing the conceptual core of disagreements between moral economy and political economy theories. His solution to the dilemma is to make an empirical case that no peasants fitting the moral economy definition are to be found, at least in Africa. He begins, quite correctly, by pointing out that communal and culturally demarcated villages are an "essential underpinning" to moral economy theories (Bates 1984: 240). Bates then rejects the idea that pre-capitalist peasant villages of this type (what he calls "natural economy" or "peasant economy" models) ever had a meaningful presence (241). This is a controversial claim, but the effort is laudable because it recognizes the conceptual problem that is central to the dispute.

The key issue Bates uses to make his point is a discussion of property rights. He understands the moral economists as contending that their culturally demarcated villages will be characterized by a tendency to support collective land rights. He argues that they see peasant revolution as village attempts to defend collective land rights against the individualization attendant upon capitalist transition (1984: 242, 1988: 501). He then goes on to show convincingly that in many cases, traditional rural cultivators *supported* private property expansion and engaged in trade. This is not quite the solution that it at first appears to be. The existence of peasant preferences for private property does not entail the absence of the strong community norms and structures that are the core of the moral economy definition. It also does not contradict moral economy claims as to when revolution is likely (see Table 11.2).

Moral economy arguments make no assumptions about the presence or absence of individual private property (see Table 11.1). They only assert that in pre-capitalist villages, social and customary patterns produce a subsistence ethic that involves practices that prevent the poorest from actually succumbing to starvation. This could take a variety of forms, including social pressure on the wealthy to hold feasts, to reduce rents in hard times, or to provide employment. It by no means entails the redistribution of land, or its collective ownership.[15] This is only one possibility among many, though it is a feature that was present in Scott's original case – Vietnam. To critique the moral economy definition of a peasantry on this basis is excessively narrow. The moral economists claim peasants revolt against extractions that place them at greater year-to-year risk of starvation, violating the subsistence ethic. They do not revolt against the market or capitalism per se, nor is the absence of collective landholding sufficient to establish the presence of rational individual decision making.

Scott also, on occasion, applies moral economy theories to contexts where their definitions may not apply. In response to political economy theories, he contends that, "any theory of revolution must make a place for the anger, revenge, hatred that are so obviously a part of the experience. Marketplace bargaining metaphors miss this entirely. If such emotions are not to be considered acts of pure madness, we are forcibly brought to the living moral economy of the participants" (Scott 1977a: 240). But marketplace metaphors might be entirely appropriate where markets have thoroughly penetrated. And moral economies cannot be presumed where their socio-cultural foundations are absent.

Hawes comes closest to recognizing directly the core conceptual difficulty in the moral economy/political economy debate. In his discussion of the applicability of Scott's theories to the Philippines, he notes,

> Though peasant rebellion has a long history in the settled, rice-producing regions . . . it has not been an important form of peasant political action since the 1950s. Subsistence crises still threaten the poor, but the *political economy of these crises has changed since the earlier rebellions*.
>
> (Hawes 1989: 269; italics mine)

In particular, Hawes points to the commercialization of the rice economy, class differentiation, and the decline of traditional patron–client ties. It is a very small step from this recognition to note that what has changed is the *type* of cultivator. With the transition to stable capitalist social relations, the variables of importance to moral economy theory cease to be effective predictors of revolt. Once marketization is complete, perhaps it is Popkin's approach that is most appropriate. Neither theory has here been falsified.

To argue that moral economy and political economy approaches to peasant revolution are incommensurable is not to contend that there is no way in which proponents of the two perspectives can engage in debate. The necessary step is to recognize that the core of the debate hinges on the nature of the peasantry, not the causes of revolution. If this is accomplished, the debate becomes centered on the domain of each theory, and the empirical issue becomes the nature of the peasantry: community-centered and risk-averse for moral economy, individualistic and self-interested for political economy. If the theoretical debate is re-framed as an empirical dispute between rival conceptualizations of a peasantry, we may gain from the interaction.

Indeed, such an empirical encounter occurs in discussions of the nature of pre-revolutionary French rural society. These disputes have explicitly been framed in terms of their implications for moral economic and more economistic conceptions of peasant society and culture (see, e.g., Hoffman 1996: 17–18). The conventional wisdom has been moral economic in its understanding of peasant society. Marc Bloch is perhaps most emphatic, stating flatly that, "early societies were made up of groups rather than individuals" (1970: 150). These communities – particularly their poorest members – resisted modernizing reforms such as enclosure and the abolition of collective property and customary rights (224–25). For both Bloch and Brenner, it was this stubborn adherence to tradition – rendered understandable in terms of its subsistence-guaranteeing functions – that for so long prevented the emergence of agrarian capitalism in France or any sort of economic modernization akin to that experienced by England at the same time (Brenner 1987: 29).

Hoffman, re-examining the case of Old Regime France, challenges this communitarian notion of the peasantry and its explicit connections to moral economic hypotheses. He correctly points out that moral economic positions assert that traditional property and customary regimes work as a form of social insurance for the poor, and that as a consequence, "peasants resist the onslaught of capitalism" (1996: 17). But, Hoffman argues, peasant communities were actually deeply divided, and the defenders of the commons were more often privileged strata, not the poor. His work shows the intense conflicts of interest within communities, rebutting the notion of a natural unity. He points out that as a consequence, collective action was unusual and where it did emerge, it frequently was accompanied by coercive measures to enforce broad-based participation.[16] It is a short step from this point to Lichbach's selective-incentive approach to peasant collective action. Root similarly points out that village institutions in Burgundian peasant communities did not level social inequalities, and that external pressures from both agricultural commercialization and the state served to strengthen, not weaken, customary practices (Root 1987: 2–3). Thus, both the underlying conceptualization and causal mechanisms central to moral economy approaches are challenged.

The point here is not to adjudicate among these works of social history. Rather, I seek to point out that this debate – framed in terms of what conceptualization of peasants is appropriate to the case – exemplifies the way that empirical evidence can fruitfully be brought to bear on the moral economy/political economy debate. If the revisionist historians are correct that community-oriented peasants do not characterize Old Regime France, Scott and Thompson's work is rendered inapplicable; it is not, however, refuted. The latter would require evaluation in cases in which it legitimately can be applied. Crucially, conceptual clarity is essential to understanding where disputes lie, and the forms of empirical evaluation that can meaningfully be brought to bear.

When conceptual disagreement is not a problem

Are all theories of peasant revolution so different that meaningful debate is impossible? Thankfully, no. It is the moral economy/political economy debate that is most affected by conceptual differences. On the other hand, the arguments of Wolf and Scott could easily be tested against each other. Both locate the root cause of peasant mobilization in the capitalist transformation of pre-capitalist peasant villages. Wolf emphasizes landholding and social subordination in his definition, while Scott emphasizes village distinctiveness as an alternative to landholding. The range of cases covered by the concept is not quite identical for each. But given the historical boundaries that both employ, they overlap empirically to a great extent. Thus, the quite different predictions that their theories make can be tested in competition with each other. Wolf expects landholding middle peasants to be the locus of rebellion, while Scott expects villages under collective threats to their subsistence to be the rebellious actor. Empirical studies could certainly adjudicate between them.

Similarly, Popkin's arguments can readily be compared with those of some other scholars. The work of Jeffery Paige likewise situates itself in the post-capitalist transformation era. He explicitly bounds his theory within the domain of modernized "agricultural export sectors [which] represent a sharp break with the pattern of subsistence cultivation" (Paige 1975: 3). As a consequence, its theoretical implications are comparable to Popkin's political economy approach. While Popkin and subsequent rational-choice inspired theorists like Lichbach emphasize leadership and the provision of selective incentives to explain rebellion, Paige hypothesizes that a non-cultivating class dependent on control over land for its income, when coupled with a wage-earning cultivating class, will produce a revolutionary explosion (58–59). Paige is careful to use the term "cultivators" to discuss his central actors, and his theory is broadly comparable to that of the political economists. While he may not call all rural actors peasants, he has a theory of all rural cultivators, as do Popkin and others. His specific hypotheses are quite different, and these *are* amenable to adjudication on the evidence. Ironically, it is wage-earning cultivators – considered by Paige as fundamentally proletarians, rather than peasants – who can be the dynamite for peasant revolution (33).

Paige's evaluation of the moral economy perspective is also carefully done within the range of cases one could reasonably include under the moral economy's definition of a peasantry. However, the empirical overlap between these two theories is exceedingly limited. Paige has selected one national case – Guatemala from 1940 to 1980 – that embodies market-oriented agro-export production, social subordination, landholding, and the persistence of strong, culturally bounded Indian communities. These peasants – barely – fit both definitions, so something of a hypothesis test is possible here. But it is not, I would argue, a strong test. Most often, these theories do not compete. Judging them on the basis of the exceedingly rare cases where they do overlap does not provide a strong evaluation of their respective core propositions. The theory test is legitimate, but it is not a strong falsification.

Theda Skocpol long ago recognized that there were serious problems arising from the differing treatments of the peasantry in theories of revolution.[17] The problem, from her perspective, was that scholars proposed competing universal definitions of the peasantry – a task she saw as hopeless. Her solution, rather than accepting any single conceptualization of the peasantry, was to wrest theoretical importance from the concept altogether. The crux of her critique of preceding scholarship is its excessive emphasis on characteristics of the peasantry in the making of social revolutions (Skocpol 1994: 226, 229).

Instead, Skocpol proposes that "revolutionary situations have developed due to the emergence of politico-military crises of state and class domination" (1979: 17). She is more interested in the political contexts in which peasants find themselves, rather than characteristics of peasants per se. Whatever one may think of the theory proposed, its conceptual domain is not restricted by any particular notion of the peasantry. Skocpol's approach is commensurable with – and should be tested against – any and all of the extant theories of revolution. Since it locates relatively little causal weight on characteristics of the peasantry itself, its predictions can validly be examined in peasantries akin to those central to moral economy, political economy, or Marxian approaches.

The use of empirical "test" cases: the two Vietnams

In this section I explore further how two theorists like Scott and Popkin could both be centrally concerned with the Vietnamese case, and yet be so fundamentally at odds. How can both produce theories of peasant revolution tailored to this case and yet not be speaking about the same peasants? The fact that both studied the same country is, I think, part of the reason why so much dispute has emerged. But did they really study the same case?

Scott's analysis of Vietnam takes as its empirical outcome to be explained the rebellions of the Great Depression. These rebellions, as Scott points out, "delivered the *coup de grace* to an agrarian order already weakened by structural changes well before 1930" (1976: 114). His central exogenous causal variable is "the growth of the colonial state and the commercialization of agriculture," which took place well before these rebellions (57). For him, peasants seek to defend a crumbling pre-capitalist economic and social order. Popkin's analysis, on the other hand, largely centers on post-WWII Vietnam. These are distinct cases. Scott is interested in transformations forty years before the period examined by Popkin, a system that apparently was, in its essentials, gone by the 1930s. Popkin analyzes a peasantry finally and forcibly drawn into full capitalist production. Popkin may well be right that the rebellions of the 1940s and 1950s were "not to destroy the market economy, but to *tame* capitalism" (1979: 245). What is not fully addressed by him is whether the movements of Scott's time period (the Depression and before) were fundamentally restorative or not.

Neither theorist disputes the fact that colonialism and the advent of export agriculture decisively changed Vietnamese society and economy. But if this is so, why would it not also fundamentally change the bases and causes of peasant collective action? Analyses of Vietnam in these two very different periods fundamentally are analyses of different cases. They are not tests of different theories in the same case. In her study of Vietnamese rebellion, Wiegersma (1988: 14) hits the nail on the head:

> Whereas others [moral economists] have seen peasants, including Vietnamese peasants, as a group caught in between old and new realities, Popkin saw them as small farmers operating according to new economic rules. Popkin viewed capitalism as having become fully established in Vietnam.

The former was true of Scott's Depression rebellions, and the latter of the period that Popkin analyzes.

While the problem with the Scott–Popkin debate was that conceptual murkiness produced two theories about two different contexts, lack of clarity can also lead to the testing of theory in inappropriate cases. Jenkins, for example, examines the case of peasant rebellion in Russia in the 1905–07 period forward, in an attempt to test the moral economy position of Scott against the Marxian approach of Paige (1983: 493). The problem is that, although the case fits Scott's conceptualization of peasant, it is a poor match for that of Paige. As Jenkins notes, prior to the emancipation of the serfs in 1861, Russian agriculture was overwhelmingly oriented toward subsistence production. In large measure, it is an analysis of a pre-capitalist peasantry – famous for its distinctive community practices – that was undergoing a particularly rapid and extractive transition to capitalist production. But Paige's theory is of social structures in export-oriented agricultural sectors (or, more accurately, commercial sectors, following Somers and Goldfrank [1979: 451]). As a structural analysis, it is not well adapted to a case in which patterns of productive relations are undergoing rapid transformation. It is precisely the necessary social structures that are Paige's independent variables that have yet to become solidified. In addition, Paige explicitly restricts his theory to cases linked via export markets to the global capitalist economy. For him, production need not be highly capitalist (hence Guatemala of the 1940s is a valid case), but the destination of production must be commercial for a case to fall within Paige's empirical domain. As a result, Jenkins' refutation of Paige's thesis is based on a case to which Paige would not apply his theory.

Conclusions

This chapter has explored how a lack of consensus in conceptualization can lead to problems of theory testing and case selection. In examining the literature on peasant revolution, I find that at least five different understandings of the term peasant are common. They are not arbitrary, but rather employ different combinations of four defining properties: (1) status as a rural cultivator, common to all, (2) the presence of social subordination, (3) cultural distinctiveness of village communities, and (4) ownership or control over agricultural land. Because they have different numbers of defining properties, the differing definitions imply widely varying ranges of cases that would fall within their boundaries.

Since conceptualization bounds the range of real-world cases covered by a term, differences in conceptualization can place strong limits on which empirical cases can be legitimate venues in which to test competing hypotheses. This problem arises in the moral economy–political economy dispute. Scott's analysis of Vietnam concerns the Depression era rebellions of a pre-capitalist economy undergoing the throes of transition to market capitalism. Popkin's analysis is of a later period, in which social structure has completed this transformation and market relations have been fully established. In analytical terms, these constitute two very different cases, with two very different peasantries. Each falls within the empirical domain of only one of the two theories. For two theories to be tested against each other, the empirical case examined must fall within the empirical scope of *both* theories. This being said, important disputes remain to be adjudicated. For instance, Scott and Wolf, or Paige and Popkin, are commensurable, and we can advance our understanding through the comparative testing of their predictions. Moreover, all these approaches stand in competition with the state-centric approach of Skocpol, whose theory does not rely in important ways on particular conceptualizations of the peasantry.

What can we take away from all of this? Put simply, scholars should devote adequate attention to conceptualization, both their own analysis and in appraising the work of other researchers. It can lead to false debates and the "testing of theory" in inappropriate settings. Just these difficulties have hindered progress in understanding the causes of peasant revolution. The sooner we recognize them, the sooner we can move forward. The lesson is also more general: because conceptualization is inseparable from hypothesis construction and testing, we should make greater efforts to explicitly integrate it into the design and execution of causal inference.

Notes

* Originally published as Marcus J. Kurtz (2000) "Understanding Peasant Revolution: From Concept to Theory and Case," *Theory and Society* 29 (1): 93–124.

1 The classic example of this is in the work of Theda Skocpol (1979). For her, the critical causes of peasant revolution lie in changes in state–society relations brought on by defeats in the international state system.
2 Obviously, these literatures derive from the path-breaking works of James Scott, Samuel Popkin, and Jeffery Paige, respectively.
3 For example, Moore (1966). Even scholars like Skocpol (1979), who locate the causes of revolution outside the peasantry, implicitly rely on a set of assumptions about what a peasant is, generally relying on the Weberian model.
4 This is the intension–extension trade-off of Giovanni Sartori (1970).
5 Scott points out how implementing broadly transformative visions based on highly abstract understandings of the workings of society can produce unintended disasters.
6 Throughout, where the intention is to speak generally about all rural producers who *might* be labeled peasants under some accepted definition, the term "rural cultivator" is used.
7 Sidney Mintz (1973) has pointed out how this makes the process of classification difficult.
8 Viewed in terms of these dimensions, it becomes easier to understand some of the debates surrounding the "correct" definition of the peasantry. It can in part be seen as a struggle over the level of abstraction at which to use the concept. In "Guidelines for Concept Analysis" (Chapter 4, this volume), Sartori argues that concepts have two aspects – their extension and their intension. The extension of a concept refers to the "class of all objects to which that word correctly applies," that is, the range of empirical phenomena for which it can he used. Intension, on the other hand, refers to the totality of characteristics or properties of a concept. The extension and intension of concepts are inversely related, and hence ascent to a higher level of abstraction implies an increase in extension (coverage) at the cost of a decrease in intension (the number or discriminating power of defining properties associated with the concept).
9 This becomes crucial because the political economy approach assumes that peasants live in more or less poorly integrated (i.e., individualistic) community systems.
10 Paige explicitly contrasts peasants – seen typically as laboring, isolated, competitive individuals – with the agricultural wage laborer who is generally "completely dependent on his fellow workers" and therefore prone to solidarity and collective action (1975: 37).
11 Magagna (1991: 22–23) and Kerkvliet (1977: 250) similarly produce distinct theories of rebellion within the moral economy tradition, focusing on when outside actors challenge deeply held village practices or disrupt traditional patron–client ties.
12 See Disch (1979: 250) for an early attempt to focus on the different empirical scopes of competing theories of revolution.
13 Hobsbawm (1973: 5) is explicit about his focus on "what happens when traditional peasants get involved in modern politics."

14 Popkin (1979: 108) comes close to conceding this when he points out that in pre-colonial Vietnam, peasants avoided conflictual, self-interested action not out of altruism but out of fear of consequences for themselves. But what, other than community norms and sanctions, would cause such fear? Mark Lichbach (1998: 410) has recently explicitly suggested, but not developed, this line of thinking. Among the possible ways of over-coming collective action dilemmas is to "explore how common belief systems solve Olson's Problem. . . ."

15 For Kerkvliet, this can simply take the form of elites' willingness to reduce rents in times of dearth. It presumes no peasant landholding at all – collective or otherwise.

16 In a telling example, he points to an example in Brittany where villagers placed a mock gallows in the village to warn their compatriots of the consequences of any effort to abet an ongoing effort at land enclosure (Hoffman 1996: 25).

17 Theda Skocpol (1994: 232) articulates the problem as a clash between theorists who see peasants as "reacting to encroaching world capitalism" and those, like Paige, who see them as "reacting from within the capitalist world economy."

References

Alexander, J. (1983) *The Classical Attempt at Theoretical Synthesis: Max Weber*, Berkeley: University of California Press.

Anderson, L. (1993) "Agrarian Politics and Revolution: Micro and State Perspectives on Structural Determinism," *Journal of Theoretical Politics* 5 (4): 495–522.

Anderson, L. and Seligson, M. (1994) "Reformism and Radicalism among Peasants: An Empirical Test of Paige's *Agrarian Revolution*," *American Journal of Political Science* 38 (4): 944–72.

Banfield, E. (1958) *The Moral Basis of a Backward Society*, New York: Free Press.

Bates, R. (1984) "Some Conventional Orthodoxies in the Study of Agrarian Change," *World Politics* 36 (2): 234–54.

Bates, R. (1988) "Lessons from History, or the Perfidy of English Exceptionalism and the Significance of Historical France," *World Politics* 40 (4): 499–516.

Bloch, M. (1970) *French Rural History: An Essay on Its Basic Characteristics*; trans. J. Sondheimer, Berkeley: University of California Press.

Brenner, R. (1987) "Agrarian Class Structure and Economic Development in Pre-Industrial Europe," in T.H. Aston and C.H.E. Philpin (eds.), *The Brenner Debate: Agrarian Class Structure and Economic Development in Pre-Industrial Europe*, Cambridge: Cambridge University Press; first published 1976.

Chiñas, B. (1972) "Comment on 'Peasantries in Anthropology and History,'" *Current Anthropology* 13 (3–4): 407–08.

Deere, C.D. and de Janvry, A. (1979) "A Conceptual Framework for the Empirical Analysis of Peasants," *American Journal of Agricultural Economics* 61 (4): 601–11.

Desai, R. and Eckstein, H. (1990) "Insurgency: The Transformation of Peasant Rebellion," *World Politics* 42 (4): 441–65.

Disch, A. (1979) "Peasants and Revolts," *Theory and Society* 7 (1–2): 243–52.

Diskin, M. (1996) "Distilled Conclusions: The Disappearance of the Agrarian Question in El Salvador," *Latin American Research Review* 31 (2): 111–26.

Ennew, J., Hirst, P., and Tribe, K. (1977) "'Peasantry' as an Economic Category," *Journal of Peasant Studies* 4: 295–322.

Hawes, G. (1989) "Theories of Peasant Revolution: A Critique and Contribution from the Philippines," *World Politics* 42 (2): 261–98.

Hempel, C. (1957) *Fundamentals of Concept Formation in Empirical Science*, International Encyclopedia of Unified Science II, vol. 2, no. 7, Chicago: University of Chicago Press.

Hoffman, P.T. (1996) *Growth in a Traditional Society: The French Countryside 1450–1815*, Princeton: Princeton University Press.

Hobsbawm, E. (1969) *Bandits*, London: Weidenfeld and Nicolson.

Hobsbawm, E. (1973) "Peasants and Politics," *Journal of Peasant Studies* 1 (1): 3–22.

Isaacman, A. (1993) "Peasants and Rural Social Protest in Africa," in F. Cooper, F. Mallon, A. Isaacman, and W. Roseberry (eds.), *Confronting Historical Paradigms*, Madison: University of Wisconsin Press.

Jenkins, J.C. (1983) "Why Do Peasants Rebel? Structural and Historical Theories of Modern Peasant Rebellions," *American Journal of Sociology* 88 (3): 487–514.

Kerkvliet, B. (1977) *The Huk Rebellion*, Berkeley: University of California Press.

Kroeber, A. (1948) *Anthropology*, New York: Harcourt, Brace, and Co.

Laitin, D. (1995) "Disciplining Political Science," *American Political Science Review* 89 (2): 454–56.

Lichbach, M.I. (1994) "What Makes Rational Peasants Revolutionary?," *World Politics* 46 (3): 383–418.

Lichbach, M.I. (1998) "Contending Theories of Contentious Politics and the Structure-Action Problem of Social Order," *Annual Review of Political Science* 1: 401–24.

Magagna, V. (1991) *Communities of Grain*, Ithaca, NY: Cornell University Press.

Marx, K. (1987) "The Peasantry as a Class," in T. Shanin (ed.), *Peasants and Peasant Society*, London: Basil Blackwell.

Migdal, J. (1974) *Peasants, Politics, and Revolution*, Princeton: Princeton University Press.

Mintz, S. (1973) "A Note on the Definition of Peasantries," *Journal of Peasant Studies* 1 (1): 93–94.

Moore, B., Jr. (1966) *Social Origins of Dictatorship and Democracy: Lord and Peasant in the Making of the Modern World*, Boston: Beacon Press.

Olson, M. (1966) *The Logic of Collective Action*, Cambridge, MA: Harvard University Press.

Paige, J. (1975) *Agrarian Revolution*, New York: Free Press.

Paige, J. (1996) "Land Reform and Agrarian Revolution in El Salvador: Comment on Seligson and Diskin," *Latin American Research Review* 31 (2): 127–39.

Paige, J. (1997) *Coffee and Power: Revolution and the Rise of Democracy in Central America*, Cambridge, MA: Harvard University Press.

Popkin, S. (1979) *The Rational Peasant*, Berkeley: University of California Press.

Redfield, R. (1955) *The Little Community: Viewpoints for the Study of a Human Whole*, Chicago: University of Chicago Press.

Redfield, R. (1987) "The Part Societies with Part Cultures," in T. Shanin (ed.), *Peasants and Peasant Society*, London: Basil Blackwell.

Root, H.L. (1987) *Peasants and King in Burgundy: Agrarian Foundations of French Absolutism*, Berkeley: University of California Press.

Sartori, G. (1970) "Concept Misformation in Comparative Politics," *American Political Science Review* 64 (4): 1033–53.

Scott, J. (1976) *The Moral Economy of the Peasant*, New Haven, CT: Yale University Press.

Scott, J. (1977a) "Peasant Revolution: A Dismal Science," *Comparative Politics* 9 (1): 231–48.

Scott, J. (1977b) "Protest and Profanation: Agrarian Revolt and the Little Tradition," *Theory and Society* 4 (1): 1–38.

Scott, J. (1979) "Revolution in the Revolution: Peasants and Commissars," *Theory and Society* 7 (1–2): 97–134.

Scott, J. (1985) *Weapons of the Weak: Everyday Forms of Peasant Resistance*, New Haven, CT: Yale University Press.

Scott, J. (1990) *Domination and the Arts of Resistance: Hidden Transcripts*, New Haven, CT: Yale University Press.

Scott, J. (1998) *Seeing Like a State: How Certain Schemes to Improve the Human Condition Have Failed*, New Haven, CT: Yale University Press.

Seligson, M. (1996) "Agrarian Inequality and the Theory of Peasant Rebellion," *Latin American Research Review* 31 (2): 140–57.

Shanin, T. (1971) "Peasantry: Delineation of a Sociological Concept and a Field of Study," *Archives Européennes de Sociologie* 12: 289–300.

Skocpol, T. (1979) *States and Social Revolutions*, Cambridge: Cambridge University Press.

Skocpol, T. (1994) "What Makes Peasants Revolutionary?," in T. Skocpol (ed.), *Social Revolutions in the Modern World*, Cambridge: Cambridge University Press.

Somers, M. and Goldfrank, W. (1979) "The Limits of Agronomic Determinism: A Critique of Paige's *Agrarian Revolution*," *Comparative Studies in Society and History* 21 (3): 443–58.

Thompson, E.P. (1971) "The Moral Economy of the English Crowd in the Eighteenth Century," *Past and Present* 50: 76–136.

Walker, H.A. and Cohen, B.P. (1985) "Scope Statements: Imperatives for Evaluating Theory," *American Sociological Review* 50 (3): 288–301.

Weber, M. (1978) *Economy and Society*, vol. 1, ed. G. Roth and C. Wittich, Berkeley: University of California Press.

Weber, M. (1979) "Developmental Tendencies in the Situation of East Elbian Rural Laborers," *Economy and Society* 8 (2): 177–205.

Wiegersma, N. (1988) *Vietnam: Peasant Land, Peasant Revolution*, New York: St. Martin's Press.

Wolf, E. (1969) *Peasant Wars of the Twentieth Century*, New York: Harper Torch Books.

Wolf, E. (1999) *Envisioning Power: Ideologies of Dominance and Crisis*, Berkeley: University of California Press.

12 Institutionalization

Unpacking the concept and explaining party change

Steven Levitsky

In a debate on the transformation of Latin American party systems, two scholars presented opposing arguments about the relationship between institutionalization and party change. Whereas one argued that the Chilean Socialist Party was able to successfully shift to the center after the late 1980s because it was well institutionalized, the other claimed that, in Argentina, Peronism's shift to the right in this same period was facilitated by its *lack* of institutionalization.[1] This difference, it turned out, was not based on opposing understandings of the causal relationship per se. Rather, it demonstrated the need for more careful conceptualization of institutionalization.

The concept of institutionalization is widely employed in the literature on political parties, but is often poorly or ambiguously defined. Taking as a starting point the idea that such conceptual ambiguity is problematic for social science research (Collier and Levitsky 1997; Sartori 1970, 1984, 1991), this chapter seeks to sort out the meanings of institutionalization that have been employed in studies of political organizations. It argues that the concept of institutionalization has been associated with different organizational phenomena that do not necessarily vary together. Using the case of the (Peronist) Justicialista Party (PJ) in Argentina, I show how these different conceptions of institutionalization can lead to very different scorings of empirical cases. Addressing these inconsistencies can clarify the causal relation between institutionalization and party change, as well as provide a new perspective on the problem that causal arguments about institutionalization can become tautological. I then examine the distinction between formal and informal institutionalization, using the Peronist case to show how intra-party processes that depart significantly from formal rules and procedures may nevertheless still be institutionalized. The chapter concludes by suggesting that analysts of political parties break down the concept of institutionalization into more specific terms: value infusion and routinization, and formal versus informal routinization.

The Peronist case is particularly useful in highlighting some of the ambiguities in the concept of party institutionalization. Peronism has been firmly entrenched in Argentine society – both organizationally and as a political identity – for more than sixty years and, despite decades of proscription and repression, PJ leaders and activists have demonstrated a high degree of loyalty to the party. At the same time, the PJ has long been fluid and unstable in its internal structure. The formal party bureaucracy, as well as its rules and procedures, routinely are ignored. Thus, Peronism is characterized by a combination of strength and endurance on the one hand, and internal fluidity and informality on the other. The dilemmas posed by the effort to characterize this set of organizational features serve to illustrate some broader issues in the study of party institutionalization.

The meanings of institutionalization

A wide range of meanings of institution and institutionalization can be found in the literature on political organizations.[2] Definitions range from a focus on formal rules (Tsebelis 1989: 94) to the inclusion of beliefs, myths, knowledge, and other aspects of culture (March and Olsen 1989: 22). Institutionalization has been associated with phenomena as diverse as bureaucratization (Wellhofer 1972: 156), organizational and electoral stability (Janda 1980: 19–28), "taken-for-grantedness" (Jepperson 1991: 147), infusion with value (Selznick 1957: 17), and the regularization of patterns of social interaction (O'Donnell 1994: 57). Perhaps because these dimensions seem intuitively to "hang together," analysts often treat institutionalization as a cluster of two or more of them. Yet as this chapter argues, many of the phenomena associated with institutionalization do not always vary together empirically, which raises the question of whether they might better be thought of as conceptually distinct.

To develop this argument, this section outlines two predominant conceptualizations of institutionalization employed in the literature on political parties: (1) institutionalization as value infusion, and (2) institutionalization as behavioral routinization. It suggests that although both of these phenomena have widely been associated with institutionalization and have at times been incorporated into a single definition, they are, in fact, distinct.

Institutionalization as value infusion

One well-known definition, which takes as its unit of analysis the organization as a whole, equates institutionalization with what might be called "value infusion" (Huntington 1968; Selznick 1957). According to this definition, institutionalization occurs when an organization becomes "infused with value beyond the technical requirement of the task at hand" (Selznick 1957: 17), or when actors' goals shift from the pursuit of particular objectives *through* an organization to the goal of perpetuating the organization per se. Scholars who employ the value infusion definition tend to be concerned with individuals' valuations of the organizations of which they are a part, and with how those valuations affect the fate of the organization as a whole. According to Selznick (ibid.: 5), a non-institutionalized organization is viewed by its members as an "expendable tool, a rational instrument engineered to do a job." Members or participants value such organizations only to the extent that they help to achieve specific goals. They do not have a stake in the organization's survival beyond its achievement of those goals and, consequently, the organization will be unlikely to survive once the goals change or are met.

Institutionalization, by contrast, is marked by a "concern for self-maintenance." It entails a "prizing of the device for its own sake," whereby the organization is "changed from an expendable tool into a valued source of personal satisfaction" (ibid.: 17–21). Because members of an institutionalized organization feel a personal stake in the perpetuation of the organization, they will seek to preserve it even after this changing or completion of its goals.

Huntington (1968: 12–15) similarly defines institutionalization as a process by which an organization becomes "valued for itself." As an organization becomes institutionalized, its members weaken their commitment to the original goals of the organization but strengthen their commitment to the preservation of the organization itself. The organization "develops a life of its own quite apart from the specific functions it may perform at any given time." Consequently, it becomes more flexible or adaptable, and thus is better able to survive in a changing environment (Huntington 1968: 15–16). Institutionalized parties, then, are those that are able to shift their programmatic or ideological goals when circumstances change. For example, nationalist parties in postcolonial states had to adapt their goals and functions in order to survive in the post-independence period. According to Huntington (ibid.: 17), those parties that undertook this organizational change, such as the Indian Congress Party, were better institutionalized than those that did not.

Institutionalization as behavioral routinization

A second approach to institutionalization takes as its unit of analysis not the organization as a whole, but rather specific patterns of behavior *within* the organization. Analysts who use these definitions focus on the "rules of the game" that shape social interaction, and they define institutionalization as the process by which such rules or patterns become routinized or entrenched (Jepperson 1991; North 1990; O'Donnell 1996). Institutionalization, then, is the entrenchment of the rules of the game.

Scholars who employ the routinization definition tend to be concerned with how behavior is regularized and made predictable. According to North (1990: 3–4), institutions "reduce uncertainty by providing a structure to everyday life." Societal institutions are thus "analogous to the rules of the game in a competitive team sport" in that they structure behavior through a combination of "rules and informal codes." Similarly, O'Donnell (1994: 57–59) defines institutions as "regularized patterns of interaction that are known, practiced, and regularly accepted," as well as the "rules and norms formally or informally embodied in those patterns." Institutionalization is, therefore, a process by which actors' expectations are stabilized around these rules and practices.

Institutionalization in this second sense is understood to constrain actors. The entrenchment of "rules of the game" tends to narrow actors' behavioral options by raising the social, psychic, or material costs of breaking those rules. According to O'Donnell (ibid.: 58), in a context of high institutionalization, individuals "come to expect behaviors within a relatively narrow range of possibilities." Although these actors may not like this narrow range of options, "they anticipate that deviations from such expectations are likely to be counterproductive." Similarly, Jepperson (1991: 148–49) argues that while institutionalized behavior patterns are reproduced through taken-for-granted routines, behavior that departs from institutionalized patterns requires "action," which often entails significant costs. Thus, change in the context of well-institutionalized rules and procedures tends to be difficult, slow, and incremental.

For these scholars, then, institutionalization entails the stabilization or routinization of behavior. When rules, procedures, roles, or other patterns of behavior are institutionalized, they are routinely repeated and taken for granted, and stable sets of expectations form around them. Institutionalized rules and behavior patterns are perceived by individual actors as permanent structures. Such regularization of behavior and expectation patterns is said to be essential for the effective functioning of regimes such as markets (North 1990), party systems (Schedler 1995b), and democracies (O'Donnell 1994).

A single concept?

Party institutionalization may be viewed as the infusion with value of a party organization as a whole, or as the routinization of the rules of the game within a party. Should these two "institutionalizations" be understood to be part of a single phenomenon, or should they be considered conceptually distinct? Scholars have frequently lumped value infusion and routinization into a single concept. In some cases, the two phenomena are simply conflated. For example, Panebianco (1988: 53) defines institutionalization as value infusion, writing that a party is institutionalized when it "becomes valuable in and of itself, and its goals become inseparable and indistinguishable from it." However, in his discussion of how to measure a party's "degree of institutionalization," Panebianco offers indicators of routinization, such as the development of a centralized bureaucracy, stable career paths, homogeneous organizational structures, and an increasing "correspondence between a party's statutory norms and its 'actual power structure'" (58–60).

Other scholars distinguish between value infusion and routinization, but include both dimensions in their concept because they see them as varying together. For example, McGuire (1997: 7–12) argues that a political party is institutionalized "to the extent that the individuals who operate within it infuse it with value, take it for granted, and behave in accordance with its incentives and sanctions." McGuire treats these dimensions as a "syndrome" of distinct, but causally related components, suggesting that value infusion may improve an organization's "capacity to shape and constrain the behavior of the individuals who operate within it." Similarly, Janda (1980: 19) defines an institutionalized party as one that is both "reified in the public mind so that 'the party' exists as a social organization apart from its momentary leaders" and "demonstrates recurring patterns of behavior valued by those who identify with it." His operationalization of the concept includes measures of organizational endurance and electoral stability, as well as the regularity and openness of processes of leadership change.[3]

However, treating value infusion and routinization as part of a single concept potentially has conceptual and analytical costs. Value infusion and routinization are distinct organizational phenomena that do not necessarily occur together. An organization may be infused with value without being internally routinized.[4] For this reason, scholars may be better off distinguishing more clearly between the two types of institutionalization, and perhaps treating them as distinct concepts. To make the case for such a conceptual distinction, the following section uses the example of Peronism, which arguably is infused with value but is not well routinized.

The case of Peronism: value infusion without routinization?

The (Peronist) Justicialista Party (PJ)[5] has been one of the most influential political forces in modern Latin American history. Created as a mass working- and lower-class movement in support of Juan Domingo Peron in the 1940s, Peronism has survived decades of proscription and repression, as well as the death of its charismatic founder in 1974. The PJ remains the largest party in Argentina today. The Peronist identity is deeply rooted in Argentine society, and the party has a strong organizational base among the working and lower classes. Nevertheless, since its founding, the PJ has been characterized by a weak bureaucratic structure, as well as fluid and contested intra-party rules and procedures. Is Peronism well institutionalized or poorly institutionalized?

By the value infusion definition, the PJ may be viewed as relatively well institutionalized. The PJ clearly is "valued for itself" by its members.[6] Peronist leaders and activists have remained committed to the party through periods of severe adversity and despite important changes in the organization's goals and strategies. Perhaps the clearest evidence of the PJ's institutionalization was its survival after the death of Peron in 1974 and its resurgence in the 1980s. Many parties of charismatic origin fail to survive the disappearance of their founders (Panebianco 1988: 162). Despite this fact, and despite the fact that the party was banned and severely repressed by the military governments that ruled between 1976 and 1983, the bulk of Peronist leaders and activists remained committed to the party. The PJ's infusion with value was also evident in the early 1990s, when the vast majority of Peronist leaders and activists remained committed to the party, despite President Carlos Menem's abandonment of the PJ's traditional socio-economic project. For most PJ members, then, the PJ is more than a tool for achieving other ends. Rather, it is widely valued for itself, and it is thus institutionalized in this sense of the term.

However, if one applies the routinization definition of institutionalization to the PJ, a different picture emerges. In terms of the rules of the game that govern the internal life of the party, the PJ is *not* well institutionalized, as intra-party rules and procedures are widely circumvented, manipulated, or contested by Peronist leaders. This under-routinization is, to an important degree, a product of party founder Juan Peron's repeated efforts to thwart the establishment of stable intra-party rules, as well as of the proscription and repression of the party throughout much of the

1955–83 period (McGuire 1997). While the Peronist "renovation" process of the late 1980s brought a greater degree of institutional stability to the party, particularly through the establishment of regular internal elections, it is still far from being internally routinized in comparison with other mass-based parties. Rather than being entrenched or "taken for granted," the rules laid out by the party charter are constantly circumvented or manipulated to suit the short-term political needs of the leadership. Provincial party charters, for example, routinely are modified to allow non-party candidates, or candidates residing in other provinces, to participate in gubernatorial and legislative elections.[7] Infra-party elections are likewise poorly institutionalized. Party leaders commonly negotiate "unity lists" that make elections unnecessary and, in some cases, elections are canceled altogether. The absence of regularized elections is particularly evident at the level of the national leadership, where in the twenty years after the party charter was reformed to permit direct elections for the National Council, not a single competitive election has been held.

The PJ is likewise poorly institutionalized in that it lacks a functioning bureaucratic hierarchy and stable career paths. Since 1989, marginal party leaders, long-time associates of President Menem, and even non-Peronist cultural and sports personalities have routinely been vaulted into the top ranks of the party. Moreover, formal leadership bodies, such as the National Council and National Congress, do not exert the independent authority with which the party charter invests them. Whenever the political orientation of the members of these organizations is out of line with that of the de facto powers in the party, these organizations become virtually irrelevant. Instead, Peronist leaders make and carry out party decisions by means of informal "summits" and parallel organizations. Thus, in terms of the rules and procedures that structure intra-party activity, the PJ must be considered relatively under-institutionalized.

The case of Peronism thus illustrates the observation that value infusion and routinization are distinct phenomena that do not necessarily vary. According to the first criterion, the PJ is arguably well institutionalized, as its members value and seek to preserve the party per se, rather than merely to pursue particular objectives through its organization. According to the second criterion, however, the PJ is poorly institutionalized, as specific organizational procedures within the party leadership structure are not routinized.

Implications for causal analysis

Poorly or ambiguously defined concepts pose a straightforward problem for causal analysis: if we cannot agree on the phenomena we are studying, then arguments about their causes and effects will be confusing and contested. In the present context, the conceptual ambiguity produced by failure to distinguish among the different phenomena associated with institutionalization may undermine our capacity to develop and assess arguments about its consequences. This problem is made clear in scholarly work on party organization.

Definitions and causal analysis

A central concern in the literature on political parties is with the capacity of parties to adapt to changing electoral and policy environments. Scholars have pointed to the degree of institutionalization as an important variable in explaining parties' capacities to adapt (Huntington 1968; Kesselman 1970; Panebianco 1988). Yet different conceptions of institutionalization are associated with opposing arguments about the causal relation between institutionalization and party change. For example, the conception of "value infusion" views institutionalization as facilitating adaptation (Huntington 1968; Roberts 1995), in that members of a valued organization will seek to preserve it even after its original goals have changed or been met (e.g., the YMCA or the March of Dimes). When individuals have a personal or professional stake in an organization's persistence, then the goal of maintaining the organization per se will override particular organizational goals. Members will, in turn, be more likely to accept changes to those goals in order to ensure the organization's survival. When an organization is not valued for itself, then its members – upon realizing that the organization is no longer an effective means to the goals they are pursuing – will be more likely to abandon the organization rather than seek to preserve it.

By contrast, the conception of "routinization" treats institutionalization, particularly formal institutionalization, as reducing adaptability (Jepperson 1991; Kitschelt 1994; Schedler 1995a). Some argue that to the extent that organizational rules, procedures, and roles become entrenched, it becomes more difficult for actors to change them. According to Panebianco (1988: 58), a high degree of institutionalization within a political party "drastically limits its internal actors' margins of maneuverability," as the organization "imposes itself upon the actors" and "channels their strategies into specific and obligatory paths." As a result, whereas weakly institutionalized parties may experience sudden transformations, organizational change in well-institutionalized parties generally takes place "slowly and laboriously." Similarly, Kitschelt (1994: 213) argues that in highly bureaucratized parties, a "plethora of rules of decision making" tends to limit the party leadership's capacity to carry out "innovation from above," while strict career paths instill conformity in lower-level leaders and thus limit "innovation from below."

Thus, the value infusion and routinization definitions are associated with opposing causal arguments about the relation between institutionalization and the capacity of organizations to adapt and survive in response to changing environmental conditions. Again, the case of Peronism helps to illustrate the analytic problems generated by this conceptual ambiguity. On the one hand, the Menem leadership's capacity to carry out far-reaching programmatic change in the PJ after 1989 can be said to have been facilitated by the party's institutionalization in the value infusion sense. Because their attachment to Peronism overrode their commitment to the party's original socio-economic project, most Peronist leaders and activists remained committed to the party even after Menem had abandoned that project. On the other hand, it can be argued that the post-1989 Peronist adaptation was facilitated by the party's under-institutionalization in the sense of routinization. Two specific factors contributed to this outcome. First, the fluidity of the PJ bureaucracy permitted the rapid rise of reformers within the party. Second, the absence of established rules and procedures to govern the party hierarchy provided the Menem leadership with a substantial amount of room for maneuver. These two factors arguably contributed to both the speed and the degree of the PJ's programmatic change (Levitsky 1995). The Peronist transformation under Menem can thus be attributed to *both high and low* levels of institutionalization, underscoring the need to unpack the concept.

The question of tautology

Another important issue concerning institutionalization and organizational adaptation involves the problem of tautology. Arguments about the relation between institutionalization and organizational adaptation have been criticized for failing to separate the explanation from the outcome they are trying to explain.[9] If, for example, organizational adaptation and survival simultaneously are treated as indicators of institutionalization and products of it, then causal inferences become meaningless (Remmer 1997; Sigalman 1979: 215; Tilly 1973: 431).

To make a causal argument about the relation between institutionalization and organizational adaptation, one must be able to show independent observations of institutionalization and adaptation. In the case of the value infusion definition, this entails demonstrating that members valued the organization at some point prior to the episode of organizational change. For example, in the case of Peronism, one could point to continued rank-and-file commitment to Peronism after the death of Peron as a prior indicator of value infusion.

In the case of the routinization definition there is less risk of tautology, because the outcome to be explained (in this case, a change in organizational goals) is not treated as an aspect of institutionalization. Rather, certain features of the organization, such as fluidity of rules or career paths, may be said to directly facilitate the change in goals. A problem of tautology arises here only if changes in rules or leadership turnover themselves were used as indicators of party transformation, rather than as facilitating conditions.

Formal versus informal routinization

In addition to the distinction between value infusion and routinization, the case of Peronism helps to highlight another distinction that has not been adequately conceptualized in the literature on political parties: that of formal versus informal routinization.[10] Guillermo O'Donnell (1996: 40) recently criticized studies of Latin American democratization for focusing almost exclusively on the formal rules and procedures of new democratic regimes, and not paying enough attention to "the actual rules that are being followed." Although these informal rules and procedures function outside the scope of formal constitutional or legal frameworks, O'Donnell argues that they are often "widely shared and deeply rooted."

The idea of informal routinization is, of course, not new. Social scientists have long pointed out that there is often a "great gap between the formal and the informal organization" (Meyer and Rowan, 1991: 43), and many contemporary "institutionalists" focus primarily on the latter (March and Olsen 1989; Powell and Dimaggio 1991). In the political parties literature, work on political clientelism and machine politics (Banfield and Wilson 1963; Scott 1969) has pointed to the divergence between formal rules and informal practices. Nevertheless, informal institutions have not been systematically incorporated into scholars' conceptualizations of party institutionalization. Much of the literature on political parties treats routinization as a process by which actual behavior is brought into line with formal rules and procedures. Wellhofer (1972: 156), for example, defines institutionalization as "synonymous with the formalization and bureaucratization of organizations," while Panebianco (1988: 58–62) associates party institutionalization with a greater "correspondence between statutory norms and the actual power structure." From such a perspective, informal behavior patterns, no matter how routinized, are viewed as phenomena that deviate from, or even undermine, institutionalization. Such an exclusive focus on the correspondence between formal rules and actual behavior runs the risk of missing important aspects of intra-party life. It leads one to ignore or understate the degree to which intra-party politics is structured by stable, regularized patterns of behavior that nevertheless depart from (or are unrelated to) formal rules and procedures.

Again, the case of Peronism is useful in developing this point. As noted above, from a formal standpoint, the PJ is poorly routinized. Yet in at least some respects, and particularly at the base level, intra-party activity is structured in a relatively stable way by informal rules and practices. One example of such informal institutionalization is the "62 Organizations," an informal trade union alliance that for decades was widely recognized by Peronists as the "labor branch" of Peronism. Although the "62" lacked formal statutes, regularized meetings, and a formal position within the party structure (McGuire 1992: 40), its role as the political representative of organized labor within Peronism was virtually unquestioned between the late 1950s and the mid-1980s.

Other examples of informal institutions can be found at the base level of Peronism. Base-level Peronist activity is, from a formal standpoint, poorly routinized. Local party branches, *unidades básicas* (base units), operate almost entirely at the margins of local party authorities. The vast majority of them are not financed by, subject to the discipline of, or even officially registered with local party authorities. In practice, any individual can open up a base unit, and in any location. Yet an exclusive focus on the formal party organization risks missing the important degree to which base-level Peronist activity is, in fact, routinized.

Despite the fact that local base units rarely carry out the functions assigned to them in the party charter, much of the activity that takes place within them is rooted in widely shared norms and expectations about how to "do Peronism." Indeed, base-level Peronism exhibits a range of practices that, while not written down in the party charter or any party manual, are widely known and remarkably similar across territorial units. These include the celebration of important Peronist dates such as

Eva Peron's birthday and Peronist Loyalty Day, organizational forms such as informal "working groups" and *agrupaciones*, and mobilizational techniques such as the singing of the Peronist March, the formation of youth graffiti painting brigades, and the use of the *bombo* (big drum) at Peronist rallies. The practice of neighborhood "social work" is particularly widespread. All Peronist base units engage in activities such as the distribution of food, clothing, and medicine, the organization of youth activities, or the operation of a retirees' center. Although they undoubtedly serve clientelistic ends, these activities entail more than the simple exchange of goods for political support. Rather, they are embedded in established and widely shared traditions, roles, language, and symbols that center around Peronist notions of "social justice" and images of Eva Peron (Auyero 1997).[11]

Peronism is by no means unique in its informal routinization. Case studies of political parties have long demonstrated how informal behavior deviates in regularized ways from formal party statutes.[12] Definitions that focus exclusively on formal rules and procedures fail to capture such routinization. Still, most comparative and theoretical work on political parties does not incorporate informal rules and procedures into discussions of party institutionalization. These informal patterns must be conceptualized and theorized in a more systematic manner.

Conclusion: unpacking institutionalization

The concept of institutionalization has not been clearly or consistently defined in the literature on political parties. The category encompasses diverse phenomena that frequently are assumed to cluster together, such as bureaucratization, electoral stability, value infusion, and regularized patterns of interaction. The case of Peronism compels us to question that assumption. The clustering of what are, in fact, distinct forms of institutionalization into a single concept is problematic for causal analysis for, as the Peronist case shows, different understandings of institutionalization generate opposing causal claims about the relationship between institutionalization and party change.

In the light of these ambiguities, it is worth suggesting that the concept of institutionalization be unpacked. Rather than lump together several different dimensions into a single concept, it may be more fruitful to break the concept down into its component meanings and to use more specific terms. This chapter argues that value infusion and routinization should be conceptualized as distinct phenomena. Value infusion is a process in which organizational actors' goals shift from the pursuit of particular objectives through the organization to the goal of preserving or perpetuating the organization per se. Routinization, on the other hand, is the regularization of patterns of social interaction, or the entrenchment of the "rules of the game." This disaggregated approach should also be extended to the formal–informal distinction. Thus, the concept of routinization can be broken down into the categories of formal and informal routinization. With a tight fit between formal rules and procedures and real patterns of behavior, these rules and procedures may be said to be formally routinized. Where behavior does not conform closely to formal rules, but nevertheless follows patterns or routines that are well established and widely shared, it is considered to be informally routinized. Finally, where no stable rules of the game (either formal or informal) structure social interaction, one may speak of non-routinization.

Parties may combine these forms of institutionalization in different ways. Some parties, such as several European social democratic parties, score high on both the value infusion and routinization, while others, like many parties in Brazil, score low on both dimensions (Mainwaring 1995). In other instances, parties' scores on the two dimensions diverge. For example, the PJ is relatively infused with value but not well routinized. Alternatively, parties may exhibit a significant degree of routinization without a high level of value infusion. Some European green parties may approach this category, in that they often exhibit a strong emphasis on intra-party democratic procedures, yet many activists prioritize ideological goals over the defense of the organization. Parties also differ on the dimension of formal versus informal routinization. Whereas European mass bureaucratic parties exhibit relatively high levels of formal routinization, clientelistic or machine-based parties may be said to be informally routinized.

These different combinations underscore the need to disaggregate institutionalization into a set of more specific concepts that refer to the particular organizational phenomena that scholars are trying to capture. The use of more specific terms would be an important step toward a much-needed clarification of this important, yet ambiguous concept. Not only would such specification permit scholars to focus more concretely on the mechanisms by which organizations or behavior patterns are reproduced, but it would also improve our analyses of the consequences of such phenomena.

Acknowledgments

Christopher Ansell, Javier Auyero, David Collier, Sebastian Etchemendy, James McGuire, and Pierre Ostiguy, as well as two anonymous reviewers for *Party Politics*, made helpful comments on earlier versions of this chapter.

Notes

* Originally published as Steven Levitsky (1998) "Institutionalization and Peronism: The Concept, the Case, and the Case for Unpacking the Concept," *Party Politics* 4 (1): 77–92.

1 Panel on economic liberalization and the transformation of Latin American party systems at the 19th International Congress of the Latin American Studies Association. See Levitsky (1995) and Roberts (1995).
2 For detailed discussions of the meaning of party and party system institutionalization, see Welfling (1973: 5–13), Janda (1980: 19–28, 143–44), Mainwaring and Scully (1995), and McGuire (1997: 7–12).
3 Janda (1980: 143–44) finds a significant degree of correlation among four of his indicators of institutionalization: party age, electoral stability, legislative stability, and leadership competition.
4 O'Donnell (1996) makes a similar argument with respect to democratic institutions in

many Latin American countries. He notes that whereas democracy itself may be valued and well established in many countries, the internal "games" within those democracies often are quite fluid.

5 It is important to clarify what is meant by "party" in the Peronist case. Following Sartori's (1976: 64) definition of a party as "any political group that presents at elections, and is capable of placing through elections, candidates for public office," I treat as part of the PJ all Peronist organizations whose primary function is to compete for party offices and candidacies. This definition does not encompass non-electoral organizations such as trade unions or the Peronist paramilitary and guerrilla organizations that existed in the 1970s. It does, however, include the wide range of local "base units," *agrupaciones* and other informal or semiformal organizations that, though not formally part of the PJ bureaucracy, participate regularly in the competition for PJ candidacies and leadership positions. This distinction is important because the formal PJ bureaucracy historically has been undervalued by Peronists, leading McGuire (1997) to conclude that the PJ is not institutionalized in the value infusion sense. Although McGuire is correct in stating that the party bureaucracy is not infused with value, I find it essential to distinguish sharply between the party bureaucracy and the party as a whole. The bulk of Peronist political activity takes place outside the party bureaucracy, but *within* other informal party organizations. While Peronists may ignore or circumvent the party bureaucracy, there is no question that they value and invest in the party as a whole.

6 This was arguably not the case in the mid-1970s, when important groups within Peronism – particularly paramilitary groups on the right and left – either ignored the party entirely or sought to use it as a tool for other ends.

7 For example, the Federal Capital PJ altered the party charter (which stipulates that candidates be registered in the district party for two years) in 1992, 1993, and 1997 to allow "outsiders" to run as Peronist candidates. A similar modification of the party charter allowed automobile racer Carlos Reutemann and pop singer "Palito" Ortega to run for governor of Santa Fe and Tucuman, respectively, in 1991.

8 In the federal capital in 1992, for example, the PJ modified its party charter to proclaim non-party member Avelino Porto the Peronist Senate candidate without an internal election (*Clarín*, March 28, 1992, p. 6). In the province of Buenos Aires, internal elections for the 1995 national deputy and mayor candidacies were canceled by the party congress, and the party leadership was given a "special mandate" to name the candidates (*Clarín*, December 18, 1994, pp. 12–13).

9 Huntingon's (1968) use of the term institutionalization has been criticized in this manner; see Tilly (1973) and Sigalman (1979).

10 Note that the formal–informal distinction made in this section applies only to the routinization component of institutionalization.

11 Auyero (1997) aptly characterizes this set of practices as "performing Evita."

12 For example, in his study of the Democratic Party in the US South, V.O. Key (1949) describes the informal rules and practices that structured intra-party life in the first half of the twentieth century. A more recent example is Appleton's (1994) study of French parties, which finds that informal practices are often more important than formal ones in structuring infra-party behavior. Other examples include work on the Daley machine in Chicago (Gosnell 1968; Rakove 1975) and the Indian Congress Party (Morris-Jones 1966; Weiner 1967). For a discussion of the emergence of informal institutions in a Leninist party, see Jowitt's (1983) work on Soviet "neotraditionalism."

References

Appleton, A. (1994) "The Formal Rules Versus Informal Rules of French Political Parties," in Kay Lawson (ed.), *How Political Parties Work: Perspectives From Within*, Westport, CT: Praeger.

Auyero, J. (1997) "Performing Evita: Brokerage and Problem-solving Among Urban Poor in Argentina," paper prepared for delivery at the 20th meeting of the Latin American Studies Association, Guadalajara, Mexico, April 17–19.

Banfield, E.C. and Wilson, J.Q. (1963) *City Politics*, Cambridge, MA: Harvard University Press.

Collier, D. and Levitsky, S. (1997) "Democracy With Adjectives: Conceptual Innovation in Comparative Research," *World Politics* 49: 430–51.

Gosnell, H.F. (1968) *Machine Politics: Chicago Model*, Chicago: University of Chicago Press.

Huntington, S.P. (1968) *Political Order in Changing Societies*, New Haven, CT: Yale University Press.

Janda, K. (1980) *Political Parties: A Cross-National Survey*, New York: Free Press.

Jepperson, R. (1991) "Institutions, Institutional Effects, and Institutionalism," in W.W. Powell and P.J. Dimaggio (eds.), *The New Institutionalism in Organizational Analysis*, Chicago: University of Chicago Press.

Jowitt, K. (1983) "Soviet Neotraditionalism: The Political Corruption of a Leninist Regime," *Soviet Studies* 35: 275–97.

Kesselman, M. (1970) "Overinstitutionalization and Political Constraint: The Case of France," *Comparative Politics* 3: 21–44.

Key, V.O., Jr. (1949) *Southern Politics in State and Nation*, New York: Alfred A. Knopf.

Kitschelt, H. (1994) *The Transformation of European Social Democracy*, Cambridge: Cambridge University Press.

Levitsky, S. (1995) "Populism is Dead! Long Live the Populist Party! Labor-based Party Adaptation and Survival in Argentina," paper presented at the meeting of the Latin American Studies Association, Washington, DC, September 28–30.

Mainwaring, S. (1995) "Brazil: Weak Parties, Feckless Democracy," in S. Mainwaring and T.R. Scully (eds.), *Building Democratic Institutions: Party Systems in Latin America*, Stanford: Stanford University Press.

Mainwaring, S. and Scully, T.R. (eds.) (1995) *Building Democratic Institutions: Party Systems in Latin America*, Stanford: Stanford University Press.

March, J.G. and Olsen, J.P. (1989) *Rediscovering Institutions: The Organizational Basis of Politics*, New York: Free Press.

McGuire, J. (1992) "Union Political Tactics and Democratic Consolidation in Alfonsin's Argentina, 1983–1989," *Latin American Research Review* 27: 37–74.

McGuire, J. (1997) *Peronism Without Peron: Unions, Parties, and Democracy in Argentina*, Stanford: Stanford University Press.

Meyer, J.W. and Rowan, B. (1991) "Institutionalized Organizations: Formal Structure as Myth and Ceremony," in W.W. Powell and P.J. Dimaggio (eds.), *The New Institutionalism in Organizational Analysis*, Chicago: University of Chicago Press.

Morris-Jones, W.H. (1966) "Dominance and Dissent: Their Inter-relations in the Indian Party System," *Government and Opposition* 1: 451–66.

North, D.C. (1990) *Institutions, Institutional Change and Economic Performance*, New York: Cambridge University Press.

O'Donnell, G. (1994) "Delegative Democracy," *Journal of Democracy* 5: 55–69.

O'Donnell, G. (1996) "Illusions About Consolidation," *Journal of Democracy* 7: 34–51.

Panebianco, A. (1988) *Political Parties: Organization and Power*, Cambridge: Cambridge University Press.

Powell, W.W. and Dimaggio, P.J. (eds.) (1991) *The New Institutionalism in Organizational Analysis*, Chicago: University of Chicago Press.

Rakove, M.R. (1975) *Don't Make No Waves, Don't Back No Losers: An Insider's Analysis of the Daley Machine*, Bloomington: Indiana University Press.

Remmer, K. (1997) "Theoretical Decay and Theoretical Development: The Resurgence of Institutional Analysis," *World Politics* 50 (1): 34–61.

Roberts, K. (1995) "The Neoliberal 'Critical Juncture' and the Transformation of Party Systems: A Comparison of Peru and Chile," paper presented at the meeting of the Latin American Studies Association, Washington, DC, September 28–30.

Sartori, G. (1970) "Concept Misformation in Comparative Politics," *American Political Science Review* 64: 1033–53.

Sartori, G. (1976) *Parties and Party Systems: A Framework for Analysis*, Cambridge: Cambridge University Press.

Sartori, G. (1984) "Guidelines for Concept Analysis," in G. Sartori (ed.), *Social Science Concepts: A Systematic Analysis*, Beverly Hills, CA: Sage.

Sartori, G. (1991) "Comparing and Miscomparing," *Journal of Theoretical Politics* 3: 243–57.

Schedler, A. (1995a) "Under- and Overinstitutionalization: Some Ideal Typical Propositions Concerning New and Old Party Systems," Kellogg Institute Working Paper 213.

Schedler, A. (1995b) "Credibility: Exploring the Bases of Institutional Reform in New Democracies," paper presented at the 19th International Congress of the Latin American Studies Association, Washington, DC, September 28–30.

Scott, J.C. (1969) "Corruption, Machine Politics, and Political Change," *American Political Science Review* 63: 1142–58.

Selznick, P. (1957) *Leadership in Administration: A Sociological Interpretation*, New York: Harper & Row.

Sigalman, L. (1979) "Understanding Political Instability: An Evaluation of the Mobilization-Institutionalization Approach," *Comparative Political Studies* 12: 205–28.

Tilly, C. (1973) "Does Modernization Breed Revolution?," *Comparative Politics* 5: 425–47.

Tsebelis, G. (1989) *Nested Games: Rational Choice in Comparative Politics*, New York: Free Press.

Weiner, M. (1967) *Party Building in a New Nation: The Indian National Congress*, Chicago: University of Chicago Press.

Welfling, M.B. (1973) *Political Institutionalization: Comparative Analyses of African Party Systems*, Beverly Hills, CA: Sage.

Wellhofer, E.S. (1972) "Dimensions of Party Development: A Study in Organizational Dynamics," *Journal of Politics* 34: 152–82.

Part III
In the academy and beyond

13 Chance, luck, and stubbornness

An autobiographical essay

Giovanni Sartori

I was born in Florence, Italy, in 1924. I thus have vivid memories of Fascism, of the war with Abyssinia, of the Spanish Civil War (in which Franco was assisted by Italian soldiers), and, of course, of World War II. It goes without saying that my lifelong concern about democracy – solid rather than advanced democracy – arises out of these "dark" memories of Fascism and Nazism. I will tell, therefore, of fortuitous side effects.

Italy's war in alliance with Hitler ended in surrender on September 8, 1943. In that year, I had expected to be and dreaded being drafted (I was nineteen) and sent to war. But the Italian military machine was, after all, Italian and thus behind schedule. My call to arms came up only in October 1943, and came from the newly installed Fascist puppet regime known as the Republic of Salò. Like most of my peers, I sought escape in hiding. The penalty for deserters was, however, to be shot on the spot, and whoever hid a deserter equally risked his or her life. I thus spent some ten months "buried" (for I was not allowed even to be seen within the household) in a somewhat hidden room until Florence was liberated from German occupation in August 1944. What does one do in just one sealed room for almost a year? Remembering *de consolatione philosophiae*, that consolation was in philosophy, I read Hegel and the two dominant Italian idealist philosophers of the time: Benedetto Croce and Giovanni Gentile. Aside from consolation, it took me one day to read ten, at most fifteen, pages of Hegel. At the end of the day I was definitely exhausted and ready for bed. So, just a handful of books (a great convenience under the circumstances) did the trick of getting me through to the end of the war in Florence. It established for future consumption my reputation as a philosopher well read in the arcana of philosophy – a reputation that brought me, suddenly and quite unexpectedly, into academe in 1950. Just as I had not intended to become a philosopher, I had not planned either to become a professor. Both happenings just happened.

I earned my doctorate in social and political sciences at the University of Florence in November 1946, and for the next four years I had nothing better to do than to linger on. The country was largely in a shambles and the university had many of its "barons" (i.e., tenured professors) under purge, suspended, or indicted for having been Fascists. Since I was considered an *enfant prodige* (remember, I was supposedly able to understand Hegel), I immediately was appointed assistant to the chair of General Theory of the State – the equivalent of the German *Staatslehre* – and in fact my assistance went as far as to do almost all the teaching in lieu of my frequently absent professor. His name was Pompeo Biondi. He never was a diligent teacher, but had a wonderfully bright mind. Pompeo (as we called him, for he was a heavy, impressive man who deserved a pompous name) implicitly taught me one thing: that intelligence *cum* ignorance (he had little time and less patience for reading) is preferable to erudition *cum* dullness. But since I could not match his wits, it struck me (second lesson) that I had to have my bibliographies in order. I have always read a lot.

Cursus honorum – career path

Now the story of how it happened that I found – or authoritatively was given – my vocation, my *Beruf*. The year was 1950. At a faculty meeting, the Dean, Maranini, told his unsuspecting colleagues that he had a promising young marvel to propose: Giovanni Spadolini, who was then 25 years old (one year younger than I was), and later became managing editor of the *Corriere della Sera* (the major Italian daily paper), minister, prime minister, and president of the Senate, and just missed by a hair's breadth the presidency of the Republic. As this record shows, Maranini had indeed picked a winner. But Pompeo, my boss, could not accept the loss of face of not having a candidate of his own. On the spur of the moment, he proposed me (as his counter-genius), and the first vacant teaching post that flashed across his mind was History of Modern Philosophy. The deal was struck – both Spadolini *and* Sartori – and I was appointed on the spot "*professore incaricato*" (assistant and/or associate professor: there was no difference at that time). I was unsuspecting and was just informed the next day that I had to teach history of philosophy (as I did for six years, 1950–56).[1] Since then, I have believed that *fortuna*, chance, luck, matters a lot in life – certainly not less than *virtù*.

Remember that philosophy was, for me, a war "accident." I was mainly interested in logic, not in philosophers. But logic was not taught in Italian universities and was, indeed, anathema for both idealistic philosophy and Marxist dialectics (the dominant schools). I had to work my way out. It would take too long to rehearse how a combination of stubbornness but also, again, of fortunate coincidences allowed me to move to political science. Skipping all the many amusing anecdotes,[2] by 1956 I had managed to have political science entered in the statute (the list of recognized and permitted teachings) of the Florence Faculty of Political Sciences, which had previously encompassed teaching on law, history, economics, statistics, geography, philosophy. I was able to switch (always as a *professore incaricato*) to this entirely novel and, for many, suspect academic discipline.

Professionally, it was not a clever move. I was told by all my friends (including Spadolini, by then a sort of twin brother) that it was a very stupid one. In order to become a full professor in the Italian academic system, one had to pass a national competition which selected three winners. Since I was alone and the discipline had little if any recognition, had I been a rational, calculating animal I would have reckoned that the date at which I could expect tenure had to be located around the year

2000 – somewhat too late for me. But at times – another lesson for posterity – one can win without expecting victory. What mattered to me was to study what I liked and to pioneer a new discipline. As for the *cursus honorum* (career path), why not leave it, again, to luck? In fact, it turned out that *fortuna* was once more on my side. By 1963 (it took me seven years of waiting, but still much less than my statistics predicted), I was the first and only tenured professor of political science in Italy. To be sure, I had to use a back door: I won a chair in sociology. But once "chaired," it was easy for me to return to political science. Against all odds, I had made it. The next and immediate task was to promote and establish the discipline.[3]

Political science in Italy

I must now take a step back. Why political science? And, further, how did I conceive the discipline and land in comparative politics? In truth, I am only a part-time comparativist. My work can be divided in three slices: (1) straightforward political theory; (2) methodological writings where methodology is understood as the method of *logos*, of thinking, not as a misnomer for research techniques; and (3) comparative politics proper.

The political theory slice is best exemplified by my writings on democracy: the early *Democrazia e Definizioni* (1957, with some ten subsequent reprints), *Democratic Theory* (1962b), *The Theory of Democracy Revisited* (1987b);[4] and also by *Elementi di Teoria Politica* (1987a). The methodological slice is represented mainly by the writings collected in the volume *La Politica: Logica e Metodo in Scienze Sociali* (1979) and, in English, by my "Guidelines for Concept Analysis" in *Systematic Analysis* (Sartori 1984), as well as by my articles on the comparative method, to which I shall come later. Finally, the comparative politics slice is represented by *Parties and Party Systems: A Framework for Analysis* (1976),[5] and recently by *Comparative Constitutional Engineering* (1994).

While I make fun of myself by saying that I am a specialist in everything, in fact there is a strong consistency among my seemingly eclectic wanderings. The backbone of all my work harks back to my philosophical beginning (in which in career terms I have invested much "lost" time, but with no regret), for a theoretical-analytical awareness underlies my comparative writings just as much as the theoretical and methodological ones. Be that as it may, let me now address my previous questions, beginning with: why did I choose to become a political scientist?

Since my student days, it had struck me that in Italy we had faculties of political sciences in which there was, in fact, no study of politics itself. In our faculties – as noted above – we had law, a fair amount of history, some economics, statistics, geography, philosophy, but no teaching that enabled students to understand politics. My long-fought battle for introducing political science in the curriculum of faculties that called themselves (with little justification) "of political sciences" was prompted, then, by what I perceived as a logical point: how can we have political sciences in the plural without a political science in the singular that explains what all the rest is about?

To be sure, I did not discover political science because I had to satisfy a logical requirement. While as a *politologo* I was largely self-taught (I had no teachers). In learning by myself, I could and did rely on the international context (the IPSA context), on my entering the path-breaking IPSA Committee of Political Sociology (where I made lifelong outstanding friends: Marty Lipset, Juan Linz, Stein Rokkan, Mattei Dogan, Hans Daalder, S. N. Eisenstadt),[6] and on the initial exposure to American political science in 1949–50, when I was in the United States on a post-doctoral fellowship.

The next question is: how did I conceive the discipline? In the Italian context, this was a relevant question because my understanding of political science did shape the views of a profession that was nurtured at the Institute of Political Science of the University of Florence and thus, willy-nilly, under my wings. In this respect, the development of political science in Italy has been unique, and symmetrically different from the German one. The German *Politische Wissenschaft* came about early on, with one large distribution of chairs which had to be filled – there was no alternative – with lateral entries. Even Voegelin, a scholar whom I personally liked and respected, but who certainly was no political scientist, returned to Germany as a *Politische Wissenschaft* professor in Munich. The converse happened in Italy: the growth was slow and, so to speak, unicentric, spreading out as it were from Florence. So, what did I teach to a selected group of post-doctoral neophytes during the mid-1960s?

My understanding of political science undoubtedly bore an American imprint.[7] In a country in which the expression "merely empirical" was derogatory – it meant that something had no heuristic value – I claimed that political science differed from political philosophy precisely in that it was an empirical science. But since I had to explain what an Englishman would know by instinct, I also stressed that empirical knowledge had to be, at some point, applied or "applicable" knowledge (Sartori 1974, 1979). It was already at this juncture, then, that I parted company with the American behavioral slant. In the United States, the discipline forsook the theory–practice connection and went wholesale for the theory–research relationship. Along this route, theory became largely atrophied into mere research design, research became a sort of end in itself, the question "science for what?" was ignored, and little was left, at the end, other than operationalization, quantification, and statistical treatment of ever growing masses of data. I have always resisted all of that.

To be sure, I endorsed the notion of a research-based science. But I never was converted to behavioralism. I have always insisted on a "theory-rich" discipline monitored by a sound training in logic and method ("methodology"); I never believed in a "superior" quantified science; and above all, as I have already pointed out, emphasis always had to be on the conversion of theory into practice, and thus on "operative" (not operational) science. In my view, political scientists are, like economists, required to know (at least better than laymen) how problems can be solved, which reforms are likely to work and, in a nutshell, to have "know-how." Economists are trained to advise, the American-bred political scientist is not. But why not? That has always been my question (see Sartori 1968c).

So, how do we acquire a practice-oriented knowledge? The test is, of course, pragmatic – that is to say, success in application. If we intervene in something, and if the outcome conforms to the intent, that is, turns out as predicted, then we have applied our applicable knowledge. But this can be a very costly test. Finding out by trial and error involves a lot of error, and we are not speaking here of laboratory tests but of human beings eventually used as guinea pigs. We must, I thought, do better than that. And, finally, here enters comparative politics.

I do not remember what came first, whether I stumbled into the importance of comparing at the 1954 IPSA Round Table in Florence, at which comparative politics was indeed the issue (and was hotly debated between the "Young Turks" led by Macridis and the senior scholars of the time, especially Carl Friedrich and Karl Loewenstein), or whether the notion that "comparing is controlling" had already been lingering in my mind in the context of my methodological ruminations. At any rate, I was at the time in charge of a quarterly, *Studi Politici*, in which I quickly published the papers of the IPSA Round Table, introduced by a preface of mine. Since then, I have argued that comparative politics was the very core of political science, for comparisons were a means, indeed the major method, for controlling our generalizations. Is it the case that working democracies are, and must be, of the Anglo-American or Scandinavian type, as Almond held in the 1950s? Do revolutions arise from relative deprivation? Did Duverger hypothesize valid laws on the influence of electoral systems? These and innumerable similar questions can and should be tested vis-à-vis the cases to which they apply, that is, by means of a comparative checking.

This has been the methodological tenet on which I have insisted in several essays since the 1950s.[8] This is actually the backbone of *Parties and Party Systems* and, more recently, of *Comparative Constitutional Engineering*. In both works, I insistently generalize and test comparatively. In the first, however, I adopt a structural-functional approach,[9] while the second leans heavily on "condition analysis." But both works are, so to speak, thickly comparative: whenever I provide causal explanations and make general assertions, I scan through, and control with, all the polities (as many as I manage to know of) that fall under any given generalization.

The American impact

Thus far, I have somewhat pictured myself as a self-propelled scholar performing on his own. I must now correct this one-sided account. While I did influence the development of Italian political science in a unique manner,[10] it is quite evident that had I not been exposed to the science of politics that blossomed after World War II in the United States, I would have been an entirely different scholar. After the early grant that brought me to New York in 1949–50 (shopping between Columbia and the New School for Social Research), I returned many times to the United States in the 1960s, first as a Visiting Professor of Government at Harvard (1964–65), and subsequently as a recurrent Visiting Professor of Political Science at Yale between 1966 and 1969. The Yale arrangement (Stein Rokkan, Shlomo Avineri, and I were supposed to rotate for a semester each) broke down in my case with the campus revolution, for under its first assaults I was elected Dean of my Faculty in Florence and had to live through the turbulence of 1969 and its aftermath in *loco*. In 1971–72, pretty much worn out by some three years of battles (it was quite rough in Italy), I went to Stanford, where I spent a delightful and fruitful year "on the hill" as a fellow of the Center for Advanced Study in the Behavioral Sciences. Thereafter, in 1976, I somewhat suddenly decided to leave Italy. Early in that year, S. E. Finer, a wonderful friend and scholar, tried to get me over to Oxford, where the sudden death of John Plamenatz had opened one of the Chichele professorships; and at exactly the same time Stanford offered me the position that Gabriel Almond was leaving for retirement. Both were very flattering offers. The last I heard about the Chichele chair (which went to Charles Taylor) was that I was one vote short. However, as Sammy Finer was telling me on the phone about my Oxford chances, I told him that Stanford had accepted my demands and that I had in turn accepted the position there. I have never known whether I had lost or might still have won the Chichele competition.

Why did I leave? Well, I had spent more than a quarter of a century (that is how I put it to myself) as a professor at the University of Florence, and I had the feeling that there was nothing more that I could accomplish there, that my Italian cycle was over. The first wave of my pupils was already well placed across the country, Italian political science had attained sufficient momentum to keep going on its own,[11] and I felt the need to work just for myself. Stanford put all the distance from Italy that I needed. But then, out of the blue, I received an offer from New York that could not be refused. After three years, in 1979, I left Stanford and became Albert Schweitzer Professor in the Humanities at Columbia University, where (since 1994) I am Professor Emeritus.

This quick account suffices to indicate the extent of my exposure to American political science. At Harvard I met, or got to know better, Carl Friedrich, Talcott Parsons, Sam Beer, Sam Huntington, Henry Kissinger; at Yale, Robert Dahl, Harold Lasswell, Karl Deutsch, Charles Lindblom, David Apter, Joe LaPalombara; at Stanford, Gabriel Almond, Marty Lipset, Robert Ward; at Columbia, Robert Merton (I had attended his class in 1950), Zbigniew Brzezinski, Severyn Bialer, and others. One always benefits from the company of good, indeed very good, minds. But reading is, as a rule, more important.

The work that perhaps influenced me more than any other was Dahl's *A Preface to Democratic Theory* (1956). When I read it, I was thunderstruck by Dahl's method, by his systematic analysis of "conditions" (an exercise that Dahl repeated in the early 1960s, under my ever-admiring eyes, at the Bellagio Rockefeller Center for the volume *Political Oppositions in Western Democracies*, 1966). In earlier days, I had been very impressed by Friedrich's *Constitutional Government and Democracy* (1946), a superb achievement considering that its first draft went back to the late 1930s. Another author to whom I owe innumerable insights is Gabriel Almond. Even though I lament that Almond did not really accomplish the structural-functional program outlined in *The Politics of the Developing Areas* (1960, a truly masterful essay), in methodology courses and teaching I have insisted that, among the competing paradigms, models, and approaches that have been flooding the discipline, structural functionalism stands out, if properly implemented, as the more fruitful scheme of analysis. Also, and to conclude the section on my intellectual debts (with some injustice, for I am obliged to be brief), the Princeton Political Development series displays, in my opinion, the very best of what American comparative politics has collectively produced to date.

An assessment

Let me now come to the straightforward question: was my moving to the United States the right step? And how should the American segment of my academic life be judged?

As my pedigree shows, I knew the United States too well to expect success. My success was in having been offered (just in time!) two prestigious positions. But by the end of the 1970s it was very clear to me that American political science had entered a path that I neither would nor could accept: the pattern of excessive specialization (and thus narrowness), excessive quantification and, by the same token, a path leading – in my opinion – to irrelevance and sterility. While sweeping generalizations must allow for many exceptions, still if one compares the *American Political Science Review* of twenty or thirty years ago to the *Review* of the last decade, the difference is striking, or even stunning. And if my methodological caveats and criticisms are correct,[12] then much of what American political science currently is producing must be quite wrong.

Based on these reflections, one might conclude that I arrived in the wrong place at the wrong time. Yet I take a kinder view of myself. While my work has never made a splash on American soil (unsurprisingly), occupying a prestigious chair and starting – in the writing business – with a text in English with an American publisher gives a scholar a strong initial edge. It took me five years to have my first Italian book on democracy translated and published in the United States. Thereafter, however, *Democratic Theory* and *The Theory of Democracy Revisited* have obtained some fifteen translations around the world. My *Parties and Party Systems* has done equally well in the international context, and *Comparative Constitutional Engineering* has likewise received wide attention and has seen a number of translations.[13] So, I cannot complain, and indeed I feel good about my overall balance sheet.

I am not happy, however, about the performance of comparative politics. Since this is the focus that I have been asked to pursue, let me close my brief by quoting the closing statement of my article "Comparing and Miscomparing" (1991a: 255) on the comparative theme:

> In the last forty years or so, we have enjoyed moving from one "revolution" to another: behavioral, paradigmatic, "critical," postpositivist, hermeneutic, and so on. But revolutions (in science) just leave us with a new beginning – they have to be followed up and made to bear fruits. We have, instead, just allowed them to fade away, as ever new beginnings hold ever new promises which remain, in turn, ever unfulfilled. In the process the basics have gotten lost. . . .

Yes, our sophistication has grown – but at the expense of an increasingly missing core. As is shown by growing numbers of comparativists (in name) who never compare anything, not even "implicitly," thus forsaking standardized labels, common yardsticks and shared parameters. Let us squarely face it: the normal science is not doing well. A field defined by its method – comparing – cannot prosper without a core method. My critique does not imply, to be sure, that good, even excellent, comparative work is no longer under way. But even the current good comparative work underachieves on account of our having lost sight of what comparing *is for*.

Notes

* Originally published as Giovanni Sartori (1997) "Chance, Luck, and Stubbornness," in H. Daalder (ed.), *Comparative European Politics: The Story of a Profession*, London: Pinter.

1 My lectures of those years were all mimeographed and for many years were unpublished, with the exception of Sartori (1966b). The material from my History of Philosophy course was later published in two volumes (Sartori 1997, vols. 1 and 2).
2 I tell some in Sartori (1986).
3 At the same time, in collaboration with colleagues, I successfully launched a general reform of Italian political science.
4 This theme recurs in many articles. For example, 1968a, 1968b, 1975, 1991b, 1992, and 1995.
5 The book (*Parties and Party Systems*, 1976), which was very slow in coming, was preceded by my article, "European Political Parties: The Case of Polarized Pluralism" (1966a) and also by "The Typology of Party Systems" (1970b). A further elaboration of the 1976 volume is "Polarization, Fragmentation and Competition in Western Democracies" (Sani and Sartori 1983). My notion of "polarized pluralism" has been much debated and the polarization variable, as I defined it, has become a standard one.
6 The experience in the Committee of Political Sociology was, for all its core members, a very enriching give-and-take affair. While my work on parties owed a great deal to our meetings on the topic, I did, in turn, reorient the approach of the group – or so I believe (see Sartori 1969).
7 The Italian political science tradition is represented by Gaetano Mosca, and it is clearly the case that I discontinued that tradition. Mosca's *Elementi di Scienza Politica*, first published in 1896, is really a text of "drawing lessons" from history, and in Mosca's time, "science" was a loosely used word. I have also been very critical of his celebrated "law" of the ruling class (see, e.g., Sartori 1987b: 145–48).
8 "Concept Misformation in Comparative Politics" (1970a) is the most quoted among these. But see, more importantly, Sartori (1971) and (1991a).
9 In *Parties and Party Systems* (1976) the structural-functional framework is not as evident as it should or would have been, because the work was conceived in two volumes and the functional argument was developed in the second one, which never appeared because my near-final manuscript was stolen. I never had the heart to undertake recreating the book, but parts of the argument have appeared in subsequent articles.
10 To wit, as in the mid-1990s, some ten political science chairholders (remember that Italy has a chair system) were trained at the so-called "Florentine School" with fellowships obtained from the Agnelli Foundation. Let me mention their names: Maurizio Cotta (Siena), Stefano Bartolini (European University Institute), Domenico Fisichella (Roma), Leonardo Morlino (Firenze), Adriano Pappalardo (Napoli), Gianfranco

Pasquino (Bologna), Giorgio Sola (Genova), Giuliano Urbani (Milano), Giovanna Zincone (Torino). The tenth was Antonio Lombardo, who died in his fifties.

11 The turning point came when the *Rivista Italiana di Scienza Politica* started in 1971 (of which I still am officially the editor). This immediately began to play a defining role in shaping the discipline of political science in Italy.

12 See not only my (1984) "Guidelines for Concept Analysis" but also, more harshly, "Comparing and Miscomparing" (1991a) and "Totalitarianism, Model Mania and Learning From Error" (1993).

13 Constitutionalism is by no means a new interest of mine. Indeed, the first article that I ever published in the United States was Sartori (1962a).

References

Almond, G. (ed.) (1960) "A Functional Approach to Comparative Politics," in G. Almond and J. Coleman (eds.), *The Politics of the Developing Areas*, Princeton: Princeton University Press.

Dahl, R.A. (1956) *A Preface to Democratic Theory*, Chicago: University of Chicago Press.

Dahl, R.A. (ed.) (1966) *Political Oppositions in Western Democracies*, New Haven, CT: Yale University Press.

Friedrich, C.J. (1946) *Constitutional Government and Democracy*, Boston: Ginn.

Sani, G. and Sartori, G. (1983) "Polarization, Fragmentation and Competition in Western Democracies," in H. Daalder and P. Mair (eds.), *Western European Party Systems: Continuity and Change*, London: Sage.

Sartori, G. (1957) *Democrazia e Definizioni*, Bologna: Il Mulino.

Sartori, G. (1962a) "Constitutionalism: A Preliminary Discussion," *American Political Science Review* 4: 853–64.

Sartori, G. (1962b) *Democratic Theory*, Detroit: Wayne State University Press.

Sartori, G. (1966a) "European Political Parties: The Case of Polarized Pluralism," in J. LaPalombara and M. Weiner (eds.), *Political Parties and Political Development*, Princeton: Princeton University Press.

Sartori, G. (1966b) *Stato e Politica nel Pensiero di Benedetto Croce*, Naples: Morano.

Sartori, G. (1968a) "Democracy," in D.L. Sills (ed.), *International Encyclopedia of the Social Sciences*, vol. 4, New York: Crowell-Collier.

Sartori, G. (1968b) "Representational Systems," in D.L. Sills (ed.), *International Encyclopedia of the Social Sciences*, vol. 13, New York: Crowell-Collier.

Sartori, G. (1968c) "Political Development and Political Engineering," in J.D. Montgomery and A.O. Hirschman (eds.), *Public Policy*, vol. 17: Cambridge, MA: Harvard University Press, 261–98.

Sartori, G. (1969) "From the Sociology of Politics to Political Sociology," in S.M. Lipset (ed.), *Politics and the Social Sciences*, New York: Oxford University Press.

Sartori, G. (1970a) "Concept Misformation in Comparative Politics," *American Political Science Review* 64 (4): 1033–53.

Sartori, G. (1970b) "The Typology of Party Systems," in E. Allardt and S. Rokkan (eds.), *Mass Politics: Studies in Political Sociology*, New York: Free Press.

Sartori, G. (1971) "La politica comparata: premesse e problemi," *Rivista Italiana di Scienza Politica* 1: 7–66.

Sartori, G. (1974) "Philosophy, Theory and Science of Politics," *Political Theory* 2: 133–61.

Sartori, G. (1975) "Will Democracy Kill Democracy? Decision-making by Majorities and by Committees," *Government and Opposition* Spring: 129–56.

Sartori, G. (1976) *Parties and Party Systems: A Framework for Analysis*, New York: Cambridge University Press.

Sartori, G. (1979) *La politica: logica e metodo in scienze sociali*, Milan: Sugar Co.

Sartori, G. (1984) "Guidelines for Concept Analysis," in G. Sartori (ed.), *Social Science Concepts: A Systematic Analysis*, London: Sage.

Sartori, G. (1986) "Dove va la scienza politica," in L. Graziano (ed.), *La scienza politica in Italia. Bilancio e prospettive*, Milan: Angeli.

Sartori, G. (1987a) *Elementi di teoria politica*, Bologna: Il Mulino.

Sartori, G. (1987b) *The Theory of Democracy Revisited*, 2 vols., Chatham, NJ: Chatham House.

Sartori, G. (1991a) "Comparing and Miscomparing," *Journal of Theoretical Politics* 3 (3): 243–57.

Sartori, G. (1991b) "Rethinking Democracy: Bad Polity and Bad Politics," *International Social Science Journal* August: 437–50.

Sartori, G. (1992) "Democrazia," in *Enciclopedia delle scienze sociali*, vol. 2, Rome: Istituto della Enciclopedia Italiana.

Sartori, G. (1993) "Totalitarianism, Model Mania and Learning From Error," *Journal of Theoretical Politics* 5 (1): 5–22.

Sartori, G. (1994) *Comparative Constitutional Engineering*, New York: New York University Press.

Sartori, G. (1995) "How Far Can Democracy Travel?," *Journal of Democracy* 6 (3): 101–11.

Sartori, G. (1997) *Croce filosofo pratico e la crisi dell'etica* and *Croce etico-politico e filosofo della libertà*, 2 vols., Naples: Il Mulino, Bologna.

14 Teacher and mentor

Cindy Skach, Edward Walker, Hector E.
Schamis, Edward L. Gibson, and
Christoph Kotowski

This chapter presents reflections, by five former students, on Giovanni Sartori's graduate course on methodology at Columbia University.

Cindy Skach

When I first interviewed for the position in the Department of Government at Harvard University, where I taught before moving to Oxford, members of that faculty expressed their admiration for the care and conceptual clarity they found in my work. Undoubtedly, many of my teachers by that time had encouraged these qualities, and whatever praise I received was in no short measure due to my training under their auspices. But the one scholar who not only taught me everything I know about democratic theory, but perhaps more crucially, incessantly stressed the importance of conceptual clarity and rigor, and helped me to build strong logical and conceptual legs for my analytic work, was Giovanni Sartori.

This training in fundamentals began in the fall of my first year of graduate school at Columbia University. Not yet the hotbed of model mania, the political science and sociology departments at Columbia at that time offered graduate students a popular course known simply as Social Science Methodology, taught by Professor Sartori.

Sartori would enter gallantly, clutching his worn leather briefcase under his arm. With the aid of a small blackboard, fighting all the ambient sounds of New York City, and with an elegance of bearing and mind that mesmerized all of us, Sartori led us through a series of drills. They were not, of course, the cartwheels and back flips of differential calculus, which seem to be most of what covers blackboards and now whiteboards across political science seminar rooms these days. Rather, Sartori took us through exercises that austerely but effectively taught us the real and now easily forgotten fundamentals of research in the social sciences: the principles of logic, the comparative pitfalls of vague versus ambiguous concepts, the circumstances that demand the use of a typology rather than a classification, the treacherous ladder of abstraction, and so forth. Sartori's demanding pedagogical style and his vast knowledge intimidated most of us, drove some of us to tears, but inspired everyone.

This course, grounded in the classic teachings of philosophical and sociological inquiry, gave us an invaluable set of tools that would enable us to become careful social scientists, to make modest but sound contributions, and to do so on the shoulders of giants. Guided by Sartori's careful and unfailing mentorship, I went on to discover the topic of semi-presidentialism, and to carve out a new research agenda on Islam and democratic theory.

I close by stressing that for those of us privileged to have worked with him, Sartori was, and continues to be, a *Doktorvater* in the original sense of the term: a world-class scholar with an incredible mind, but concurrently, an amazing teacher with an even more incredible, and incredibly generous, heart.

Edward Walker

When I arrived at Columbia as a Ph.D. candidate in political science in 1987, Giovanni Sartori was a legend, albeit a rather intimidating one. He was said to be the most brilliant scholar in an outstanding department, but he did not suffer fools gladly. Enrolling in his seminar on epistemology and methodology in the social sciences, and later his class on parties and party systems, I learned that half of this reputation was entirely warranted. He was certainly brilliant. But he also turned out to be rather less intimidating than expected, with great Old-World charm and a dry sense of humor. He was also deeply committed to his graduate students and to teaching.

As a result, I became a member of what turned out to be something of a cult of Sartori at Columbia in those years. Being a member of the cult entailed not only taking his classes and admiring his scholarship, but embracing his literary style, conceptual lexicon, and unique idiom as well. Those who used terms loosely were "concept stretchers"; those who used terms inconsistently were "equivocators"; those who knew a great deal about one country only (e.g., the Soviet Union) lacked "comparative control"; those who claimed that a very old argument was entirely new were "novitists"; those who claimed that they were moving "beyond" conventional scholarship without merit were "beyondists"; arguments that were unconvincing were simply "feeble." At one point I remember Sartori encouraging us to keep a written record of the most common "fallacies" that we encountered in the discipline, which I took to mean a record of common stupidities. I still have my list of fallacies on my computer, which I occasionally share with graduate students. He also told us to come up with useful names for these fallacies, although he lamented that we would be unlikely to create appropriate neologisms, because we lacked Latin and Greek.

Above all, Sartori emphasized clarity in thought and language, and the relationship between logic and language. Logic and precision of exposition were necessary, albeit hardly sufficient, conditions for progress in the discipline. This was a traditional idea that he strongly embraced, as did I. Correspondingly, Sartori's own scholarship is dense and rich, and it demands the closest of scrutiny. Even though I studied authoritarian regimes in general and Soviet-type systems in particular, his *Parties and Party Systems* and *The Theory of Democracy Revisited* were enormously rewarding for me in their exploration of the dynamics of democratic politics, and of democratic breakdown.

In truth, Sartori had a greater impact on my intellectual development than any scholar with whom I have had personal contact, then or since. I suspect that was true for many of us. It was a privilege to have had Sartori as a teacher at Columbia.

Hector E. Schamis

Back in graduate school, Giovanni Sartori was not your typical university professor in the United States. In his tailored Italian suits, he was always stern and very demanding. In class, he used to address us by our last names, and in small seminars he would go around the table, asking us our views on the issue under discussion. I clearly remember his, "And what do you think, Mr. Schamis?" To get Professor Sartori's approval was not easy. We used to feel somewhat intimidated by his presence. How to say something, or write something, that could impress Giovanni Sartori? And of course, that intimidation was the result of the extraordinary quality of his mind and the unparalleled breadth of his scholarship. Sartori is a giant: the constitutionalist, the democratic theorist, the expert on party systems, the insightful philosopher, and methodologist of the social sciences, and in many fields he is a mandatory first or second footnote. In other words, Sartori is, and has been for several decades, a living classic.

From all the "multiple Sartoris" I have known, there is one that impressed me deeply from the beginning, one that I have carried with me beyond Columbia. From the very first to the most recent of my publications, I seek to engage prevalent research programs in comparative and Latin American politics at a conceptual level, and always with reference to Sartori's contributions. In my work on Latin American authoritarianism, I highlight the risks of ignoring such Sartorian themes as "conceptual stretching" and "homonymy," once changes in the political economy of military rule made it incompatible with the dominant notion of bureaucratic-authoritarianism. In my work on the field of democratization, I argue that a "frenzy of novitism" has developed in the recent construction of diminished forms of democracy, generating a true "Babel" of types and subtypes that has been conducive to "ambiguity" – i.e., lack of rigor in the connection between meaning and word; and "undenotativeness" – i.e., looseness in the linkage between meaning and referent. In my article on the different types of left in Latin America (Schamis 2006), like Sartori I emphasize the importance of defining the *fundamentum divisionis* – that is, "the basis of division of the different types and subtypes" ex-ante and according to logically consistent rules.

In other words, all these years I have just tried to be Sartorian. My Sartori folder is never in the file cabinet and my Sartori books are never on the shelves. They are always on my desk.

Edward L. Gibson

The course was entitled Social Science Methodology. It was the only "methodology" course I took during the Ph.D. phase of my graduate education. This was

1986, and those were very different times. Of all the courses I took during my Ph.D. training at Columbia, Professor Sartori's course, Social Science Methodology, had the most enduring effect on my thinking and my writing. More than a technical methods course, it was a course on how to think as a social scientist. Today, it might be placed under a "philosophy of the social science" category and, while accurate to some extent (we spent a great deal of time discussing the epistemological bases of positivist social science), the course was also a powerful training ground for how to slice the empirical world in analytically useful ways, how to construct concepts rigorously, and how to prepare the intellectual terrain to embark on the most exciting of social science endeavors – that of discovery.

In fact, I remember little of the "testing" components of the course. They were there, but given the overwhelming emphasis on this task in current methodological training, they have probably gotten blended in with much of what I have heard in the twenty years since I sat in that small and memorable class with Professor Sartori. What I remember vividly, and what I apply regularly in my work, is what I have seldom heard from the field of political science since then: the power of language and analytical thinking in the construction of concepts that not only help us to "seize the object" in a messy empirical world, but also help shape the way we subsequently ask questions and make discoveries about important political phenomena.

In Sartori's class, we spent little time on the definition and operationalization of small variables. The focus was on the largest and most contested of concepts – "development," "authoritarianism," and "revolution." Despite the complexity of these troublesome concepts, Sartori gave us strict and simple rules by which to tackle them and to greatly reduce the confusion and ambiguity that tend to cloud their use. These rules were based on a clear understanding of how to move along "ladders of abstraction," of how to peel away properties associated with concepts until the "defining" properties were identified and isolated, and how to make clear their relationship to "contingent" properties. These basic rules exposed us to a dynamic understanding of important political phenomena, and the power to analyze them in fruitful and exciting ways. In recent years, scholars have advocated more flexible approaches to concept formation, but I have yet to see heuristic payoffs in works applying those more flexible approaches that can be seen in those employing Sartori's more "stringent" approach.

Thanks to my exposure to Sartori's training, my comparative research has usually begun with an exercise in Sartorian conceptualization. My first book, *Class and Conservative Parties* (1996), which sought to define the "conservative" concept in a way that was useful to the study of party politics, was profoundly influenced by Sartori's teaching. Looking to the sociological bases of party politics, I identified "conservative" parties as those that draw their core constituencies from the upper social strata, and, taking this social base as their defining characteristic, separated it from "contingent" characteristics such as ideology. This helped me to compare a variety of conservative parties across time and continents, and to analyze their evolution by exploring, among other things, the changing interaction between upper strata core constituencies, other social constituencies, and ideological dynamics. This has sparked numerous debates with other scholars who prefer broader or more ideologically-based definitions of conservative parties. However, I have always felt that while it leaves many parties out of the "pool" that scholars would like to include, the discipline behind the conceptualization has produced analytical dividends that are well worth the costs of restriction.

Of my subsequent works, one on "populism" (one of the most contested and widely used concepts in Latin American politics) similarly zeroed in on a defining characteristic that limited the pool to a number of concrete cases of populist electoral mobilization. Thanks to this definition, I was led in my research on the topic to dynamics of populist movements that had not been previously uncovered in the comparative literature. And more recently, my work on federalism, subnational authoritarianism, and even my ongoing work on party systems in federalized countries (work that is critical of Sartori's own substantive research on parties), similarly benefited from Sartori's insistence that good social science begins with clear concept formation and definition.

We find an exemplary analytic template here. Without first mastering the "basic unit of thinking" in any scholarly work, our ability to discover the unseen, or to critically analyze the arguments of our colleagues, will be much impaired.

Christoph Kotowski

I credit Professor Sartori with helping me think more clearly. First you classify, categorize, and typologize, not just so you can put things in tidy buckets, but so that you can identify the key fault lines between things. The "things" in question can, of course, be just about anything, from ideal concepts like "revolution," to concrete world historical events like specific revolutions. But whatever you are looking at, the first job is to understand and define the fault lines.

My first course with Professor Sartori was a seminar called Social Science Concepts, I believe in 1980, which was his first year at Columbia. I had read his *Parties and Party Systems* as an undergraduate, and had some inkling of what I was in for. However, as I remember, most of the other students in the class were from the School of International and Public Affairs (i.e., pre-professional students), to whom Social Science Concepts sounded like an easy class. We were all in for a bit of a shock.

It was certainly the most rigorous course any of us took that semester, and those who had not done the reading or thought it all through would inevitably be dissected – in the most charming and courteous manner, to be sure, but dissected nonetheless. For me, this course was one of those coming of age moments in which I realized that I was no longer just writing term papers, but that I was expected to be a professional and make a real contribution.

The other thing from that course that has really stayed with me ever since is the concept of "setting the semantic field." None of my undergraduate professors had ever talked in these terms, and although I took a number of "philosophy of language" courses as an undergraduate, I had not yet come across the idea – crucial to Sartori's thinking – of "setting the semantic field." Scholars are forever defining their terms, but the more I thought about it, the more I found that definitions are pretty lifeless without understanding how a term fits with related terms. This, again, was one of those life lessons for me: figure out how people set the semantic field and you will see how people speak past each other all the time.

For my seminar paper, I chose the topic of revolution. It had been a focus of mine at the time. At the end of the term, Professor Sartori asked me if I would like to have him include it in the volume *Social Science Concepts* that he was editing. I was thrilled and accepted immediately. Of course, "It needs a little work . . .," he said. Needless to say, a big part of the next year was devoted to multiple rewritings of the paper. Busy as he was, he was always most generous with his time, always full of comments, always calm, gracious, charming, and encouraging – but always, always very exacting as well. I will always be grateful for that effort, both for making "Revolution" a much better article and for teaching me the dedication and rigor it takes to create a substantial piece of work.

Reference

Schamis, H E. (2006) "A 'Left Turn' in Latin America?," *Journal of Democracy* 7 (4): 20–34.

15 Giovanni Sartori
Biography and bibliography

Oreste Massari

Giovanni Sartori, born in Florence, May 13, 1924, is Albert Schweitzer Professor Emeritus in the Humanities, Columbia University, New York (since 1994), and Professor Emeritus at the University of Florence.

Education

Doctorate in Political and Social Science, University of Florence, 1946
Habilitation in History of Modern Philosophy, 1954
Habilitation in State Theory, 1955

Academic career

Assistant Professor of History of Modern Philosophy, University of Florence, 1950–56
Assistant Professor of Political Science, University of Florence, 1956–63
Professor of Sociology, University of Florence, 1963–66
Professor of Political Science, University of Florence, 1966–76
Professor, European University Institute, 1974–76
Professor of Political Science, Stanford University, 1976–79
Albert Schweitzer Professor in the Humanities, Columbia University, 1979–94
Professor of Political Science, University of Florence, 1992–94

Other academic appointments

Visiting Professor of Government, Harvard University, Fall 1964–65
Visiting Professor of Political Science and Fellow of the Concilium on International and Area Studies, Yale University, 1966–67
Visiting Professor of Political Science, Yale University, Fall 1968–69
Senior Fellow by courtesy, Hoover Institution, Stanford, 1976
Visiting Scholar, American Enterprise Institute, Washington, DC, Fall 1982
Visiting Fellow, Russell Sage Foundation, New York, 1988–89

Honors and awards

President of the Italian Republic's Gold Medal for Cultural and Educational Merits, 1971

Fellow of the Center for Advanced Studies in the Behavioral Sciences, Stanford, 1971–72

Foreign Honorary Member, American Academy of Arts and Sciences, 1975

Guggenheim Fellow, 1978–79

Ford Foundation Fellow, 1979

Accademia dei Lincei, 1992

Doctor *Honoris Causa* of the University of Genoa, 1992; Georgetown University, Washington, DC, 1994; University of Guadalajara, 1997; University of Buenos Aires, 1998; Complutense University of Madrid, 2001; University of Bucharest, 2001; Università di Urbino, Italy, 2005; University of Athens (Panteio), 2005; UNAM (Universidad Nacional Autonoma de México), Mexico City, 2007

Award of the President of the Council of Ministers for the Social Sciences, Italy, 1994

Outstanding Book Award of the American Association of Political Science (APSA) for *Parties and Party Systems: A Framework for Analysis* (1976), 1998

Commendador, Ordem do Cruzeiro do Sul, Republic of Brazil, 1999

Festschrift in honor of Giovanni Sartori: *La scienza politica di Giovanni Sartori* (Gianfranco Pasquino, ed.), Bologna, Il Mulino, 2005

Lifetime Achievement Award, ECPR (European Consortium for Political Research), 2005

Prince of Asturias Prize in the Social Sciences, Oviedo (Spain), 2005

Lifetime Achievement Award, Qualitative Methods Section of APSA, for Exceptional Contributions to Social Science Methodology, 2006

Freedom Prize, Fundación Internacional para Libertad, Buenos Aires

Further academic and professional appointments

Director, Institute for Political Science, University of Florence, 1966–76

Executive Committee and Program Committee, International Political Science Association (IPSA), 1967–76

Dean of the Faculty of Political Sciences, University of Florence, 1969–71

President of the Committee for Conceptual and Terminological Analysis (COCTA) of IPSA, the International Sociological Association (ISA), and the International Social Science Council (ISSC), 1970–79

Executive Committee of the European Consortium for Political Research (ECPR), 1973–76

Director of the Center for Italian Studies, Columbia University, 1980–85

Founder and editor of the *Rivista Italiana di Scienza Politica*, 1971–2003

Publications

Books, monographs, and other texts

1951 *Da Hegel a Marx: la dissoluzione della filosofia hegeliana*, mimeographed, University of Florence

1953 *Etica e libertà in Kant*, mimeographed, University of Florence

1955 *La filosofia pratica di Benedetto Croce*, mimeographed, University of Florence

1956 *Croce etico-politico e filosofo della libertà*, mimeographed, University of Florence

1957 *Democrazia e definizioni*, Bologna: Il Mulino; third expanded edition 1969; 8th reprint 1989

1959 *Questioni di metodo in scienza politica*, mimeographed, University of Florence

1962a *A teoria da representação no Estado representativo moderno*, in "Revista Brasileira de Estudios Politicos," Minas Gerais

1962b *Democratic Theory*, Detroit: Wayne University Press; 2nd edn., New York: Praeger, 1965 (reprinted 1967); Indian edn. New Delhi: Oxford & IBH Publishing Co., 1965; Spanish edn. Mexico: Limus Wiley, 1965; Brazilian edn. Rio de Janeiro: Fondo de Cultura, 1965; French edn. Paris: Colin, 1973; reprinted in the United States in 1973 by Greenwood Press

1963 (ed.) *Il parlamento italiano 1946–1963*, Naples: Edizioni Scientifiche Italiane

1965 *Partiti e sistemi di partito*, mimeographed, Florence: Editrice Universitaria

1966 *Stato e politica nel pensiero di Benedetto Croce*, Naples: Morano

1970 (ed.) *Antologia di scienza politica*, Bologna: Il Mulino

1973 (ed.) *Correnti, frazioni e fazioni nei partiti politici italiani*, Bologna: Il Mulino

1976 *Liberty and Law*, Institute for Human Studies: Menlo Park; reprinted in K.S. Templeton (ed.), *The Politicization of Society*, Indianapolis: Liberty Press, 1979; translated in "Libertas" (ESEADE), October, 1986

1976 *Parties and Party Systems: A Framework for Analysis*, New York: Cambridge University Press; Spanish edn. Madrid: Alianza Editorial, 1980, 1987, 2nd edn. 1992, 1994, 1997, 3rd edn. 1999, 2000, 2002, 2003; Brazilian edn. Universidade de Brasilia, 1982; Japanese edn. Tokyo: Waseda University Press, 1980; South Korean edn. 1986; Chinese edn. Beijing: Commercial Press (forthcoming); new edition as an ECPR (European Consortium for Political Research) Classic, ECPR Press, University of Essex, 2005; Czech translation, Brno, 2005

1977 *Il cittadino totale: partecipazione, eguaglianza e libertà nelle democrazie* (with R. Dahrendorf), Torino: Centro Einaudi

1978 (ed.) *Eurocommunism: The Italian Case* (with A. Ranney), Washington, DC: AEI-Hoover Press

1979 *La politica: logica e metodo in scienze sociali*, Milan: SugarCo., 2nd edn. 1980; Brazilian edn. Editora Universidade de Brasilia, 1981, 1997; Mexican edn. Fondo de Cultura Económica, 1984, 1987, 1988, 2nd edn. 2000, 2002, 2003

1982   *Teoria dei partiti e caso italiano*, Milan: SugarCo

1984   (ed.) *Social Science Concepts: A Systematic Analysis*, London: Sage

1987   *Elementi di teoria politica*, Bologna: Il Mulino, 2nd edn. 1990, 3rd edn. 1995, 2002; Spanish edn. Madrid: Alianza Editorial, 1992, new edn. 1992, 2002

1987   *The Theory of Democracy Revisited*, 2 vols. Chatham, NJ: Chatham House. Vol. 1, *The Contemporary Debate*; vol. 2, *The Classical Issues*. Reprinted in 1990. Distributed since 2004 by CQ Press, Washington, DC. Spanish edn. Madrid: Alianza Editorial, 1988, 1995, 1997, 2000; Bulgarian edn. 1992; German edn. (*Demokratietheorie*), Darmstadt: Wissenschaftliche Buchgesellschaft, 1992, and Darmstadt: Primus Verlag, 1997; Slovak edn. Bratislava: Archa ed., 1993; Turkish edn. Ankara: Turkish Political Science Association, 1993; Chinese edn. (censored), 1993, 2nd complete edn. 1998; Brazilian edn. Editora Atica, 1994; South Korean edn. 1994; Polish edn. Varsavia: Naukowe, 1994; Albanian edn. Tirana: Dituria, 1994

1991   (ed.) *La comparazione nelle scienze sociali* (with L. Morlino), Bologna: Il Mulino

1992   *Seconda Repubblica? Sì, ma bene*, Milan: Rizzoli

1993   *Democrazia: cosa è*, Milan: Rizzoli, 4th reprint; in BUR Supersaggi, 1994, 1995, 1996, 1997, 2000; Albanian edn. Dituria, 1998; Mexican edn. 1993, 1997, 2003; Spanish edn. Taurus, 2003; Hungarian edn. Budapest: Osiris Kialo, 1999; Serbian edn. Belgrade: Cid, 2001, 3rd edn. 2007

1993   *La Democracia después del Comunismo*, Madrid and Buenos Aires: Alianza Editorial (this is the Appendix to *Democrazia: cosa è*; excerpts appeared in *Mondo Operaio*, August–September, 1992: 90–99, October, 1992: 73–85)

1994   *Comparative Constitutional Engineering*, New York: New York University Press; London: Macmillan, 1994; 2nd edn. 1997; Mexican edn. Fondo de Cultura, 1995, 1996, 1999, expanded 2nd edn. 2001, 2002, 2003; Chilean edn. 1995; Italian edn. Bologna: Il Mulino, 1995, 1996, 1998, 4th edn. 2000, 5th edn. 2004; Brazilian edn. Editora Universidade de Brasilia, 1997; Turkish edn. Ankara: Turkish Democracy Foundation, 1997; Taiwanese edn. 1998; Czech edn. Prague, 2001; Japanese edn. Waseda University Press, 2000; Lithuanian edn. 2001; Romanian, Editura Mediterana, 2002; Hungarian edn. Budapest: Akadémiai Kiado, 2003

1995   *Come sbagliare le riforme*, Bologna: Il Mulino

1997   *Croce etico-politico e filosofo della libertà*, Bologna: Il Mulino

1997   *Croce filosofo pratico e la crisi dell'etica*, Bologna: Il Mulino

1997   *Homo Videns: televisione e post-pensiero*, Rome and Bari: Laterza, 2nd edn. 1998, 1999, 2000, 2003; Polish edn. Warsaw: Televiwize Polska, 2005; Spanish and Mexican edn. Taurus, 1998, 2nd edn. 2000, 2003; Brazilian edn. EDUSC, 2001; Turkish edn. Karakutu Yayinlari, 2005

2000   *Pluralismo, multiculturalismo e estranei: saggio sulia società multietnica*, Milan: Rizzoli (3rd reprint), 2nd expanded edn. 2002 (Superbur); Spanish and Mexican edn. Taurus, 2000, 2nd edn. 2002; French edn. Editions des Syrtes, 2003

2003 *La terra scoppia: sovrappopolazione e sviluppo* (with G. Mazzoleni), Milan: Rizzoli, 2nd expanded edn. 2004; Spanish and Mexican edn. Taurus, 2003

2004 *Mala tempora*, Rome and Bari: Laterza (fifth reprint)

2004 "Where is Political Science Going?," *PS: Political Science and Politics* 37 (4): 785–87. Published in Mexico in *Politica y Gobierno* 2, 2004; in Spain in *Revista Española de Ciencia Politica*, April 2005; in Greece in *Greek Political Science Review*, November 2005

2005 *Semantics, Concepts and Comparative Method*, Greek edn.: Serafim Sepheriades (ed.), Athens, Papazisis

2006 *Mala costituzione e altri malanni*, Bari: Laterza, 2006

Essays in edited volumes

1958 "La democrazia americana di ieri e di oggi," in F. Rossi-Landi (ed.), *Il pensiero americano contemporaneo: scienze sociali*, Milan: Comunità, pp. 299–357

1960 "Gruppi di pressione o gruppi di interesse?," in *I contributi italiani al IV Congresso mondiale di Scienze politiche* (various authors), Milan: Vita e Pensiero, pp. 94–129. An expanded version appeared in 1959 in *il Mulino* 1: 7–42

1961 "I significati del termine 'élite,'" in *Le élites politiche* (various authors), Bari: Laterza, pp. 94–99

1962 "Dittatura," in *Enciclopedia del diritto*, vol. 11, Milan: Giuffré, pp. 1–16 (in the 1964 edition, vol. 13, pp. 356–72)

1963 "Dove va il parlamento?," in G. Sartori (ed.), *Il parlamento italiano 1946–1963*, Naples: Edizioni Scientifiche Italiane, pp. 270–386

1963 "The Political Meaning of Liberty and Equality," in *Values in Conflict* (various authors), Toronto: University of Toronto Press, pp. 65–70

1965 "Gli studi politici nella Facoltà di Scienze politiche," in *Atti del III congresso nazionale di Scienze politiche e sociali*, Milan: Vita e Pensiero, pp. 41–55

1966 "European Political Parties: The Case of Polarized Pluralism," in J. LaPalombara and M. Weiner (eds.), *Political Parties and Political Development*, Princeton: Princeton University Press, pp. 137–76. Reprinted in R.A. Dahl and D.E. Neubauer (eds.), *Readings in Modern Political Analysis*, Englewood Cliffs, NJ: Prentice Hall, 1967; translated in *Revista de Estudios Politicos*, Madrid, May–August, 1966

1967 "Members of Parliament in Italy," in J. Meynaud (ed.), *Decisions and Decision-Makers in the Modern State*, Paris: UNESCO, pp. 156–73

1968 "Democracy," in *International Encyclopedia of the Social Sciences*, vol. 4, New York: Crowell-Collier, pp. 112–21. Translated 1969 in appendix to *Democrazia e definizioni*, 3rd edn., pp. 321–51

1968 "Representational Systems," *International Encyclopedia of the Social Sciences*, vol. 13, New York: Crowell-Collier, pp. 465–74. Translated 1969 in appendix to *Democrazia e definizioni*, 3rd edn., pp. 352–78

1969 "From the Sociology of Politics to Political Sociology," in S.M. Lipset (ed.), *Politics and the Social Sciences*, New York: Oxford University Press, pp. 65–100. Reprinted 1990 in P. Mair (ed.), *The West European Party System*, New York: Oxford University Press, pp. 150–82. Partially reprinted 1969 in *Government and Opposition* 4 (2): 195–214

1969 "Political Development and the Objectives of Modern Government: Comment," in R. Braibanti (ed.), *Political and Administrative Development*, Durham, NC: Duke University Press, pp. 136–42

1970 "Per una definizione della scienza politica," in G. Sartori (ed.), *Antologia di scienza politica*, Bologna: Il Mulino, pp. 11–28

1970 "The Typology of Party Systems," in E. Allardt and S. Rokkan (eds.), *Mass Politics: Studies in Political Sociology*, New York: Free Press, pp. 322–52

1971 "Appunti per una teoria generale della dittatura," in K. Von Beyme (ed.), *Theorie und Politik*, Den Haag: Nijhoff, pp. 456–85. Translated 1987 in *Opciones* (Chile), May–August

1972 "La scienza politica," in L. Firpo (ed.), *Storia delle idee politiche, economiche e sociali: Il XX Secolo*, vol. 6, Torino: UTET, pp. 665–714. Reprinted 1972 in *Rivista Italiana di Scienza Politica* (April and August): 3–26, 227–63

1973 "Governed Democracy and Governing Democracy," in L.E. Shaw (ed.), *Modern Competing Ideologies*, Lexington: Heath & Co., pp. 213–33

1974 "Rivisitando il pluralismo polarizzato," in F. Cavazza and S.R. Graubard (eds), *Il caso italiano*, Milan: Garzanti, pp. 196–223

1975 "Demokratie als Elitenherrschaft," in F. Grube and G. Richter (eds.), *Demokratietheorien*, Hamburg: Hoffmann and Campe, pp. 67–75

1975 "The Italian University System," in P. Seabury (ed.), *Universities in the Western World*, New York: Free Press, pp. 246–56

1975 "The Tower of Babel," in G. Sartori, F. Riggs, and H. Teune (eds.), *Tower of Babel: On the Definition and Analysts of Concepts in the Social Sciences*, Pittsburgh: International Studies Association, University of Pittsburgh, Occasional Paper 6: 7–37

1978 "The Relevance of Liberalism in Retrospect," in Research Institute of International Change, Columbia University, *The Relevance of Liberalism* (various authors), Boulder: Westview Press, pp. 1–31. Translated 1980 as "Il liberalismo che precede i liberalismi," in *Biblioteca della Libertá* 76: 127–39

1978 "Calculating the Risk," in A. Ranney and G. Sartori (eds.), *Eurocommunism: The Italian Case*, Washington, DC: AEI-Hoover Press, pp. 165–81

1978 "Lo scenario del compromesso storico," in J. LaPalombara, G. Sani, and G. Sartori (eds.), *I comunisti al governo. E dopo?*, in *Biblioteca della Libertá*, July–August, Torino, Centro Einaudi: 79–108

1979 "Liberal Democracy in Western Europe," in W.S. Livingston (ed.) *A Prospect for Liberal Democracy*, Austin: University of Texas Press, pp. 199–214.

1979 "Opinione pubblica," in *Enciclopedia del Novecento*, vol. 4, Rome: Istituto dell'Enciclopedia Italiana, pp. 937–49. Reprinted 1987, 1990, 1995, 2002 in *Elementi di teoria politica*, Bologna: Il Mulino

1981 "Pragmatismo e ideologia," in *Italia e Stati Uniti: concordanze e dissonanze* (various authors), Rome: Veltro Editrice, pp. 159–69. Reprinted 1981 in *Rivista Italiana di Scienza Politica* 1: 137–46

1981–82 "Western Europe: Are We Losing Contact?," in *Proceedings of the General Education Seminar* 10, New York: Columbia University, pp. 11–15

1983 "Le radici dell'ingovernabilità," in A. Levi (ed.), *Ipotesi sull'Italia*, Bologna: Il Mulino, pp. 33–50

1984 "Guidelines for Concept Analysis," in G. Sartori (ed.), *Social Science Concepts: A Systematic Analysis*, London: Sage, pp. 15–85

1985 "Perfeksjonisme og Utopi," in B. Hagtvet and W. Lafferty (eds.), *Demokrati og Demokratisering*, Oslo: Aschehoug & Co., pp. 187–207

1986 "Dove va la scienza politica," in L. Graziano (ed.), *La scienza politica in Italia: Bilancio e prospettive*, Milan: Angeli, pp. 98–114. Translated 1990 in *Estudios Politicos* (Mexico), October–December; 1991 in *Revista de Ciencia Politica* (Chile), 1–2

1986 "The Influence of Electoral Systems: Faulty Laws or Faulty Method?," in B. Grofman and A. Lijphart (eds.), *Electoral Laws and their Political Consequences*, New York: Agathon Press, pp. 43–68. Translated 1985 in *Estudios Publicos* (Chile) 17; and 1988 in *Cuadernos de Capel* (Costa Rica) 27

1986 "Partiti e sistemi di partito: i sistemi competitivi," in *I sistemi di partito* (various authors), Milan: Angeli, pp. 167–245. Translation of Chapter 6 of *Parties and Party Systems*, 1976

1990 "A Typology of Party Systems," in P. Mair (ed.), *The West European Party System*, New York: Oxford University Press, pp. 316–49. Appeared as Chapters 5, 6, and 9 of *Parties and Party Systems*, 1976

1991 "Comparazione e metodo comparato," in G. Sartori and L. Morlino (eds.), *La comparazrone nelle scienze sociali*, Bologna: Il Mulino, pp. 25–37. Also published 1990 in *Rivista Italiana di Scienza Politica* 3: 397–416. Spanish edn. Alianza Editorial, 1994, 1999

1991 "Market, Capitalism, Planning and Technocracy," in G. Thompson et al. (eds.), *Markets, Hierarchies and Networks*, London: Sage, pp. 154–62

1992 "Democrazia," in *Enciclopedia delle scienze sociali*, vol. 2, Rome: Istituto della Enciclopedia Italiana, pp. 742–59. Translated in *Revista de Ciencia Política* (Chile), 1–2: 117–51

1993 "La sinistra? È l'etica," in G. Bosetti (ed.), *Sinistra punto zero*, Rome: Donzelli Editore, pp. 109–115

1994 "Compare Why and How: Comparing, Miscomparing and the Comparative Method," in M. Dogan and A. Kazancigil (eds.), *Comparing Nations*, Oxford: Basil Blackwell, pp. 14–34

1994 "Neither Presidentialism nor Parliamentarism," in J.J. Linz and A. Valenzuela (eds.), *The Failure of Presidential Democracy*, Baltimore, MD: Johns Hopkins University Press, pp. 106–18. Italian edn., Rome: Arel, 1991; published 1995 as "Né presidenzialismo né parlamentarismo," in J.J. Linz and A. Valenzuela (eds.), *Il fallimento del presidenzialismo*, Bologna: Il Mulino, pp. 181–200; Spanish edn. 1992 in O. Godoy (ed.), *Cambio de Regimen Político*,

Santiago, Ediciones Universidad Católica de Chile, 1992, and 1993 in *Novos Estudos* 35

1996 "La democrazia," in F. Roversi Monaco et al. (eds.), *Leggere il mutamento nella società di fine millennio*, Florence: Vallecchi, pp. 57–69

1996 "L'Italia tra sbagli e abbagli costituzionali," appendix to the 1996 edition of *Ingegneria costituzionale comparata*, Bologna: Il Mulino, pp. 221–34. Previously presented at the annual lecture of the Association "il Mulino" (Bologna, November 4, 1995) as "La democrazia delle idee sbagliate"

1996 "Per una difesa della logica scientifica" (response to Angelo Panebianco, *Il sartorismo imperfetto*), in *Cambiare la Costituzione* (various authors), Rome: Liberal/Atlantide Editoriale, pp. 157–67

1997 "Chance, Luck and Stubbornness," in H. Daalder (ed.), *Comparative European Politics: The Story of a Profession*, London and Washington, DC: Pinter (reprinted 1999), pp. 93–100. Translated 1998 as "Azar, suerte y tozudez," in *Revista Argentina de Ciencia Politica* 2: 193–202

1997 "Democratic Government by Leading Minorities, Responsiveness and Responsibility," in E. Etzioni-Halévy (ed.), *Classes and Elites in Democracy: A Reader*, New York: Karland, pp. 168–73 (excerpts from *Theory of Democracy Revisited*, 1987)

1997 "Hay que terminar con las ideas sobre la democracia que primaron en 1968," interview in *Gobernabilidad: un reportaje de America Latina*, Mexico: PNUD – Fondo de Cultura, pp. 310–23

1998 "Il fiasco della bicamerale," appendix to the 1998 edition of *Ingegneria costituzionale comparata*, Bologna: Il Mulino, pp. 235–41

1998 "Les Partis," in R. Darntorn and O. Duhamel (eds.), *Démocratie*, Paris: Editions du Rocher, pp. 135–39

2000 "Incapacità di riforma e bastardi istituzionali," appendix to the 2000 edition of *Ingegneria costituzionale comparata*, Bologna: Il Mulino, pp. 243–52

2000 "The Party Effects of Electoral Systems," in P. Mair and R. Hazan (eds.), *Parties, Elections and Cleavages*, London: Frank Cass, pp. 13–28. Reprinted in *Israeli Affairs* 1: 13–29

2000 "Relevant Parties," in R. Rose (ed.), *The International Encyclopedia of Elections*, Washington, DC: CQ Press, pp. 275–77

2001 "Elezioni e legge elettorale," in *Il Libro dell'Anno 2001*, Istituto dell'Enciclopedia Italiana, pp. 231–48. Reprinted 2001 as "Il sistema elettorale resta cattivo," *Rivista Italiana di Scienza Politica* 3: 471–79, and with the same title in G. Pasquino (ed.), *Dall'Ulivo al governo Berlusconi. Le elezioni del 13 maggio 2001 e il sistema politico italiano*, Bologna: Il Mulino, 2002, pp. 107–15

2001 "The Party Effects of Electoral Systems," in L. Diamond and R. Gunther (eds.), *Political Parties and Democracy*, Baltimore, MD: Johns Hopkins University Press, pp. 90–105. This is an abridged version of an essay that appeared in 2000 in P. Mair and R. Hazan (eds.), *Parties, Elections and Cleavages*, London: Frank Cass

2002 "Conflitto di interessi," in F. Tuccari (ed.), *Il Governo Berlusconi*, Rome-Bari: Laterza, pp. 21–33

2004 "Definizione della democrazia ottocentesca," in G.M. Bravo (ed.), *La Democrazia tra libertà e tirannide della maggioranza nell'Ottocento*, Florence: Olschki, pp. 1–6

2004 "Opposizione e oppositori," in F. Bassanini (ed.), *Constituzione una riforma sbagliata*, Florence: Passigli Editori, pp. 269–73

2004 "Preface," in O. Massari, *I partiti politici nelle democrazie contemporanee*, Rome-Bari: Laterza, pp. ix–x

2004 "Preface," in L. Pellicani, *Jihad: le radici*, Rome: Luiss University Press, pp. 5–9

2004 "Verso una costituzione incostituzionale?," appendix to the 2004 edition of *Ingegneria costituzionale comparata*, Bologna: Il Mulino, pp. 219–34

Journal articles

1952 "Critica al concetto di volontà generale," *Studi Politici* 2: 299–305

1952 "Saggio su la propaganda," *Studi Politici* 2–3: 198–38, 369–411

1952 "Scienza politica e conoscenza retrospettiva," *Studi Politici* 1: 52–74

1953 "Intellettuali e 'intelligentzia,'" *Studi Politici* 1–2: 29–53

1953 "Filosofia della politica e scienza empirica della politica," *Studi Politici* 3–4: 348–77.

1954 "L'identificazione di economia e politica nella filosofia crociana," *Studi Politici* 2–3: 288–312

1954 "Lo studio comparato dei regimi e dei sistemi politici," *Studi Politici* 1: 7–25

1957 "La rappresentanza politica," *Studi Politici* 4: 527–613

1957 "La teoria dello stato in Benedetto Croce," *Studi Politici* 2: 153–81; 3: 351–82

1958 "Electoral Studies and Democratic Theory," *Political Studies* 1: 9–15

1960 "Democrazia, burocrazia e oligarchia nei partiti," *Rassegna Italiana di Sociologia* 3: 119–36

1960 "Der Begriff der Wertfreiheit," *Politische Vierteljahresschrift* 1: 12–22

1960 "Parlementarisme et démocratie," *Res Publica* 2: 112–20

1960 "La ripresa della scienza politica in Francia," *Rivista Internazionale di Scienze Sociali* 5: 461–69

1961 "La sociologia del parlamento: linee di interpretazione," *Studi Politici* 2 (3–4): 131–59, 352–82

1961 "Les Parlementaires Italiens," *Revue International des Sciences Sociales* 4: 647–66. Reprinted 1967 in *Decisions and Decision Makers in the Modern State*, Paris: UNESCO; and 1971 in M. Dogan and R. Rose (eds.), *European Politics: A Reader*, Boston: Little, Brown

1961 "Una disciplina derelitta: la sociologia politica," *Rassegna Italiana di Sociologia* 2: 159–69

1962 "Constitutionalism: A Preliminary Discussion," *American Political Science Review* 4: 853–64. Reprinted 2003 in N. Dorsen et al. (eds.), *Comparative Constitutional Law: A Reader*, St. Paul, MN: West Group Publishing

1962 "Cosa è propaganda?," *Rassegna Italiana di Sociologia* 4: 563–85

1962 "Metodologia della scienza politica," report for the *Centro Studi Metodologici*, Torino, October 27–28. Reprinted 2002 in S. Paolini Merlo (ed.), *Annali della Fondazione Luigi Einaudi*, vol. 35, Florence: Olschki, pp. 281–321

1963 "Considerazioni sui concetto di propaganda: risposta a P. Facchi," *Rassegna Italiana di Sociologia* 4: 616–22

1964 "Costituzionalismo: un riesame," *Rivista Internazionale di Filosofia Politica e Sociale* (January–March): 41–68

1964 "L'Avenir des Parlements," *Bulletin SEDEIS, Futuribles* 74: 40

1964 "Nota sul Rapporto tra Stato di diritto e Stato di giustizia," *Rivista Internazionale di Filosofia del Diritto* 1–2: 310–16. Reprinted 1963 in *Dommatica, teoria generale e filosofia del diritto – Atti del VI Congresso Nazionale di Filosofia del Diritto*, vol. 2, Milan: Giuffrè

1964 "Osservazioni sulla teoria della dittatura," *Storia e Politica* 2: 180–97

1965 "Modelli spaziali di competizione partitica," *Rassegna Italiana di Sociologia* 1: 7–29

1965 "A quando le Facoltà di Scienze politiche e sociali?," *Rassegna Italiana di Sociologia* 4: 503–14

1965 "A Rejoinder on Constitutionalism," *American Political Science Review* 2: 441–44

1966 "Opposition and Control: Problems and Prospects," *Government and Opposition* 2: 149–54. Reprinted in R. Barker (ed.), *Studies in Opposition*, London: Macmillan, 1971

1966 "La teoria empirica della politica di Carl J. Friedrich," *Il Politico* 1: 61–73

1967 "Bipartitismo imperfetto o pluralismo polarizzato?," in *Tempi Moderni* (Fall): 1–34. Reprinted 1972 in P. Farneti, *Il sistema politico italiano*, Bologna: Il Mulino, pp. 287–309; and 1982 in *Teoria dei partiti e caso italiano*, Milan: SugarCo, pp. 7–44

1967 "La scienza politica," *Il Politico*, 4: 689–701. Reprinted 1969 in *Le scienze dell'uomo e la riforma universitaria*, vol. 2, Bari, Laterza, pp. 83–101

1968 "Alla ricerca della sociologia politica," *Rassegna Italiana di Sociologia* 4: 597–639

1968 "Political Development and Political Engineering," *Public Policy* 17: 261–98 (J.D. Montgomery and A.O. Hirschman eds.). Partially reprinted 1990 in P. Mair (ed.), *The West European Party System*, New York: Oxford University Press, pp. 75–77

1968 "Tipologia dei sistemi di partito," *Quaderni di Sociologia* 3: 187–226. Translated 1980 in M. Dogan and D. Pelassy (eds.), *La comparaison internationale en sociologie politique*, Paris: Litec. Partially reprinted 1972 in D. Fisichella (ed.), *Partiti e gruppi di pressione*, Bologna: Il Mulino, pp. 197–206

1969 "Liberalismo e democrazia," *Biblioteca della Libertà* (January–February): 1–23

1969 "Politics, Ideology and Belief Systems," *American Political Science Review* 6 (2): 398–411. Reprinted 1972 in D.D. Nimmo and C.M. Bonjean (eds.), *Political Attitudes and Public Opinion*, New York: McKay Co., Chapter 4; by Bobbs & Merrill Reprints, PS-547; and 1979 in *Revue Européenne des Sciences*

Sociales 46, Geneva: Droz, pp. 91–114. Translated as "Ideologia," *Elementi di teoria politica*, Bologna: Il Mulino, 1987, 1990, 1995, 2002

1970 "Concept Misformation in Comparative Politics," *American Political Science Review* 64 (4): 1033–53. Reprinted and translated in many anthologies. Abridged version in M. Dogan and D. Pelassy (eds.), *La comparaison internationale en sociologie politique*, Paris: Litec, 1980, pp. 77–81

1970 "La cultura liberale in Italia: difficoltà e prospettive," *Liberalismo '70*, Reggio Emilia, Fondazione Einaudi: 56–64

1971 "La politica comparata: premesse e problemi," *Rivista Italiana di Scienza Politica* 1: 7–66. Reprinted 1973 in G. Urbani (ed.), *La politica comparata*, Bologna: Il Mulino, pp. 59–85

1971 "Proporzionalismo, frazionismo e crisi dei partiti," *Rivista Italiana di Scienza Politica* 3: 629–55. Reprinted 1973 in *Correnti, frazioni e fazioni nei partiti politici italiani*, Bologna: Il Mulino, pp. 9–36

1971 "Technological Forecasting and Politics," *Survey* (Winter): 60–68

1973 "Il potere del lavoro nella società post-pacificata," *Rivista Italiana di Scienza Politica* 1: 31–91. Reprinted 1976 in G. Urbani (ed.), *Sindacati e politica nella società post-industriale*, Bologna: Il Mulino, pp. 77–127

1973 "Scienza politica e politica estera," *Affari Esteri* January: 18–26

1973 "What is Politics?," *Political Theory* 1 (1): 5–26

1974 "Il caso italiano: salvare il pluralismo e superare la polarizzazione," *Rivista Italiana di Scienza Politica* 3: 675–87. Reprinted 1978 in A. Lombardo (ed.), *Il sistema disintegrato*, Milan: SugarCo, pp. 57–72

1974 "Philosophy, Theory and Science of Politics," *Political Theory* 2: 133–61

1974 "Tecniche decisionali e sistema dei comitati," *Rivista Italiana di Scienza Politica* 1: 5–42

1975 "Will Democracy Kill Democracy? Decision-making by Majorities and by Committees," *Government and Opposition* (Spring): 129–56. Translated 1984 in B. Guggenberger and C. Offe (eds.), *An den Grenzen der Mehrheitsdemokratie*, Wiesbaden: Westdeutscher Verlag, pp. 83–107

1978 "Anti-Elitism Revisited," *Government and Opposition* (Winter): 58–80

1978 "Frammentazione, polarizzazione e cleavages: democrazie facili e difficili" (with G. Sani), *Rivista Italiana di Scienza Politica* 3: 339–61. Translated 1983 as "Polarization, Fragmentation and Competition in Western Democracies," in H. Daalder and P. Mair (eds.), *West European Party Systems: Continuity and Change*, London: Sage, pp. 307–40; and 1980 in *Revista de Ciencia Política* (Chile) 1–2. Also published 1980 in Universidad Nacional de Educación a Distancia, Madrid, Fall

1978 "Lo scenario del compromesso storico," *Biblioteca della Libertà* 11: 79–108

1979 "A Tribute to Charles Frankel," Newsletter of the International Council on the Future of the University, New York (November): 6–7

1981 "Pragmatismo e ideologia in Italia e negli Stati Uniti," *Rivista Italiana di Scienza Politica* 1: 137–46

1982 "Il pluralismo polarizzato: critiche e repliche," *Rivista Italiana di Scienza Politica*, 1: 3–34

1983 "The Market, Planning, Capitalism and Democracy," *This World* (Winter): 55–83

1984 "Comment on Maddox," *American Political Science Review* 78 (2): 497–99

1984 "Le 'leggi' sulla influenza dei sistemi elettorali," *Rivista Italiana di Scienza Politica* 1: 3–40

1986 "Localismo e Globalismo," *Biblioteca della Libertà* (October–December): 7–19

1984 "Pluralismo polarizzato e interpretazioni imperfette," *il Mulino* 4: 674–80

1986 "Razionalità pratica e sapere applicato," *Nuova Civiltà delle Macchine* 3–4: 72–7. Reprinted 1986 in *Ragioni Critiche* (September): 3–6

1987 "Le prospettive degli Stati Uniti: riflessioni sul sistema presidenziale," Atti Seminario Relazioni Esterne IRI, Rome, December 14: 1–12, 28–35, 41–45, 50–54, 72–77, 80–82

1988 "Come curare i mali istituzionali," interview by G. Torlontano, *Nuova Antologia* (January–March): 100–06

1988 "Intervista di Mario Stoppino," *Politeia* Winter: 20–27

1988 "I mass media e il futuro della democrazia," interview by A. Lombardo, *Mondo Operaio* 8–9: 36–40

1989 "The Essence of the Political in Carl Schmitt," *Journal of Theoretical Politics* 1: 63–75. Translated 1989 in *Actas* (Mexico) 3: 88–106

1989 "A Response to Paul Gottfried," *Journal of Theoretical Politics* 3: 369–70

1989 "Undercomprehension," *Government and Opposition* (Fall): 391–400. Translated 1990 in *La Jornada Semanal* (Mexico), August 26

1989 "Video-Power," *Government and Opposition* (Winter): 39–53. Translated 1989 as "Videopolitica," *Rivista Italiana di Scienza Politica* 2: 185–98. Also translated 1991 in *Revista de Ciencia Política* (Chile) 1–2

1991 "Comparing and Miscomparing," *Journal of Theoretical Politics* 3 (3): 243–57

1991 "Consideraciones sobre alternativas semipresidenciales y parlamentartas de gobierno" (roundtable), *Estudios Publicos* (Chile) (Fall): 7–44

1991 "Parlamentarismo e presidenzialismo," report to the "Parlamentarismo e presidenzialismo: dibattito sulla proposta di G. Sartori" (with Amato, Barbera, Elia, Galeotti, Manzella, Miglio), *Il Politico* (April–June)

1991 "Rethinking Democracy: Bad Polity and Bad Politics," *International Social Science Journal* (August): 437–50 (also in French). Spanish translation 1992 in *Examen* (Mexico) (February)

1993 "Tecnologia e globalismo," opening address, *Atti dell'Accademia dei Georgofili*, Florence, pp. 47–54

1993 "Totalitarianism, Model Mania and Learning From Error," *Journal of Theoretical Politics* 5 (1): 5–22

1995 "La democrazia delle idee sbagliate," *il Mulino* (Lettura) (November–December): 959–69

1995 "Elogio del semipresidenzialismo," *Rivista Italiana di Scienza Politica* 1: 3–20

1995 "How Far Can Democracy Travel?," *Journal of Democracy* 6 (3): 101–11. Reprinted 1995 as "Exporting–Importing Democracy," in S.C. Yang (ed.),

Democracy and Communism, Seoul: The Korean Association of International Studies, Seoul Computer Press, pp. 27–39

1995 "Parlamento," *Quorum* (Mexico) 37: 13–38.

1995 "Una repubblica di aria fritta," *MicroMega* 1: 41–50

1996 *"Constitutional Engineering and its Limits,"* 3rd Conferencia de la Unión Interamericana de Organismos Electorales (Mexico), July

1996 "Hay una crisis de representación?," *Este País* (Mexico) (August): 2–8. Translation of the paper "Failure of Representation or Failure of Understanding?," presented at the symposium *The Crisis of Representation*, Forum International des Sciences Humaines, Paris, October 26–29, 1995. Reprinted 1997 as "A Proposito de la Representación en democracia," *Nueva Revista de Politica Cultura y Arte* (Madrid) (June): 37–49

1996 "Límites de la ingenieria constitucional," *Justicia Electoral* (Mexico) 8: 45–52. Also published 1996 in *Memoria: III Conferencia de la Unión Interamericana* (June) and in *Cuadernos de Capel* (Costa Rica) 41

1997 "El Pluralismo y sus Interpretaciones," *Revista de Occidente* (January): 131–47. Reprinted 1997 as "Understanding Pluralism," *Journal of Democracy* (October): 58–69; as "Capire il pluralismo" in *Atti Accademia dei Lincei* (Rome), lecture, on March 7; and in an expanded version as "Pluralismo, multi-culturalismo e estranei," *Rivista Italiana di Scienza Politica* 3: 477–99

1998 "In Defense of Representation," conference at the Chamber of Deputies for the 20th Anniversary of the Spanish Constitution, Madrid, December. Published 1999 as "En defensa de la representación política," *Claves* (Madrid) (April): 2–6

2000 "About Constitutional Engineering," opening address, Nagoya, Japanese Political Science Association, October

2001 "Le illusioni del multiculturalismo" (interview), *Mondo Operaio* (April): 63–64

2001 "Signor Presidente, sul conflitto di interessi non è possibile tacere: lettera aperta," *MicroMega* (June): 7–12

2002 "Premierato forte e premierato elettivo," *Rivista Italiana di Scienza Politica* 2: 285–93

2002 "Videopolitica: medios, informacion, y democracia de sondeo," (Instituto Tecnológico de Monterrey, Mexico): 37–77

2004 "Norberto Bobbio e la scienza politica italiana," *Rivista Italiana di Scienza Politica* 1: 7–11

2004 "Where is Political Science Going?," *PS: Political Science and Politics* 27 (4): 785–86

2005 "Party Types, Organisation and Function," *West European Politics* 28: 5–32

Notes

* Updated from Oreste Massari (2005) "Nota bio-bibliografica," in G. Pasquino (ed.), *La scienza politica di Giovanni Sartori*, Bologna: Il Mulino.

Acknowledgments to reprint previously published material

The work in this collection has been published previously in a variety of different forms. We would like to thank the publishers for granting permission to use the following copyright material:

Giovanni Sartori (1970) "Concept Misformation in Comparative Politics," *American Political Science Review* 64 (4): 1033–53. © The American Political Science Association, published by Cambridge University Press, reproduced with permission.

Giovanni Sartori (1973) "What is Politics?," *Political Theory* 1 (1): 5–26. Reproduced with kind permission of Sage Publications Ltd.

Giovanni Sartori (1975) "The Tower of Babel," in G. Sartori, F. W. Riggs, and H. Teune (eds) *Tower of Babel: On the Definition and Analysis of Concepts in the Social Sciences*, International Studies Association, Occasional Paper No. 6, University of Pittsburgh, Chapter 1.

Giovanni Sartori (1984) "Guidelines for Concept Analysis," in G. Sartori (ed.) *Social Science Concepts: A Systematic Analysis*, Beverly Hills: Sage Publications, Chapter 1. Reproduced with kind permission of Sage Publications Ltd.

Giovanni Sartori (1991) "Comparing and Miscomparing," *Journal of Theoretical Politics* 3 (3): 243–57. Reproduced by permission of Sage Publications Ltd (© Giovanni Sartori, 1991).

Giovanni Sartori (1987) *The Theory of Democracy Revisited*, Chatham, NJ: Chatham House, pp 131–181.

Giovanni Sartori (1993) "Totalitarianism, Model Mania, and Learning from Error," *Journal of Theoretical Politics* 5 (1): 5–22. Reproduced with kind permission of Sage Publications Ltd.

Gary Goertz (2006) *Social Science Concepts: A User's Guide*, Princeton: Princeton University Press, Chapter 3, Goertz, Gary, "Concept Intension and Extension". © 2005 Princeton University Press, reprinted by permission of Princeton University Press.

Marcus Kurtz (2000) "Understanding Peasant Revolution: From Concept to Theory and Case," *Theory and Society* 29 (1): 93–124.

Steven Levitsky (1998) "Institutionalization and Peronism: The Concept, the Case, and the Case for Unpacking the Concept," *Party Politics* 4 (1): 77–92. Reproduced by permission of Sage Publications Ltd (© Levitsky, 1998).

John Gerring and Paul A. Barresi (2003) "Putting Ordinary Language to Work: A Min-Max Strategy of Concept-Formation in the Social Sciences," *Journal of Theoretical Politics* 15 (2): 201–32. Reproduced by permission of Sage Publications Ltd (© Gerring & Barresi, 2003).

Giovanni Sartori (1997) "Chance, Luck, and Stubbornness," in H. Daalder (ed.) *Comparative European Politics: The Story of a Profession*, London: Pinter. By kind permission of Continuum International Publishing.

Collier, David and Steven Levitsky (1997) "Democracy with Adjectives: Conceptual Innovation in Comparative Research," *World Politics* 49:3 (1997), 430–451. © The Johns Hopkins University Press. Reprinted with permission of the Johns Hopkins University Press.

Every effort has been made to contact copyright holders for their permission to reprint material in this book. The publishers would be grateful to hear from any copyright holder who is not here acknowledged and will undertake to rectify any errors or omissions in future editions of this book.

Index